Past and Present Publications

Crime in seventeenth-century
England

This book is published as part of the joint publishing agreement established in 1977 between the Fondation de la Maison des Sciences de l'Homme and the Press Syndicate of the University of Cambridge. Titles published under this arrangement may appear in any European language or, in the case of volumes of collected essays, in several languages.

New books will appear either as individual titles or in one of the series which the Maison des Sciences de l'Homme and the Cambridge University Press have jointly agreed to publish. All books published jointly by the Maison des Sciences de l'Homme and the Cambridge University Press will be distributed by the Press throughout the world.

Crime in seventeenth-century England is the first of an informal series of joint publications by the Maison des Sciences de l'Homme and the Cambridge University Press on the history of crime and criminal justice. The series will be edited by HERMAN BIANCHI, Professor at the Criminologisch Instituut, Vrije Universiteit, Amsterdam; YVES CASTAN, Professor at the Université de Toulouse II (Le Mirail); and J. A. SHARPE, Lecturer in History, University of York.

This book is also published in association with and as part of Past and Present Publications (Cambridge University Press and *Past and Present*), a series designed to encompass a wide variety of scholarly and original works, monographs and anthologies, primarily concerned with social, economic and cultural changes.

Volumes published by the Cambridge University Press are:
Family and Inheritance: Rural Society in Western Europe 1200–1800, edited by Jack Goody, Joan Thirsk and E. P. Thompson*
French Society and the Revolution, edited by Douglas Johnson
Peasants, Knights and Heretics: Studies in Medieval English Social History, edited by R. H. Hilton*
Towns in Societies: Essays in Economic History and Historical Sociology, edited by Philip Abrams and E. A. Wrigley*
Desolation of a City: Coventry and the Urban Crisis of the Late Middle Ages, by Charles Phythian-Adams
Puritanism and Theatre: Thomas Middleton and Opposition Drama under the Early Stuarts, by Margot Heinemann*
Lords and Peasants in a Changing Society: The Estates of the Bishopric of Worcester, 680–1540, Christopher Dyer
Life, Marriage and Death in a Medieval Parish: Economy, Society and Demography in Halesowen 1270–1400, Zvi Razi
Biology, Medicine and Society 1840–1940, edited by Charles Webster
The Invention of Tradition, edited by Eric Hobsbawm and Terence Ranger
Industrialization before Industrialization: Rural Industry and the Genesis of Capitalism, Peter Kriedte, Hans Medick and Jurgen Schlumbohm*
The Republic in the Village: The People of the Var from the French Revolution to the Second Republic, Maurice Agulhon*
Social Relations and Ideas: Essays in Honour of R. H. Hilton, edited by T. H. Aston, P. R. Coss, Christopher Dyer and Joan Thirsk
A Medieval Society: The West Midlands at the End of the Thirteenth Century, R. H. Hilton
Winstanley: 'The Law of Freedom' and Other Writings, edited by Christopher Hill
The Development of the Family and Marriage in Europe, Jack Goody*

*Also issued as a paperback

Crime in seventeenth-century England

A county study

J. A. SHARPE
Lecturer in History, University of York

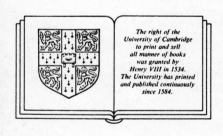

Cambridge University Press

Cambridge
London   New York   New Rochelle   Melbourne   Sydney

and

Editions de la Maison des Sciences de L'Homme
Paris

Published by the Press Syndicate of the University of Cambridge
The Pitt Building, Trumpington Street, Cambridge CB2 1RP
32 East 57th Street, New York, NY 10022, USA
10 Stamford Road, Oakleigh, Melbourne 3166, Australia
and Editions de la Maison des Sciences de l'Homme
54 Boulevard Raspail, 75270 Paris Cedex 06

First published 1983
Reprinted 1985

Printed in Great Britain at
the University Press, Cambridge

Library of Congress catalogue card number: 82-23490

British Library Cataloguing in Publication Data

Sharpe, J. A.
Crime in Seventeenth-century England.—
(Past and present publications)
I. Title   II. Series
364′.9426′7   HV6950.E/

ISBN 0 521 25074 9
ISBN 2 901725 84 8 (France only)

Contents

List of maps   *page* vi
List of figures   vi
List of tables   vi
Acknowledgements   viii

Part 1 Introduction
1 Problems, sources and methods   3
2 Essex: a county and its government   15

Part 2 The face of disorder
3 The regulation of economic life   39
4 Drink offences   49
5 Sexual morality and sexual offences   57
6 Riot and popular disturbances   71

Part 3 Offences against property and the person
7 Property offences   91
8 Crimes of violence   115

Part 4 General themes and wider issues
9 Punishment   141
10 Crime and the local community   154
11 Overall patterns of crime in Essex, 1620–80   182
12 Concluding observations   211

Abbreviations and conventions   219
Notes   220
Bibliography   272
Index   285

Maps

1 The Essex economy in the seventeenth century   *page* 16
2 The administration of seventeenth-century Essex   20
3 Riots and popular disturbances in Essex, 1640–2   85
4 Place of last settlement of vagrants passing through Chelmsford and Colchester houses of correction, 1620–80   165
5 The Essex hundreds   186

Figures

1 Survival of Essex assize files and quarter sessions rolls, 1620–80   13
2 Broad trends in indicted crime in Essex, 1620–80   189
3 Assault indictments at the Essex quarter sessions, 1620–70   190
4 Recognizances on Essex quarter sessions rolls, 1620–80   194
5 Presentments on Essex quarter sessions rolls, 1620–80   195
6 Property offences at Essex assizes and quarter sessions, 1620–80, and wheat prices   199
7 Property offences in four selected hundreds   203

Tables

1 Trades allegedly practised without seven years' apprenticeship: indictments and informations at Essex assizes and quarter sessions, 1620–80, by quinquennia   42
2 Thefts at Essex assizes and quarter sessions, 1620–80, by quinquennia, and type of goods stolen   93

3 Verdicts in theft cases at Essex assizes and quarter sessions, 1620–80, by type of goods stolen   94

4 Treatment of theft suspects at Essex assizes and quarter sessions, 1620–80   95

5 Treatment of theft suspects at Essex assizes and quarter sessions, 1620–80, by quinquennia   96

6 Treatment of burglary and housebreaking suspects at Essex assizes and quarter sessions, 1620–80   108

7 Treatment of burglary and housebreaking suspects at Essex assizes and quarter sessions, 1620–80, by quinquennia   109

8 Value of goods stolen in burglary and housebreaking cases tried at Essex assizes, 1620–80, compared with capital convictions   110

9 Treatment of persons accused of assault at Essex quarter sessions, 1620–80   117

10 Treatment of persons accused of assault at Essex assizes, 1620–80   118

11 Relationship of social status of male offenders to amount fined in assault cases at Essex assizes and quarter sessions, 1620–80   119

12 Treatment of homicide suspects at Essex assizes, 1620–80   124

13 Method of killing in homicide cases, Essex assizes, 1620–80   128

14 Variations in homicide rate and convictions for homicide at Essex assizes, 1620–80, by quinquennia   134

15 Treatment of persons accused of infanticide at Essex assizes, 1620–80, by decades   136

16 Capital punishments inflicted at Essex assizes, 1620–80, by quinquennia   143

17 Use of remands and transportation for property offences, Essex assizes, 1620–80, by quinquennia   148

18 Offenders at Chelmsford house of correction, 1620–80   151

19 Offences indicted at Essex assizes and quarter sessions, with Essex King's Bench indictments, 1620–80, by quinquennia   183

20 Offences indicted at Essex assizes and quarter sessions, with Essex King's Bench indictments, 1620–80, by hundreds   184

21 Essex assize, quarter sessions, and King's Bench indictments, 1620–80, by quinquennia and hundreds   187

22 Presentment of unlicensed alehouse-keepers at Essex quarter sessions, 1620–80, by quinquennia   197

23 Broad categories of indicted offences in six selected Essex hundreds, 1620–80   202

24 Overall criminality and population in Essex hundreds in selected periods   205

25 Overall criminality and poverty in Essex hundreds, 1665–9   206

Acknowledgements

No work of this type can be carried out without the assistance of a large number of individuals and institutions. Of the latter, the most important was the Essex Record Office, whose staff, under the then County Archivist, the late Mr K. C. Newton, offered constant help and interest; I should like to express special thanks to Miss Nancy Briggs, supervisor of the Students' Room of the E.R.O., and to Mr Arthur Searle. I should also like to thank the Controller of H.M.S.O. for permission to quote Crown-copyright records in his custody, and the staffs of the Public Record Office, the Bodleian Library, and the J. B. Morrell Library of the University of York.

This book is a substantially rewritten version of my Oxford Doctor of Philosophy thesis, and the ideas developed in it owe much to help and stimulation I received at this earlier stage. My greatest intellectual debt is to my erstwhile supervisor, Keith Thomas, of St John's College, Oxford, whose advice, criticism, and interest added much to both the content and the coherence of my thinking on early modern crime. N. D. Walker was kind enough to supervise my work for a term, and added some useful criminological insights. Mrs H. Gardner, Mrs E. Griffiths, Mrs J. Trythall and Mrs J. Eastwood all typed various drafts of the typescript, and I am grateful for their patience and accuracy. Professor David Flaherty's insistence that my thoughts on crime in Essex should go into print was a great source of encouragement, while I am grateful to a number of friends, colleagues and students at the universities of Oxford, Durham, Exeter and York for advice, comment, and moral support at various stages in the development of those thoughts. It is, perhaps, invidious to single out individuals from among them, but I am happy to acknowledge a special debt of gratitude to Dr G. E. Aylmer, Dr M. J. Ingram, and Mr C. S. L. and Mrs K. M. Davies. Indeed, it was working for undergraduate tutorials under Cliff Davies that first aroused my interest in seventeenth-century social history: I hope that he will not regard this book as too chastening a reminder of the importance of long-term causes.

All dates are in old style, but with the new year beginning, according to modern practice, on 1 January. Quotations are in the original spelling, although capitalisation and punctuation have been modernised where necessary.

Bishophill, York
August 1981

Part One

Introduction

1. Problems, sources and methods

Until recently, crime has ranked as one of the 'strangely neglected topics' of history. As long ago as 1873 an early student of the subject remarked that it 'could hardly have been considered either unimportant or uninteresting in itself',[1] but there was a gap of nearly a century before crime attracted much serious attention from professional historians. To a large extent, this was one aspect of the general tendency to treat social history as a poor relation; writers of textbooks, for example, were content to include crime in a generalised discussion of social problems, thus eschewing either precise definition or deep analysis.[2] Only recently have historians turned to the detailed study of crime; their work has demonstrated the truth of our nineteenth-century observer's belief in the importance and interest of the subject. Despite this work, and despite the widely held view that the history of crime is one of the major growth areas of social history, the subject is one which, among historians of England at least, is still in its formative stages: as yet, the problems involved in studying it have been only tentatively and imprecisely formulated. Nevertheless, the history of crime has already proved to be a subject worth serious study, both intrinsically, and for the light it throws on other areas. It affords the student rare insights into the interactions between government and the governed. British historians have been keen enthusiasts for order, for the wise legislator, the 'strong king' making 'good laws'; the history of crime involves an examination of the impact of these laws upon society, and of the legal and administrative machinery of the state at its lowest levels. Studying crime, paradoxically enough, is one of the best ways of understanding why society coheres. Moreover, court archives arguably provide a unique method of gaining entry to the isolated world of the mores and mentalities of even the lowest social groups, either through their overt actions or through such details of their sentiments as officialdom chose to record.

The neglect of crime by historians of society constitutes a stark contrast with the established nature of legal history. The criminal law has not received as much attention as some other areas of legal development, but a number of scholars have examined it in detail, and it continues to provide fertile ground for study. The magisterial work of Sir Leon Radzinowicz,[3] the continued detailed studies of J. H. Baker,[4] and the bold essays in

3

comparative legal history of J. H. Langbein[5] all demonstrate that the sensitive study of changes in the law and its administration can yield far more useful insights into a society and its crime than the products of the dry-as-dust legal historians of earlier generations might suggest. On the other hand, even the most adventurous legal history remains, in the last analysis, legal history. The volumes produced by Radzinowicz demonstrate this premise: his interest in the administration of the law led him to examine criminal cases in the past, and his descriptions of eighteenth-century crime go far beyond the anecdotal. His perspective, however, remains that of the legal rather than the social historian; his central concern is to explain how and why the law changed. Patterns of crime are adduced as a background to the shifting attitudes of central government, the judiciary, and reformers, but they are not studied for themselves. The history of the criminal law should not be equated with the history of crime.

Breaking from the traditions of legal history, however, leaves the would-be historian of crime searching for methodologies appropriate for studying his chosen subject. Despite the comparatively new and still somewhat protean nature of the history of crime, a number of approaches to it have already emerged. The first of these, the broad attack on a general level, was exemplified more than a century ago by Luke Owen Pike.[6] Pike took as his starting point the proposition that there had been many 'histories of civilization', but not one 'history of crime', and set out to remedy this defect. Despite his engaging enthusiasm, his work demonstrates some of the limitations and drawbacks inherent in general studies of this nature. Although he was aware of, and sometimes used, documentary sources, his emphasis was on the dramatic, well-known case, easily accessible from legal history textbooks or printed sources. His approach was essentially anecdotal, his book a miscellany of everyday crime, religious offences, state trials, and the unruly doings of the overmighty subject. Several later writers have adopted Pike's methodology, and failed to improve much on it. J. Bellamy's volume on the later medieval period, for example, is a collection of anecdotes, some of them culled from Pike, and offers few general insights apart from the familiar and somewhat sterile truism that there was a relationship between effective kingship and the maintenance of law and order.[7] J. J. Tobias's study of nineteenth-century crime[8] is more imaginative in its attempt to link criminality with social and economic change, but it fails to be as penetrating as the subject demands. It is, however, a recent book by Michael R. Weisser[9] which best demonstrates the flaws in the general approach to this subject; despite its courage in trying to link the history of crime with the broad lines of socio-economic change, the book fails largely because we as yet lack the information upon which wide-ranging, interpretative essays must be based. The problem is similar to that lamented by an historian of witchcraft a decade ago: there is little point in attempting to write general books until a number of more limited, more specific studies, preferably based on archival sources, have been produced.[10]

The possibility of generalising in a stimulating fashion from limited studies has been demonstrated by the early researches on eighteenth-century crime carried out by E. P. Thompson and his colleagues.[11] Written from a more or less Marxist standpoint, this group's work attempts to understand how the law mediates and determines class relationships, and aims, moreover, to present crime as an ideal vehicle for the writing of 'history from below'. This perspective is a valid and exciting one, and of fundamental importance: unfortunately, it is limited by its concentration on only one aspect of the problem of crime. As is admitted, the preoccupation of this school is the ' "good" criminals, who are premature revolutionaries or reformers, forerunners of popular movements – all kinds of rioters, smugglers, poachers, primitive rebels in industry. This appears as "social crime".'[12] The fundamental belief of this school, that law is ultimately a vehicle for class oppression, is, on one level, a correct one; moreover, their contention that certain types of crime might best be interpreted as forms of class warfare has much to recommend it. However, they confess their inability to produce any convincing conceptual framework for dealing with 'those that commit crime without qualification',[13] while the concentration on the use of the law as a means of mediating relationships between classes obscures the frequency with which it was used to settle disputes between members of the same social group. Even so, this work has constituted an important contribution to our understanding of the complexities of what crime and law enforcement in the past might have been about.

It is, perhaps, an indication of the difficulties involved in the subject, especially at this still comparatively early stage of investigation, that collections of essays dealing with the history of crime have generally been more successful than monographs or broad, general works.[14] These collections have demonstrated the variety of sources and perspectives which can be employed by the historian of crime, thus confirming that his field is both an exciting one and one which will see rapid developments in the next few years. Numerous questions will emerge, and numerous methodologies will be developed for resolving them. The student rejecting the broad anecdotal approach is confronted by a whole range of alternatives, of which that employed by Thompson and his colleagues is the only one which has so far been developed on more than an initial level. Among these alternatives are the study of specific offences, few of which (apart from poaching) have so far received any very detailed study.[15] The writings of past moralists and social commentators might be used as a starting point for the study of opinion about crime and punishment.[16] Popular literature, in the form of ballads, pamphlets, and, from the mid seventeenth century onwards, newspapers, provides the medium through which another set of attitudes towards the criminal might be studied.[17] The microscopic study on a village level, given adequate record survival, might be used to place the offender and his victim firmly in their social context.[18] All of these represent valid methods of studying crime in the past; to them might be added the method adopted in this book, that is, an exhaustive study of the crimes coming before the courts of an English county over a limited period.

This line of approach was suggested many years ago by the early editors of the quarter sessions documents which figure so prominently in the publications of the county record societies which proliferated in the later nineteenth century. Pioneer work by A. H. A. Hamilton and J. C. Jeaffreson presented edited versions of the raw materials for the study of crime in early modern England.[19] The pointers that these writers gave to the possibilities inherent in a history of crime involving the quantification of the types of document they handled continued to be ignored for many years. Indeed, despite the presence of some essays using this approach,[20] and of two studies employing it for the medieval period,[21] only one full-scale monograph has appeared on the dimensions of crime in one county in early modern England, that written by Joel Samaha.[22] Briefly, Samaha argues from his study of recorded crime in Elizabethan Essex that the social and economic changes of the period were reflected in criminal statistics. These changes produced a substantial mass of poor agricultural labourers and a ruling stratum of rich, capitalist landowners. The consequent polarisation of society created a harsher attitude towards the defence of property among the rich, and a greater predisposition to steal among the poor. This situation, heightened in times of harvest failure, brought about a reorganisation of local government and what the author describes as 'the emergence of modern courts'. Samaha's work has many flaws,[23] but there is much of value in his basic argument, and in his methodology. The book, in its objectives if not in its attainment, marks an important step forward: it attempts to study crime through the medium of the records of the assizes and quarter sessions of one county.

Samaha's approach, like the one adopted initially in the present work, was to produce a statistical analysis of crime brought before these courts, and then to infer the relationship of crime with other social phenomena from his statistics. Any quantification in historical studies is, of course, a risky enterprise, especially when early modern materials are involved; nor is it an end in itself. Even so, such questions as the relative frequency with which different offences reached the courts, and the response that they evoked there, are ones which are well worth asking. The results of such investigations provide, if nothing else, the essential framework within which problems of a more qualitative nature might be formulated. In recent years, therefore, a number of historians have overcome the general reluctance to derive statistical evidence from court materials. Reference has already been made to the work of Joel Samaha. J. S. Cockburn, using similar materials, has set out to analyse the nature and incidence of crime in Elizabethan and Jacobean England; while J. M. Beattie, in his study of crime in Surrey and Sussex 1660–1800, has given an object lesson in how to handle early modern criminal statistics, and how to relate them to the wider context of the period from which they are drawn.[24] The historian contemplating the statistical analysis of court archives as a first step to understanding crime in the past might, therefore, feel reassured by the prior existence of a number of studies which use such an approach to good effect.[25]

He or she might also be encouraged by the use that foreign historians have made of this approach in studying the history of crime in their respective countries.[26] In the United States, for example, court records of seventeenth-century Massachusetts provided the basis for two pioneering studies. The first of these, by Edwin Powers, is a general account based firmly on court records.[27] The second, by Kai T. Erikson, is more theoretical in its approach and is a rare example of a sociologist making sensible use of historical materials.[28] More recent work, notably Douglas Greenburg's study of crime in colonial New York,[29] continues to demonstrate the value of such studies. In France, provincial historical journals have published a number of articles on crime and the localities, while yet others have appeared in the pages of *Annales E. S. C.*[30] These and other exploratory articles have been followed by a number of monographs, of which perhaps the most relevant is that written by Nicole Castan.[31] The quality of the best of this American and French work must strengthen the conviction that the systematic exploitation of court records dealing with a limited chronological and geographical area offers an important perspective upon the study of crime.

Moreover, such an approach helps resolve two basic methodological problems. Firstly, it offers a ready answer, at least for immediate purposes, to the knotty problem of how 'crime' should be defined. As G. R. Elton has pointed out,[32] the word was unknown in its present sense in the sixteenth and seventeenth centuries, and the imprecision which he traces in its use in that period is mirrored by a corresponding confusion among modern historians. Crime has variously been described as an act which breaks the law or as an act which leads to prosecution at a court, while the work of Thompson and his school has emphasised that crime has a social as well as a legal dimension. These problems are compounded when dealing with a period when contemporaries did not make a clear-cut division between sin and crime, and in which a sharp distinction between criminal and civil offences was still a relative novelty.[33] 'Crime' is, at best, a very imprecise descriptive term: this imprecision is even more marked when crime in the early modern period is under discussion. However, the acceptance of what might be described as an 'institutional' definition – a crime is an act which breaks the law and can be tried before a court – imposes some consistency in the use of the term. This 'institutional' definition is not, of course, an exhaustive one,[34] but its use at least allows initial study of the history of the phenomenon to take place.

Secondly, the exploitation of local court archives forces coherence upon the historian of crime by focusing his attention upon both a limited period and a limited geographical location. Crime did not exist in isolation, and the historian of the subject should attempt to relate it to other social phenomena. Court records studied over time might reveal variations in court practice and fluctuations in recorded criminality, fluctuations and variations which might well be linked to other socio-economic variables and structures. In most respects, the county provides an appropriately sized unit of study. In some ways, perhaps, it is too small; it provides only a limited sample of some types of offence, popular disturbances for example. In others, as the intimate portrayal of crime and law enforcement afforded by village studies suggests, it is too large. Moreover, any conclusions based on the assize and quarter sessions records of any one county must be extremely tentative. Despite these reservations, the county still seems to offer the most seasonable mean between the general and the particular. It is additionally attractive to the historian of crime as many of the courts with whose archives he must deal were organised on a county basis, while the historiographical tradition of analysing English society between the fifteenth and the nineteenth centuries through county studies means that he will be placing his findings in a familiar context.

Selecting a period of study presented more problems. It was decided, after some initial investigation, that a run of sixty years represented a suitable compromise between the depth of study envisaged and the need for a relatively long-term perspective. Finally, the years 1620 to 1680 were chosen, largely because they encompassed a series of governmental changes and experimentations. These years witnessed the 1631 re-issue of the Book of Orders; the subsequent period of 'Thorough'; the Civil Wars; the following republican and Cromwellian regimes, generally thought to have introduced new personnel into local government and new attitudes towards the 'Reformation of Manners'; and the period following the Restoration, usually thought of as an era of slackness in local government energies, a contrast to the years of puritan ascendancy. The sixty years in question therefore provide ample opportunity for examining how crime and related problems were treated by different regimes.

The choice of the county to be studied was dictated more by the exigencies of record survival. The most important sources for the student of English crime in the seventeenth century are the records of the courts of assize and quarter sessions. Until the middle of the century assize records are not available in anything like a continuous series for any area other than that covered by the Home circuit, comprising the counties of Kent, Essex, Hertfordshire, Sussex and Surrey. Eventually Essex was chosen. The survival of assize files for the county is at least as good as that for any other county on the circuit, and Essex also possesses a run of quarter sessions rolls almost unbroken until the 1670s. The attractiveness of this county as an area of study is further enhanced by the existence of ample surviving records to supplement those of the quarter sessions, including a reasonable selection of borough court archives.[35]

This study will, therefore, be based primarily on the records of the Essex assizes and quarter sessions, and we must now turn to a discussion of the most relevant types of document produced by those courts. The most important was the indictment. This was 'a written accusation of one or more persons of a crime or misdemeanour, preferred to, and presented upon oath by, a grand jury',[36] in effect, the formal accusation upon which the alleged offender stood his trial. The information given on an indictment included the name of the accused, his 'style' (i.e. his occupation or rank), his place of residence, the name of the person allegedly offended against, and, at least in most cases of felony tried in Essex, some details of punishment. An accurate description of the accused was demanded by statute,[37] and this formed the basis for the legal commonplace that errors of fact in an indictment invalidated it.[38] The theoretical premium placed on accuracy in indictments would seem to make them an ideal source for the social historian.

In practice, comparison of indictments with other sources indicates that certain types of information given on them is frequently suspect. J. S. Cockburn has demonstrated the unreliability of assize indictments in the Elizabethan and Jacobean periods,[39] and many of his findings are relevant to the sources used in connection with this study. Firstly, clerks both of the assizes and the quarter sessions seemed to equate the residence of the accused with the place where the alleged offence took place. Thus, although the location of the crime as given on the indictment is usually correct, the home parish of the accused as stated on the indictment is often inaccurate. Secondly, the 'style' of the accused given on indictments is frequently at variance with that given on other documents. The issue is further obscured by the tendency of assize clerks, as the century progressed, simply to describe all males below gentry rank as 'labourer'. It is hoped, therefore, that the reader will insert mentally the words 'described as' before any description of status or occupation given in this study which has been drawn from an indictment. Details of punishment seem generally to have been accurate,[40] but sometimes persons sentenced to death were later reprieved. It was therefore found necessary to check details given on indictments against those given on gaol delivery rolls, the formal returns of the fate of prisoners after trial. The details of stolen goods given on indictments were also frequently false, since many indictments were adjusted to place the value of goods stolen below the shilling that separated grand from petty larceny.[41] It has also been suggested that the dates given on assize indictments are suspect, but the nature of assize documents used in this study precludes investigation of this point.[42]

These reservations must impose severe restraints upon the uncritical use of the indictment. It is now obvious that a number of the questions that might be posed if indictments are taken at their face value can no longer legitimately be answered. The social status of criminals as revealed by the style of indicted persons; the geographical mobility of criminals manifested by differences in the place of residence of the criminal and the location of the offences as given on indictments; the seasonality of crime as shown by the dating of offences as given on indictments – all of these are problems which can no longer be solved solely by the use of this class of document.

There are, however, some indications that Cockburn's extreme pessimism over the accuracy of indictments may be somewhat unjustified, certainly when applied to indictments later in the seventeenth century. A check of the details given on a sample of indictments and coroners' inquests in homicide cases tried on the Northern circuit in the 1660s against other documentation[43] shows them to have been more reliable than Cockburn's findings on earlier indictments might suggest. Certainly details of the date and location of the offences seem to have been accurate. It is, of course, probable that a greater premium would be placed on accuracy in indictments for homicide, as this was obviously regarded as a more serious offence. Recent research by Alan Macfarlane on a group of property offenders from Westmorland in the 1680s, however, suggests that they too were tried before a court which was anxious to frame the charges against them correctly.[44] Moreover, although Cockburn's doubts about the description of a man's style are well founded, they must be at least partially modified by some of the broad trends that are discovered when large numbers of indictments are analysed. To take the most obvious example, Essex assize and quarter sessions clerks described 45 of the 261 males accused of homicide as gentry or yeomanry, but only attributed these styles to 72 of the 2,381 males accused of theft.[45] Again it is possible that the clerks were more anxious to be accurate in homicide cases, but it would surely be difficult to negate the conclusion that these figures do provide a very rough indication that thefts in this period tended to be carried out by the poor, whereas violence was more widespread socially.

It should also be remembered that reservations about indictments are at their most persuasive when applied to felony. Trial for misdemeanour could involve traversing the indictment, in which case the accused was allowed counsel. This would imply that indictments for misdemeanour were more likely to be accurate; the defending lawyer would not have missed the opportunity to unearth any faults.[46] Such considerations lend weight to assertions about the social status of persons indicated for misdemeanours, notably assault, where nearly a third of males indicted are described as gentlemen or yeomen.[47] Doubts about the reliability of a man's style can, of course, best be resolved by knowing more about his real economic and social status. It is therefore interesting to note that microscopic studies of two Essex villages in the seventeenth century indicate that the impression given by the breakdown of styles given on assize indictments is generally correct: theft was usually the prerogative of the poor, while violence was indulged in by most social groups.[48]

Moreover, it is possible to suggest reasons why indictments were becoming more reliable as the century progressed. As Cockburn has suggested,[49] many of the irregularities in the indictments he has studied arose from the need of the assizes to deal with the rapidly expanding volume of criminal business in the Elizabethan period. Possibly, as these pressures receded, and as the clerical staff of the assizes became more professionalised,[50] the indictment became a closer reflection of reality. Nevertheless, our present state of knowledge dictates that the indictment be treated as an unreliable source for many purposes.[51]

The presentment was a less formal allegation of an offence. In the Essex records of this period three main types of presentment survive. The most weighty of them, in the eyes of contemporaries, was doubtless the presentments made by the assizes and quarter sessions grand juries. These could be concerned with everything from the minor (although presumably persistent) offender, through the general nuisance, to the use of the presentment as a statement of political opinion. Greater in bulk were the presentments drawn up for each hundred, presumably resulting initially from the action of parish constables, which swell most of the quarter sessions rolls. More specific evidence of the constables' activities comes in their returns to set articles, which occasionally survive.[52] These last two categories covered a wide range of petty offences, and, since they are usually of an informal nature, frequently include local comment on offenders. Presentments in Essex rarely carried details of punishment, although they often formed the basis for a more formal indictment.[53]

Further information about the enforcement of law and order is provided by the recognizance, described by one contemporary as 'a Bond of Record, testifying the Recognizer to owe a certain summe of Money to some other; and the acknowledging of the same is to remain of Record; and none can take it but onely a Judge or Officer of Record'.[54] Recognizances surviving in the Essex quarter sessions records and in the archives of the borough courts performed two functions. The first was that of binding persons over to appear in court, either to answer charges or to give evidence. The second was the prohibition of individuals from performing certain acts, on pain of forfeiting the money they owed, the most common example of which was binding over to keep the peace. The recognizances, therefore, afford insights into areas of crime and disorder which never reached the courts in the form of an indictment. They also provide supplementary information about offenders and their alleged offences.

The fourth major type of document used in this study is the evidence taken by justices known variously as examinations, depositions, or, where appropriate, confessions. Tudor legislation[55] had empowered justices of the peace (JPs) to take statements from accused persons before bailing them or committing them to gaol, and the evidence of the accuser and witnesses was often added to that of the accused. These depositions vary in quality, according to the conscientiousness of the examining justices, from full and lengthy descriptions of crimes to the scantiest details. At their best, they can provide a setting within which the bare outline of an offence given on indictments can be placed. Such elusive information as the previous relationship of the victim and offender, or their respective places in the social hierarchy, is given on a good deposition, while the evidence of witnesses can offer much information both about the facts of individual cases and attitudes towards certain kinds of offence.

Any study of the crime tried at the seventeenth-century assizes and quarter sessions must, therefore, rest upon these four main types of document – the indictment, the presentment, the recognizance, and the deposition. They survive in sufficient quantity for Essex to make a study of crime in the period 1620–80 a viable project, but certain gaps in record survival must be borne in mind. Recognizances and (save a few random survivals) depositions do not survive in the Essex assize records for these years, and, as figure 1 demonstrates, even the rolls which contain the indictments and presentments do not enjoy anything like an unbroken run before 1645. Essex quarter sessions records survive in much greater continuity. Quarter sessions rolls, containing indictments, presentments, and recognizances, with the exception of the odd lost roll, and of deficiencies in recognizances and presentments in the 1630s, exist in an almost unbroken series until the early 1670s. At this point, as figure 1 shows, their survival becomes more erratic. Depositions enjoy a similar level of survival, at first with other informal documents in the quarter sessions bundles, and later as part of the material included on the rolls. No class of document used in this study exists in an unbroken series from 1620 until 1680; conversely, no year within this period is without documentation of some form, and ample materials survive upon which to base a study of the type envisaged.

The main objective of this book, then, is to study crime in seventeenth-century England by focusing attention on the offenders and offences tried

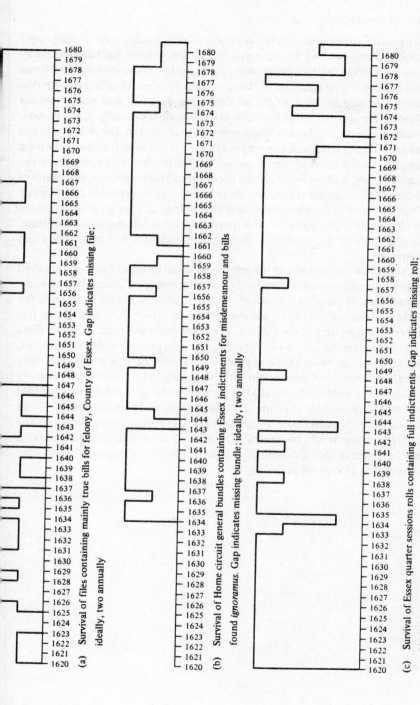

(a) Survival of files containing mainly true bills for felony, County of Essex. Gap indicates missing file; ideally, two annually

(b) Survival of Home circuit general bundles containing Essex indictments for misdemeanour and bills found *ignoramus*. Gap indicates missing bundle; ideally, two annually

(c) Survival of Essex quarter sessions rolls containing full indictments. Gap indicates missing roll; ideally four annually

Fig. 1 Survival of Essex assize files and quarter sessions rolls, 1620–80

before the assizes and quarter sessions of one county over a sixty-year period. After a second introductory chapter, providing background information on Essex and its government, this study will be divided into three main sections. The first two of these will study types of offence, with one section devoted to what might be described as petty and non-felonious offences, the second to more serious crimes against property or the person. Despite frequent mention of fluctuations in prosecution, the analysis of the various offences tried will, in many ways, be a static one. It will concentrate upon the background of the prosecution of offenders, the reaction of the courts to them, and (as far as can be ascertained) their motives. For many of the crimes discussed, evidence on these points is so scattered as to make any direct connection between them and chronological change impossible. In the closing section, however, the more important 'changes through time' that the study of the records of these courts suggests will be isolated and discussed.

It should be reiterated that the approach to the history of crime employed in this book, the systematic study of court archives for a limited period and a limited area, is only one of many, and that confusion still surrounds the whole problem of how to tackle the history of crime. As G. R. Elton has written so engagingly of the subject, 'these are early days and . . . some of the snags are at present only dimly discerned'.[56] The present writer is, however, convinced of the value of the approach envisaged here; a solid, archivally based examination of crime in an English county in the seventeenth century would make a useful addition to the growing number of similar studies that have been completed on crime in other periods of English history. These studies have demonstrated that, however valid other approaches to the history of crime might be, the most important advances, given the current state of research into the subject, are now to be made through the detailed examination of county archives.

2. Essex: a county and its government

Essex, like most English counties during this period, was not a socially or economically homogeneous entity, and it is possible to trace several economic subdivisions within it.[1] The county was very populous, with a total number of inhabitants rising from perhaps 100,000 to 120,000 in the course of the seventeenth century, and most contemporaries agreed that it was very prosperous.[2] This prosperity was, to a large extent, a consequence of the growth of the London food market.[3] Essex was renowned as a supplier of meat, poultry, eggs and dairy produce to the capital. It also enjoyed a less publicised trade in wheat, barley and hops with London, while from the middle of the seventeenth century a flourishing market-gardening trade, again stimulated by metropolitan demand, developed in the south-western corner of the county. In general, the agricultural life of Essex depended upon mixed farming geared increasingly to the needs of the capital. The agriculture of the county was, by the standards of the time, advanced, and was characterised by long-established enclosures.

This overall picture is subject to a number of local variations. The north-west of the county constituted something of an exception to the broad pattern. Despite scattered evidence of open-field cultivation in the east and north of the county, this was the only part of Essex where open-field organisation predominated, a result, perhaps, of this having been the first area of the county to have been heavily settled. It was also the only region of the county where nucleated settlements were common, most villages in Essex having their origins in scattered settlements cleared from the forest that had once covered much of the county.[4] The soil of this north-western region was extremely fertile, a chalky boulder clay ideal for corn growing, but the area had to support a dense population of small peasant farmers attempting to make a living on or just below the poverty line. Investigation of poor relief in one north-western parish in the period 1560–1640 has revealed that perhaps half the population was in need of assistance,[5] and that 42.5% of households in this region were exempted on grounds of poverty from the 1671 hearth tax.[6] This open-field area thus serves as a corrective to contemporary writers' assertions of Essex's prosperity.

More substance is given to such claims by conditions in the centre and south of the county. Around Chelmsford Hundred there lay an area of

15

16   *Introduction*

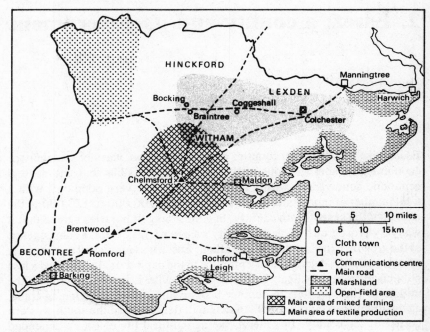

Map 1 The Essex economy in the seventeenth century

relatively prosperous mixed farming, with larger farms than those found in the north-west corner and a less dense population. Wheat was the main crop of this region, and large numbers of sheep, cattle, and horses were kept.[7] The tendency towards larger farms and a thinner spread of population became more marked further south, along the coastal strip of marshland. Here alluvial deposits, when drained, provided excellent corn-growing soil, although the area was perhaps best known for livestock farming. Horses were bred and raised on the marshes, but the most significant activity in the region was the fattening of livestock for the London market. Cattle came from as far afield as Yorkshire to pasture in this part of Essex, and sheep from Leicestershire and Lincolnshire. Farming in the coastal strip was further diversified by widespread dairy farming, again to meet metropolitan demand. Moreover, in addition to stimulating so many economic developments within the county, the capital was already beginning to change the nature of those parts of Essex adjacent to it. By the end of the century a ribbon of houses joined the eastern suburbs of the city to the western parishes of Essex, and the more polite parts of those parishes were beginning to acquire an almost suburban air as successful London businessmen settled in country houses.[8]

The influence of London was further reflected in the extensive maritime activity around the Essex coast. A survey of 1600 estimated that there were 130 small harbours and landing places along the Essex shore, most of them presumably serving local needs, and there also existed a number of more substantial ports. Some of these were heavily involved in fishing, an industry employing between 200 and 300 boats and a labour force of between 500 and 700 men in the second half of the century. Barking, the most important fishing port in the county, was firmly attached to the needs of the Billingsgate market by the time that Defoe was writing, while Harwich regularly supplied lobsters and cod to London. The seafood most readily associated with Essex during this period was, however, the oyster, which was cultivated along the coast from Shoebury to St Osyth, and Essex oysters were highly prized in the capital. Nevertheless, the county's ports were not concerned purely with fishing. Harwich, with its good harbour and lack of any significant hinterland, was a vital link in the coastal trade from Newcastle to London, and was also of some strategic importance in a century which saw constant warfare in the Low Countries. Maldon in 1600 was an important outlet for grain and dairy produce destined for the London market; it seems, however, that as the century progressed this trade became less significant. Although better known as a textile centre, Colchester, with its satellite port of Wivenhoe, was involved in both fishing and the coastal trade, as were a number of lesser ports, such as Leigh and Manningtree.

Communications and trade with the capital and the wider world were not, of course, exclusively seaborne. Both the administrative and the economic life of the county were affected by the Great Essex road, part of the main route from London into East Anglia, which bisected the county from its south-west to its north-east corners. This thoroughfare was to achieve great importance a little after our period, when William III's wars placed a special premium upon good communications between the capital and Harwich. Throughout the seventeenth century, however, the road was much used by travellers of all sorts, including drovers, carriers, and pedlars; by 1681 there were fifty coach and carrier services between Essex and the capital, most of them using the Great Essex road at some stage.[9] The traffic along the road encouraged the growth of a number of towns which added catering for the needs of travellers to their function as local marketing centres. Brentwood, Ingatestone, and Kelvedon all fall within this category, while Chelmsford, the county town with a population of perhaps 3,000, was essentially a marketing and communications centre.

The emphasis so far placed upon the agricultural life of the county, and the influence of the London market, should not obscure the presence in the north and north-east of the county of a highly developed textile industry, concentrated in Hinckford and Lexden Hundreds.[10] Although the industry was based upon a putting-out system (many families in the area, it seems, combined involvement in the textile industry with small-scale pasture farming), a number of towns in this region enjoyed a national reputation as clothing centres, among them Bocking, Braintree, Witham, Coggeshall, and, above all, Colchester. This last town was the only really large urban centre in the county, with a population perhaps slightly in excess of 10,000 in the early 1660s. Cloth production was long established in Colchester and Lexden and Hinckford Hundreds, but by 1620 the Essex clothing areas were given over entirely to the manufacture of the new draperies, bays, says, and other varieties of cloth. The new draperies had become increasingly important from the 1570s,[11] and were usually associated with the arrival of refugees from the Low Countries, of which the most celebrated group was the 'Dutch' community at Colchester. By 1629 a workforce of perhaps 35,000 was employed in the trade, the bulk of them domestic workers, with spinners as the most numerous element. From the late sixteenth century to the late eighteenth the fortunes of the trade in new draperies affected the economic well-being of nearly half the inhabitants of the county.

This dependence had serious disadvantages. The Essex textile industry was subject to violent booms and slumps,[12] largely as the result of forces far outside the control of those involved in cloth production. The light cloths woven in the county were marketed mainly in the Iberian peninsula and the Mediterranean. The new draperies were, therefore, geared to an export trade which was extremely vulnerable in the event of European warfare. Any outbreak of hostilities in western Europe seems to have resulted in a disruption of textile exports through an intensification of activity on the part of privateers and pirates, of whom those based at Dunkirk seem to have caused Essex special trouble. Actual warfare between England and Spain involved an immediate 'stop of trade' which had serious repercussions throughout the textile industry. In such times of crisis the inherent weaknesses in the organisation of the new draperies became more apparent. The cloth-owner (normally, at least before the Civil Wars, a small-scale operator) was enmeshed in a highly developed system of credit between himself and the London merchant community, so that at the best of times a bankrupt or dishonest merchant could mean ruin for the clothier. In periods of commercial disruption, the merchant aiming at cutting his losses would have recourse to immediate disinvestment, a process made easier by the mobile nature of capital within the trade. The resultant difficulties faced by the provincial cloth-owner would, in turn, be passed on speedily to the labour force. Even in good times the position of the wage-earner in the new draperies was precarious. Wages were, to the cloth-owner, the most important single element of production costs (often, in fact, amounting to more than half) and were, furthermore, the only element in those costs that had to be met regularly with cash. A large pool of cheap labour was therefore essential to the industry, both to keep wages low in slack and normal times, and to meet the demands of any sudden boom. In times of slump, the clothier would be obliged to attempt to cut employment and wages, a process which had serious implications for the workforce and which was, in the last resort, detrimental to the social stability of the weaving districts. The defects of the Essex new draperies were summed up neatly by a clergyman in the late eighteenth century, when the industry was falling into its final decline: 'too much work today, none at all tomorrow, no constant medium'.[13] These words were equally applicable to the industry in its seventeenth-century heyday.

Apart from the broad areas of economic activity represented by mixed farming, fishing, communications, and the textile industry, there existed a number of minor industrial and agricultural pursuits, most of them of only local importance. Saffron was extensively grown in the north-west of the county, and was one of Essex's most famous products, significant enough to lend its name to the most important town in the area, Saffron Walden. Hop growing (and the attendant industry of the production of hop-poles) was widely dispersed throughout the county, although there was something of a concentration in Hinckford Hundred, in the region of the Hedinghams. Some pottery was produced at Stock, while brickmaking was carried out in some parts of the county, an essential activity in an area lacking suitable deposits of building stone. Above all, Essex fostered a diverse and growing body of tradesmen, craftsmen, and artisans serving the needs of local commerce and agriculture.

Despite the existence of economic fluctuations, some of them quite serious, the basic economic structures of the county remained unchanged in the period under review. Developments in agriculture were slow, and rarely involved radical innovations or abrupt discontinuation of previous practices. The shift towards market gardening, the increased emphasis on stock raising, the use of better drainage and more varied manures did little to break the continuity of Essex agricultural life. The population growth that had marked the previous century was slackening by 1630, and the number of inhabitants of the county does not seem to have risen much before 1680.[14] There was no great change in settlement patterns within Essex,[15] while after 1650 both rents, and, insofar as wage assessments at the quarter sessions reflected reality, wages were static.[16] There was a tendency towards larger units in both agriculture and the textile trade, but in general the period was one of continuity in the basic patterns of economic life.

A similar underlying continuity characterised the administration of law and order in the county throughout the seventeenth century. The system depended upon a number of courts[17] and a variety of officers which are familiar enough to students of local government in the Stuart era. Of the courts concerned with the suppression and punishment of crime, the quarter

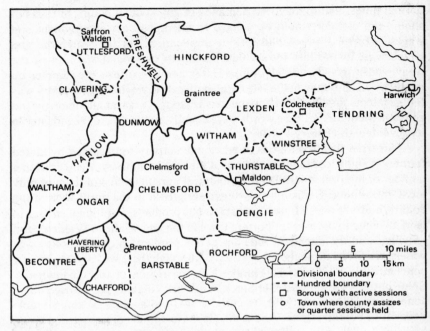

Map 2 The administration of seventeenth-century Essex

sessions is perhaps that best known to the general historian.[18] Since the fourteenth century the quarter sessions, held four times annually, had constituted an indispensable part of the machinery of law and order. By 1620, however, the Essex quarter sessions (held almost invariably at Chelmsford) were dealing mainly with non-capital offences. More serious crimes were reserved for the assizes,[19] and arguably the suppression of crime was by that date a less important part of the quarter sessions' business than their role as the medium through which the administration of the county was exercised and subjected to constant scrutiny by the ruling gentry. Nevertheless, the quarter sessions continued to play a vital role in the maintenance of order: petty criminals were still tried by them, while the common practice of enforcing local government policies through indictment makes any clear distinction between the quarter sessions' criminal and administrative business meaningless. The quarter sessions did not, however, enjoy unlimited jurisdiction over the county. The liberty of Havering, and the boroughs of Maldon, Harwich, Saffron Walden and Thaxted held their own sessions. Of these, though, only Colchester was empowered to hold gaol deliveries and punish felonies, and was thus the only borough to enjoy judicial powers on a par with the county quarter sessions.

A number of lesser meetings of justices served as auxiliaries to the main court. As the work of local government became more complex, it grew apparent that three months was too long a hiatus in the work of co-ordinating the activities of justices. Pressure of work forced the justices to meet on an *ad hoc* basis to consider administrative problems, such as the upkeep of bridges, paternity in bastardy cases, and the licensing of alehouses.[20] Early attempts to formalise these meetings into a coherent framework of petty sessions, ranging from a statute of 1541[21] to a Privy Council order of 1605,[22] proved abortive. It was not until the 1631 Book of Orders, with its provision for monthly meetings of justices to supervise the high constables, petty constables, churchwardens and overseers of the poor, that a formal and enduring system of meetings was instituted.[23] This order was also important in that it afforded formal recognition to the divisional system, by its assumption that meetings would be held over groups of hundreds. The division had apparently taken shape in the late sixteenth century, hundreds or half-hundreds being lumped together, in Essex in groups of three, for certain administrative purposes.[24] By 1620 the division was a well-established entity, presentments to the quarter sessions, for example, being grouped on a divisional basis.

It is difficult to give more than an impressionistic portrayal of the work of the petty sessions. Apart from a few returns under the Book of Orders,[25] the business dealt with by them is recorded only in stray references in the quarter session rolls. These suggest that the justices in their meetings were most consistently concerned with the licensing of alehouses and other forms of regulation of the drink trade.[26] However, a broad spectrum of other business was attended to: a woman was bound over to answer for violent behaviour; fines on those failing to attend church were enforced; and reluctant masters were bound over for refusing to take parish apprentices.[27] Such references suggest that these meetings of justices were of considerable importance in the interconnected problems of administration and law enforcement. Moreover, it is noteworthy that the system was flourishing less than a century after a similar scheme had been discarded because of the lack of interest of those charged with administering it.[28] The socio-economic changes of the late sixteenth and early seventeenth centuries had evidently impressed the virtues of active involvement in the system of law enforcement upon the ruling stratum.

The novel and haphazard nature of the petty sessions forms a striking contrast to the antiquity and majesty of the assizes. Their origins lay in the twelfth century, their evolution being a lengthy process in which an institutional framework was developed capable of ensuring royal control over local courts, the full collection of the profits of justice, and the meeting of the popular demand that this justice should be speedy and efficient.[29] For the historian of crime, the most important element in this evolution was the development of the system of gaol delivery, a process which was virtually completed by the end of the thirteenth century.[30] From this time onwards the biannual journey of the assize judges into the counties of England was one of the main events in the legal calendar.

By the seventeenth century the assizes enjoyed a threefold function. They dealt with civil actions, usually under a writ of *nisi prius* taken out of the common law courts at Westminster. Notes on such cases were entered into a *postea* book, and the full details returned to the appropriate court for certification. The court also heard criminal cases, the accused being dealt with through indictment. By the seventeenth century the most serious offences – treason, homicide, rape, burglary and witchcraft – were usually reserved for the assizes, although the court also dealt with the less spectacular matters of petty theft and minor administrative cases. Moreover, the assizes were an important link between central and local government. The justices of assize had a supervisory role to play over the local administration that was equivalent to their superior jurisdiction in criminal cases, and they were also responsible, through their charges to jurors, for transmitting the nuances of royal policy to the localities. Equally, the assize grand jury, composed of members of the middling gentry, was an important medium for articulating county opinion before these representatives of the central government.[31]

This was made easier since the assizes, like the quarter sessions, constituted an important event in the county calendar.[32] Every year the judges rode out, in pairs, on their respective circuits. At the borders of each shire the judges were met by the sheriff and his retinue, who would conduct them to the town, normally Chelmsford in the case of Essex, where the assizes were to be held. The assizes were prefaced by the assize sermon, a literary form which constituted almost a separate genre in the seventeenth century. It was usually of a stereotyped nature, consisting of general and conventional observations on law and order in normal times, and more specific comments on the duty of obedience in times of crisis.[33]

The conduct of criminal trials, to which the judge dealing with the crown side would then turn, is a familiar subject, and it would be otiose to describe it in more than the barest detail here.[34] Proceedings were prefaced by a charge, which normally consisted of a recapitulation of the main areas of concern to the court, ostensibly for the benefit of the grand jury. At the assizes this charge was delivered by the judge, at the quarter sessions by a senior JP acting as the deputy for the *custos rotulorum*. The grand jury was responsible for determining which indictments were sufficiently well founded to provide a basis for prosecution. Those that were rejected were marked *'Ignoramus'* or 'No True Bill' and proceedings against those named on them dropped. Those thought good enough to warrant further investigation were marked 'True Bill' and filed separately.

These preliminaries normally took up the morning of the first day of the court's sitting. After a midday meal, trials for felony began. The accused was brought into court, had his indictment read to him, in English, and was asked by the clerk how he wished to plead. If he pleaded guilty, he was put on one side until time of judgement. If he pleaded not guilty, the clerk asked him how he wished to be tried, the standard response being 'by God and the country'. The clerk would reply 'God send thee a good delivery', and call the next of the accused, until as many as could be dealt with by a trial jury, normally between two and six, were in court. Trial then commenced. The accused stood at the bar, witnesses gave their evidence, and relevant examinations and depositions were read out by one of the clerks. The petty jury would then reach its decision on each case,[35] and those who had stood trial were set aside to await judgement if convicted, or to be delivered by proclamation if found not guilty.

One aspect of trials in this period was the degree to which assize judges were willing to direct trial juries, and the willingness of these juries to follow such direction. J. S. Cockburn has remarked that by the end of a trial 'few juries can have entertained doubts about the attitude of the judge',[36] and that they were generally willing to adopt it. The assize judge, then, had considerable influence over the progress and outcome of a trial, even when he felt it unnecessary to indulge in the coercion and browbeating of juries that was such a feature of the criminal proceedings of the period. It was probably this direction which allowed the assizes to cope with the growing volume of business which came before them from the late sixteenth century.

When the felonies had been dealt with, trial of misdemeanours began, either through the procedure employed in trying felony, or through the accused pleading a traverse against the charge.[37] This latter course allowed the accused to contest the details on the indictment, rather than merely giving a blanket plea of not guilty, and to have recourse to an attorney, a luxury not allowed to the prisoner in trials of felony. When all cases had been heard, judgement was given on felons and those accused of mis-demeanour who had elected for trial by jury. Those whose indictments had been returned *ignoramus*, or who had been acquitted at their trial, were delivered by proclamation. Those who had been found guilty had sentence passed upon them, by the judge at the assizes, or by the chairman of the bench at quarter sessions. They were then handed over to the sheriff for punishment.[38]

The most serious penalty imposed was death. In England hanging had early established itself as the standard method of execution, although other forms were employed in exceptional circumstances. The peerage enjoyed the privilege of being beheaded, while persons convicted of treason were singled out for special treatment. Convicted traitors were dragged to the place of execution on a hurdle, where male traitors were subjected to the barbarities of hanging, drawing and quartering, and females burnt at the stake.[39] The law could also take the lives of those obstinately refusing to plead at their trial. Those who stood mute suffered the *peine forte et dure*, and were pressed to death.[40]

A large proportion of those convicted on theoretically capital felonies escaped through the loophole offered by benefit of clergy.[41] This anomaly had its origins in the legal problems attendant upon the twelfth-century struggle between church and state, one consequence of which was the concession to the church of the right to try clerks accused of felony. The initial test of clerical status – tonsure – was invalidated by the statute *Pro Clero* of 1350, which extended the privilege to secular clerks (clerical assistants, such as doorkeepers). From this point the clergy came gradually to be extended to the public at large, proof of clerical status coming to rest in an ability to read.

Various abuses of the system were tackled by a statute of 1489,[42] which laid down the procedure in operation in the period under review. Convicted felons claiming benefit of clergy and not in orders were branded with a hot iron on 'the braun of the left thumb', with M for murder or T for theft. On a second conviction, any felon already thus branded was hanged. This legislation was augmented by 18 Eliz. I cap. 7, which gave the judge the power to supplement branding by sending the offender to gaol for up to a year, and 21 Jac. I cap. 6, which extended benefit of clergy to women convicted of stealing goods worth less than 10/-. Statutory exceptions making certain offences non-clergyable proliferated in the Tudor period, and in the years 1620–80 these exceptions included treason, piracy, murder, arson, burglary, housebreaking and putting in fear, highway robbery, all other forms of robbery, stealing from the person to the value of more than a shilling, buggery and rape. The most common offences for which clergy was granted were simple grand larceny and manslaughter.

Other fates could await those convicted. Petty thieves were sentenced to 'bee openly whipped on their backs till their bodyes bee bloody',[43] either at the end of a cart or at the whipping post. Even those convicted of non-clergyable felony could escape hanging through reprieves, pardons, or, later in the century, transportation to the colonies. Those convicted of misdemeanours were most often punished by fining, the amount being either laid down in the statute defining the offence in question, or, if it were a common law misdemeanour, at the discretion of the court. The more exotic forms of punishment so beloved by antiquaries[44] – the stocks, pillory, or carting – were rarely inflicted by the assizes or quarter sessions during this period.

Although this study is concerned primarily with the criminal business of the assizes and quarter sessions, reference will be made at some points to other courts, and it is necessary to describe the most frequently mentioned of these. The most significant in the institutional hierarchy was the court of King's Bench at Westminster.[45] The origins of this court, like those of so many governmental organs, are obscure, its antecedent being the pre-Conquest supervision of hundred courts by the king's court. The court continued to exercise these supervisory powers after the Conquest, its importance growing proportionately with both the increasing sophistication of the machinery of justice and the firmness of royal control over that machinery. By the seventeenth century the court of King's Bench, located at Westminster, had developed from the personal court of the monarch into the most important of the common law courts.

Control over the lesser courts was exercised in three main ways. Firstly, the court enjoyed in theory an original jurisdiction over all other courts, and, again theoretically, the right to try any common law offence. The other two methods of supervision were through the transfer to the King's Bench of cases first tried at an inferior court either on a writ of error or, more usually, in the seventeenth century, on a writ of *certiorari*.[46] Despite these theoretically wide powers, the scope of criminal business coming before the King's Bench in the seventeenth century, on the evidence of Essex cases for the period 1620–80, was more limited.[47] The most important categories of offences were misdemeanours involving violence – assault, riot and forcible disseisin – the accused often being persons of a relatively high social status. These cases were almost invariably removed from the assizes or quarter sessions on a writ of *certiorari*. To offences of this type can be added a surprisingly wide variety of minor misdemeanours and nuisance offences, while the King's Bench records also contain coroners' inquests on suicides, deaths of prisoners in the county gaol, deaths by divine providence, accidental deaths, and a few cases of homicide. Apart from this last, felony committed by Essex inhabitants was never prosecuted in the King's Bench in the period under review. Printed King's Bench records for the years 1477–1547 indicate that even at this date the court was concerning itself mainly with misdemeanours.[48]

At the opposite end of the spectrum of courts from the King's Bench lay the manorial courts,[49] subdivided by seventeenth-century legal theory into two main institutions, the court baron and the court leet. The court baron was the customary court of the manor, and the organ of its lord; in the period under review it was concerned mainly with recording land transfers and purchases, and hence is of only secondary importance to the history of crime. The court leet, on the other hand, was, theoretically, a royal court, and had once enjoyed extensive powers, including trial of felony. By the seventeenth century this jurisdiction over serious offences had been lost, but the leet was far from universally moribund. The Webbs discovered that many leets were still active in the 1680s[50] while in a few towns which grew rapidly but did not achieve borough status, the leet remained the organ of local government until well into the nineteenth century.[51] In Stuart Essex such important towns as Chelmsford and Braintree[52] were still being governed efficiently through the leet.

In addition to its administrative function, the leet was still, at least in the first half of our period, an important organ for dealing with a wide variety of petty offences.[53] It is tempting to concur with the Webbs' assertion that:'In fact, it is difficult to find any kind of personal conduct, whether intrinsically innocent or plainly criminal, and whether or not expressly included among statutory offences, which might not, at one period or another, have found its way, as a common nuisance, into the presentments of a Court Leet Jury.' The range of offences that could be dealt with, therefore, was considerable, and of some importance when local government was virtually synonymous with the suppression of common nuisances. Leets could only punish through fining. If a definite offence (for example, an assault) had been committed, the fine would be levied in the normal way, although a jury faced with semi-permanent grievances could 'order the reforming of them under a pain'.[54] Examples of this treatment of leet offenders can be found in the Essex records of this period; four persons presented for failing to clean ditches at Braintree were to incur a 20/- fine if the ditch were not cleaned within a month or so of the sitting of the court.[55] It was this type of flexibility which prolonged the active existence of the leet, even though its business no longer included serious offences.

Lastly, a description of the courts relevant to a study of crime in seventeenth-century Essex must include those of the church. A hierarchy of ecclesiastical courts existed parallel to that of the lay courts,[56] and although the scope of the present study precludes a detailed examination of the impingement of all these institutions upon Essex inhabitants in this period, some reference must be made to the work of the archdeacon's court, which was the church court most concerned with the perennial problems of the enforcement of social discipline.[57] With the exception of a handful of parishes that were located in the peculiar of Bocking, or fell under the direct jurisdiction of the Bishop of London's Consistory Court, all Essex parishes were under the jurisdiction of one of three archdeacons. Seventy-eight parishes in the north and north-west of the county lay within the Archdeaconry of Middlesex, which sprawled over parts of Middlesex, Hertfordshire, and Essex. The Archdeaconry of Essex covered 155 parishes in the south of the county, and the Archdeaconry of Colchester comprehended roughly as many in the east and north-east.[58]

The archdeaconry court had powers of correction over a variety of religious and moral offences. The religious responsibilities of the court included the enforcement of conformity and attendance at church, the upkeep of church fabric and furnishings, and the supervision of the clergy.

The moral offences within the cognisance of the archdeacon's court were numerous, and the sanctions against them, if operated thoroughly, would have constituted an important contribution to overall control. They included such offences as adultery, fornication, incest, defamation, sorcery, usury, blasphemy, profaning the sabbath, drunkenness, and frequenting alehouses during service time.[59] Detection of such offences depended upon a considerable degree of public co-operation, and those finding themselves before the archdeacon were likely to have offended parish opinion, represented by either 'common fame' or the local oligarchy from which the churchwardens were drawn, rather than to have been presented as the result of 'police' action by any outside authority. Presentments before the archdeacon are important, therefore, in that they in many cases give information about popular rather than official attitudes to wrongdoers. Even the punishments awarded by the archdeaconry courts were obviously attuned to the idea of reaffirming community standards. Excommunication (in its social rather than its theological implications) was only a serious sanction if exclusion from the community was conceived as a major disadvantage. Apart from fines, the other penalty commonly imposed by the archdeaconry courts was penance, which normally involved the guilty party standing before the congregation in service time, dressed in a white sheet, carrying a white wand, and confessing the fault that had incurred punishment. Given its overtones of public humiliation, penance was obviously a form of chastisement likely to afford considerable satisfaction to an outraged community.

The presence of such a complexity of courts seems to have offered curiously little obstruction to justice through competing jurisdictions. After the Wray reforms of 1590 the justices at quarter sessions seem to have been happy to pass 'difficult' cases on to the assizes, which implied that capital offences were no longer tried at the sessions. In the latter half of the sixteenth century many of those tried at Essex quarter sessions had been executed,[60] but the only capital convictions at the sessions after the starting date of this study arose out of one case of buggery, and a handful of thefts, the last of these occurring in 1634.[61] Similarly, there is little evidence of jurisdictional rivalry between the borough courts and the county quarter sessions and assizes, such disputes as there were being more likely to have arisen from disputes over taxation rather than criminal matters.[62] This lack of conflict even extended to relations between the lay and the ecclesiastical courts, with the rare example of overlapping jurisdiction being smoothed over without difficulty. A case of adultery presented to the quarter sessions in 1620, for example, was dismissed because it was a spiritual offence, and presumably passed on to the archdeacon.[63] Such co-operation seems to have been more normal than inter-jurisdictional rivalry: in general, the impression remains that the courts provided a useful machinery for the maintenance of law and order and the punishment of the criminal, capable of dealing with a wide range of offences. That there was so little friction between the courts must be attributed to a combination of established legal demarcations of their respective areas of competence, a tacit division of responsibility among those empowered with running them, and the unusually homogeneous nature of the ruling class of Essex during most of the period under review.[64]

The main contribution of this county elite to the smooth running of the system of law and order was, however, the willingness of its members to hold unpaid office within that system. The most familiar aspect of this is, of course, the service that the upper stratum of county society rendered as justices of the peace (JPs).[65] The office had its inception in the fourteenth century, from which point onwards its duties were extended and diversified by statute. This tendency accelerated in the fifteenth and sixteenth centuries, so that by 1600 the JP was involved to some extent in every sphere of local administration. It has been calculated that 133 statutes extending the powers of the justice were passed between the institution of the office and 1485, and a further 176 had reached the statute books by the time Lambarde wrote *Eirenarcha* in the 1580s. The next century was not one of large-scale innovation in the JP's duties, and the description of them given in Lambarde's great work corresponds with those of the Essex justice of the seventeenth century.[66]

As well as dealing with the steadily growing body of administrative work imposed on them by statute, the justices exercised extensive powers in more strictly criminal matters. The wording of the commission of the peace declared that it was incumbent upon the justices at sessions

to hear and determine all and singular the Felonies, witchcrafts, Inchantments, Sorceries, Magick-Arts, Trespasses, Forestallings, Regratings, Ingrossings, Extortions, Unlawful Assemblies, Indictments aforesaid, and all and singular under the premises, according to the Laws and Statutes of England, as in the like case hath been used or ought to be done: And to chastise and punish the said persons offending and everyone of them for their offences, by Fines, Ransoms, Amercements, Forfeitures, or otherwise as ought and hath been used to be done, according to the Laws and Customs of England, or the form of the Ordinances and Statutes aforesaid.[67]

Given these powers, Coke's opinion that the justice and the quarter sessions constituted 'such a forme of subordinate government for the tranquility and quiet of the Realm, as no part of the Christian world have the like, if the same be duly executed', seems fully justified.[68]

By 1600 the English JP was normally drawn from the elite of landed society,[69] and the Essex bench followed this national pattern. In the eighty years preceding the Civil Wars the county was governed by a large body of justices (numbering ninety at the end of the sixteenth century) who were, in terms of attendance at the universities or the Inns of Court, better educated than their forebears.[70] Naturally enough, those named on the commission did not form a monolithic body. The Privy Councillors and peers who headed the list rarely attended sessions, and were not the most active justices. These notables, together with the major gentry whose interest in the magistracy lay in its political rather than its administrative functions, formed roughly a third of the justices. Half the bench came from county families of established fortune and local prestige, and it was this group who were most involved in the everyday duties of magistracy. The remainder of the bench was made up of new arrivals. The proximity of London meant that Essex attracted more than its fair share of *nouveaux riches*, and more than one county family owed its rise to merchant wealth or successful royal service. The tyros on the bench also included representatives of the minor branches of established families.

This tripartite division of the Essex bench seems to have operated throughout the period 1620–80, and the ruling gentry apparently suffered from internal strife and the impact of national events to a lesser degree than those of some other counties. In the two decades before 1642 the political machine developed by the Earl of Warwick and Sir Thomas Barrington imposed an unusual degree of unity on the Essex gentry, a unity which was to blossom into effective opposition to Charles I.[71] This control by the established county families, working with a common purpose, was only broken in the aftermath of the Second Civil War. The complicity of a number of the county's elite in the Royalist machinations of 1648 necessitated both a moderate purging of the bench and the introduction of new men with a stake in the regime; even so, a hard core of representatives of the old families remained.[72] The position after the Restoration is more obscure, and awaits further investigation. The county gentry must have been temporarily unified in 1660 by a general feeling of relief, but, as the memoirs of one of their number demonstrate, the county was affected by political faction within a decade.[73]

Throughout the period there existed a permanent lack of uniformity in the contribution of individual justices to the work of administration, and it is difficult to estimate how much time an Essex JP might be forced to spend on his magisterial duties. For some, the responsibilities of office must have been heavy; it was these justices who were most often responsible for taking recognizances, who were most often recorded as committing suspects to prison, and who took the most detailed depositions. Such men emerged in every part of the period under review, regardless of political change at the centre. In the two decades before the Civil War, for example, a very heavy burden was carried by four justices. Two of them, James Heron of Panfield Hall and Henry Gent of Steeple Bumpstead, lived in Hinckford Hundred, where the population was dense, poverty widespread, and justices few and correspondingly busy. The other two, Thomas Heigham and Nicholas Coote, lived in the south-west of the county, where the proximity of the metropolis caused its own problems.[74] In the Interregnum, two of the busiest justices were Isaac Alleyn and Christopher Muschamp.[75] Alleyn was a member of the minor branch of a family which had supplied the county with a number of justices and other officials, and was to continue to do so after 1660; his record of diligence in the decade previous to that year, therefore, marks an important continuity in the county's administrative history.[76] Muschamp, on the other hand, is an obscure figure who disappears from the commission of the peace after 1655. It is instructive that two men with such different degrees of previous attachment to the county should combine to be two of its most effective governors. After the Restoration, however, the day of such interlopers as Muschamp, no matter how efficient, had clearly passed. The old families returned to the bench in strength. The most active justices of the 1660s,[77] Thomas Bowes, Samuel Hare, and Henry Appleton, were unremarkable men with a record of long and efficient service.

For these dedicated men the burden of office must have been considerable, and the time spent on official business proportionately long. For many members of the bench, however, the duties of office cannot have been very onerous, and it is difficult to accept at face value the legend of the overworked JP which has gained such currency among general historians.[78] No diary kept by an Essex justice is known to survive from this period, but two documents exist which provide insights into the extent of a JP's workload. Carew Mildmay, JP and Commissioner of Sewers for the Liberty of Havering, made a brief note of his official activities in his copy of *Gallen's Almanack* for 1669. This suggests that he spent forty days in a year on his duties, a figure approximately confirmed by the notebook of William Holcroft, who recorded the various magisterial duties he carried out in the 1670s and 1680s.[79] For the working justice, official business was a constant irritant rather than an oppressive load; this should not, however, diminish our admiration at the diligence with which this business was generally conducted.

The work of the justices could not have functioned efficiently without the assistance of the clerk of the peace and his staff.[80] The clerk's responsibilities fell into two broad categories. Firstly, since the ancient office of *custos rotulorum* was by now a purely honorary one, the clerk was entrusted with the care of the documents of the quarter sessions.[81] Secondly, the clerk co-ordinated all aspects of the work of that court. He was responsible for drafting the numerous documents used at the sessions, for recording the orders of the court in the order books, and for evaluating and filing the less formal documents that came to him in the form of letters, complaints, and petitions. In short, the smooth running of the court, the care of its archives, and the co-ordination of the justices' activities out of sessions, depended on the clerk of the peace. The clerk and his staff formed the professional element in the system of magistracy.

Examination of the careers of such men as Edward Eldred (clerk 1611–22),[82] Richard Pulley (clerk 1641–8),[83] and Thomas Goldsborough (clerk 1648–60),[84] suggests that the Essex clerk of the peace was normally a member of the petty gentry, and had usually some grounding in the law and local administration. Eldred, perhaps the most efficient of the clerks in the period under review, came from an impressive dynasty of minor office-holders, and had previously served as deputy clerk. Pulley had been bailiff of Barstable Hundred and a deputy vice-admiral for the county, which suggests that he was the protégé of the Earl of Warwick. He also acted as an informer in prosecutions on a number of occasions, and served on the committee for compounding during the Civil War. For such men, holding the clerkship represented the summit of their career. The post was attractive enough to induce them to fill it during their last years of active life, rather than use it as a stepping-stone to something higher.

In contrast, the office of sheriff was becoming steadily less appealing to those who might be called upon to hold it.[85] The erosion of the power of this office since its medieval heyday had, by 1600, made the post largely honorary; this loss of power, however, was accompanied by a steady rise in the expenses attendant upon it. At best it was extremely costly. Substantial fees had to be paid on entry, and the incidental expenses, notably those incurred in entertaining assize judges and keeping up a retinue in proportion to the dignity of the office, were heavy. The sheriff was also responsible for money due to the crown left uncollected during his year of office, a responsibility which was never light, and which could reach terrifying proportions in the ship money years.[86] He was bound to reside in the county where he held office, another disadvantage in the eyes of the socially or politically active man. It is hardly surprising, therefore, that there exists evidence of a lack of enthusiasm for the office among the country's elite. Early in the century, for example, Sir William Wiseman was reputedly paying Ben Jonson (then influential in court circles) an annual retainer of £50 to prevent his being chosen sheriff, while a generation later Ralph Josselin recorded drawing up a petition to the House of Lords to save his patron, Richard Harlackenden, from a second year in the office.[87]

Despite the unpopularity of the shrievalty, it still played a vital part in the preservation of law and order. The sheriff and his staff performed an important executive function in the meeting and operation of the assizes and the quarter sessions. The tasks of making the dates of courts known, empanelling juries, keeping gaol calendars, serving process on those due to appear, and punishing convicted felons fell upon the sheriff and his men. It was they who served and returned the writs not only of the assizes and quarter sessions, but also of the central common law courts at Westminster.

Moreover, it was the sheriff who met the assize judges on the border of the county and conducted them to the assize town, and it was he who was responsible for their lodging and entertainment, and for that of the JPs, both at assize and quarter sessions time.

The sheriff was aided in his work by a substantial staff. By the seventeenth century most of the administrative work of the shrievalty was carried out by the undersheriff, with a number of bailiffs beneath him. There were bailiffs errant, directly responsible to the sheriff, and hundred bailiffs, who were responsible for aiding the sheriff but who normally held their bailiwick for life and who were normally appointed not by the sheriff but by others. It is significant that the most prominent feature of the sheriff's relationship with his staff was his anxiety to indemnify himself against the legal and financial repercussions of their negligence or wrongdoing, this usually being done by extracting a bond from the undersheriff and bailiffs. One writer commented that the sheriff could not 'sleepe quietly, and take his repose in safety' until he had obtained 'bonds and covenants of the undersherife & his friends'.[88]

Despite such precautions, it has been claimed that the chief defect in the sheriff's office was 'the performance of most of its duties by irresponsible under-officials'.[89] The most serious problem was presented by the bailiffs. Both kinds of bailiff regarded their office essentially as a means of making profit, and this attitude, combined with the contemporary tendency to blur distinctions between legitimate fees, bribes, and extortion, caused considerable trouble. Over sixty indictments were made against bailiffs in the period 1620–80, including twenty-eight for taking extortionate fees, four for extorting money on a false warrant, four for accepting bribes, and seventeen for acting as a bailiff without being first sworn by an assize judge. This last problem was aggravated by the employment of unsworn underbailiffs, which was presented as an abuse by the quarter sessions grand jury in 1649.[90]

Another, and equally troublesome, area of the sheriff's responsibilities was the upkeep of the county gaol and the welfare of the prisoners in it.[91] In Essex the county gaol had from the thirteenth century been located in Colchester castle. By the early seventeenth century this structure was in a state of ruin. At the Hilary 1631 assizes the grand jury requested that the gaol be moved to Chelmsford on the grounds of the castle's general dilapidation, and at about the same time prisoners were left up to their knees in water after a heavy storm.[92] This state of affairs was conducive neither to the good health of the prisoners, nor to the security of their incarceration. Perhaps a hundred prisoners died in the gaol between 1620 and 1650, with particularly heavy mortality during the winter of 1623–4, before the Hilary 1626 assizes, and during the mid 1640s.[93] Almost as many prisoners were lost through escape as through gaol fever. The problem was endemic, while on occasion mass gaol-breaks took place. In 1627 thirteen prisoners broke gaol, and the gaoler fled the county to avoid indictment for negligence.[94] The most dramatic incident, however, occurred in 1644, when forty-four prisoners awaiting trial escaped.[95] In the first half of the century, then, disease and gaol-breaks kept many felons from the courts; both problems became less serious after the transference of the county gaol from Colchester to the 'Crosses Keyes' in Chelmsford, a move ordered in 1659.[96]

The normal hazards of prison life included the gaoler, another of the sheriff's staff,[97] who was usually either negligent or hostile towards the prisoners, and sometimes both. Gaolers, like bailiffs, were rarely men of the best character. Stephen Hoy, gaoler in the 1620s, was constantly on the brink of trouble with the law, and was fined in 1628 for drunkenness and swearing.[98] Again, like bailiffs, the gaoler was dependent on fees for his livelihood, and, predictably, both Hoy and his predecessor Peter Clayse were indicted for taking extortionate fees.[99] Such men were unlikely to be over-careful of the well-being of their prisoners, of whom the poorer elements lived in squalor and hunger. The conditions in which they existed might be deduced from a complaint by one of the richer prisoners who claimed that after falling out with the gaoler over the rent of his room he had been placed in 'the Common Gaole amongst the most notorious felons, which is a place very noisome'.[100] Further insights into prison life in Colchester castle are afforded by a number of inquests on dead prisoners dating from the dearth years of 1649–50, which alleged that death had been caused by starvation resulting from the negligence or tight-fistedness of the gaoler.[101]   Given the financial burdens of the office, the political disadvantages it might incur, and the problems presented by its underofficers, it is hardly surprising that the shrievalty should become steadily less attractive to the county elite of Essex.[102] From about 1620, the upper gentry were increasingly unwilling to assume the office. The tendency after this date was to appoint recent arrivals in the county whose links with Essex were either tenuous or newly formed. Representatives of the leading families continued to serve in some years; Henry Mildmay of Graces who served in 1628–9 can hardly be dismissed either as a nonentity or a parvenu, and scions of the Smiths, Herrises, Mildmays and Wisemans served in the 1630s.[103] This mixture of members of established families and newcomers continued to fill the office until about 1665, after which the newcomers predominated. The social background of Essex sheriffs after this date awaits further investigation, but the list of their names shows few traces of established families. On this index, the attractiveness of the shrievalty had fallen even since 1600.

Another official of medieval origins whose early powers had suffered a decline was the coroner.[104] By the seventeenth century the coroner's most important function was to enquire into cases of unnatural or unexplained death, for the twin purposes of keeping the king's peace and ensuring that the profits of justice, whether in the form of confiscated felons' goods or deodands,[105] went into the royal treasury. On the report of a suspicious death (parishes failing to report such fatalities were theoretically liable to heavy financial penalties),[106] the coroner viewed the corpse and called a jury to ascertain the cause of death. In cases of suicide, death by divine providence, or accidental death, copies of inquests were returned to the King's Bench.[107] Homicides, or deaths where there was a strong suspicion of foul play, were reported to the assizes. The coroner had power to bind over suspects and witnesses to appear at the assizes; he could also commit suspects to prison, and he was empowered to take depositions. Few details survive of the actual conduct of these duties, or of how inquests were run. It is probable that in most cases the jurymen followed the directions of the coroner in reaching their verdict. Inquests were prefaced by a lengthy charge,[108] in the style of the assizes or quarter sessions, setting out the legal rules concerning death, and it is unlikely that the coroner would not make his views on the case plain.[109]

It is likely that the coroner enjoyed both a degree of social standing and some familiarity with the law. Essex coroners in this period (in theory chosen by the body of the freeholders at the county court, in fact by now usually royal nominees) were drawn from the same stratum of legally educated minor country gentry as that which provided the clerks of the peace. Typical of them was William Chevely, of Coopersale Hall in Theydon Garnon. Chevely came from a family that had extensive legal connections in London, and before his appointment as coroner had served as high constable of Ongar Hundred and as churchwarden of his parish. His term of office, 1641–51, was apparently marked by diligence, for numerous inquests held by him survive in the King's Bench records.[110]

As Chevely's career suggests, the minor gentry, and those prosperous yeomen with pretensions to gentility, served as high or hundred constables. Despite the hundred's decline as an administrative unit, the high constable was still a significant figure. Chosen by the bench,[111] usually for a three-year period, the high constable constituted a link between the justices and the parish constables, and hence formed yet another element in the chain of command by which the wishes of the central government were transmitted to the localities. Temporary shifts in the preoccupations of central or county government could be passed on to the petty constables by set articles of enquiry, and the results of these enquiries passed back to Chelmsford in the form of presentments. At all times, the hundred constable was responsible for co-ordinating the work of the parish officers.

The parish or petty constable came at the very base of the law-enforcement system.[112] In theory, the constable's main concern was still what had been his original function, that vague task of keeping the king's peace. The constable's role in this was largely a preventive one. Lambarde, writing on the constable's duties in keeping the peace, postulated a three-fold division: 'that is to say, first in foreseeing that nothing be done, that tendeth either directly or by meanes, to the breach of the peace: secondly, in quieting or pacifying those that are occupied in the breach of the peace: and thirdly, in punishing such as have alreadie broken the peace'.[113] This ancient responsibility had been augmented by the tendency for the constable, like the JP, to have his duties extended by statute, notably by Tudor legislation against rogues and vagabonds. His other *ex officio* duties included the detection and apprehension of minor offenders and suspected felons; to this end the constable was empowered to supervise watch and ward, and to make search of suspect inns and alehouses. To these police duties were added the collection of certain national and local rates and taxes, a responsibility which could add considerably to the constable's problems and strain his relations with the parish. By the early seventeenth century, however, the bulk of the constable's work lay simply in carrying out the instructions of the justices.

The exact social status of parish constables awaits detailed examination. Traditionally, they were selected annually by the court leet, either by the steward or by the leet jury, although in parishes where no leet functioned they were chosen by the bench.[114] In theory, all suitable candidates (which excluded clergymen, women, children, lunatics, 'scandalous livers', or 'malitious and contentious men')[115] were liable for service, on pain of being fined. At the beginning of the century there is evidence that constables were expected to be 'sufficient'. John Norden, in 1594, remarked with satisfaction that the large numbers of yeomen in the county ensured a good reservoir of talent to fill parish offices.[116] Such detailed research as has so far been carried out on individual Essex parishes has shown that constables, like other parish officeholders, tended to be recruited from among the more substantial villagers:[117] indeed, the presentment of Goldhanger parish in 1624 for appointing as constable a poor man, 'having no estate to live by, but ownly his daie labour',[118] indicates that contemporary expectations were that the constable should be a man of some substance.

The constable could be confronted with a wide variety of problems while trying to carry out his duties. Constables were frequently the victims of assault, and were often subjected to other forms of abuse and obstruction. Numerous cases could be cited like that of the constable of Aveley who was injured with a bill while trying to disperse a disorderly crowd,[119] or that of the constable of Great Burstead who was reviled while carrying out his duty of correcting vagrants.[120] In spite of such difficulties, and the fact that the powers of the office were in many ways limited, there is a body of evidence which shows Essex parish constables performing an important function in enforcing law and order. Scattered references illuminate isolated acts of efficiency; in one such case, for example, we find the constables and watch of Barling, at 3 a.m., apprehending a thief with a stolen pig in his sack.[121] There is, moreover, evidence of more systematic diligence, perhaps most commonly in the forms of the numerous returns of presentments made by constables.[122] If these are to be trusted, it would seem that the constables were able, at least on occasion, to carry out effective routine searches for rogues, vagabonds, and other disorderly persons. The constable should not, therefore, be entirely discounted as an agent of law enforcement. This is not to deny, of course, that it would be totally inaccurate to claim that the parish officers of this period, local men operating without remuneration, represented anything like a modern police force.

This reliance upon unpaid[123] amateurs to enforce the law at a grass-roots level had obvious disadvantages. Any body of quarter sessions materials of this period contains accounts of negligent, corrupt, or partial parish officers. Even so, despite such examples, and despite occasional references to individuals refusing to serve, the system does not seem to have worked too badly within its own terms of reference. Historians would do well to discard Dogberry as their archetypal parish constable.[124] Such officers existed, but, on the evidence of rural Essex, there was also present a number of constables who were responsible and sometimes thoughtful men. Even they, of course, would often be caught between the dictates of the law and the opinions of their neighbours, or between their duty to keep the peace and their own instincts of self-preservation, and in such circumstances would fail in their responsibilities. Due credit should, however, be given for the extent to which the parish constables did manage to carry out the tasks entrusted to them: as one historian has remarked: 'Parliament was a wonderful institution; but the unpaid parish constable was much more remarkable.'[125]

It is hoped that this chapter will render later references to the officers described in it more intelligible. Some of them, notably the Essex justices and the constables, are worthy of lengthy research in themselves. Moreover, certain offices have been ignored. The Lord Lieutenant and his deputies were ultimately responsible for the maintenance of public order in the county, although they provided such a distant sanction that they can safely be ignored in a study concerned primarily with the more mundane lawbreaker.[126] Churchwardens had an important part to play in law enforcement on a parochial level, but detailed study of their work falls outside the range of a study concentrating upon the assizes and quarter sessions. It is to the offenders and offences with which these two courts dealt that attention must now be turned.

Part Two

The face of disorder

3. The regulation of economic life

One of the major objectives of the law in early modern England was to regulate economic activities. The ideology behind this intended regulation was essentially conservative, and the letter and spirit of legislation often found itself opposed to the ethics, which were gradually becoming customary, of what was a developing capitalist economy. Such a situation necessarily produced infringements of economic regulations, some 362 of which were indicted or informed against at the Essex assizes and quarter sessions in the years 1620–80.[1] The most common offence of this type was infringement of those provisions of the 1563 statute requiring that those exercising a craft or trade should be qualified by seven years' apprenticeship,[2] 204 such cases having been recorded. There were also sixty-six cases of keeping false or deficient weights and measures, sixty-two of engrossing, regrating or forestalling, and thirty miscellaneous cases, including such minor offences as selling groceries without licence or working on the sabbath. These offences together constituted some 4.5% of all indictments, their greatest contribution to the overall figures coming in the quinquennium 1660–4, when they formed over 9% of indictments.

No study of crime arising from the breach of regulations concerned with economic and commercial activity can be written without mention of the complications arising from the influence of the business ethic. The distinction between acceptable business practice and criminal behaviour is often a very subjective one. Realisation of this has produced the concept of 'white collar' crime, defined as 'crime committed by a person of respectability and high social status in the course of his occupation',[3] and has led some criminologists to conclude that a society based on capitalistic free enterprise is criminalistic in terms of both its organisation and its ideology.[4] It is unlikely that this attitude would have seemed altogether alien in the seventeenth century. Defoe was voicing established opinion when he commented that 'There is some difference between an *honest man* and an *honest tradesman*', and that 'there are frauds in trade, with which tradesmen daily practise, and which notwithstanding they think are consistent with their being honest men'.[5] The wider moral aspects of this problem fall outside the limits of a work based on court rather than literary records; nevertheless, the prosecution of fraud and other forms of dishonesty dictates that the problem must at least be raised here.

Isolated cases of fraud were tried in the Essex courts of this period, although it seems likely that courts other than those under consideration here dealt with most cases of this type. Thus one relatively sophisticated deception, involving affixing counterfeit Colchester bay seals to 'other bays of a meaner condition', manufactured at Bocking, is known to have been tried in Star Chamber in 1632.[6] Similar deceptions may be recorded in the central court archives, but those brought before the assizes and quarter sessions involve naive peasant cunning rather than commercial chicanery of a high order. Frauds tried in Essex courts include stuffing a leg of lamb with cloth to improve its appearance, cheating a man of a cow worth 32/- and cheese worth 2/-, cozening a clothier of 26 lb of wool by means of a false token, or millers attempting to cozen a yeoman of bran and wheat.[7] Such petty swindles can hardly have constituted more than a very minor irritant for the inhabitants of the county.

Even so, the annoyance caused by these cozenings might well have reinforced feelings of antipathy towards those engaged in commercial life. Although the urge to embark on a wider discussion must again be resisted, mention must be made of what has been described as the 'medieval' attitude towards trading, which according to one writer had given the merchant and tradesman 'a notorious name for his fraudulent business habits' which was well entrenched by the sixteenth century.[8] Exact definition of this 'medieval' ethic is difficult, but one of its fundamental elements is conveyed in Holdsworth's description of it as a view of business life in which prices were determined 'not by the law of supply and demand, but by considering what amount would be a fair return to the producer, having regard to the cost of production; and that consequently any manipulation of the market with a view to manipulating of price in the interests of either buyers or sellers was illegal'.[9] The longevity of this attitude is demonstrated by the assertion that eighteenth-century food riots could have as their ideological basis a 'popular consensus as to what were legitimate and what were illegitimate practices in marketing, milling, baking, etc.'.[10] Again we are faced with the problem of popular distinctions between criminal and non-criminal activity in commerce.

A key area of divergence between what might be called the 'medieval' business ethic and that of modern commerce lies in prosecutions for engrossing, forestalling, and regrating. These offences, of medieval origin,[11] were given the definition current in the seventeenth century by the statute 5 & 6 Edw. VI cap. 14. This legislation defined a forestaller as one who purchased or contracted to purchase goods while they were *en route* to market or who attempted to produce an artificial shortage by persuading others not to come to market or not to bring goods there. A regrator was a person buying corn or other provisions in a market and selling them at the same market or at another within a radius of ten miles. An engrosser was defined as one who bought growing corn or goods wholesale in order to sell them again. All three offences were punishable in the first instance by forfeiture of the value of the goods involved. The whole tenor of the act was conservative; underlying it was antipathy towards the middleman, an individual as suspect to proponents of the 'medieval' ethic as he is essential to an expanding capitalist economy. The old ideal was the 'face-to-face' transaction, implying, in the corn trade for example, that: 'The owner, countryman or urban dealer, placed his open sacks of grain upon the regular corn market, and standing before them awaited a purchaser, either a poor customer, or the servant of the rich merchant or industrial employer'.[12] More complex forms of transaction were current by the seventeenth century, and Essex's importance to the massive London food market had long since rendered the 'face-to-face' transaction obsolete.

Only sixty-eight cases were tried under this statute at the courts under consideration in the years 1620–80, and, as table 19 indicates,[13] it is difficult to see any clear fluctuations in prosecution coinciding with what is known of changes in food prices. Years of dearth,[14] on the evidence of existing records, were not marked by a wave of prosecutions of middlemen. The crisis years of 1629–31 provide only isolated examples. One engrosser was indicted at the King's Bench,[15] while two cornsellers were reported to the Privy Council for failing to carry out an agreement to keep Colchester supplied with grain. The Council's reaction to these two latter offenders was a very traditional one: they were ordered to sell their wares at 6d a bushel below market price, and to serve the poor first.[16] Similarly, the bad harvests of the late 1640s and of 1661 did not occasion a rash of prosecutions under this statute. Prosecution of engrossers and forestallers was seemingly motivated by considerations other than an awareness of an impending food crisis.

Fluctuations in prosecutions of this type of offence could be caused by the activities of the professional informer.[17] Thus eleven of the nineteen prosecutions recorded in the years 1640–5 resulted from two groups of informations brought before the Trinity 1641 assizes.[18] Initiatives by local minor officers could also result in flurries of prosecution, although this is only rarely reflected in the comparatively lofty heights of an indictment. Seventeen forestallers and engrossers were presented by the grand jury as part of an attempt to curb abuses in Chelmsford market,[19] while a steady flow of indictments and presentments of engrossers and forestallers, as well as of other market offenders, in Rochford Hundred can best be interpreted as evidence of some local sensitivity to the problem.[20]

Attempts to analyse accusations of forestalling and engrossing by the type of commodity involved provide no clear pattern. The informations mentioned for 1641 were concerned mainly with livestock; a group of eight indictments brought against inhabitants of Rochford Hundred in 1641 all involved poultry, and a group of five informations brought in 1650 were

Table 1 Trades allegedly practised without seven years' apprenticeship: indictments and informations at Essex assizes and quarter sessions, 1620–80, by quinquennia

	1620–4	1625–9	1630–4	1635–9	1640–4	1645–9	1650–4	1655–9	1660–4	1665–9	1670–4	1675–80	Total
Grocer	—	—	—	—	4	5	1	1	3	8	2	1	25
Baker	1	1	2	8	14	1	5	1	18	4	—	2	57
Butcher	—	1	—	—	—	1	—	—	25	1	1	2	32
Cheesemonger	—	—	—	—	—	—	—	—	1	—	—	—	1
Brewer	1	2	—	2	—	—	—	—	1	—	—	—	6
Miller	—	—	—	—	—	—	—	—	—	—	1	—	1
Poulterer	—	—	—	—	—	—	1	—	—	—	—	—	1
Chandler	—	—	—	—	—	—	1	—	—	—	—	—	1
Mercer	—	—	1	—	—	—	—	—	—	—	—	—	1
Linendraper	—	—	—	—	1	—	2	—	—	—	—	—	3
Woollendraper	—	—	—	—	1	—	—	—	—	1	—	—	2
Hatmaker	—	—	—	—	1	—	—	—	—	—	—	—	1
Weaver	—	—	—	1	—	—	—	—	—	—	—	—	1
Tailor	—	—	—	—	—	—	—	3	—	—	—	—	3
Collarmaker	—	—	—	—	—	—	—	—	—	1	—	—	1
Fuller	—	—	—	—	—	—	—	—	—	1	—	1	2
Tucker	—	—	—	—	—	—	—	2	—	—	—	—	2
Clothworker	—	—	—	—	—	—	—	2	—	1	—	—	3
Clothier/Fuller	—	—	—	—	—	—	—	—	—	3	—	—	3
Clothier	—	—	—	—	—	—	—	—	—	—	8	—	8
Cardmaker	—	11	—	—	—	—	—	—	—	—	—	—	11
Building trades	1	—	2	—	1	—	—	—	7	1	—	—	10
Barber	1	—	1	—	1	—	—	—	10	1	—	1	14
Miscellaneous	1	—	2	2	—	3	3	1	2	1	1	3	17
Total	4	15	8	13	21	10	13	9	66	18	15	12	204

Notes: building trades includes 2 brickmakers, 5 glaziers, 2 plumbers, and 1 painter/stainer. Miscellaneous includes 3 cordwainers, 4 blacksmiths, 1

concerned with groceries.[21] Forestalling or engrossing in grain was prosecuted surprisingly rarely; only about a dozen such cases were recorded. The amount and value of the goods involved were as varied as their nature, ranging from the 100 capons, 500 chickens, 5,000 eggs and 1,000 lb of butter allegedly engrossed by a yeoman in 1641, to quantities as small as 10 lb of butter.[22]

Punishments are rarely recorded, although if large quantities of goods were involved fines could be correspondingly heavy. Two forestallers were apparently fined £150 in 1627, and a few years earlier a pardon had been issued to a Hockley man for the fine of £80 which he owed the king for engrossing oats.[23] Lesser offenders suffered smaller fines. Harwich borough sessions punished forestallers of fish with fines of 10/- or 6/8d and there is also mention of an engrosser of bread being fined £5 and placed in the pillory at Epping.[24] In another case a Rochford higgler, imprisoned for failing to pay a fine incurred for engrossing, petitioned the bench for release on the grounds that he was at last able to pay.[25] Generally, indictments at quarter sessions indicate that fines for these offences were small and arbitrary, rather than being linked to the value of the goods involved, as laid down in the statute.[26]

Attempts to control trades by ensuring that all those exercising them had served seven years' apprenticeship,[27] as laid down by the Statute of Artificers, demonstrate a conservatism similar to that underlying the distrust of the middleman. Surviving records reveal 204 such cases in the period under review, and as table 1 indicates, the occupations allegedly exercised in contravention of this Act cover a wide range of economic activities. The figures register a shift from the sixteenth-century situation, in which prosecutions of this type were mainly concerned with the textile trade.[28] Some 60% of prosecutions in this sample involved the food distribution trades and it could be argued that this reflects a rise in their importance. Setting aside the prosecution of fourteen barbers, the remainder of the cases involve a wide variety of rural crafts, building trades, and textile occupations. No coherent long-term pattern can be traced, prosecutions of non-apprenticed tradesmen being subject as much to localised fluctuations[29] as were cases of forestalling and engrossing. Labourers, yeomen, and husbandmen must often have been tempted to try their hands at more specialised trades. In some cases, of course, the alleged transition from one calling to another was an easy one; from nailer to blacksmith, tailor to mercer, or ship's carpenter to cooper.[30] That seventeen of the twenty-seven prosecutions tried in the 1670s were found *ignoramus* suggests that such flexibility in occupation was beginning to be regarded as normal.

A vital area of consumer protection lay in the regulation of weights and measures. One writer commented that if these were unfair, 'your commerce is a perfect cheat; the Buyer goes away satisfied that he hath so much as he bargain'd for, for his money, when indeed he hath not'.[31] Ensuring that traders used honest and standard weights and measures was of constant concern to the Essex authorities in this period, sixty-six indictments being brought for this offence between 1620 and 1680. The problem was not a new one, while the lack of standardisation of weights and measures which forms the backcloth for prosecutions of this offence was to complicate the buying and selling of commodities well into the nineteenth century.[32]

Most of the indictments for this offence were brought at the quarter sessions (forty-six in the period 1674–80) after the appointment of Nicholas Nicholls and his helpers to what were virtually positions of weights and measures inspectors for the county.[33] For the remainder of the period quarter sessions must have been a fairly remote sanction against the keeper of false weights and measures: like others involved in minor infringements of marketing regulations, he was more likely to be dealt with at the court leet. The market officials of all leets had control of weights and measures, and a rare leet document among Maldon borough papers indicates how difficult the maintenance of uniformity and honesty could be. Twelve traders (including an apothecary) were listed as keeping false weights and measures, twenty-one others failed to bring their weights in for inspection, fourteen were found to have unsealed measures, and a widow who kept an alehouse was fined 3/4d for using a non-standard pot.[34] Evidence for the county as a whole is provided by a sheriff's notebook for the 1630s, which contains lists of numerous fines levied on the keepers of false weights and measures.[35] The problem must have caused constant annoyance to all those engaged in commercial transactions, and was to provoke occasional grand jury presentments which portrayed false or non-standard weights as a general nuisance to the county.[36]

Two ancient institutions designed to protect the consumer and enforce a uniform relation between cost and amount sold were the assizes of ale and bread.[37] Infringements of these venerable laws were rarely indicted at the assizes and quarter sessions during this period.[38] There were, however, 149 presentments for selling beer at more than a penny a quart at the quarter sessions, 106 of them in 1631, presumably in response to the 1630 Book of Orders which enjoined that renewed attention should be given to the keeping of assizes.[39] A number of cases of this type were indicted at the assizes and quarter sessions,[40] though breakers of the assizes of bread and ale were more often dealt with at the leet, where this was still functioning. At Braintree, for example, there were 201 presentments for breaking the assize of beer between 1620 and about 1640, the bulk of them against two groups of persistent offenders who were fined almost annually to the value of a few shillings.[41]

Indictment of those working on the sabbath[42] was very infrequent, only four such cases being recorded at the assizes and quarter sessions during this period. In addition, thirty-seven presentments were made at the sessions against those working on the sabbath (or, during the Interregnum, fast days), thirty-one of these in the 1640s and 1650s, when the church courts, which were also empowered to punish this offence, ceased to function. The evidence of the secular courts, therefore, indicates that the offence was one rarely prosecuted, and the present writer's partial examination of archdeaconry act books suggests that it was rarely presented before that court. Even so, in parishes where puritanism was strong, the sabbath-breaker could become an object of real odium. There is, for example, a note of genuine indignation in a complaint to the bench in 1651 that a Boreham woman kept her shop and alehouse open on Sundays '& maketh the lord's day as a Com[m]on market day'.[43]

Another theoretical constraint on the rise of a free-market economy lay in the regulation of wages under the Statute of Artificers. This enacted that maximum wages for various types of employment were to be laid down annually by the justices, employers paying more than the prescribed rates being open to prosecution.[44] Infringements of these regulations were not indicted in the period 1620–80, and a study of the economy of the county in the late seventeenth and early eighteenth centuries has found only one such indictment, in 1685, which was found *ignoramus*.[45] This dearth of prosecutions probably indicates that the law was generally ignored rather than rigorously adhered to, and contrasts with complaints about the breach of the legislation late in the century. The grand jury at the Easter 1677 sessions called for the more energetic application of this section of the statute, and at the Michaelmas sessions that year it was thought expedient to stir the hundred constables into action by sending them copies of the wage assessments and ensuring that statute sessions were held.[46] A printed circular of 1684 from the bench commented that 'the Insolences and Disobediencies of Servants are grown almost insufferable; by exacting greater Wages than are now limited and appointed by the justices', and repeated the call for more strenuous action against the abuse.'[47] The presentment of hundred constables for failing to keep statute sessions some two years later is a sad commentary on the response to this call.[48]

Another offence infrequently prosecuted was usury,[49] defined by an Act of 1571 as either selling goods and then buying them back at a lesser price, or charging more than 10% interest. The offence was punishable at the assizes or quarter sessions by the confiscation of three times the value of the money or goods involved, a fine, and imprisonment.[50] Only seven accusations under this Act are recorded, an information against a Romford yeoman in 1627, another brought against a Clavering man in 1641, and a group of five indictments brought against two Colchester inhabitants in 1677.[51] The first two cases were brought by professional informers, while the two Colchester men were both accused by one of their debtors, which suggests that motives other than outrage at the breach of the medieval business ethic lay behind these prosecutions. Usury could be presented in the church courts, but a cursory inspection of archdeaconry records suggests that it was rarely brought before them in seventeenth-century Essex.[52]

The study of economic offences is complicated by the presence of the professional informer.[53] The informer could claim half of the sum due to be forfeited under a wide range of penal statutes governing economic activity, there being 115 such statutes in the middle years of the reign of James I.[54] The profits to be drawn from a successful information could be great. Tradesmen who had not served their seven years' apprenticeship were liable to pay £2 for every month in which they exercised the illegal occupation, although really big money lay in successfully informing against engrossers and forestallers. Informations were laid at the Essex quarter sessions against engrossers of goods worth £194/13/4d, £280, or even £600,[55] half these sums being due to the informer if the prosecution were successful.

Such a system was intrinsically vexatious and was open to serious abuse. It seems that the informer was unlikely to press a case that was contested, but was more interested in effecting a composition with the accused, and settling out of court. This could be done legally, on a licence from the Exchequer, or extra-legally, by means of private arrangement. The latter course was attractive to both parties, especially in the golden age of the professional informer, before the 1624 statute[56] which enacted that all informations, with a few exceptions, should be tried in the county where the alleged offence took place. Prior to this, informations could be laid at the Exchequer, and a disinclination for the expense and trouble involved in a Westminster lawsuit could constitute a potent incentive for composition on the part of the accused. Even after the worst excesses of this type were curbed, informers were not popular figures. Coke, hardly a prominent critic of the legal system, had some hard words to say about them,[57] and there exists an order in the Essex quarter sessions records for the Michaelmas 1646 sessions that all informers against bakers should enter securities to pay the costs of unsuccessful prosecution.[58] Compounding survived the 1620s. Thus we find Thomas Styles, in trouble for taking a composition in 1637, promising the bench that if he were excused 'he will never com[m]it the like any more, neither will he ever practise as an Informer Agayne'.[59]

The most serious case of the extortionate informer is provided by Robert Marrion. A frequent participant in prosecutions of economic offences, Marrion overreached himself when in 1623 he attempted to bring a charge of engrossing against Robert Aylett, a gentleman of Aythorpe Roothing, as a preliminary to bringing him to a composition. Aylett responded with an accusation that the prosecution was malicious, and it was this action which probably prompted two similar indictments by more lowly sufferers.

Subsequent investigations revealed something of Marrion's methods. He would serve subpoenas on those accused, telling them that for a small sum of money (in one case 16/8d) he would sue at the Exchequer for a 'License of Concord', presumably as a preliminary to legal composition. He also, according to two witnesses, made a habit of sending messages to offenders, informing them on Friday afternoons that he intended to prosecute them at the Exchequer on Monday if he had not heard from them by ten or eleven o'clock, in which case a mutually satisfactory arrangement would be made.[60] If Marrion was typical of informers, it is no wonder that they were held in disrepute.

The informer could contribute considerably to the level of prosecution of economic offences. As has been mentioned,[61] forestalling and engrossing cases were boosted in the early 1640s by the activities of three informers at one assize, while twenty-two of the sixty-six prosecutions of non-apprenticed tradesmen in the period 1660–4 are accounted for by a group of informations laid by William Piddocke at the Trinity 1663 assizes.[62] The self-interested and venal informer was not, however, the only agent to prosecute such cases. John Stone, who informed against thirty-two breakers of the assize of beer in 1631, was just one of several public-spirited informers who renounced their share of fines in favour of the poor.[63] More remarkable is the case of a prosecution for potmaking without apprenticeship brought by the potters of Buttsbury in 1622, a rare case of artisans taking action against interlopers.[64] Despite these examples, the most consistent opponent of the economic offender was the local man, whether he were a rural counterpart of the large-scale London informer who was so active against Essex tradesmen at the assizes, or some form of local market official. The initiatives of such people lay behind the bursts of localised prosecutions that are so characteristic of economic offences.

The evident defects of the informing system and the problems inherent in dependence upon local prosecutors could only be met by the appointment of local government officers with responsibility for enforcing economic regulations. The career of Nicholas Nicholls, who seems to have progressed from quasi-professional informer to county weights and measures inspector in the 1670s, is therefore illuminating. Nicholls, with his assistants William Kelsey and Thomas Hart, was largely responsible for the upsurge in presentments and indictments of keepers of illegal weights and measures that mark that decade.[65] He was first recognised in his official capacity in 1677, when it was announced at Michaelmas sessions that the grand jury had appointed him to inform against those breaking the laws concerning weights and measures, but this elevation followed many years' involvement with the courts. He had appeared as witness against forestallers in the late 1660s, and had for several years been receiving payments from the Eastern Division Fund for Charitable Uses for 'service done to the county'. After his official appointment he set out on a campaign against keepers of faulty weights and measures, eventually extending his interest to other forms of economic offenders, and even to poachers. Nicholls was not above bribery, and was indicted for taking 2/6d from William Love to show him favour under colour of his office shortly after his appointment.[66] Despite such lapses, Nicholls's career suggests that the servants of the Essex bench were developing a 'professional' attitude to some of the problems they faced. Moreover, the effects of his activities on the level of indictment of economic offenders serve as a useful illustration of the impact that variations in the efficiency of law enforcement agencies could have on certain types of criminal statistics.[67]

This last consideration re-introduces the fundamental problem of the gulf between actual and reported crime. As has been demonstrated, several economic offences (notably the payment of wages in excess of those fixed by the bench) were rarely indicted. It is tempting to interpret this paucity of prosecutions as evidence of public indifference rather than of a low rate of offences. The difficulties involved in envisaging a sufficient motive for prosecution tend to support this hypothesis. The informer, of course, would be motivated by a straightforward desire to make money, and the prosecution of traders who had not served their apprenticeship could result from a desire to remove competitors. However, indignation at violations of a popular 'medieval' business ethic, although sufficient to provoke a grain riot, was unlikely to have overcome the reluctance that those of lowly status would have felt about taking, say, a large-scale engrosser to law. Lesser malpractices, such as market offences, could be remedied cheaply in the leet, and hence were unlikely to be taken to a higher court. It must be concluded that the number of prosecutions for economic offences at the assizes and quarter sessions during this period seriously underrepresent the real extent of those offences.[68]

4. Drink offences

The connection between the consumption of drink and criminality, one of the commonplaces of nineteenth-century social reformers,[1] was well established in the seventeenth century.[2] Although the social basis of the Victorian interpretation – the equation of the 'criminal' classes with the 'drinking' classes – had not yet been clearly articulated, the drunkard was seen as a potential repository of every sort of vice.

> All sins whatsoever in a drunkenman
> Doe meet like Rivers in the Ocean,[3]

wrote the poetaster clerk of the peace of the County Palatine of Lancaster, Joseph Rigbie, and Jacobean legislation against drunkenness was partly justified on the grounds that inebriation was 'the root and foundation of many other enormous sins, as bloodshed, stabbing, murder, swearing, fornication, adultery, and such like'.[4]

Drunkenness was encouraged by a wide social acceptance of over-indulgence in drink. William Prynne claimed that 'why this gangrene or leprosie of Drunkennesse doth so dilate, and propalate itselfe, is the ill example of some great men, Clergiemen, and others'.[5] This view is supported by such cases as that of the future Essex justice whose youthful courtship was abruptly ended after he had paid his respects to the object of his affections while drunk and had vomited in her lap.[6] The widespread acceptance of heavy drinking rested partly on the lack of alternative beverages; until tea, coffee and chocolate became commonly available and cheap,[7] the domestic production and consumption of alcohol formed a basis for its abuse. In this period, therefore, drink was clearly perceived by legislators, magistrates and moralists as a social problem, in many ways intimately connected with crime. Naturally, prosecution of drunkenness or other offences concerned with the drink trade constituted one of the most important elements of the regulative activities of local government agencies. Essex was no exception; 1,182 indictments against infringements of the drink laws were brought before the county assizes and quarter sessions between 1620 and 1680. This figure constitutes some 14% of all indictments, and must be supplemented by numerous presentments and an unknown total of summary convictions. Attempting to curb the abuse of alcohol was evidently one of the central concerns of the county authorities.

An obvious starting point in the struggle against drunkenness lay in the control of premises where drink could be bought and consumed. Jacobean legislation[8] provided the framework within which justices worked during this period. A statute of 1604 provided a clear summary of what was considered to be the traditional and legitimate functions of such premises, namely 'the Receit, Relife, and Lodging of Wayfaring People travelling from Place to Place, and for such supply of the wants of such People as are not able by greater Quantities to make their provisions of Victuals, and not meant for Entertainment and Harbouring of lewd idle People to spend and consume their Money and Time in lewd and drunken manner'.[9] At its best the large, prosperous wayside inn was a respectable institution, according to one widely travelled contemporary the finest of its type in the world.[10] Such establishments existed in Essex; one of them, The Angel at Kelvedon, was thought worthy of lodging William III *en route* for Harwich and the Low Countries in 1693.[11] The county could, of course, boast few inns of this standard; even so, the lodging and refreshment of travellers was an important service industry.[12] The number of alehouses in existence, however, indicates that their clientele was not limited to travellers; it was estimated in the 1630s that there were about 800 alehouses of all types in Essex, or one for every 125 inhabitants of the county.[13]

The licensing policy of the Essex bench was set out in detail in the 'Justices' Orders Concerning Alehouses' of 1656.[14] These orders, based on a legislative framework tempered by local experience, describe what was standard practice throughout the century. Alehouses were to be licensed in public at justices' divisional meetings, the licences to be signed by at least two JPs. Licensees were to be of honest life and conversation, and had to produce certificates to this effect witnessed by the minister and three or more of the well-affected of the parish. They were bound over for £40, with two sureties of £20 apiece, to be paid by persons of sufficient estate who were not themselves alehouse-keepers, servants, or bailiffs. The premises were to have at least two beds to accommodate travellers, and to have stabling for four horses,[15] and were to be on the open road, 'not in blinde lanes or Corners out of the road'. Details of alehouses licensed or suppressed were to be returned by the justices to the sessions, where they were to be read out in open court. The 'Orders' ended, significantly enough, with encouragement to the justices to keep their monthly meetings and to ensure that the inferior officers were diligent in seeking out and presenting unlicensed alehouses.

Prosecutions for unlicensed alehouse-keeping continued throughout the century, evidence of the tenacity of both law-enforcement agents and illicit drinkers. There were 1,682 presentments of unlicensed alehouse-keepers at the quarter sessions, and a total of 878 indictments for this offence were lodged at that court and at the assizes.[16] Even allowing for repeated prosecutions, the figures are imposing. They give, however, only a very limited impression of the scope of the problem, for the unlicensed alehouse-keeper could be dealt with by other methods than indictment or presentment. The offence could, by statute, be punished by a summary fine of 20/-;[17] the offender might simply be bound over to desist from selling drink; and from the 1650s the persistent unlicensed alehouse-keeper was committed to the house of correction.[18] It would seem likely, therefore, that those who were indicted for the offence were either offenders who had not proved amenable to milder forms of coercion, or were the victims of unwonted efficiency on the part of local officers. The county authorities never solved the problem of the unlicensed alehouse, for, seemingly, as soon as one such institution was suppressed, another would open. Some idea of the number of such premises in the county, more accurate than that derived from the details of indictment, can be gleaned from the special returns of 1644. These mention eighty-six unlicensed alehouses in some fifty parishes.[19]

The disquiet felt by the local authorities at the prevalence of drunkenness and the unlicensed alehouse was intensified in periods of dearth.[20] Bad harvests in seventeenth-century England characteristically provoked 'a quite spectacular intensification of regulative social control',[21] one of the most outstanding features of which was a heightened awareness of the need to supervise and limit the sale and consumption of drink more closely.[22] The conviction that the grain used in brewing should, in times of dearth, be used for bread lay at the basis of this sensitivity; as Sir Thomas Barrington wrote in the crisis period of March 1631, 'it were farr more sufferable for ye poore to drinke whaye & water this sommer, than to want the staff of bread'.[23] The impetus given by harvest failure to the authorities in their fight against the drunkard and the illicit or disorderly alehouse was, therefore, dramatic; the reaction in crisis years should not, however, obscure the point that drink offered consistent and long-term problems to those seeking social discipline. As Wrightson has commented:

There were good economic reasons for keeping an eye on the alehouse and all men in authority would do so in time of dearth. It was not this, however, which drew the hostility of the most consistent critics of the alehouses, the puritans. They contributed to such arguments, but their prime concern was with the minimising of the social functions of the alehouses.[24]

Essex sources suggest that many participants in the local government of the county, puritan or not, shared the view of the godly pamphleteers. The battle against the disorders engendered by drink was by no means restricted to famine years.

The most consistent cause of hostility against the unlicensed alehouse was disquiet at the misbehaviour that occurred there. As pamphleteers and legislators saw the drunkard, potentially at least, as a general sinner, so petitioners to the bench regarded alehouses as 'one of the chiefe rootes upon which a world of diabolicall wickedness growes which spreads into the whole kingdom, and doth poyson many townes' familyes'.[25] In the absence of alternative leisure facilities, however, the alehouse was a vital centre of social life within the village. Despite the strictures of puritan critics, the concept of 'good-fellowship' in the alehouse was an integral part of popular culture. One writer put 'the bare pleasure of drink' seventh on a list of inducements to drinking.[26] The list was headed by good-fellowship and the preservation of friendship, and included, interestingly enough, 'the preventing of that reproach which is put by the world on those that will in this be stricter than their neighbours'.[27]

Examples of drink-induced bucolic merrymaking were common in this period. The West Hanningfield churchwardens presented to the archdeacon two men who in May 1627 had come into the parish 'and there not only made a songe [but a] most dissolute and ribaldrye songe in the alehouse to the greate scandall of all the p[ar]ishes and doth the like in other townes. The scandalous wordes used in this songe are that for the greatest p[ar]te the wyves are whores and theire husband[es] cuckolds.'[28] Ambrose Sutton, a victualler of Grays Thurrock, was presented before the same court in 1621 'for sufferinge on the XIth. of November last past in the time of divine service Idle persons of other townes adioyning drinking and mispending their time from the church w[i]th pyping and fidlinge'.[29] This tendency for the inhabitants of Stuart Essex to have a wider view of the functions of the alehouse than contemporary legislators led to 164 indictments for disorderly alehouse-keeping during this period.[30] Like that for unlicensed alehouse-keeping, this figure must represent merely the tip of the iceberg. Only in rare cases are details of the type of disorder involved given; these include allowing drunkenness or tippling, permitting gaming, or keeping disorder in sermon time.

A number of those accused of keeping disorder in their houses were apparently guilty of little more than entertaining friends or relatives. Thomas Roydon of Kelvedon, presented before the archdeacon for allowing tippling in his house on the sabbath, claimed that 'there were certain children of one Pollard who came to towne for goose berrys & cherryes, w[hi]ch were in his house & did call for a iugg of beer'.[31] William Stanley of West Ham, also presented before the archdeacon, replied that he was simply entertaining his brother and sister-in-law, on their arrival, with a jug of beer one Sunday afternoon.[32] In a period when many households brewed their own beer, the dividing line between such hospitality and keeping an unlicensed alehouse was an easy one to cross. The 1644 enquiry into alehouses produced a report from Stebbing of three inhabitants who had sold beer during the recent fair, 'butt beinge by us admonished they have hereafter p[ro]mised to forbeare'.[33] This type of 'alehouse' must have been almost impossible to suppress, and the disorders associated with it almost impossible to eradicate.

Despite its overtones of conviviality, the unlicensed and disorderly alehouse constituted a genuine social problem. The type of immoderate drinking encouraged in such establishments exacerbated the problem of poverty.[34] Jacobean legislation against drunkenness lamented 'the over-throw of many good arts and manual trades, the disabling of divers workmen, and the general impoverishing of many good subjects';[35] and the archetype of the labourer spending more money in the alehouse in a day than he earned in a week was familiar to contemporary writers.[36] It is no accident that the poverty-stricken weaving area of Hinckford Hundred provided a large proportion of indictments for drink offences,[37] and occasionally more specific insights are provided into the connection between poverty and drink. A Bocking man was presented for living in drunkenness, refusing to support his wife and family, and failing to follow any calling.[38] Nathaniel Smith and his wife Mary were complained against for keeping a disorderly alehouse where not only were poor men encouraged to spend their money, but also 'if they come in without money, if it be possible they wil make them pawn something for beere befor they will let them goe'.[39]

Gaming increased the threat that the alehouse posed to the economic well-being of the poor man. It was reported in 1627 that two brothers had played cards with stakes of 5/- a game and had run through 50/- in two days.[40] The keeper of an alehouse at Moreton was fined 40/- for allowing persons to play unlawful games. Depositions in this case reveal that at one time twenty people were there playing cards, while four strangers to the parish appear to have spent the greater part of January 1636 playing slideboard.[41] The presence of cheats and cardsharpers made the risks inherent in gambling greater. John Aylett complained that he was cheated of 8/- in a Chelmsford alehouse where the company played at 'cross and pile, hide under hatt, at cards, tables and dice'.[42] One indictment for cheating at cards survives, the guilty party being pilloried for cozening money while playing a game called 'my card before thy card'.[43]

The alehouse could also loosen the ties of social discipline by offering a leisure centre for apprentices and servants. A disorderly house run by Thomas Stanes offered a series of temptations to Nicholas Moore, an apprentice who in 1634 went there

one the Saboth to spend his money to valluw of three shillings after e[ve]ning prayer. At his partten the said Thomas Stanes did request him to come the next saboth day & he would requit him for his money spended the saboth day before & the said Stane's wife at this apprentice's departten desired him to com when her husband was not at home.[44]

Six alehouse-keepers were presented for running disorderly alehouses and entertaining other men's servants in 1630,[45] while a few years earlier John Been of Springfield was presented for entertaining servants and other poor men, 'who being reproved, moketh and flouteth such reprovers of these disorders'.[46] Robert Culpitt of Great Burstead was presented for allowing men's sons and apprentices to waste their time and money on 'tobacko and small kannes of beare',[47] and Thomas Hammond, reproved by the authorities of his parish in 1645 for entertaining young people and apprentices on the sabbath, retorted 'this was not a tyme to curbe servant[es] or restrayne them of their libertyes'.[48]

Despite such cases, the outstanding problem associated with the disorderly alehouse was drunkenness. The statutory penalty for drunkenness was a 5/- fine or a spell in the stocks,[49] and there is scattered evidence of these penalties being inflicted. Thomas Wells, for example, who while 'surcharged with drink' disturbed the minister of All Saints parish, Maldon, during service time, was 'commited to the stocks there to sitt sixe howres for that he refused to pay the vs. penalty for the said offence & the same could not be levyed of his goods'.[50] Like other types of drink offence, however, drunkenness was most often dealt with by summary conviction, of which surviving documentation provides only infrequent evidence. More formal prosecutions include 88 indictments for drunkenness at the assizes and quarter sessions,[51] with a further 163 presentments (half of them dating from the 1620s) at quarter sessions. Drunkards could also be presented before the archdeaconry courts, although this practice seems to have been restricted to those inebriated on the sabbath.[52]

Drunkenness, legally defined, amounted to almost total incapacity. Dalton wrote that it could be diagnosed when 'the same legs which carry a man into the house cannot carry him out again',[53] an opinion that was echoed by a Maldon man who in 1624 criticised the borough authorities for putting a friend of his in the stocks, 'seeing he was not drunck, for he that was drunck could not stand nor goe'.[54] Given a willingness to reach this level of intoxication, the contemporary equation of drunkenness with a type of voluntary insanity,[55] and the behaviour associated with it, are perfectly understandable. Certainly the modern view which emphasises the role of drink in releasing inhibitions[56] was already current in the seventeenth century. The writers of the period had very pessimistic expectations of the conduct to be expected from the drunkard. This pessimism was well founded; details of misconduct in disorderly alehouses supported it, while other links between drink, disorder, and crime existed.

Thus Robert Cole, a Romford shoemaker, was presented before the Archdeacon of Essex, 'for a most notorious and common drunkard, infamous and offensive to the whole p[ar]ishe, who in his drunken fitt[es] walketh about the streetes w[i]th his naked sword breakinge the windows, quarrellinge and raylinge, bravinge and cursinge after a fearfull manner'.[57] Two men styling themselves gentlemen were drunk when they assaulted the Rayleigh watch in 1629, while Richard Wiseman, presented for brawling and wifebeating, explained a little lamely that 'Some tymes beinge amongst Companye he doth drinke to muche'.[58] A Dagenham innkeeper was habitually drunk, in which condition he beat his wife and threatened the neighbours, and was eventually indicted for assault.[59] Brawls were not uncommon in alehouses, drink having its normal effect of loosening inhibitions, even if the participants were not actually drunk.[60] One of the best documented murders of the period took place in a Maldon tavern after card play.[61] Another Essex murder committed under the influence of drink, when William Purcas stabbed his mother in 1608, prompted a lengthy broadside ballad replete with warnings against the demon alcohol.[62] These examples, which could be multiplied, suggest that the pamphlet-writers' fears of the connection between drink and violence were fully justified.

Drunkenness could not yet be pleaded as an extenuating circumstance in criminal cases (this defence seems to have followed the arrival of widespread spirit-drinking)[63] and one is left with the impression that, to the tract-writers at least, drunkenness would constitute an aggravating factor. There are, however, a number of instances in which persons accused of theft pleaded that they were drunk when the offence took place, obviously in the hope of more lenient treatment. The hope was not always fulfilled. Men making this claim were whipped[64] or branded[65] in common with sober thieves, while justice Holcroft recorded sending to prison Samuel Wheeler who, apprehended when driving two stolen hogs, began 'pretendinge yt he was in drink'.[66] No indictment has been found, however, against a Toppesfield labourer who, accused of housebreaking, replied that after drinking three quarts of beer he found himself 'somewhat light in the head' and went into one of his accuser's outhouses to sleep it off.[67]

One must conclude that as long as the sale and consumption of alcohol, institutionalised in the alehouse, was socially acceptable, the struggle against drunkenness and the disorderly alehouse was doomed to failure. The alehouse continued to be a social centre, and also performed other useful functions. Alehouse-keeping was seen, for example, as a form of out relief. A petition on behalf of an invalid who was too sickly to work and who made his living from an alehouse that the parish authorities were trying to close down received the support of Sir Robert Mildmay.[68] In 1671 an old man from Coggeshall, a former scot-and-lot payer, was 'now through his age and disabilitie of bodie . . . no wayes able to bring in a livelyhood for ye supportac[i]on of himselfe and family if not licensed to keep an Alehouse';[69] a similar petition survives from a man who had lost his goods through fire.[70]

The inn and alehouse received their most striking official recognition through the custom, necessitated by the lack of alternative public buildings, of justices holding meetings and petty sessions at inns. Numerous returns from such sessions survive in the quarter sessions records giving the name of an inn as the place of meeting,[71] and on one occasion the floor collapsed under 200 people attending the justices at The White Hart at Bocking.[72] These occasions were not perhaps invariably decorous. Indeed, one critic of the bench alleged in 1684 that the justices of the southern division of Essex were drunk when they met at The Robin Hood in Leytonstone.[73] This allegation was without doubt totally false. On the other hand, there lingers the underlying irony that the administrators of a system which devoted so much time and energy to the suppression of drunkenness and the unlicensed alehouse should conduct their business at meetings held at an inn.

5. Sexual morality and sexual offences

One of the more distinctive characteristics of the work of the courts in our period was their continual involvement in attempts to punish a variety of behaviour which the modern observer would think the proper concern of personal morality rather than of a criminal court. A number of forms of sexual misconduct were felonies throughout the period under review: rape, of course, but also buggery and bigamy. All of these were tried at the assizes, and thus fall within the orbit of the historian of crime. Other forms of sexual behaviour, which today would more definitely be regarded purely as breaches of morality, were also punishable by the courts, notably adultery and fornication. It might be argued that since these transgressions were, for most of our period, dealt with by the church courts, they have only a peripheral importance for the present work: however, the attempts to punish adultery, fornication and incest at the assizes and quarter sessions in the 1650s, and the constant involvement of the JP in bastardy cases, make some discussion of sexual morality inevitable.[1] Such a discussion is made more desirable by a second consideration: the interest shown by contemporaries in suppressing 'whoredom' was one aspect of a wider desire to achieve a disciplined society. Fornication, like idleness, pilfering, swearing and drunkenness, was one of the distinguishing activities of the disorderly. A study of crime in Stuart England must, therefore, include some investigation of contemporary attempts to regulate sexual morality.

It is, of course, impossible to quantify the extra-marital sexual activities of our Stuart forebears. Bridal pregnancy rates, which give at least a minimal impression of pre-marital intercourse, have yet to be studied in Essex, and any investigation of this topic must attempt to cope with the question of contraception.[2] Similarly no work has yet been published on bastardy rates in Stuart Essex.[3] It is the suspicion of the present writer that any attempt to quantify this phenomenon would rest on evidence too shaky to be of more than slight value. Church court records provide some insight into the extent of fornication and adultery.[4] In the village of Kelvedon Easterford, for example, with a population of about 600, an average of five people were presented annually before the archdeacon's court for these two offences in the period 1600–40.[5] This figure is in itself of little value, except that it does indicate a widespread indulgence in extra-marital intercourse, or, perhaps more accurately, of a widespread suspicion of such indulgence.

One area of sexual activity which is relevant to a study of crime and which might have been expected to leave traces in court records is prostitution. The Middlesex sessions records for the Jacobean period reveal that the prostitute and the brothel were established features of metropolitan life,[6] but they do not seem to have been common in Essex. Examination of church court records may reveal more examples, but there are only two indictments for brothel-keeping in the assize and quarter sessions records during the period 1620–80,[7] although the position is somewhat obscured by a tendency to include sexual misbehaviour in the catalogues of complaints against disorderly alehouses.[8] Similarly, prostitution, strictly defined as the granting of sexual favours for cash or goods, was not recorded in the Essex assize or quarter sessions records during this period. Although the terms 'whore' and 'harlot' were bandied about in defamation cases at the church courts, it seems that few specific accusations were made before them. Mary Bradley of Fobbing complained to the archdeacon's court that 'Marie Smith the wife of Jeremie Smith had raised a slander of her sayinge that she tooke xiid. of a Dutchman to lye w[i]th him',[9] and it was reported that Christopher Cole of Stebbing had promised Grace Hood that he 'should give her a shoulder of mutton for lyeing with her'.[10] It would be unwise, however, to make very much of such cases.

Despite the lack of evidence of intercourse on a purely commercial basis, a number of women reported to the courts for bastardy or fornication may have been at least semi-professional prostitutes.[11] Elizabeth Rudd was presented in 1680 for committing adultery with William Phillips '& cum multis alii [*sic*]'.[12] A number of sometimes surprisingly casual relationships described in bastardy depositions may be concealed references to prostitution. Rachel Pepper of Colchester confessed to being made pregnant by 'a stranger whome she never sawe before';[13] this and similar cases indicate that intercourse could follow a very short acquaintance, although mention is never made of cash payment. Microscopic research on individual communities might reveal examples of women who may safely have been presumed to have been prostitutes. Such a case is provided by the widow Joan Hoye of Maldon. Hoye was presented before the archdeacon in 1623 on vehement suspicion of being with child, and in the following year for 'whoredom' with Richard Hurrell. A deposition by Hurrell, in which he confessed to intercourse with Hoye 'about hay season last, Twice w[i]thin one fortnight', survives in the Maldon archives. The outcome of this liaison was that Hurrell was now 'in great hazard & p[er]rill of his life' from venereal disease. Four years previously Hoye's sexual conduct had been reported to the borough magistrates by Margaret Wiseman, who recounted how

upon tweskay last about ix of the clock in the evening she understanding by her girls that the widdow Hoye had gotten a man in her chamber being a p[ar]ler the doors &

windows shutt about, & her children shutt into ther room she thrust by a window w[i]th her hand & saw her & the man now present before Mr. Bayliffe upon the bedd, she being all unbeard & her Clothes open, And they were together in such sort that he had the use of her bodie or ell[es] no man ever had the use of any woman's bodie.

Hoye's history suggests strongly that prostitution existed in Essex during this period, although there is no mention of cash payment in any of the relevant sources.[14]

The most concrete evidence of extra-marital intercourse was the arrival of an illegitimate child. Even so, a number of factors might prevent a bastard birth being reported to the secular authorities: local indifference; successfully concealed infanticide; the mother taking to the road; or the couple marrying to the satisfaction of their neighbours. Such bastards as did come to the attention of the justices were important primarily because of the problems of maintaining them; in particular, justices and the local community alike shared the wish that the illegitimate child should be supported by its parents rather than by the parish. Statutes[15] set up the system whereby the bench could order payments for maintenance, with a mechanism for distraint on the father's goods if he refused to meet his obligations; the mother was punished with a year in the house of correction.

The importance of finding financial support for bastards accounts for the emphasis placed on persuading girls in labour to reveal the identity of the father of the child. At worst, the midwives might refuse to officiate,[16] and at best their reminders that the dangers of childbirth put the mother sufficiently close to the next world to make truthfulness in such matters advisable must have aggravated an already traumatic experience.[17] Despite the efforts of the midwives, girls were known to lie about the father's identity,[18] cases of disputed paternity were not unknown,[19] and evasion on the part of suspected fathers can be found. A man enjoying sexual relations with his fourteen-year old servant girl told her that should she get with child 'she might lay it to a soldier in the army and he would take such a course that she should not want',[20] and on at least two occasions girls were offered £5 by fathers of their bastards to accuse other men of being responsible.[21] The problems of the authorities did not end with the discovery of the father. Suspected or confessed fathers could run away,[22] and by 1662 one such could claim that joining the army exempted him from responsibility.[23] Fathers sometimes refused to pay maintenance, and on one occasion an overseer of the poor was assaulted while trying to collect bastardy money.[24]

A systematic study was made of references to bastardy in the quarter sessions 1650–9, in order to obtain a more detailed impression of the phenomenon. By gleaning depositions, presentments, house of correction calendars, and bastardy orders, a total of 145 cases was found, many of them being referred to in more than one type of document.[25] In fifty-one cases out of the seventy-five in which the parish of residence of both parents is given on recognizances, that of the father and mother differ. It might therefore be possible that a case was more likely to be taken to sessions when the maintenance of the child involved members of different parishes. The description of the occupations of the alleged fathers, even if normal allowance is made for the problems involved in the recording of a man's 'style', suggests that the very lowest levels of society were under-represented. Against nine labourers must be set thirteen yeomen, fifteen husbandmen, and thirty artisans or tradesmen, together with three gentle-men, one clerk, one 'infant', and two youths described as 'junior', one of them a husbandman's son. This analysis suggests either that the very poor were unusually chaste; or that they were better able to abscond if this type of trouble came their way, having less of a stake in the community; or that illegitimacy among them was less likely to arouse the interest of the parish authorities.

Less can be learnt about the social status of the mothers. A very large proportion of them were domestic servants. At least nineteen of the forty-nine mothers of bastards whose examinations survive from the 1650s were servants, their master being the alleged father in no less than eleven cases, and a fellow servant in three others. It is interesting to mention here the case of William Bickner, a yeoman of Hatfield Peverel, who was bound over in 1646 for lodging all his servants in one room after an ex-servant of his, Sarah Tiboll, had produced a bastard who was chargeable to the parish.[26] The other striking feature of these unmarried mothers is their insistence that they had been promised marriage before consenting to intercourse.[27] In many cases, of course, it is probable that such statements were made in the hopes of arousing as little hostility as possible from the examining justice. On the other hand, it is tempting to interpret them as evidence of that popular contemporary attitude which held the contract, and not the marriage service, to be of primary importance in establishing marital status.[28] Martha Johnson of Maldon, for example, when presented before the archdeacon for sexual incontinency, was at pains to make it clear that intercourse happened 'after the said contract and not before'.[29] Popular opinion on such matters constituted an area where bending, if not actually breaking, the moral code was acceptable.[30]

Scattered evidence of adultery and fornication, whether in archdeaconry court presentments or bastardy depositions, provides a background to the workings of the ordinance of 10 May 1650 'for suppressing the detestable sins of Incest, Adultery, and Fornication'.[31] This made adultery by a married woman felony without benefit of clergy, punishable by death for both parties; gave incest by either sex the same status and punishment; made simple fornication punishable by three months' imprisonment followed by being bound over to keep the peace for a year; and introduced whipping and branding for brothel-keepers. Certain precautions were written in which indicate that the legislators were aware of the seriousness of introducing the death penalty for incest and adultery: justices and assize judges were empowered to examine defence witnesses on oath; confession by one member of a couple accused of a sexual act did not incriminate the other; and husbands and wives were not allowed to give evidence against each other.

Puritan writers had been demanding for some time more serious punishment for fornication and adultery than that offered by the church courts, and the argument that adultery was a more serious offence than theft or murder and therefore worthy of the death penalty was a familiar one. The ordinance of 1650 was not, however, a great success. Whereas presentment for adultery occurred at almost every sitting of the archdeaconry courts before 1642, only seven persons were indicted for the offence at the assizes and quarter sessions in the 1650s, and none of them was hanged. Fourteen others were accused of fornication, six of them being found guilty and imprisoned for three months, and four were accused of incest, none of whom, it seems, was executed.[32] Hence a total of only twenty-five people were tried in ten years under the 1650 legislation, as many as might have been presented for the offences covered by this act at any one sitting of the archdeacon's court. This low total must be accounted for partly by the differences in the relation of the various courts to the people. The quarter sessions and assizes represented a more distant sanction than the arch-deacon's court, and it was more troublesome and possibly more costly to bring a prosecution at the lay courts. Even after making allowance for this, however, it is difficult not to interpret the relative dearth of prosecutions as evidence of an unwillingness to expose offenders of this type to a punishment more rigorous than penance.

This suggestion must be modified by an awareness of the role played by neighbourly indignation in bringing the adulterer or fornicator to court, even if it were insufficient to generate a crop of hangings in the 1650s. The control of sexual morality in early modern England depended upon members of the community minding each other's business. Burn probably wrote a truism when he commented: 'Presumption of guilt may go sometimes for a proof of the aforesaid crimes; as when a man and a woman are seen in bed together, this is allowed to be sufficient evidence; for such crimes will scarce admit of other proof',[33] but seventeenth-century court documents reveal a general willingness to seek out this proof and report it. Numerous examples could be provided similar to Margaret Wiseman's evidence against the widow Hoye, quoted above. A Harwich woman recounted how Susan Plumber called her out and told her 'that her kinswoman Elizabeth Morfield was playing the whore with her man Blose; and said Goe & see ye pimpinge Jade for there he is now'.[34] Two servants accused of breaking a wall of a house at Great Coggeshall explained that 'they were called by Mrs Goodwyn to see ye said Thomas Till and his mayde in bedd together' and observed the couple through a cranny in the wall which became enlarged.[35]

This type of community interest in sexual transgressions could produce peasant satire of sexual lapses, the cuckold being a major object of amusement. Leaving aside Peter Christmas of Maldon, presented 'for being in drinke and abusing him selfe in the streete in making of hornes w[i]th his fingers and casting of a horne after auncient men and women as they rod by',[36] as being too general in his aspersions, it is possible to find deliberate use of the cuckold's horns as a form of ridicule. A Colchester man, Edward Raynes, was reported to the bench in 1657 for setting up horns at a fellow tradesman's door,[37] and Henry Merivall, a young carpenter, was bound over in 1647 to answer John Clay because he 'did make a libell by signes against the said John Clay and his wife in hanging a horne on Raileigh church gate when the said John Clay and his wife were coming to the same Church to be married'.[38] Formalised local comment of this type, in addition to the type of neighbourly supervision of sexual conduct discussed above, suggests that fornication and adultery were not consistently ignored.[39] Conversely, the evidence of the 1650s indicates that there was no widespread desire to see adulterers hanged and fornicators imprisoned. Contemporary attitudes towards sexual immorality were evidently complex, sophisticated, and, one suspects, generally adjusted to suit individual cases.

This conclusion reinforces our contention that any discussion of sexual morality in Stuart England must perforce remain tentative. The court records consulted for this study afford little assistance in assessing either the extent of, or changes in, the incidence of sexual immorality in Essex. It is improbable that we will ever fully understand the sexual mores of our ancestors, and even a partial understanding will not be achieved until more extensive work has been carried out on bastardy, bridal pregnancy, and cases of sexual immorality presented before the church courts. The impression remains that fornication and perhaps adultery were fairly common in Essex during this period, and that the breaking of the code of sexual morality constituted an important divergence between the standards set by the authorities and those of the populace at large. Nevertheless, there is little evidence of the imminent collapse of sexual morality which agitated some puritan pamphleteers.[40] Their fears that 'sexual indiscipline was more widespread . . . than ever before'[41] may have been correct: certainly the preliminary investigation of long-term fluctuations in bastardy would support them.[42] Nevertheless, court records suggest that 'whoredom', although common enough, was not a major threat to society. Organised prostitution was uncommon, sexual promiscuity seems to have been rare, and the unmarried mothers questioned by the Essex justices, with a few striking exceptions, were characteristically girls betrayed by their intended spouses rather than members of a bastardy-prone subculture.[43] Sexual immorality was certainly one aspect of the disorders of the meaner sort, but it had no special impact on the work of the Essex bench or assizes.

A comprehensive portrayal of those sexual transgressions which were punishable by death through our period – rape, bigamy, and buggery – is equally difficult to reconstruct. Certainly contemporary official opinion regarded them as serious matters; they were, for example, like other major felonies and treasons, exempted from general pardons.[44] None of them, however, was brought frequently before the courts, probably largely as a result of under-reporting. The 'dark figure' of unreported crime is notoriously high in sexual offences; indeed, one recent study has suggested that only 5% of sexual offences committed in modern England and Wales come to the knowledge of the police.[45] It is likely that the situation was much the same in the seventeenth century; there must have been many cases like that of the ten-year-old Colchester girl, the alleged victim of what was either rape or indecent assault, who dared not complain about it 'in feare of her father in lawe beating of her'.[46] The study of sexual offences, in any period, is fraught with other difficulties. Conviction in such cases requires stringent standards of proof, this problem being complicated by the need, in cases of rape and indecent assault, to scrutinise the relationship between victim and offender.[47]

All of these considerations affected the reporting and trial of rape cases. In the seventeenth century rape was defined as 'the unlawfull and carnall knowledge of any woman above the age of ten years against her will, or of a woman child of ten years with her will, or against her will',[48] and the offence had been made felony without benefit of clergy by the statute 18 Eliz. I cap. 7. It was not, however, a frequently indicted offence in Essex in the years 1620–80. Thirty-one cases survive in the assize records, two more in the quarter sessions rolls, and a further eight appear in the fragmentary Colchester sessions rolls. These name a total of thirty-six accused, seven of whom were found guilty (and six of them hanged), fifteen acquitted, and ten found *ignoramus*. The remaining cases were accounted for by one example in which the accused is recorded as being at large and for which no other details of punishments are given, and two others in which the accused were respectively bailed and imprisoned to the next assizes, no further details being forthcoming. Hence even if those cases in which no punishment is recorded resulted in a hanging, barely a quarter of those accused suffered the maximum penalty. Judges and juries were evidently very sceptical in their treatment of evidence in rape accusations. It was probably such scepticism which accounts for the stretching of the law implied when a Walthamstow man found guilty of rape was sentenced to be fined, whipped, and to make a public apology to the parents of the girl involved.[49] The low conviction rate in this admittedly small sample of indictments is perhaps a reflection of the generally accepted difficulties of proof in such cases. Hale, commenting on a rash of malicious prosecutions for rape in post-Restoration Sussex which followed a capital conviction for the offence, remarked: 'It is true rape is a most detestable crime, and therefore ought severely and impartially to be punished with death; but it must be remembered, that it is an accusation easy to be made and hard to be proved, and harder to be defended by the party accused tho' never so innocent.'[50] The general scepticism of jurors in rape cases may be deduced from Blackstone, who, commenting on the time limits within which a rape accusation had formerly to be brought (twenty-four hours under Norman law, forty days under the Statute of Westminster), thought that although no such limit was fixed in his day, yet 'the jury will rarely give credit to a stale complaint'.[51]

The absence of assize depositions prevents the construction of any clear impression of the background to rape, although other sources provide some information. A handful of quarter sessions depositions reveal that the attitudes of rapists were generally opportunist, and that the victim and offender usually knew each other.[52] Despite Dalton's contention that conception was proof of consent in rape cases,[53] one pregnant girl attempted to bring rape charges against the supposed father of her child; the indictment, whether through respect to Dalton or the inherently suspicious nature of the charges, was found *ignoramus*.[54] William Holcroft recorded a case in 1687 which commenced when a woman servant at an inn attempted to bring charges of paternity against the lieutenant of a regiment quartered in the area, after which the affair escalated into accusations of rape against him and his quartermaster.[55] Informations concerning a slanderous accusation of rape taken to the Star Chamber in 1620 reveal how a background of sexual licence could result in what seem to have been very slight grounds for a rape indictment.[56]

Depositions taken at Colchester, however, suggest that the most consistent background to rape cases, especially of young children, was one of sexual experimentation which went too far. The problem is obscured by the lack of an elaboration of sexual offences in this period to correspond with the modern one. Attempted rape was, of course, indicted as common assault,[57] and this must also have been the only means for dealing with the related offence of indecent assault. Despite the absence of a legal definition for either of these offences, isolated examples of unseemly sexual conduct falling short of rape can be found. One report of indecent assault, in which a girl's pudenda were so roughly handled that her clothes were bloodied, was probably the outcome of a long history of sex-play.[58] Another girl complained that a visitor to her master's house 'in a very uncivill manner laid hands of her and tooke up her Coates, but what his intent was she knoweth not'.[59] Mary Whoods, a Roydon maidservant, was the victim of an indecent exposure when she was sent on an errand to Leigh in 1623. She was accosted by William Stace of Horndon, who attempted to press his favours upon her. She declined, whereupon he threatened her '& drew out his privy members, and swore that she should goe no further, untill he had the use of her bodye'. Mary escaped by running home to her master.[60]

Many accusations of rape must have resulted from the natural consequences of such incidents, and from the Colchester evidence young children were often left surprisingly vulnerable to sexual interference by older children and even adults. John Hynone, aged about twenty, left to mind the children of the house when the master and his wife went to church, indecently assaulted their five-year-old daughter, 'and did endeavour what he cold then to have had the Carnall use of her bodie but he saieth he could not enter her'. He then tried to do the same with a second girl of about the same age.[61] A man of seventy-four allegedly indecently assaulted a young girl on a number of occasions. He 'gave her some tyme bread and butter & sometime Apples & sometyme Rost mete', and eventually had intercourse with her.[62] When the parents of a girl of twelve discovered that their daughter had sore genitals, investigations revealed that the man responsible had indulged in sex-play with her for a long time 'but did not hurt her, neither did she crie out nor make it known nor would not have spoken of it but that she was forced thereunto by her father'.[63] Scattered evidence suggests that such incidents were not atypical. A Chelmsford man was committed to the house of correction in 1638 for 'offering abuse to the body of a little woman child',[64] and the only multiple rapist to be tried at the assizes was hanged for raping four girls aged between ten and twelve.[65] The English also apparently took these usages with them to the colonies. In Massachusetts the first penal code did not include the death penalty for rape, this being introduced in 1641 after a scandal involving four girls, all aged under ten, and various household servants. One of the girls had apparently 'grown capable of a man's fellowship, and took pleasure in it'.[66]

Perhaps even more serious than rape in contemporary legal opinion was buggery or sodomy. Coke defined this offence as 'a detestable and abominable sin, amongst Christians not to be named, committed by carnall knowledge against the ordinance of the Creator, and order of nature, by mankind with mankind, or with brute beast, or by womankind with brute beast',[67] while to Blackstone it was 'the infamous *crime against nature*, committed with either man or beast'.[68] This severe legal attitude seems to have originated with the statute 25 Henry VIII cap. 6, which claimed that the offence had 'not yet sufficient and Condign Punishment' under English law, and sought to remedy this by making it felony without benefit of clergy. The statute, along with other Henrician innovations, was repealed in Mary's reign,[69] but was re-established by 5 Eliz. I cap. 17. The preamble to this Act voiced governmental worry about the prevalence of the offence, and claimed that since the repeal of the previous legislation, 'divers evil disposed Persons have been more bold to commit the said most horrible and detestable vice of Buggery'. Once more, however, the level of prosecution did not match the degree of governmental anxiety; indeed, only one indictment for sodomy survives in the Essex records in the period under consideration. A London grocer was indicted for committing the offence at Waltham Holy Cross in 1669, the indictment being returned *ignoramus*.[70] It would therefore seem that homosexuality, however common in London or in court circles, was not a widespread phenomenon in rural Essex.

To the one case of sodomy can be added nine of buggery with animals. Only three of those indicted were hanged, one after conviction at the quarter sessions in 1634, the others, a pair of Steeple Bumpstead labourers, at the assizes in 1664.[71] Of the remaining accused, two were acquitted and four had their bills found *ignoramus*. Stray references to the offence exist to supplement the evidence of indictments, but are hardly numerous enough to suggest a widespread indulgence in bestiality which failed to be reported. Richard Bickmore, committed for buggery with a mare, died in gaol in 1626 before his case could come to trial,[72] and an eighteen-year-old sailor was reported to have attempted the carnal knowledge of a bitch in a Colchester inn.[73] These two examples do not modify the overall conclusion that despite the horror with which the offence was viewed by legal writers, it was rarely indicted and not unduly likely to result in a conviction. Penetration, as in rape cases, had to be proved to ensure conviction, and at least one of the accused was apparently saved by the jury's strict adherence to this rule. William Spiller, a yeoman's son of Hatfield Broad Oak, was seen following a bullock in a close, having 'his yarde in his hand stiffe standing', but his explanation that he was prevented from committing buggery because 'the Bullocke would not stand still' apparently succeeded in obtaining an *ignoramus* for his indictment.[74] It is also noteworthy that no reference has been found either in legal writings or court records of the period to seventeenth-century English examples of the carrying out of the biblical recommendation that the animal involved in a buggery case should be destroyed.

The almost total absence of references to homosexuality helps to confirm an impression that the sexual practices of the inhabitants of Stuart Essex were relatively straightforward. Quarter sessions and assize records contain few references to perversions, and a cursory inspection of archdeaconry court records makes it seem unlikely that details of many will be found among ecclesiastical records. One such allegation, however, came in 1645, when Edward Shepheard, minister of Great Maplestead, attempted to accuse his servant of theft. The girl retaliated by claiming the clergyman had enjoyed sexual relations with her over a long period, and had given her presents from time to time. On several occasions, she claimed, Shepheard had broken off from intercourse to beat himself with white rods, exclaiming 'cannott I curb this sinfull flesh of mine, I will curbbe this sinfull flesh of mine'. It is hardly surprising that she rejected a gift of a petticoat from her employer on the grounds that 'folke talked enough allreadie'.[75] This deposition is, however, the only explicit evidence of irregular sexual practices of this type to be found in records consulted for the present study.[76]

One form of sexual misconduct which does appear is bigamy. Defined as marrying a second time while possessing a living spouse, the offence was made felony in 1604.[77] Benefit of clergy was not excluded, however, and several grounds for defence were set out. The accused could plead seven years' separation without confirmation that the other party to the marriage was alive; that the marriage had been nullified or ended by divorce; or that the spouse in the first marriage was under the age of consent when the marriage took place.

Twenty indictments for bigamy survive in the assize files, one other case being found in the Colchester sessions rolls, the accused including seventeen men and four women. Of the men, one was hanged; four pleaded their clergy and were branded; two were recorded as being at large; one was remanded; no details of punishment survive in two cases; and the remainder were either acquitted or found *ignoramus*. Of the women, three were sentenced to be hanged (of whom two were subsequently reprieved while the other pleaded pregnancy successfully), and one was described as being at large. In other words, of those accused of the offence only one, a West Bergholt tailor convicted in 1621, is definitely known to have been executed.[78]

Blackstone, who preferred to call the offence 'polygamy', did not think it a major threat to the institution of marriage among the English, as 'in northern countries the very climate seems to reclaim against it'.[79] It is probable, however, that factors other than the weather were affecting marital stability at this time. Not enough is known about migration in the sixteenth and seventeenth centuries, but it seems likely that a combination of geographical mobility and bad communications could lead husbands and wives to lose touch with each other, or facilitate separation when one or both partners desired it. The wording of the 1604 statute suggests that governmental anxieties over this point formed the basis of that legislation. Moreover, as one recent writer has commented, in the conditions operating in England at this time, the practical difficulty in proving that a person was committing bigamy was considerable.[80] When Symon Warner was questioned by the Colchester authorities in 1623 about his recent marriage to Alice Norris, who had gone home to her mother on hearing rumours that he was already married, he gave an account of his movements over the past few years that must have been typical. Warner told how he had married a woman in Suffolk about sixteen years previously, but some ten years later, 'being in debt and danger', he had moved to Kirby-le-Soken, his wife going to stay with relatives in Stowmarket, and that since then they had not been in contact.[81] Confusion of this sort was probably worsened by the Civil Wars; one complaint, for example, reached the quarter sessions of how a man returning from the conflict maliciously claimed to be the husband of a woman who had remarried.[82] Equally suggestive is the case of a man who would not marry the woman with whom he cohabited on the grounds that he refused to believe that her husband was dead. He overcame these doubts when he got her with child.[83]

A second problem involved in any consideration of bigamy was the difficulty, for any but the very rich, of obtaining a divorce.[84] Among the poor, marital incompatibility must have frequently resulted in separation, either by mutual consent or through the desertion of one of the partners. One curious example of what appears to have been separation by mutual consent is recorded on a gaol calendar for 1666, which includes Stephen Muttitt and his wife Elizabeth, 'for that they being lawfully coupled in matrymoney the said Stephen did marry one Elizabeth Sacke, and one Robert Peach did marry the said Elizabeth Muttitt'.[85] Another cause of marital breakdown, the tendency for female adherents of extreme sects to put away their less enthusiastic husbands,[86] is also recorded in Essex court documents. Mary, the wife of John Pickis, was reported to have declared that 'John Alexander was the said Maries husband & she was his wife & he was given her of God; and that John Pickis was none of her husband'. Alexander, a weaver, was examined by the magistrates and informed them that 'Rose that was his wife (& still liveing) is now none of his wife but is a widowe ... he is dead to Rose his late wife, & she is dead to this examinant, & that a misterie'.[87] It is probable, however, that most separations were carried out on a less exalted spiritual level.

If the bigamist was unknown in the area where the second marriage took place, the chances of detection were slight. Most of the cases tried in Essex in this period were detected soon after the second marriage, although in one case the accusation came fourteen years after the second and twenty-five years after the first marriage.[88] Many bigamous marriages must, however, have passed undetected, and the rarity with which the extreme penalty was exacted for this offence indicates that it was not regarded very seriously by judges and juries.

Another sexual offence punishable in this period was incest. Incest is, according to anthropologists, a sexual transgression which arouses a peculiar horror in all societies, and it was one which was universally condemned by moralists and legislators in early modern England.[89] It also figured prominently in the Elizabethan and Jacobean drama, particularly in the Italianate revenge tragedies which enjoyed such a vogue at the time. This prominence has caused one writer to comment that 'the theme of incest runs like a scarlet thread through the turgidities of the drama' of the period, the subject always being 'broached in an atmosphere of tension and horror'.[90] Neither official sanctions for dealing with the offence, nor the frequency of its prosecution, however, suggest that it was perceived as a great problem on a local level. Except in the decade after the ordinance of 1650, it was a church court offence, punishable like other church court offences by penance and excommunication;[91] and as with other sexual offences other than simple fornication or adultery, it was very rarely prosecuted.

Incest was defined as sexual relations or wedlock within the prohibited degrees of marriage.[92] This was a fairly wide definition, by no means restricted to blood relations. Even so, it seems that sexual relationships between blood relations were more seriously regarded than those between in-laws, even when these latter fell within the prohibited degrees. Certainly Macfarlane's findings suggest that this was the case; his conclusion, based on an extensive study of church court records, is that most presentments were for incest in its narrow definition.[93] In any case, the citation of an Inworth man for getting his wife's sister with child, accompanied by citation of the churchwardens for failing to present him, indicates that in incest, as in other cases, indignation at the offender was not invariably so great that it could not be modified by personal factors or by the lethargy of local officers.[94]

Accusations of incest sometimes tell us more about the living conditions of the period than about its sexual morality. Families forced by poverty to sleep several to a bed were vulnerable to charges of incest. Ann Ellis of Kelvedon was presented before the Archdeacon of Colchester on a suspicion of incest after her sixteen-year-old son was overheard announcing 'that he desyered to fele other children's secrett p[ar]t[es] saying further that he Lyinge nightly with his mother and grandmother knewe ther secrett p[ar]t[es] to be hearye'.[95] A similar case involved a woman who, when accused of incest with her son, claimed that he had been sick, and that she had been obliged to stay in his chamber with him.[96]

Only three indictments for incest were brought under the 1650 ordinance which made the offence felony without benefit of clergy.[97] A Wickford labourer was accused of incest with his mother, the indictment being found *ignoramus*,[98] while the other two cases concerned an incestuous marriage at Doddinghurst between a husbandman and the daughter of his deceased wife's previous marriage. Perhaps because of the relatively concrete evidence of marriage the couple were found guilty. Even so, the man was reprieved after being sentenced to be hanged, and the woman probably shared this fate, as she was ordered to stay in gaol after the assizes.[99] Apart from these indictments, the only evidence of Essex inhabitants falling foul of the 1650 ordinance for incest is provided by a man bound over to answer at the quarter sessions for marrying his late wife's sister.[100] Ecclesiastical court archives suggest that incest was not a major problem for those tribunals; the presentment of Ann Ellis of Kelvedon was, of 756 presentments of inhabitants of that parish before the archdeacon's court between 1600 and 1642, the only one to involve incest.[101]

It would therefore seem safe to conclude that, despite the odium attached to them by moralists and legislators, serious sexual offences were neither frequently reported nor unduly likely to result in a conviction even when tried. Indictments for sexual offences, including those of the 1650s for fornication and adultery, amounted to only just over 1% of all those tried at the assizes and quarter sessions. Without doubt, the number of cases reaching court was a severe underrepresentation of the number of occasions on which indictable behaviour occurred. Even so, it seems unlikely that there was a mass of unreported sexual offences being perpetrated. The harsh sentiments about sexual offences expressed by legal writers, and the fears of commentators that sexual morality was collapsing, are best interpreted as evidence of official preoccupations rather than as a reflection of reality.

6. Riot and popular disturbances

Popular disturbances in seventeenth-century England, despite their obvious importance to the social historian, await thorough investigation.[1] The infrequency of large-scale popular rebellions in the period, compared with the experience of some contemporary European states,[2] suggests a surprising degree of social cohesion. Detailed research, however, indicates that this suggestion must be modified by the presence of a constant undercurrent of small-scale rioting, and future investigation of court records will doubtless reveal more previously unknown disturbances. The study of this topic is, unfortunately, obscured by the wide definition of the term 'riot'. Legal theory saw three stages in public order offences, summed up by Lambarde as follows: 'And thus (upon the whole reckoning) an *unlawful assembly* is the first degree, or beginning: a *Route*, the next step, or proceeding: and a *Riot*, the ful effect and consummation, of such a disordered and forbidden action.' This disorderly behaviour showed two main characteristics; it involved three or more people, whose 'being together do breed some apparent disturbance of the Peace'.[3]

Resources for dealing with large-scale riots were hardly adequate, and central and local authorities were forced to use a number of expedients to suppress them. The first statute to deal specifically with riot, enacted in 1393, depended upon the sheriff and the power of the county.[4] Further legislation, in 1411 and 1414[5] respectively, enabled two or three justices to call out the *posse comitatus* and enacted that it should include every able-bodied male adult, all such being legally and morally bound, as the king's loyal subjects, to assist in putting down breaches of the king's peace. Tudor statutes made it felony without benefit of clergy for an unlawful assembly of twelve or more persons to continue riotously for more than an hour after being ordered to disperse by a justice, and indemnified those killing any members of the unlawful assembly if it was necessary to disperse them by force when the hour expired.[6] This legislation was the obvious forerunner of the famous Riot Act of 1715,[7] which contained little that was very novel in its provisions. What was new, in the early eighteenth century, was the availability of an efficient tool for implementing such legislation in the shape of a standing army.[8] Before that time the authorities were dependent upon more amateur forces than the military for the suppression of the large-scale riot.[9]

Most riots in Essex in the period under review were not serious enough to have caused major alarm to the county or national governments. Behaviour classed as riotous, sharing the broad characteristics of being conducted by three or more persons, and tending to cause or actually having caused a breach of the peace, comprehended a multitude of activities, most of them essentially undramatic. A total of one hundred and thirty-nine prosecutions for riot were brought between 1620 and 1680, thirty-six of them at the King's Bench, a further eighty-four at the quarter sessions, and nineteen at the assizes.[10] These cases covered a wide range of misconduct, from poaching expeditions to what looks like an early example of machine breaking. Almost all of them, apart from a few serious incidents such as the riots of 1640-2, which were tried by special commissions, were proceeded against by indictment. Analysis of these indictments into subdivisions of types of riot is difficult, although a few obvious categories, such as riot in church or against taxation, do emerge. The majority of riots, however, were simple affairs involving purely interpersonal violence, rather than action against somebody or something perceived as an offence or a threat to communal values. Most riot cases were simply assaults in which three or more persons were accused.

A number of difficulties obscures the interpretation of these small-scale riots: the divergence between the dramatic events recounted on indictments, and what happened in reality; the problem of prosecutions brought on slight or malicious grounds; and the ever-present dangers involved in accepting descriptions of a man's 'style' at face value. Even when allowances are made for these complicating factors, however, a distinct impression emerges that violence was indulged in by a wider range of social groups in this period than in modern England. Twenty-eight of these cases involved persons described as gentlemen, some of them identifiable members of leading county families. William Wiseman of Great Baddow, Esq., was indicted for a riot committed in 1618, in which he allegedly led five husbandmen in a breach of the peace on Arthur Page and his son.[11] In 1649 a gentleman and a clerk led a riotous assault upon another gentleman in Berden Church,[12] and more gentry violence occurred at Berden in 1669 when a gentleman-led gang assaulted Margaret Grove, the owner of Berden Hall, in her home.[13] Cases of gentry leading groups to attack the wives of owners of property in their homes also occurred at Great Horkesly and Chignall Smeally.[14] These examples provide more indications that the gentry were not yet above acts of violence.

Further proof of the predilection of the landed orders for violent and disorderly behaviour might be derived from cases of forcible entry and forcible disseisin. These offences, defined as 'violently taking or keeping possession with menaces, force, and arms, of lands and tenements, without the authority of the law',[15] were, by the seventeenth century, a familiar feature of English rural life. Disseisin has been described as the distinctive crime of the medieval upper classes,[16] and continued to be a problem as the middle ages waned.[17] In Essex, forcible entries and disseisins were prosecuted regularly in the sixteenth century: eighteen indictments for these offences appear on the three surviving Marian session rolls, while details of a further sixty cases survive for Elizabeth's reign.[18] A hundred and forty-seven examples have been traced for the period 1620–80, twenty-one of them in the King's Bench records, the remainder in assize and quarter sessions documents. It might be argued that forcible entry and forcible disseisin would continue as long as violence was a widely accepted method of achieving ends, and as long as the possession of land continued to be the major objective of most socially aspirant Englishmen.

Such an argument must be modified by a suspicion that the realities which underlay prosecution for forcible disseisin were often far removed from the accounts of armed and violent entry given on indictments. The contemporary land law depended heavily on the use of legal fictions, especially in those actions of ejectment which had such a close connection with forcible disseisin,[19] and it is possible that some of this fictitiousness has permeated records of criminal offences connected with the land. The earliest statute dealing with forcible entry, enacted under Richard II, implied that violence in such cases was a genuine problem. It directed that 'none from henceforth make any entry into Lands and Tenements, but only in peaceable and easy manner'.[20] By the seventeenth century, however, violence and mob action were no longer inevitable ingredients in forcible entries and disseisins.

Indeed, legal theory accepted that the amount of force involved in a forcible disseisin could be minimal. Lambarde observed that it could be 'rather intellectual than actuall', while Dalton wrote that force might be so defined purely in legal terms, 'which accounteth every private Tresspass to be a force'.[21] A forcible entry, therefore, like a riot or an assault, could be more dramatic on parchment than in reality; in one Essex case, for example, the force involved amounted to entering a cottage in the absence of its owner and changing the lock on the door.[22] Moreover, entry might be effected not as an act of wanton violence, but rather with the intention of initiating or furthering legal proceedings. Forcible disseisin had constituted an important tactical move in many medieval lawsuits involving landownership,[23] and it has been claimed that by the sixteenth century 'most intrusions were made with the intention of drawing on a suit of trespass by which title could be tried, rather than defying the law'.[24] Indeed, some accusations of forcible disseisin were founded upon nothing more violent than a desire to remove tenants in arrears with their rent. In 1637 John Totman complained to the bench that 'the Last Quarter Sessions his landlord John Chalke did (unknowne to this Petitioner) frame an Indictment against him for Forcible entry, whereupon a writt of Ejection was granted against him by this court', with the result that Totman and his family found themselves on the parish. Other witnesses suggested that Totman was, in fact, seriously behind with his rent.[25]

Such considerations make it impossible to use the incidence of forcible entry and forcible disseisin prosecutions as an index of violence or disorder; nevertheless, a number of cases did involve the use or threat of real violence. One justice reported how when he was called to view a disseisin in 1652 he 'found Samuel Smyth of Great Yeldham and Joseph Reeve of Co[ggesh]all being barred into the roome with two irons on the sides of the door & a crosse wooden barre in the midle'.[26] During a riotous entry engendered by a dispute over the ownership of the schoolhouse at Elmdon in 1664 the schoolmaster was threatened by the rival claimant and his son, these being armed with a pikestaff and a hammer respectively.[27] Indictments for forcible disseisin might be accompanied by indictments for other forms of violence or disorder, such as assault, closebreaking and barratry, and riotous assault,[28] while one would-be perpetrator of a forcible entry attempted to enlist the aid of a gang of labourers from East London on the pretext that he was hiring them to carry bricks.[29] Even when no violence was offered to persons, property might be damaged in the course of a disseisin; indeed, since the cutting of trees of corn constituted a trespass *vi et armis*,[30] it is possible that normal husbandry might be construed as damaging. Thus we find one case in which six fishermen accused of disseising some coastal land were also alleged to have removed £5 worth of oysters, and another in which a disseisin was accompanied by threatening words and the removal of hay.[31]

Forcible entry and forcible disseisin did not constitute felony, and, as with other misdemeanours, details of punishments are only rarely given on indictments. Of the seventy-six cases tried at the quarter sessions, fourteen resulted in the property in question being returned on a writ of restitution, six were punished by fining, seven were returned *ignoramus*, and one led to the accused being bound over to keep the peace. The frequency with which the writ of restitution was used without fining gives added weight to the theory that many cases were concerned with testing property rights rather than with the real use of force. Even so, a number of these cases involved violence, and were often similar in nature to other forms of violent offence.

The motives behind simple, interpersonal riots are even more obscure than the circumstances underlying a prosecution for forcible disseisin. Many of them must have been isolated incidents in a history of long-term interpersonal tensions, but it is difficult to arrive at more precise insights. Such problems as the exact nature of the grudge that led three Maldon tradesmen to remove riotously Heybridge parish stocks in 1650, or the grievance that prompted seven inhabitants of Wickham Bishops to pull down a cottage there belonging to Thomas Strutt,[32] must remain intractable. Only rarely is it possible to reconstruct a history of conflict between the parties involved in a riot, and thereby place the incident indicted in some sort of context.

One such history can be reconstructed in connection with a riot of 1654. This allegedly involved nine men, led by a yeoman named Robert Aylett, who riotously assembled at Stisted and broke a wooden gate, valued at 8/8d, belonging to John Alston.[33] Examination of the history of Stisted parish and of the relationship of the Ayletts and the Alstons makes this rather odd case more comprehensible. Both families held considerable land in the parish, and considered themselves to be on the fringe of gentility. Alston had annoyed his neighbours by altering the church path from Rayne Hatch to Stisted church, and was presented for this offence at the quarter sessions in 1636 and 1654. He was also indicted in 1655 for failing to scour his ditch abutting the highway and for allowing overgrown trees to obstruct it, the witness against him in each case being Robert Aylett. Although the naming of several other yeomen on the riot indictment suggests that Alston was not generally popular with his peers, further investigation reveals a long history of particular tension between his family and the Ayletts. The Alstons were no strangers to parish politics. Henry Alston and his father John were reported to be refusing to pay rates in 1652, while eight years previously Henry, who was then churchwarden, offered Ralph Josselin a £10 bribe when that worthy minister visited the parish (which he described as a sad and divided community) to 'assist in the choice of a minister'. In 1643 the Alstons had attempted to discredit the Ayletts by bribing two of their maidservants to swear false information against them. The girls alleged that Robert Aylett, Thomas Aylett, and others had entered the Alston residence at night and indulged in a sexual orgy and in black magic there, proceedings being further enlivened by the introduction of fiddlers from Coggeshall and Sir William Maxie's maid, who played on the virginals. These accusations were quashed, but as the cross-indictments of 1654–5 indicate, the feud lived on. It is possible that other cases of riot enjoyed a similar background to this exceptionally well-documented example.[34]

Although most riots resulted from interpersonal antagonism of the above type, a number of them can more properly be ascribed to community action. These could, of course, arise from motives as varied as those prompting the purely interpersonal violence which formed the background of the majority of cases. An unusual example occurred in 1673, when about thirty persons gathered to destroy the town stocks, whipping post, and cage at Hornchurch, the actual destruction being carried out by three men who had been paid by local gentlemen among the onlookers. The riot was almost certainly occasioned by the location of these instruments of punishment, which had been presented in 1670 and 1672 before the local leet on the grounds that they blocked the main street of the parish.[35]

Other riotous manifestations of community feelings took more familiar forms. The most obvious of these, enclosure riots, were few in Essex, probably because the county had been enclosed at a very early date. Nevertheless, a few disturbances which may have been connected with enclosure or similar problems were recorded. In 1626 at Stratford Langthorne a wood was broken into and several trees chopped down, the incident being sufficiently alarming to warrant being dealt with by a special commission.[36] Complaints of various troubles at Hatfield Forest in 1638, during which wood was cut and coppices burnt, probably refer to some sort of community action.[37] Another incident related to enclosing came in May 1677, with a riot at Canewdon involving upwards of 120 persons from the surrounding parishes. This case was probably part of the lengthy conflict about rights over the Walfleet oyster beds between the lords of Burnham manor and the local populace that had been in progress since 1641, court leet documents revealing that two of the victims of the riot had been granted licences to fish the Walfleet about a month before the riot.[38]

Despite such suggestive examples, only one enclosure riot proper is known to have occurred in Essex in the period under review, at Nazeing in 1622. Its occasion was an attempt by Sir Edward Denny, Lord of Waltham manor, and since 1604 Baron Denny of Waltham, to enclose Nazeing wood. This was common land used for grazing and had never, according to local opinion, been part of Waltham manor. The commoners were therefore perturbed when Denny enclosed the wood and began to cut down the oak trees which provided acorns upon which their animals fed. There were fears that he wished to 'improve and inclose the said wood and make a kind of depopulation', or make it 'a warren for conies'. The Sunday before the riot, John Tey, a gentleman who seems to have attempted to organise and lead opposition to Denny, had discussed matters with several other substantial tenants, claiming that he had consulted the relevant statutes and had found Denny's actions illegal. It was against a background of growing tension, then, that a riot broke out when Denny's servants suddenly impounded all the sheep grazing in the wood, these apparently numbering 1,200. A mob, composed mainly of women armed with sticks and, in one case, a pitchfork, went to the wood to confront the lord's men. One of the women, asking a Denny servant 'what would become of them if they shoulde loose their good[es]?', received the harsh reply that 'they should have their maintenance in the house of correction'. It was probably comments of this sort that earned another Denny minion, William Gardiner, the manhandling from which, according to his employer, he later died.[39] The women continued to occupy the wood, and when informed that the parish officer had been called they replied 'they neith[er] cared for Lorde nor constable, and they would give them (if they were there) so much as they had given Gardiner'. They were eventually dispersed, although the outcome of the matter is unknown.[40]

Grain riots were as infrequent as enclosure riots. The most serious of them, at Burrow Hills in 1629, came at the end of what had been a troubled decade for the county. The 1620s had seen the first stirrings of that political unrest among the gentry that was to continue until the end of the First Civil War, while the lower orders were affected by the more immediate problems of bad harvests, plague, and a depression in the textile industry. As early as February 1624 a Colchester weaver was reported for loose words about a rising of the poor,[41] and in the summer of that year a shadowy figure was seen removing royal proclamations from the town square.[42] By the late 1620s poverty in the county was serious enough to provoke fears of social unrest. The 'Briefe declaration concerninge the State of Manufacture of Woolls in the Countie of Essex' of 1629 was a terrible portrayal of poverty in the textile areas, and commented on growing tension between rich and poor.[43]

The situation was aggravated by the dislocation caused when various Stuart expeditionary forces passed through the county. Disorder invariably accompanied the passage of soldiers. The county trained bands were mobilised in 1624 to police troops on their way to join Count Mansfield's protestant forces in the Palatinate.[44] Captains conducting soldiers to Harwich in the following year were instructed to prevent straggling and the sheriff was warned to be ready to put down 'tumultuous and disordered assemblies'.[45] Troops sent up to Harwich in 1627 mutinied, apparently because they were billeted on ships rather than on the town, and when they deserted in large numbers and broke open the town gaol to release six ringleaders who had been imprisoned, the local trained band refused to assist the soldiers' officers in restoring order. When the Privy Council ordered the Essex bench to hold a session to deal with the offenders, the justices replied, a little lamely, that they were awaiting 'ye comminge downe of a justice of Assize and a seriant at Law for that purpose'. Eventually one deserter was hanged.[46]

Troop movements in 1628 provoked a serious riot at Witham. Soldiers returning from the Rhé expedition were billeted in the county and committed the usual outrages. One soldier was killed by a servant while attempting to rape a widow.[47] Depositions taken at Witham reveal a background of petty thefts and unpaid bills by the troops,[48] and at Maldon the company of Irish troops who were involved in the Witham incident provoked a note in the borough sessions recording 'their mutinous carriage & other insolencies'.[49] This contingent does not seem to have caused any real trouble at Witham until 17 March, St Patrick's day. Friction then arose after a local boy tied red crosses, similar to those sported by the Irish in honour of their patron, on the whipping post, and onto a dog's tail. A series of confused incidents followed, in the course of which the master of the boy originally responsible for the affair and the town constables were beaten up, with the troops' officers assisting and encouraging their subordinates rather than attempting to restrain them. The climax came when the captain of the company attempted to march his men through the town with swords drawn, colours flying and drums beating, and was shot in the head by a hidden marksman. Several townsfolk and soldiers were injured, two more of the latter receiving gunshot wounds, and order was only restored when neighbouring justices called out the trained bands and disarmed the troops.[50]

Against this background of disorder the Burrow Hills riot of May 1629 was as unremarkable for its short-term and localised nature as was the Privy Council's response for its unusually sharp tone. The riot, according to reports sent to the Privy Council, was directed initially at a ship lying at Burrow Hills laden with grain which was bound for Hull. At least a hundred people, many of them women, gathered from Totham (at which parish the ship lay) and a number of other parishes, some coming from Bocking and Braintree, a distance of twelve miles. The crowd set upon the chief of the merchants, a Mr Gamble, who only escaped after paying them £10. The rioters then took fifteen quarters of rye from the ship, two quarters of rye being stolen from a barn at the same time. The report received by the Privy Council emphasised the role played in the affair by Agnes Clark, a Maldon woman who had ridden through the countryside calling people together, and distributing letters to mobilise the countryfolk. Governmental reaction was swift. Three of those who robbed the ship were hanged by the special commission of Oyer and Terminer sent to punish offenders, and another was reprieved, only to break gaol subsequently. Of those that stole grain from the barn, two were hanged, two branded, and one acquitted. The authorities congratulated themselves for discouraging 'a general inclination for all who pretended poverty to rise and do mischiefe', and remarked upon the fact that all those punished were in work at the time of the incident, and that corn was at 'wonderfull easie rates'.[51]

The Burrow Hills incident was not isolated. Early in the year reports reached the Privy Council of interference with the transport of grain by armed bands,[52] and in March a serious incident occurred near Maldon. This disturbance seems to have been very similar to the riot at Burrow Hills, which it preceded by a few weeks. Once again it was sensitivity over the export of grain which stimulated the mob; a body of women emptied a ship of grain, one of them declaring that 'the owners of the said vessell were dunkirckes & yt was pittie they were suffered to lye there'. The authorities were obviously uneasy at the growing social tension in the area, and participants in this affair were asked if they had been 'procured to riot'. All of them denied it, one woman declaring roundly that 'the Crie of the Country and hir own want' had been encouragement enough.[53] After what must have been an almost identical disturbance, a Frances Cousin was committed to gaol before the Trinity assizes for 'animating of poore people to the number of sixe or seaven score to the Earle of Rivers house saying there was gold & silver enough and stayinge of corne by the waterside'.[54] A riot at Brightlingsea in September, in the course of which a mill was broken into and the millstone removed, may have been prompted by hard times.[55] The events at Burrow Hills were only the most dramatic incidents in a period of acute tension.

Perhaps the most interesting feature of the Burrow Hills riot, the Maldon disturbance and the Frances Cousin affair was that it was the export of corn which seems to have provoked the anger of the poor. Evidence from Colchester later in the century provides more examples. In March 1674 a merchant carrying corn on a pack horse had it taken from him by 'diverse lewd people', one of whom declared 'it was pity anie corn should be carried awaie in yt manner', to which a woman added that 'if they would be ruled by her the next yt came by w[i]th corn theie would be theire Butchers'.[56] In the course of a serious riot in the town in October 1675 a woman was heard encouraging the mob to attack a grain merchant 'for selling ye corne out of ye land'.[57] Another incident occurred at Harwich in 1644, when a grain ship was prevented from sailing by a mob which removed its mast.[58] There is little evidence of direct subsistence rioting, examples being limited to the sacking of a barn containing grain in 1640,[59] and the committal of two women to Colchester house of correction for 'makeing a Turmoill in the m[ar]ket place about the price of coal' in March 1630.[60] The cases detailed here do indicate that hunger, or the fear of hunger, could help motivate the poor to riot, but they can hardly be presented as indicative of unrelieved misery throughout the period.[61]

Resistance to taxation, a feature of disturbances in France at this time,[62] caused some unrest in Essex, although the relatively low levels of taxation imposed on the English labourer and small producer do much to explain the country's freedom from large-scale unrest on the French pattern. The heavy taxation of the Civil Wars and Interregnum, on the evidence of assize and quarter sessions records, provoked surprisingly little resistance. There were a few minor incidents, such as an assault on subsidy collectors at Rettendon,[63] but no serious rioting in the county. Many may have agreed with the blacksmith of Stansted Mountfitchet who, seeing a company of travellers on the road in 1654, declared that 'Theise are Parliament rogues and I am faine to work hard to get money with ye sweat of my browse to maintain such Parliam[en]t rogues',[64] but there were few prepared to translate their discontent into action. Other isolated examples of anti-taxation riots occurred after the Restoration, notably an attack on an excise officer in 1664,[65] and a riot by over forty persons, led by a merchant, against a tunnage and poundage collector at Colchester in 1679.[66]

The imposition resisted most in Essex during this period was the hearth tax, which seems, from the moment of its introduction, to have attracted an unusual degree of odium. The tax was sufficiently unpopular to render collection by parish constables impossible, and the subsequent decision to farm it heralded a series of attacks on collectors which resulted in fatalities in Dorset, Somerset, and Hertfordshire.[67] Nothing so drastic occurred in Essex, although there was widespread hostility to the tax. In 1669 a collector at Great Waltham was informed by John Poole that 'it was unjust, and if everyone were of his mind they would fight up to the eares in bloud before they would pay it'.[68] Rueben Barker, a Hempstead blacksmith, expressed the opinion that 'the chymney money was graunted for nothing but to maintain rogues and shaggs'.[69] A yeoman of Little Oakley refused to pay the tax, adding that he 'cared not a fart' for the king's officers,[70] and a woman at Leigh, a member of the tumultuous Osborne family, attempted to spit a tax collector and the parish constable with a pitchfork.[71] Another collector provoked a riot headed by the owner of a horse which he had attempted to distrain in lieu of payment of chimney money, after being offered more sullen resistance by three innkeepers at Horndon; this trio was indicted for refusing to serve him.[72]

There was only one full-scale riot against the tax, and it took place, perhaps significantly, at Colchester. Two hearth tax officers rode into St Giles parish in March 1668 to make an initial survey. There they saw a boy who sounded a horn on sight of them, thus mobilising a crowd of about a hundred people who pelted the officers with dirt and stones. The officers complained to the justices, who were apparently meeting at the time, either by coincidence, because they were performing a routine duty to meet the assessors, or because of some premonition of trouble.[73] No details of official action survive, but the incident, in that it involved surveyors rather than collectors of the tax, demonstrates both the degree of hostility the hearth tax engendered, and an unusual state of preparedness on the part of the Colchester mob, which evidently possessed some form of corporate consciousness.

Work on rioting in the eighteenth and early nineteenth centuries has revealed that disturbances by groups of workers were often controlled demonstrations aimed at what could be considered as legitimate objectives. One writer has even discovered a pattern of what he describes as 'collective bargaining by riot'.[74] Despite Essex's heavy involvement in the textile industry, there is little evidence of similar disturbances in our period. Disorder among textile workers may have been endemic in periods of economic dislocation, but (with the exception of the Colchester riot of 1675, described below) there is little evidence of their having rioted over pay and conditions. This is not to deny the existence of social tensions in the textile areas; in 1629, for example, the reports which reached Westminster of poverty in the Essex clothing towns described a sharpening of bitterness among the poor. At Bocking it was feared that the clothworkers 'having noe employment will make the place verie hazardous for men of better Ranke to be amongst them'. In response to this the Privy Council instructed the local justices to 'make diligent search and enquire to discover and finde out such lewd p[er]sons as aforesaid, that belonge not to the trade of Clothing and do ioyne themselves with the poore workmen to increase their disorders'. A 'Mutine' was only prevented by the timely arrival of the Earl of Warwick and Lord Maynard.[75]

Riots involving large numbers of textile workers occurred at Great Coggeshall in 1621 and 1674. The earlier of these, with its seven named participants and mention of numerous 'others' on the indictment, was probably some type of community, and possibly 'industrial', action.[76] Disturbances at Bocking in 1646, involving a London weaver who was felt to be a ringleader, were taken fairly seriously by the county authorities, although it is impossible to discover the exact nature of the incidents.[77] A riot which was more definitely motivated by working conditions occurred at West Ham on 11 August 1675, when a workshop was broken into and engine looms to the value of £110 removed by a crowd of indeterminate number led by a labourer. This disturbance coincided with three days of rioting in London directed against new engine looms that threatened unemployment among silk weavers.[78]

The best-documented workers' riot in this period occurred at Colchester on 11 October 1675, and was concerned with rates of pay. One witness deposed how, five days previously, he had heard weavers 'speaking of the weaveing of bayes at 9 shillings. He heard some say theie would rise to get it at 10 shillings a bay & goe to tradesmen's houses.' On the day of the riot the mob was brought out by a horn being blown. The fifty people initially involved expanded to an estimated five hundred, who began to demonstrate before the houses of various clothiers. Informed that troops would be called if they did not disperse, they replied that 'theie were strong enough & if theie would not do they could have many in the towne & a thousand out of the country'. One of their number was then chosen to present a petition to the mayor, naming those employers unwilling to pay more than 9/- a bay. So far the affair adhered to the usual pattern of 'collective bargaining by riot', a premeditated and largely peaceful demonstration aimed at presenting what was felt to be a legitimate grievance.

At this point a group of townswomen attempted to direct the ire of the mob towards the person and property of John Furly, an ex-mayor of the town who had retired from politics at the Restoration and was now combining quakerism with various business enterprises, including dealing in grain. The indignation of the women was aroused because Furly was thought to be responsible for exporting corn, and one woman described how she had been encouraged to 'goe to Furly's house and pull Furly out by ye eares' because of his activities. Order was eventually restored, and several ringleaders were imprisoned. Some of these may have been pilloried and whipped, while others had impossible fines placed upon them. Following this show of strength by the authorities, the ringleaders received a royal pardon after a petition for mercy on the grounds that they were poor, ignorant, and misled men.[79] Once again, the authorities had demonstrated both their power and their capacity for mercy.

As the foregoing pages have suggested, small-scale popular disturbances were common enough in seventeenth-century Essex: it was, however, only in the years 1640–2 that anything like a serious threat to public order on a county-wide level can be perceived. Three critical factors were operating at this time: general political unrest; the presence of large bodies of troops, raised to fight the Scots; and the blossoming of an *ad hoc* ideology of discontent focused on Laudian innovations in church affairs. In the event, the ruling segment was remarkably successful at advancing its own opposition to the Stuarts without letting the masses get out of hand. At certain points within these years it must have felt such an outcome uncertain.[80]

The extent of popular disturbances in 1640–2 raises the problem of sedition and opposition to the existing social and governmental status quo. Sedition constantly exercised the vigilance of Tudor and Stuart regimes, and the numerous cases of seditious words tried at the Essex assizes and quarter sessions are probably better interpreted as evidence of governmental sensitivity rather than of a continuous underground current of potential rebellion. Numerous such cases were reported in the Elizabethan period,[81] and every regime in the period under review attracted adverse comment. It is unnecessary to catalogue these, especially since, as has been suggested, they tell us more about governmental anxieties than anything else. Individuals were indicted or bound over for language whose modern equivalent, if prosecuted with complete efficiency, would result in the incarceration of most of the population. Even the immediate post-Restoration period provided little more than isolated mutterings, with loose talk of massacres or impending invasion of covenanting Scots,[82] which seems tame when compared to the county's record of opposition to Charles I. Interestingly enough, the central government seems to have been less worried by such utterances than it had been a century earlier: vigilance had to be exercised, and the low-born critic of the regime chastised, but nobody indicted before the Essex assizes and quarter sessions in our period for seditious words is known to have been executed. This is a striking contrast to Elizabeth's reign, when a number of the county's inhabitants suffered death for words spoken against the queen or her regime.

Despite suspicion that too much weight should not be placed on isolated examples of seditious words, it cannot be denied that puritanism, if only in the form of an incoherent anti-Laudianism, provided an important quasi-ideological motivation for many riots in the years 1640–2. Evidence of opposition to certain aspects of the established church could also be listed at length, although the problems of the clergy in the years before the Civil War fall outside the scope of this work.[83] It should be remembered, however, that difficulties between a clergyman and his flock were not limited to theological differences. Disorders against clergymen continued throughout the century, and it is not always easy to ascertain what particular issue was at stake. A strange incident, for example, occurred at Ardleigh in 1676, when two local tradesmen employed a pair of postboys to blow their horns in church during service time. Forty other persons riotously assembled there, some of whom declared that they would put the vicar in the stocks if they could get him out of the church. The causes of the incident remain impenetrable, although the quarter sessions obviously took the incident seriously, inflicting a £30 fine on one of the instigators.[84]

A more detailed impression of what could happen when good relations between a clergyman and the parish broke down is provided by the culmination of Edmund Hickeringill's career as vicar of Boxted. Hickeringill had come to Boxted after a varied life, the most recent developments in which had been ordination as a loyal supporter of Charles II, and subsequent preferment to the vicarship of St Peter's and then All Saints', Colchester, where he was apparently a popular preacher. His stay in Boxted lasted two years and was not a happy one, being marred by a feud between him and some of his parishioners. The first sign of overt tension came when a John Maidstone enlivened divine service one Sunday by standing in the belfry and urinating on the congregation. A few days later Hickeringill found several boys, including a scion of the Maidstone family, playing in the church, and upbraided them, reminding them how Maidstone had 'pissed' in the church. 'You piscopal priest,' retorted the young Maidstone, 'I have as much to do hear as you', at which the vicar set upon him and beat him. The final incident came in March 1664, when a riot broke out at the burial of Richard Dyer's wife. Hickeringill first tried to prevent the burial because the deceased had been an infrequent attender at church, and then attempted to read the burial service over the coffin, to which the relatives objected. An unseemly scuffle resulted, in the course of which a child fell into the grave, and one of the mourners expressed the wish that 'Mr Hickeringill's fatt gutts' were there too. Another man called Hickeringill a 'hireling', and exhorted the rioters against being led astray by this priest and deceiver.[85] Given such incidents as these, it may be presumed that it was probably not merely theological *Angst* that made Ralph Josselin dream of anabaptists throwing bricks at him.[86]

The disturbances of 1640–2 must, therefore, be understood against a background of small-scale rioting, some of it directed against ministers, but all of it symptomatic of a general turbulence. This turbulence is itself indicative of a willingness on the part of Stuart Englishmen to resort to direct action to achieve their ends, whether these were to do violence in the pursuit of a private quarrel, to defend community rights, or to attain a more godly ministry. In 1640, however, the crucial catalyst in the outbreak of rioting was the presence of large bodies of soldiers. Raising troops caused some trouble on a parish level. John Wise of Rettendon declared roundly that 'If I were prest for a souldier the Kinge should bee the first that I would aime att',[87] and harsh words spoken against the constable of St Osyth by the wife of a recruit were later to figure in suspicions of witchcraft when the officer fell sick.[88] Instructions to the nation at large to mobilise the trained bands in order to control the troops is evidence that the Privy Council expected more dramatic problems.[89] Despite such precautions, the levies raised in the county in 1640 were to prove much more troublesome than their predecessors of the 1620s.

Popular prejudices against the outward manifestations of the Laudian church lent coherence to the actions of the soldiery and their civilian supporters. Even if the attacks on church property at this time are part of a long history of ecclesiastical problems in the county, the rioting in 1640 was unique in its scope and intensity. Early rumblings of trouble had come in March, with a near-riot at Chelmsford accompanying the elections to the Short Parliament,[90] and with anti-Catholic disturbances at Whitsun in Colchester.[91] The first incident in the mainstream of rioting seems to have been a 'Mutiny and Tumult' among troops at Chelmsford on 12 July 1640 which prompted immediate requests for a commission of Oyer and Terminer to be sent to inflict exemplary punishment. Edward Greene, presumably a recusant or known government supporter, reported an attack by fifty or so troops on his house at Stanford Rivers, which he forestalled with 'money, victualls, and fayre speeches'. Later in the month reports filtered through that the soldiers, apparently suspicious of their officers' religious affiliations, were insisting that their superiors took communion with them. Early in August it was reported that troops stationed at Saffron Walden had struck down their officer, and it was probably these men that had removed images from the church at nearby Radwinter and burnt them in the streets of Walden.[92]

Troops all over central Essex took to tearing down and burning altar rails. At Panfield the minister was forced to leave his family for fear of his life. At Bocking the parson sent the soldiers a gift of 50/-, on which they promptly got drunk, tore down the altar rails, and burnt them in front of their captain's lodgings. Soldiers also attacked a Mr Clark, husband of a notorious recusant, at Stebbing, and destroyed the altar rails at Dunmow, with a soldier nick-named Bishop Wren taking a leading part. At Witham the vicar was beaten for crossing a child in baptism.[93] The records of a commission of Oyer and Terminer, preserved in the quarter sessions rolls, reveal that

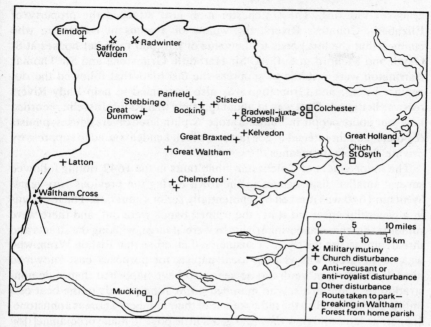

Map 3 Riots and popular disturbances in Essex, 1640–2

similar incidents took place at Kelvedon, Stisted, Bradwell-juxta-Coggeshall, Great Braxted, Elmdon and Great Holland.[94]

The disturbances of 1640 burnt themselves out fairly quickly, the various commissions sent into the county, together with the efforts of the local authorities, being sufficiently strong to re-impose order. Even so, isolated disturbances continued. At Latton, early in 1641, a group of apprentices and servants, encouraged by a widow, drank beer in the church and burnt the altar rails by the whipping post.[95] The windows of Chelmsford church were broken in November 1641.[96] At Radwinter the long history of troubles between the vicar, Nicholas Drake, and his parishioners reached a climax early in 1642 in a series of incidents which included a small riot.[97] At Great Witham four women tore up a hood and surplice.[98] In the summer of 1642 the deterioration of the political situation coincided with another upsurge of rioting. One element in this was an epidemic of attacks on the royal deer in Waltham Forest. Numerous yeomen and gentlemen were among the 187 persons tried by the commission of Oyer and Terminer sent to deal with the problem, and fines of between 3/4d and £3 were levied.[99] The summer of 1642 also saw serious attacks by the townsfolk of Colchester on Sir John Lucas, a noted royalist sympathiser who was believed to be harbouring arms for the king. The Colchester mob also attacked the property of Elizabeth, Countess Rivers, the widow of a recusant nobleman, who claimed that she lost goods to the value of £50,000 from her houses at St Osyth and Melford in Suffolk. Sir Harbottle Grimstone and Sir Thomas Barrington were ordered to suppress the disorders that followed the riot against Lucas, and Grimstone was also instructed to help Lady Rivers recover her goods.[100] It was at about this time that Ralph Josselin recorded how 'our poore people in Tumults arose, & plundered divers houses, papists & others, and threatened to goe farther, which I endeavoured to suppress by private & publique meanes'.[101]

The involvement of Colchester inhabitants in the 1642 rioting followed several smaller disturbances in the town during the previous two years. Whitsun 1640 was marked by a potentially serious situation. The town was in a generally unsettled state, the trained bands were out, and there were rumours that two wandering Irishmen were at large, walking the streets and threatening to fire the town. A suspicion then arose that Bishop Wren, who was in the area, was visiting local papists for purposes best known to himself. Nothing more dramatic seems to have happened than a demonstration by apprentices, who marched on St John's fields to the beat of a militia drum owned by the father of one of their number, Thomas Johnstone. Johnstone later told how they 'did gett a little boye to make proclamac[i]on & to saie that all gentlemen prentices should p[re]sentlie resorte unto Snt John's Feildes'. The affair was contained by the local authorities, although an anonymous gentleman wrote to the Privy Council implying that the incident had not been handled strongly enough, and the impression lingers that the mayor and his subordinates tried to play it down.[102] In November 1640 the altar rails of Chelmsford church were torn down by Samuel Ferman, a Colchester man described as 'crazy in his brains'.[103] Incidents in Colchester continued throughout 1641, as when rails and pales outside the house of Thomas Bullock were torn down,[104] or when a crowd, estimated at a hundred, attempted to rescue a lunatic named Stephen Warner from the custody of the county gaoler.[105]

Such incidents were probably endemic nationally in the two years of political crisis which followed the calling of the Short Parliament. They were invariably disturbing to high-placed observers, and probably became even more so when they were carried out by social groups generally thought of as volatile, such as the Colchester clothworkers. On the other hand, control, in Essex at least, was reasserted fairly quickly, and the county witnessed no further mass rioting on a scale equal to that which prefaced the outbreak of the First Civil War. The confused and often elusive events of 1640–2 do, however, serve to raise a number of questions about the popular disturbances of the seventeenth century as a whole, and, in particular, re-emphasise the problems involved in attempting to classify riots. A nineteenth-century legal historian, describing the law of treason, commented how 'unlawful assemblies, riots, insurrections, rebellions, levying of war, are offences which run into each other, and are not capable of being marked off by perfectly definite boundaries'.[106] The study of riot is further complicated by reservations about treating riot as a normal criminal offence. Obviously many small riots, hardly differing from common assault in their motivation, outcome, and punishment, can safely be classified as criminal. On the other hand, the disturbances of 1629, 1640–2, and 1675, although illegal, were something more than purely 'criminal' in the eyes of both the authorities and the participants. To the former they offered a threat to the social order, to the latter they represented a defence of interests, or what were conceived of as interests. Evidence of organisation – Agnes Clark calling out the country, the Colchester mob activated by the blowing of horns or the beating of drums, and the poor of Coggeshall rallying by the beat of a drum to hinder 'ye carrying away of corne' in 1695[107] – suggests that the lower orders of Essex possessed something approaching a class consciousness and were, if only in the short term, capable of concerted and organised action in defence of their interests. It is remarkable, however, how rarely real violence was used in major riots. Even in 1640–2 the popular fury against the church was expressed in breaking altar rails rather than attacking persons. Perhaps some Laudians and papists were lucky to escape with their lives, but as far as is known no one was killed in Essex by mob violence. Throughout this period, if rioting involved violence, it was more likely to be directed at property than at persons.[108] In any case the wrath of the mob tended to be of short duration.

This was just as well, given the manifest inability of the local authorities to deal with a serious riot. A Hampshire JP who set his thoughts on the subject to paper recommended his fellows to pacify the mob with 'good words', and then 'proceed against the ringleaders' when things had quietened down. It is difficult to see what else could have been done.[109] The trained bands could be called out, but these were not invariably trustworthy. The continual dependence on commissions of Oyer and Terminer provides ample demonstration of the incapacity or unwillingness of local authorities to deal with popular disturbances. It is probably this incapacity as much as any direct involvement on the part of the gentry which explains such references as exist to upper-class connivance in riots.[110] Even in the political crisis of 1640–2 there is no direct evidence of upper-class encouragement of riots, although the attitude of grand jurors towards Laudian clergymen at the summer 1639 assizes demonstrates how opposition to at least the religious status quo cut across class barriers. The events of these three years were exceptional, and the ruling sector must have regarded the continual rioting of the period with dismay. Nevertheless, the student of the popular disturbances in early modern England might be excused for thinking the widespread fear of the masses current at the time[111] somewhat overdrawn. Enclosure riots, disturbances provoked by dearth, and even industrial riots among textile workers were not as numerous in Essex in the years under consideration as the realities of life among the lower orders might lead the modern observer to expect. The pre-industrial riot is a fascinating phenomenon, and sensitive study of it reveals much of the fundamental workings of society, and of the fundamental attitudes current in that society. Paradoxically, however, the limited objectives and attainments of the riot demonstrate ultimately the robustness of early modern English society rather than its fragility.[112]

Part Three

Offences against property and the person

7. Property offences

Property offences constituted by far the largest category of serious crimes tried in Essex between 1620 and 1680. They totalled 3,206, outnumbering homicides and infanticides combined by over ten to one, and assaults by about five to one. Such a pattern was probably fairly typical of early modern England, and was certainly not new: other studies have shown the overwhelming numerical preponderance of property offences in the Home circuit in the sixteenth and seventeenth centuries,[1] and have also demonstrated that, in some areas at least, a less marked version of the same situation was current in the early fourteenth century.[2] It is, therefore, perfectly understandable that by the Elizabethan period trials for theft traditionally dominated criminal court proceedings, and that most contemporary complaints of rising crime centred on offences against property.[3] Analysis of the nature, extent, and treatment of such offences would therefore seem to be of prime importance to any study of crime in seventeenth-century England. If only because of their sheer numbers, thefts, burglaries, breaking and enterings, robberies and pickpocketings demand serious attention from the historian of crime.

The legal definition of theft or larceny was essentially simple. Coke described it as 'the felonious and fraudulent taking and carrying away by any man or woman, of the meere personal goods of another, neither from the person, nor by night in the house of the owner'.[4] However, the treatment of theft cases was complicated by the distinction, dating from approximately the reign of Edward II, between grand and petty larceny.[5] The former, involving theft to the value of one shilling or upwards, was classed as felony punishable by hanging, although with a few statutory exceptions benefit of clergy might be claimed. The latter, involving thefts to the value of less than one shilling, was in theory punished at the judge's discretion, although by this period the standard punishment for petty larceny was whipping. The prescribed punishment for grand larceny – hanging for those stealing goods worth one shilling or more, if they were unable to read – was very harsh, and was attracting adverse comment by the middle of the century.[6]

The rigorous legal attitude to theft had long been modified by the practice of the courts. The decision as to the value of the goods stolen – and hence whether the offence in question constituted grand or petty larceny – lay with juries, which from the fourteenth century onwards had been saving thieves from the gallows by giving false returns of the sums involved.[7] Blackstone described how

the mercy of juries will often make them strain a point, and bring in larceny to be under the value of twelvepence, when it is really of much greater value: but this, though evidently justifiable and proper, when it only reduces the present nominal value of money to the antient standard, is otherwise a kind of pious perjury, and does not at all excuse our common law in this respect from the imputation of severity.[8]

This 'pious perjury', which was to result in the virtual suspension of many capital statutes by the early nineteenth century,[9] was already commonplace by the seventeenth. It is also certain that the test of literacy applied to those claiming clergy was not always a strict one. Both these points will, of course, be dealt with more fully in the wider context of the flexibility of sentencing;[10] they are raised here simply to render the discussion of the treatment of property offenders more understandable.

Larceny was the most commonly indicted crime at the Essex assizes and quarter sessions, 2,653 cases involving 2,777 accused being tried between 1620 and 1680.[11] A further ninety-two cases survive among the fragmentary Colchester sessions rolls, and the Maldon archives contain scattered references to thefts. Given the poor survival of assize documents of the 1620s and 1630s, two decades when property offences were heavily prosecuted, the total of 2,653 surviving indictments must be a serious understatement of the total prosecutions. They do, nevertheless, provide a large enough sample for analysis, the most logical starting point for which is to subdivide indictments by the type of goods allegedly stolen, and then to consider the treatment of the accused. Most of the categories of goods described are self-explanatory, and problems of classification are discussed as they arise. Initially, therefore, let us turn to a commentary on tables 2–5.

The most common form of larceny on the evidence of surviving records was sheep-theft, nearly a fifth of all thefts falling into this category. Sheep-thefts were common throughout the county and follow no obvious geographical pattern, apart from a tendency to be concentrated in the clothing districts of the north of the county, and the London peripheries where sheep were constantly passing *en route* for the markets of the capital. The number and value of sheep allegedly stolen varied considerably. One labourer was charged with four thefts involving sheep valued at £19/18/-, and other indictments involved eleven wethers each valued at 10/-, or nine wethers at 13/-;[12] the number of sheep-thieves whipped indicates that in at least sixty cases the sheep stolen were priced at less than a shilling. This cannot be attributed to fluctuations in the price of sheep over the century. At the Epiphany 1626 sessions, for example, the value of single ewes allegedly stolen ranged from 10d to 6/8d.[13] The value of sheep given on indictments must frequently have been understated, and it is sometimes possible to find

Table 2 *Thefts at Essex assizes and quarter sessions, 1620–80, by quinquennia, and type of goods stolen*

	1620	1620–4	1625–9	1630–4	1635–9	1640–4	1645–9	1650–4	1655–9	1660–4	1665–9	1670–4	1675–9	1680	Total	Percentage of theft 1620–80
Sheep	3	41	80	69	45	20	56	52	30	33	22	18	25	2	496	19%
Cattle	2	4	25	17	11	9	14	16	10	10	5	5	11	—	139	5%
Horses	5	6	28	14	21	12	47	27	16	22	23	11	20	—	252	9.5%
Other Livestock	1	10	14	9	6	7	13	5	3	3	3	14	7	—	95	4%
Poultry	—	18	24	20	21	10	7	25	10	12	11	10	2	—	170	6%
Clothes and household linen	2	29	50	51	51	30	23	43	26	25	19	9	20	—	378	14%
Cloth	—	6	12	14	11	8	18	15	3	3	3	1	5	—	99	4%
Tools/ Materials	3	16	23	25	34	10	13	22	15	17	10	4	6	1	199	7.5%
Wheat	—	16	30	42	25	8	18	20	10	21	16	2	9	—	217	8%
Food	1	5	18	19	17	5	9	10	7	3	4	1	6	—	105	4%
Money	3	12	14	18	9	9	10	10	8	7	9	8	8	—	125	5%
Miscellaneous	4	20	46	42	43	32	34	42	25	23	27	16	22	2	378	14%
Total	24	183	364	340	294	160	262	287	163	179	152	99	141	5	2653	—
Percentage of theft 1620–79	—	7%	14%	13%	11%	6%	10%	11%	6%	7%	6%	4%	5%	—	—	—

Notes: the 1620 column represents cases committed before 1620 but tried in or after that year. The 1680 column represents cases committed and tried in 1680

Table 3 *Verdicts in theft cases at Essex assizes and quarter sessions, 1620–80, by type of goods stolen*

	Hanged	Read as a clerk, branded	Whipped	At large	Acquitted	Ignoramus	No details	Other	Total
Sheep	15	176	60	23	121	78	14	25	512
Cattle	15	50	2	12	39	16	18	11	163
Horses	59	–	–	22	57	54	31	48	271
Other livestock	3	24	15	8	27	21	8	6	112
Poultry	3	19	60	18	59	44	11	9	223
Clothes and household linen	8	14	133	17	91	56	9	20	348
Cloth	–	30	12	10	27	17	6	6	108
Tools/Materials	2	24	57	21	55	38	32	3	232
Wheat	4	48	56	10	80	36	10	7	251
Food	1	10	46	10	21	19	6	7	120
Money	7	24	12	6	47	34	6	12	148
Miscellaneous	12	73	69	34	86	75	27	20	396

Notes: totals are inflated, as persons accused of more than one type of theft have been included more than once

Table 4 *Treatment of theft suspects at Essex assizes and quarter sessions, 1620–80*

	Hanged	Read as a clerk, branded	Whipped	At large	Acquitted	Ignoramus	No details	Other	Total
Male subtotal	105	485	394	167	557	412	121	140	2,381
Females									
Widow	—	5	16	6	21	13	5	2	68
Spinster	4	20	55	16	46	41	9	11	202
Married	1	14	25	6	47	29	5	4	131
Female subtotal	5	39	96	28	114	83	19	17	401
Total	110	524	490	195	671	495	140	157	2,782
Percentage	4%	19%	17.5%	7%	24%	18%	5%	5.5%	—

Notes: totals here and in table 5 differ from those in table 3 because persons indicted for stealing more than one type of goods have been counted once, the most serious penalty being the one noted. Hence an accused whipped for poultry-theft but acquitted for sheep-theft appears twice on table 3, but once as whipped, here. The male styles, as given on indictments, were: gentleman, 25; yeoman, 47; husbandman, 223; craftsman or tradesman, 449; labourer, 1,601; no details, 26

Table 5 *Treatment of theft suspects at Essex assizes and quarter sessions, 1620–80, by quinquennia*

	Hanged	Read as a clerk, branded	Whipped	At large	Acquitted	*Ignoramus*	No details	Other	Total
1620–4	10	26	55	30	45	10	8	7	191
1625–9	18	65	74	38	94	52	24	34	399
1630–4	28	94	84	28	87	25	8	17	371
1635–9	7	62	67	23	69	62	11	16	317
1640–4	2	31	23	29	49	38	4	3	179
1645–9	6	52	23	14	60	55	18	27	255
1650–4	12	59	53	18	63	85	9	8	307
1655–9	2	36	28	3	44	44	17	6	180
1660–4	7	39	25	4	55	37	18	9	194
1665–9	5	9	27	2	44	34	6	13	140
1670–4	3	24	7	3	25	16	13	8	99
1675–9	10	27	24	3	36	27	4	9	140
Total	110	524	490	195	671	485	140	157	2772

evidence of this practice: a Yorkshire vagrant indicted for the theft of a ewe worth 10d in 1651 had already deposed that the animal had been purchased by him and a friend for 6/-.[14]

As table 3 indicates, sheep-thieves were unlikely to be hanged, only some 3% of those accused suffering the extreme penalty. These tended to be the more serious offenders, in terms of the value of the sheep stolen, and also included several accused who were also convicted for other types of theft and burglary. The last hanging of a sheep-thief proper was in 1634, when two men were sentenced to death for this offence at the Hilary assizes.[15] The high proportion of those branded for sheep-theft – 34% as against 19% for all thefts – must be taken as evidence of an unwillingness on the part of the courts to press for a capital conviction in this type of case.

Depositions reflect no clear pattern of victim–offender relationship that might help explain this. Sheep were already being marked in this period, which added to the difficulties of stealing sheep from members of one's own village.[16] Even so, depositions suggest that established members of the community occasionally came under suspicion of stealing sheep from their neighbours. A number of these cases must have involved genuine mistakes, perhaps when a neighbour's sheep was accidentally penned with those belonging to the accused. If a grievance already existed between the two parties accusation of theft could ensue, as at Birchanger in 1648, when a suit already existed between the prosecutor and defendant in a case that involved the penning of sheep that had strayed onto the latter's land.[17] Stray sheep also offered temptations to the opportunist criminal among the rural poor. A Tollesbury labourer recounted how he came upon a stray sheep on desolate Tiptree Heath 'and stealing closelie to her did sodenly flye upon her and then bound her and carried her to his Mother's house', where the animal was promptly skinned and butchered.[18] Similarly Edward Wright, examined at Maldon, confessed that, while visiting his married brother in the borough, he was directed by his sister-in-law to 'go into the fields by a howse that stoode emptie & there were sheep & that he might goe w[i]thout feare. And he went Accordinglie thither & did drive the sheep into the lane', one of them being subsequently killed and butchered.[19] Such thefts were, on occasion, easily detected when search was made of the suspect's house: evidence of a freshly butchered sheep was considered adequate grounds for bringing an indictment when few labourers could afford to buy meat in such quantities.[20] Sheep were not, of course, vulnerable merely to the resident poor; vagrants might come across stray sheep, and carry or drive them off with the object of selling them.[21]

Horse-theft was regarded more seriously than most forms of larceny, Tudor legislation having made it felony without benefit of clergy.[22] As tables 2 and 3 demonstrate, fifty-nine horse-thieves, or 21.75% of those accused, were hanged, a further fourteen reprieved, and five transported, this accounting for the unusually high proportion of horse-thieves placed in the 'other' category. On the evidence of 'styles' as given on indictments, the social composition of alleged horse-thieves was also unusual, twenty-eight of the accused (10.25%) being described as yeomen or gentlemen, and only three of the accused being women.

All but fifteen horse-thefts were prosecuted at the assizes, and the familiar problem of the absence of assize depositions makes it difficult to evolve a clear picture of the horse-thief. It is noteworthy, however, that one Essex writer of the sixteenth century thought horse-traders especially dishonest, so that 'an honest meaning man shall have very good luck among them if he be not deceived by some false trick or other',[23] and a Jacobean writer describes 'Jinglers' whose Smithfield base would have enabled them to make frequent forays to Essex horse fairs.[24] Given the existence of such men in the horse trade, it seems likely that a number of those indicted for horse-theft were horse-dealers, although this is impossible to prove. One such case may be provided by that of Raphe Barker, incarcerated in Colchester castle on suspicion of horse-theft. His wife Mary rode to town 'to see howe he did' on a horse which, the borough authorities suspected, was stolen. The woman claimed that her husband had 'swapped' it for another at Romford fair.[25]

Thefts of cattle, pigs, and other forms of livestock require little comment. It is, perhaps, surprising that cattle-theft was only about half as frequent as horse-theft, although our knowledge of the relative numbers of these two animals in seventeenth-century Essex is limited. Hanging for cattle-theft tended to be most common in the early half of the century, only two examples being recorded after 1655. Given that even the most merciful jury would boggle at valuing cattle, normally priced on indictments at several pounds, at less than a shilling, it is understandable that only two of those accused of cattle-theft were whipped. Again the high proportion of those claiming clergy successfully is striking, and once more it seems likely that this is attributable to an unwillingness on the part of the courts to hang cattle-thieves rather than to widespread literacy. Similar conclusions may be reached from the thefts of other livestock (of which ninety-five cases involved pigs, although goats, mastiffs, a tame doe and a ferret were also included in this category). It would seem, moreover, that thefts of livestock other than sheep tended to be a predominantly male activity. Only 3% of those accused of stealing cattle and 10% of those accused of stealing other livestock were female.

It is perhaps with poultry that we are confronted with a different type of theft, the petty thieving that played a major role in the struggle for survival of the poor, and which has obvious links with poaching, gleaning, and hedgebreaking. Whereas the theft of cattle, horses, and in many cases, sheep, must have called for considerable initiative and presented difficulties of disposal, poultry was much more vulnerable to the village poor, this vulnerability being perhaps reflected by the high proportion of females accused of poultry-theft, 17.5% as opposed to 14.5% overall. Easily stolen, poultry could be dressed, cooked, and eaten quickly, with none of those problems of disposal which could lead to the downfall of a sheep-thief. An example of this type of theft is provided by two Latton men who went poaching rabbits at Harlow, but finding none, stole two geese which they concealed in their breeches.[26] Investigation was hampered by the problem of identifying the stolen goods. When a Panfield man tried to claim a stolen hen from a neighbour, he was attacked by the suspect and his wife, who 'offered to beat him out of the yard, telling him that he came to cony catch him'. The prosecutor claimed that the hen in question had been mutilated to evade detection, but the jury was apparently unimpressed, and the accused were acquitted.[27]

The punishments inflicted on chicken-thieves suggest that their activities were not taken too seriously by the courts. One of the three persons hanged for poultry-theft, a labourer at the Hilary 1620 assizes,[28] was charged solely with this offence, but the two others were also convicted of burglary and pig-theft. The high proportion of accused whipped, and the low proportion of those branded, are probably a natural result of the low value of poultry compared with livestock.

A total of 217 cases concerned the theft of grain, involving 251 accused.[29] Of these only four were hanged, one of them being also convicted for horse-theft, which is probably the charge which resulted in capital punishment.[30] Of the remainder, one is a unique case of a father prosecuting his son, a Hockley yeoman, for the theft of £3 of barley at the Hilary 1621 assizes;[31] another is unusual in that the indictment states that the accused was unable to read his book and claim clergy,[32] and the third is one of the rare quarter sessions indictments resulting in a hanging.[33] From the low incidence of death sentences for grain-theft it may be deduced that this offence was not regarded as a major threat to the social fabric. It seems probable that many such thefts were committed by harvest workers who would take advantage of the chance to carry off grain after their labours. The problem is further complicated by the custom of gleaning, for the pretensions of the lower orders to gleaning rights and those of the landowner to his property had been a source of tension since at least the late thirteenth century.[34] As we shall see when discussing crime and the community, such tensions formed the background to many accusations of grain-theft in seventeenth-century Essex.

Obviously related to thefts of grain is larceny involving foodstuffs. Given that hunger was a common experience for much of the population of the county in the seventeenth century, it is surprising that only 105 cases of theft of food, constituting 4% of all thefts, are recorded for the period 1620–

80. There are a number of reasons that might be suggested to explain this. Firstly, prepared foodstuffs might normally have been stored indoors, although it should be pointed out that few burglary indictments involved taking foodstuffs.[35] Secondly, detection could be difficult – a vagrant stealing a pie, for example, would be able to dispose of the evidence fairly quickly. Thirdly, there may have been a disinclination to prosecute thefts of small amounts of food, whether through humanity or through a feeling that it was too much trouble, and it seems probable that many rural property-owners would turn a blind eye to the theft of small amounts of food. Indeed, the paucity of indictments for thefts of this type demonstrates the difficulties involved in making statistically based assertions about the crime of the period: the post-Restoration era might have been less grim for the county's poor than the two decades before the Civil Wars, but it is unlikely that the seventeen recorded thefts of food in Essex represent the real extent of such larcenies in the years 1660–80. This apparent tolerance of persons stealing food was paralleled by the leniency with which they were treated by the courts. A labourer accused of stealing assorted consumables valued at £1/14/- was hanged in 1634,[36] probably as an object of exemplary punishment after a decade of disruption and high theft rates in the county. He was, however, the only person to be executed for stealing food in our period; the overwhelming majority convicted for this offence were whipped.

Similarly, reported cases of thefts involving textiles are fewer than might be expected in a county where cloth production was so important. Only ninety-nine cases of this type survive from the county assizes and quarter sessions, and even in Colchester, a town dependent on the clothing trade, only ten of the ninety-two cases of theft recorded on the borough sessions rolls between 1619 and 1639 involved the taking of textiles.[37] This situation is at variance with that existing in the Elizabethan period, when trial of some 206 thefts and burglaries (roughly an eighth of all cases in these categories) involving textiles were recorded at the assizes and county quarter sessions in the years 1558–1602.[38] There is no ready explanation for this, and as table 2 indicates, thefts of wool and cloth cannot be directly linked to what is known of fluctuations in the fortunes of the textile industry.

Exact information on the relationship of victim to offender is elusive. In an industry dependent on outworking it is likely that some textile thefts are accounted for by workers attempting to appropriate the materials given to them to process. This could be classed as embezzlement, punishable by a spell in the stocks: a number of Colchester clothworkers convicted of stealing yarn they had been given to work suffered such punishment.[39] There are, however, few references to embezzlement in the assize and quarter sessions records, and it would seem that offenders of this type were dealt with as simple thieves; certainly, a number of cases exist in which the accused were, in all probability, outworkers.[40] Even so, it is impossible to calculate with any certainty how many of the accused were clothworkers. In only seventeen cases were persons described as textile workers, or wives of textile workers, accused, although many of the labourers or spinsters charged with cloth-theft must have been involved in the industry.

As might be expected, textile-thefts were concentrated in clothing centres. Bocking and Braintree witnessed eight and nine cases respectively, the Coggeshalls a further ten, with more cases in the smaller centres dependent on the Coggeshall trade: Rivenhall, Kelvedon, and Great Braxted. Similarly, although only two cases from Colchester proper reached the county assizes and quarter sessions, textile-thefts occurred in many of the villages in Colchester's economic orbit: Greenstead, Langham, Wivenhoe, West Bergholt, Boxted and Dedham. Despite four cases at Chelmsford, and a handful more in the south-west of the county, cloth-thefts were normally committed in those parts of the county most heavily involved in textile production.

Thefts of clothes and what might be described as household linen – sheets, tablecloths, and such related objects as mattresses and pillows – totalled 378 cases and involved 408 persons. The goods stolen within this category varied in size and value from a shirt or smock to substantial quantities of clothing or bedding, although the high proportion of whippings inflicted for thefts of this type (32.5% of those accused) suggests that most thefts within this category were either small-scale or unlikely to arouse great indignation. Nevertheless, a few persons were hanged for stealing clothes or similar items, although such cases fall into no very discernible pattern. As elsewhere, capital convictions cannot be related to the value of the stolen goods. Although a spinster was hanged in 1664 for stealing clothes and oddments to the unusually high value of £9/16/-,[41] other thieves were hanged for taking clothing or household linen valued at 17/2d, 10/6d[42] and for two thefts of less than thirty shillings.[43]

Analysis of the bulk of the cases reveals that thefts of clothing and household linen must be regarded as typically minor larcenies; they were usually opportunist and carried out by the less terrifying criminal elements, an assertion supported by the fact that 30% of those charged with this type of theft were female. Depositions support the suspicion that clothes and household linen were most often stolen by the opportunist petty thief. The practice of drying clothes and similar articles on bushes or hedges facilitated their theft, and several vagrants fell into the temptation offered by laundry left in this fashion.[44] Moreover, the vagrant was not above stealing sheets or linen from the alehouse where he lodged,[45] or even from those whose charity he sought.[46] Drying washing was not, however, at risk only to thefts by vagrants; cases involving women stealing laundry from their neighbours occurred,[47] the goods in question sometimes being identified by initials stitched into them.[48] When not being dried, clothes and linen were especially vulnerable to servants, whose opportunities for taking and selling off these articles must have been very good. Clothing was sometimes included in the property taken when dismissed or absconding servants decided to depart with some of their late employer's goods.[49]

Thefts of tools and materials were also common, 199 cases involving 232 accused being recorded. A wide range of articles falls within this category, although, as might be expected, the normal equipment of husbandry and rural crafts was most frequently taken: iron wedges, plough hooks, harrow teeth, pales, hop poles, and such materials as iron, lead, or coal. Despite the generally miscellaneous nature of the stolen goods, it is possible in some cases to detect a direct connection between the thief and his spoil. Thus cases occurred of a carpenter stealing wood, a joiner stealing carpenter's tools, a glover stealing calf skins, a tailor stealing silk and buttons, and a shoemaker stealing leather.[50] It is such links as these that must account for the unusually high proportion of persons described as craftsmen and tradesmen being involved in thefts of this type, 21.5% in contrast to 16% for all thefts.[51] Characteristically, only tools or materials of little value were stolen, and thieves were therefore unlikely to arouse great indignation on the part of judges or juries. Only two persons were hanged for thefts of this type, one in 1629 for the theft of tools valued at 5/4d, the other for two thefts totalling £1/9/6d worth of tools in 1630.[52] Given that nearly a quarter of those charged with stealing tools or materials were whipped, it may be concluded that larceny in this category was usually minor in character.

Thefts of money, although not negligible, are not as widespread as might have been expected, this being perhaps a reflection of the difficulties of detection in such cases. A total of 125 thefts of money are recorded, involving 148 persons, 7 of whom were hanged. The study of thefts of money is, of course, complicated by the existence of pickpocketing as a distinct offence. Stealing from the person without knowledge of the victim had been made felony without benefit of clergy during Elizabeth's reign.[53] This is an indication of the seriousness with which the offence was viewed, and it is interesting that Blackstone was to describe this statute as 'a most severe law'.[54] Eighteen cases of pickpocketing reached the Essex assizes and quarter sessions during this period, involving twenty-three accused, of whom five were hanged, nine acquitted, and five discharged on an *ignoramus*.

Pickpocketing required a level of expertise which suggests that some of those accused were professional or semi-professional criminals. Certainly the preamble to the Elizabethan statute against pickpockets and cutpurses would support such a view, with its reference to 'a certain Kind of evil-disposed Persons, commonly called Cutpurses or Pick-purses . . . who do confeder together, making among themselves as it were a Brotherhood or Fraternity of an Art or Mystery, to live idly by the secret Spoil of the good and true Subjects of the Realm.'[55] This may have been an accurate description of the situation in Tudor London, but there is little evidence of this degree of organisation in Stuart Essex. A unique example of a semi-professional pickpocket is provided by fourteen-year-old Edith Harding, last settled at St Giles-in-the-Fields in London, taken on suspicion of pickpocketing at Colchester in 1629. She admitted the offence, adding 'that ever since her owne father died about fower years since she hath used picking of purses and that once before this shee picked a man's pocket in this towne a great while since'.[56]

Gatherings of any sort attracted pickpockets. William Kemp recorded how the throng that came to see him dance at Brentwood in 1600, during his nine-day morris-dance from London to Norwich, included two female vagrant pickpockets who were whipped as rogues by the town authorities.[57] Similarly, Colchester corn market and the butter and cheese market provided an opportunity for pickpockets,[58] and there is one complaint of a pocket being picked by a maid during a scuffle in an alehouse.[59] Apart from these cases there is little qualitative evidence concerning the offence.

Thefts of money excluding pickpocketing show few salient features. The value of coin stolen varied from a few pence[60] to a record 2,000 Spanish pieces of eight stolen at Grays Thurrock in 1675. The money was valued at £450, and four sacks worth 6d were included on the indictment for good measure, although the two labourers accused of the theft (a father and son team) were acquitted.[61] No other thefts of money reached this level, the highest other sums recorded being £70, £50 and £56/14/4d.[62] As in other types of theft, it is difficult to discern any pattern behind the bringing of capital convictions. Certainly the amount of money stolen cannot be related to the employment of the death penalty. In the 1630s, for example, thefts of £3 and £1/14/8d were punished by hanging,[63] at the same time as thefts of £10/1/-, £2/11/- and £3/16/- resulting in the accused being branded.[64]

Stolen goods classed as miscellaneous include a wide variety of articles, a few of them bizarre in nature, including such oddities as the sail from a windmill, and a treble viol.[65] The more ambitious thief might take a cockboat (valued at £13, with £2/15/- of accessories),[66] while the more sacrilegious would not scruple at church property, such as the silver cup from Little Stambridge church for which a thief was hanged in 1626, or the cup and clothing stolen from the churchwardens of Frinton in 1630.[67] Two other unusual thefts which have been placed in this category are that occurring in 1633, when a labourer was whipped for stealing the parish stocks at Bulmer, and that committed by Henry Argoe, whipped in 1653 for stealing 'iron from a whipping post', which was the property of the parishioners at Writtle.[68] These last cases demonstrate not only eclecticism on the part of the early modern thief, but also an admirable contempt for authority.

Of the 378 cases within this category, 88 involved goods so various as to defy analysis. These were mostly small in value, although one indictment mentioned miscellaneous items to the value of £108/13/4d.[69] This subdivision has, however, been used to include some types of theft which, although not frequent enough to warrant separate treatment, have been placed under this heading for convenience. Among these are thefts of household implements, such as plates, bowls, dishes and skillets. These thefts ranged from small quantities of cheap pewter to quite expensive items of gilt or silverware; one case of this type, involving silver and gold dishes worth £8/10/-, resulted in a hanging.[70] Also included in this category are thefts of firewood, and of spoons, firearms, and gold rings, none of which contributed more than a handful of cases to the total. Overall, little clear pattern emerges from a study of this kind of offence. Even so, the very variety of goods stolen lends weight to the theory that theft at this period was an essentially opportunist activity.

Another important impression that emerges from the study of theft as recorded on indictments is the rarity of cases involving violence. Theft with violence was classed as robbery, and was felony without benefit of clergy,[71] thus forming a legal entity distinct from larceny proper. Robbery was an extremely rare offence,[72] however, and it has therefore been dealt with here. Not only was it rarely prosecuted, but when it was the reaction of the courts to robbers was not an especially severe one. When two husbandmen were indicted for this offence in 1622, the details of the stolen goods were stricken from the indictment, and one of the accused fined 6d for simple assault,[73] the other being at large. Other cases of robbery – for example of oats, or of a fowling piece – resulted in returns of *ignoramus*, or of no clear conclusion being reached.[74] Only two men are known to have been hanged for robbery, both of them in the 1620s.[75] The impression from court records is that violence was only rarely used to further a theft – surprisingly rarely if the predilection of the age for violent behaviour is remembered.

An exception must be made for highway robbery. The highway robber, destined to become perhaps the most romantic figure in English criminal history, was already active in the sixteenth century, and surviving records indicate that over sixty offenders of this type were tried in Essex in Elizabeth's reign.[76] Seventy-nine highway robberies were indicted in the period 1620–80, a total of one hundred and nine persons, all male, being accused. Of these, thirty-eight were hanged; five others remanded after judgement; one sent to the house of correction; and another, although the offence was theoretically, like other forms of robbery, not clergyable, branded. Thus although highway robbery was not prosecuted frequently enough to justify the notoriety that has been attached to it,[77] it was, by the standards of the time, one of the more common serious offences, and produced a steady crop of executions long after capital punishment had become uncommon for most types of simple theft.

Highway robberies tended to be clustered around the peripheries of London, which suggests the presence of highwaymen based on the metropolis making occasional forays into the London hinterland. Some highwaymen were certainly professional criminals. One diarist recorded in 1637 the execution of a group of gentlemen robbers who, with the assistance of 'many confederates and attendants', had plundered travellers in a number of eastern counties, Essex among them.[78] In 1681 Carew Harvey Mildmay, JP, was given information about a group of professionals carrying out burglaries and highway robberies on the fringes of the capital, and Claude Duval, one of the more celebrated highwaymen of the post-Restoration period, operated in the county.[79]

Despite the evidence of the activities of professional criminals, and the emergence of the romantic archetype of the highwayman, it is likely that most highway robberies were mundane crimes committed by mundane people. Most highway robbers describing themselves as gentlemen probably had only the most tenuous connection with gentle blood, and even less with gentlemanly behaviour; in 1675, for example, a minor scion of the Verney family found himself in Chelmsford gaol on a charge of highway robbery, and was eventually hanged after frantic attempts to escape by turning king's evidence.[80] Court records suggest that Essex highway robbers cut an inferior figure to the silk-clad daredevil gentleman of romantic fiction. A witness described how, in 1681,

about one of the clocke this morning Peter Hall (in company w[i]th four men more) did in the rode in the parish of West Ham tooke hould of his horse's bridell he beinge upon his backe and did bid him stand, upon w[hi]ch Mr Riman quitted his horse and tooke hould of the said Peter Hall (the others running away) and carryed him to the constable who brought him hither.[81]

A similarly unimposing highway robber was foiled in 1635 when his proposed victim thwarted him by the simple expedient of hitting him over the head.[82] These two examples suggest that the highway robber was not always the most confident of malefactors. Moreover, the spoils taken in highway robberies suggest that many offenders were amateur rather than professional criminals. Fifteen of the indictments were brought for robbery of goods or money valued at less than £1, and although it is possible that the professional might have been unlucky enough to choose a poor victim, it is unlikely that he would have put his life in danger for the hat and petticoat valued at 1/5d allegedly taken from a woman in 1655, or for the contents of a pedlar's pack stolen in 1634.[83]

The degree of violence offered by highway robbers varied. The widely travelled Fynes Moryson commented in the 1630s that: 'Theeves in England are more common than in any other place, so farre as I have observed or heard, but having taken purses by the high way, they seldom or never kill those they rob', a state of affairs that led the stalwart Moryson to advise his readers to attack their would-be robbers and take them before a justice.[84] John Clavel, an early Stuart highwayman who set out his thoughts on his former craft when pardoned, advised those being robbed to resist where possible and give in gracefully where not, making it plain that in either case the robbers would be unwilling to risk taking a life.[85] Only one murder in the course of a highway robbery has been recorded in the Essex assize documents within the period of this study, in 1668,[86] although by the 1690s there were pitched battles between travellers and highwaymen in the county.[87] There is some evidence of non-fatal violence. In one case a Hertfordshire man was knocked off his horse and robbed after drinking in an alehouse with his assailant,[88] and an unlucky Scotsman was robbed of £11/15/-, and then bound by the malefactors and 'forced to goe three quarters of a mile to gett himself unbound after the theeves left him'.[89] Other travellers may have suffered similar troubles, although details of such cases are now lost, but serious violence must have been the exception. It is also noteworthy that the chronological spread of highway robberies in the county between 1620 and 1680[90] does not readily support the claim that it was the presence of large numbers of disbanded troops in the aftermath of the Civil Wars which really established highway robbery as a major problem in England.[91]

Although less readily open to romanticisation than highway robbery, burglary and housebreaking were far more common. By the seventeenth century the term burglary was used loosely to cover all forms of theft involving entry of a house, but in its strict definition, to quote Dalton, it occurred when

one or more in the night time, do break or enter into another's dwelling-house feloniously, wherein some person is, or a Church, or the Walls or Gates of a City, or Walled Town, with an intent to rob, or do any other Felony, although he or they do not execute same, or do take or carry away nothing; yet it is Felony of Death, and the offenders shall not have the benefit of their Clergy.[92]

Two elements made burglary a more serious offence than simple theft,[93] and hence not clergyable. Firstly, it was committed at night, which, to Coke, 'doth aggravate the offence, sith the night is the time wherein Man is to rest, and wherein Beasts runne about seeking their prey'.[94] Secondly, the fact that burglary was committed in the home of the victim led to its being considered as a more direct threat to society than straightforward larceny. Burglary offered a serious affront to the security to which a man might feel entitled in his own house.

This stricter definition of burglary was, in the seventeenth century, a relatively recent one. Pollock and Maitland, although stating that in medieval England 'the thought that crimes committed at night are to be punished more severely than similar crimes committed by day was not far from our ancestors', found it impossible to give any 'precise account of the genesis of burglary'.[95] The insistence that burglary was housebreaking carried out at night seems to have been a sixteenth-century innovation,[96] and the other major element of burglary, putting the victim in fear, was probably first made explicit by the statute 1 Edw. VI cap. 12.[97] Late sixteenth-century legislation also made housebreaking by day, under certain circumstances, a more serious offence, the most important statute being that of 1597 making breaking a house and stealing goods worth more than 5/- during the daytime felony without benefit of clergy.[98]

Three hundred and thirteen indictments for burglary were brought between 1620 and 1680, and one hundred and sixty-four for housebreaking by daylight, these two categories combined constituting some 6% of all indictments. Seven hundred and eleven persons were indicted under these two headings, details of their social status and treatment being given in tables 6 and 7. As table 6 indicates, burglary was a predominantly male activity during this period, only 16% of those accused being women. As in most property offences, those indicted were described as being from the lower orders, 70% of them as 'labourer'. Details of punishment demonstrate that, despite the less stringent legal penalties for those breaking and entering by day, there was no great divergence between the treatment of burglars and daytime housebreakers. It is also remarkable that, even though burglary constituted felony without benefit of clergy, almost as many people initially accused of burglary were branded or whipped as were hanged.

This can only be interpreted as a manifestation of the practice of the courts of modifying the more draconian aspects of the legal code. Many judges and juries must have felt the execution of lesser burglars somewhat excessive, and by the eighteenth century legal textbooks were sufficiently aware of clemency in favour of this type of offender to warn that although 'a judge ought to be tender in such cases, and use much discretion and moderation, yet this must not pass for law'.[99] Two ploys were used to modify legal theory. In many cases juries brought a verdict of not guilty of burglary but guilty of felony, allowing the accused to take his chance with the book, or, where appropriate, undergo a whipping. Less commonly, the court resorted to the attractive expedient of striking out from the original indictment the word 'burglariously', the details of the housebreaking, and the clause stating that the offence was nocturnal, thus altering the charge to one of theft. A number of indictments altered in this fashion survive.[100]

The factors affecting the decision to extend clemency in such cases must remain imponderable. The absence of assize depositions (burglary, as a serious felony, was usually tried at the assizes) here, as elsewhere, precludes detailed investigation of offenders. Attempts to relate capital convictions to the value of goods taken, on the hypothesis that a more substantial haul would be more likely to result in a hanging, provide no

Table 6 *Treatment of burglary and housebreaking suspects at Essex assizes and quarter sessions, 1620–80*

	Hanged	Read as a clerk, branded	Whipped	At large	Acquitted	*Ignoramus*	No details	Other	Total
Male subtotal	142	100	26	49	121	51	53	50	592
Females									
Widow	2	4	3	—	6	—	—	—	15
Spinster	12	6	8	—	14	3	5	9	57
Married	10	5	—	—	19	7	6	—	47
Female subtotal	24	15	11	—	39	10	11	9	119
Total	166	115	37	49	160	61	64	59	711
Percentage	23.5%	16%	5.5%	6.5%	22.5%	8.5%	9%	8.5%	—

Notes: male styles, as given on indictments, were: gentleman, 7; yeoman, 12; husbandman, 18; craftsman or tradesman, 42; labourer, 501; no details, 12

Table 7 *Treatment of burglary and housebreaking suspects at Essex assizes and quarter sessions, 1620–80, by quinquennia*

	Hanged	Read as a clerk, branded	Whipped	At large	Acquitted	Ignoramus	No details	Other	Total
1620–4	7	7	3	4	7	1	1	3	33
1625–9	20	13	7	9	18	3	—	10	80
1630–4	44	15	9	12	32	3	—	7	122
1635–9	8	7	—	—	6	—	2	1	24
1640–4	3	8	4	9	15	2	4	1	46
1645–9	2	12	1	3	12	4	9	3	46
1650–4	17	13	6	12	14	18	19	10	109
1655–9	15	7	3	—	15	7	13	2	62
1660–4	16	17	1	—	16	13	4	10	77
1665–9	5	1	—	—	9	7	8	2	32
1670–4	21	4	—	—	9	1	—	2	37
1675–80	8	11	3	—	7	2	4	8	43
Total	166	115	37	49	160	61	64	59	711
Burglary only	126	84	20	44	109	37	42	40	502
Percentage	25%	17%	4%	9%	22%	7%	8%	8%	—
Housebreaking only	40	31	17	5	51	24	22	19	209
Percentage	20%	15%	8%	2%	24%	12%	10%	9%	—

Table 8 *Value of goods stolen in burglary and housebreaking cases tried at Essex assizes, 1620–1680, compared with capital convictions*

Value of goods	1d to 11d	1/- to 19/11d	£1 to £4/19/11d	£5 to £9/19/11d	£10 to £19/19/11d	£20 to £49/19/11d	£50 to £99/19/11d	£100 plus
Cases	14	71	146	27	24	19	9	7
Capital convictions	—	16	29	13	6	10	4	3

conclusive proof. As table 8 indicates, the value of goods taken varied from a few pence to several sums of over £100, the most serious burglary in this period involving £760 in money allegedly taken by two burglars at Southchurch in 1649.[101]

Thus just over a third of assize cases involved goods worth less than £1; a roughly similar proportion fell in the £1–£4/19/11d bracket, the remainder being above £5. Those accused of burglaries involving more than £5 were twice as likely to be hanged as those accused of taking less than this sum, but the failure of this trend to continue into the £10–£19/19/11d bracket prevents any easy generalisation. No burglar taking goods worth more than 1/- had any guarantee of escaping the noose, while it was possible to be hanged merely for breaking and entering with intent to steal.

The type of goods stolen varied as widely as their value. About half the assize cases involved ordinary household goods – sheets, clothes, pewterware, silverware, and other domestic chattels. In just over eighty cases the main component of the accused's alleged gains was money, in thirty-eight cases food. Sometimes the goods taken were too diverse to permit analysis – the alleged burglar might take small quantities of food, a shirt or two, and a few shillings in coin. General household goods and money were, as might be expected, the most frequent target of the burglar.

It is tempting to speculate that many burglaries were committed by vagrant or 'professional' criminals, especially as local men would experience serious difficulties in evading detection or disposing of stolen goods after committing a serious burglary. Certainly housebreaking and burglary tended to be group activities when compared to other types of felony, with 118 indictments involving more than one person. Isolated examples survive of burglaries by as many as eight or ten persons,[102] although any attempts to describe these groups as 'gangs' must rest upon intuition rather than anything more concrete. There is, however, evidence of what seem to have been organised groups at work in some areas. A labourer accused of two burglaries at Bocking in January 1627 was also a member of a group accused of various thefts and burglaries in the north of the county in the previous month.[103] Another group operated in central Essex in 1653, committing burglaries at Inworth, Great Totham, and Langdon Hills.[104] Such cases are suggestive, but any hypothesis that a large proportion of burglaries were carried out by vagrant bands must be modified by the details of the geographical distribution of burglary and housebreaking cases, which do not show the tendency to cluster around main roads that might be felt to have been a corollary of this theory. Moreover, the low value of goods stolen in most of these cases suggests that they were often prosaic offences committed by minor, local offenders. The small body of relevant depositions in the quarter sessions and in the Colchester borough archives demonstrates that the Stuart poor felt no deep-seated objections to burgling the houses of their co-parishioners.

This activity was facilitated by the flimsiness of many of the houses of the period. Doors were not proof against the determined felon, while there are a few references to the employment of picklocks to assist the burglar. William French of Colchester, for example, used 'an instrument that he puld out of his pockett' to open a door and effect a burglary in 1634.[105] A greater degree of pertinacity was shown by Richard Seares, committed for stealing £6 from a house, in the process 'breakinge upp 4 iron lockes thereby to obteyne his wicked designe'.[106] Windows were a favoured means of entry,[107] and John Lock, a Colchester 'cunning man' employed to recover stolen yarn in 1651, could explain his tardiness in carrying out his task on the not unreasonable grounds that 'he was troubled how to cawse the yarne to bee brought in at the same windowe it was stoolen out at'.[108] Given the houses of the time, however, even breaking windows or doors could be superfluous, for there exist a number of cases in which entry was gained simply by breaking through a wall. A Norfolk labourer, on the road at West Bergholt, broke through the wall of a house to effect a theft, but was frightened off by the wife of the owner and took only a pair of gloves.[109] Similar examples occurred at Colchester,[110] and even the house of an Ulting clergyman was not safe from this type of treatment.[111] Given that houses could be blown down in this period – a Purleigh man, for example, returned home in December 1662 to discover that his house had been destroyed by high winds and that two men were busily engaged in removing timber from the ruins[112] – it is not surprising that the meaner dwelling-house provided no obstacle to the burglar.

Surprisingly few burglary cases involved violence. The 'putting in fear' of the victim may have been an important element in the legal definition of burglary, but there is little reference to actual or threatened violence in Essex court records. The most serious example occurred in 1675, when ten men descended on a house on isolated Vange Island, assaulted the occupant, his daughter, and a servant, and took assorted goods worth

£6/9/6d and £21/13/2d in money.[113] There were few other such cases, and some of the burglaries involving violence were much less sinister affairs. These were characterised by that rustic aggression found in assault cases, as when a Corringham widow in 1662 broke into a house in the parish, stole 32/-, and attacked one of the household in the process.[114] In general, although burglary was a widespread phenomenon, it did not represent a major threat to the social fabric, rarely involved physical violence, was infrequently carried out by gangs of 'professional' criminals, and did not provoke an unduly harsh response from the courts. Moreover, as table 7 suggests, it was an offence which was prosecuted less frequently in the second half of the period under review than in the first. Like theft, burglary was most often prosecuted in the years 1625–34, and it was also the early 1630s which saw the greatest number of executions of burglars.

The theft, robbery, or burglary of any articles other than those intended for the offender's immediate use or consumption presupposes the existence of some means of selling or bartering them. A sophisticated system of 'fencing' was well established in London during this period,[115] while stolen goods were sufficiently familiar nationally for a writer of a handbook for gentlemen to warn that buying them was morally as reprehensible as the original theft.[116] In Essex the thief likewise enjoyed outlets for his acquisitions, although these were not as regularised as those found in the metropolis. Alehouses, as part of their illicit function of providing an informal support system for the rural criminal, acted as centres for receiving stolen goods, and the authorities issued warrants against alehouse-keepers who entertained criminals, and on occasion prosecuted them.[117] Specific examples of alehouse-keepers receiving are not lacking. A stolen pig, for example, could be offered to a beerseller for 2/-,[118] and it was felt to be important evidence of guilt that a woman suspected of theft had been seen going to the alehouse with 'her lap full of linin'.[119] Stolen goods could be exchanged directly for beer, and an alehouse-keeper accused of stealing a chicken could claim that it had been brought to him by two men wishing to use it to settle a bill.[120]

Outlets for stolen goods were not restricted to the alehouse. 'One Betts a taylor' of Hutton told a travelling woman that 'if she could lay her hand[es] on any duck or geese or steale any other thing yf shee should bring it to his house he would give her money for it, & intertaine her'.[121] A tailor and his servant combined to steal turkeys, sold them off to neighbours, and divided the profits between them.[122] Following the theft of harrows in 1650, Thomas Prior went to William Bateman, a blacksmith of Great Chrishall, 'whome this Examin[an]t hath useth to buy stolen goodes', and asked him to report any attempted sales,[123] while there is some evidence of the disposal of stolen goods to those likely to have a use for them, for example the sale of stolen lead to a Chelmsford glazier.[124] Stolen goods could also be pawned.

Lambskins stolen in 1621 were pawned with a Writtle tailor for 2/6d,[125] and a shirt stolen by a harvest worker at Rettendon in 1675 was similarly disposed of for 2/-.[126]

Conversely, there is evidence of unsuccessful attempts to sell stolen goods. A blacksmith at Great Bardfield, offered a lock that he thought to be stolen, circularised the surrounding area, and a Maldon glover, offered some stolen sheepskins, apprehended the thief and notified the town authorities.[127] These examples cannot destroy the impression that the thief normally experienced little trouble in disposing of stolen goods, although it is difficult to establish how formalised this process was. There is certainly little evidence of organised theft, with a receiver 'employing' a team of professional thieves. In the context of rural England in this period such operations would have been difficult, and it is probable that only London was large enough to offer the combination of continual rich pickings and anonymity for such organisation.[128]

Isolated examples of organised thieving exist, but the organisation involved was essentially local and very temporary in character, a typical example being provided by the group of thefts and burglaries committed in 1620 by a gang supported by John and Rose Fuller, a Little Coggeshall couple.[129] Some individuals, especially innkeepers, may, like the William Bateman mentioned above, have enjoyed a local reputation for receiving, and the records give a distinct impression that the thief in possession of stolen property normally had a good idea of where to get rid of it. This impression is strengthened by such cases as that of Sara Bryett, a Colchester spinster who was given a 22/- piece to dispose of by her brother Thomas, who had stolen it from his employer. She took the coin straight to The Cross Keyes at Wivenhoe, where it was changed (perhaps significantly, at a discount of 2/-) into less conspicuous money.[130]

This example, and others like it, although suggestive of at least some degree of sophistication in the receiving of stolen goods, hardly undermines the suspicion that organised theft was virtually unknown in the county in the period of this study. The resident poor stealing poultry or scrap-iron, and the migrant worker or vagrant breaking into empty houses as they passed,[131] obviously had little trouble in disposing of their spoils, whether to the public at large or to tradesmen or inn-keepers who habitually received stolen goods as a sideline. Moreover, as we have seen, some vestiges of 'professionalism' among criminals can be found when examining horse-thieves, pickpockets, and highway robbers. It would be unwise, however, to elevate these phenomena into meaningful proof of the existence of some organised rural 'criminal underworld'.[132] The overall impression is that the attitude of most thieves was opportunistic and that larceny was usually unpremeditated in more than general terms. Property offences were undeniably the most common form of felony indicted in Essex in the seventeenth century; but they were characteristically the work not of the organised criminal, but rather of the poor in general. Legislators and social commentators might, on occasion, express disquiet at the spectre of the professional thief or burglar; but, as we shall see in a later chapter, it was economic dislocation and high grain prices which formed the background to increases in thefts and burglaries, not the emergence of a criminal class.[133]

8. Crimes of violence

Violence is a subject of obvious interest to modern industrial man. Violence, violent behaviour, and the violent offender are foremost among the current preoccupations of social debate, and the terms in which this debate takes place often presuppose an historical context: claims that society is becoming more violent rest on the assumption that, at some past stage, it was less so. Proponents of this assumption rarely take a long view of the problem, and rarely extend their arguments back much beyond the beginning of the twentieth century. Recent work by Alan Macfarlane has, however, signposted the importance of the early modern period in any discussion of the history of violent behaviour in England.[1] Briefly, Macfarlane has attacked the view that late medieval and early modern England was a society experiencing a transition from a brutal and violent stage to an orderly one. He argues that, even in marginal areas, crime was essentially modern, its basic impulse being economic gain rather than peasant brutality. This view has much to recommend it, although, as we shall see, there do appear to have been important differences between seventeenth-century and twentieth-century English violence. There are, however, a number of difficulties, particularly those associated with underreporting, which make any easy comparison between violence in the two periods very risky. Conversely, analysis of criminal violence as recorded in court archives provides the fullest impression of violence in the past that the modern student is likely to come by. This chapter will, therefore, be devoted to an examination of the three most important classes of criminal violence: assault, homicide and infanticide.

Assault was one of the most frequently indicted offences in the years 1620–80. A total of 652 indictments are recorded, 579 at the quarter sessions, where assaults constituted 17% of all indictments, 52 at the assizes, and a further 21 at the King's Bench. Overall, assault was the third most frequently indicted criminal offence in Essex during this period, exceeded only by grand larceny and unlicensed alehouse-keeping, and formed nearly 8% of the total of indictments.[2] The records of other courts provide further evidence of assault and similar acts of violence. The borough archives of Colchester, Maldon, and Harwich all contain references to assault cases, although few indictments survive. Leets could try minor cases of assault and bloodshed, a 6/8d fine being imposed for an assault in 1620 by Braintree leet, for example.[3] Even archdeaconry records contain stray references to violent behaviour, usually in connection with other offences, which would have provided grounds for an assault prosecution at the assizes or quarter sessions. Presentment of certain members of the Harris family of Danbury before the Archdeacon of Essex in 1621 for a variety of delinquencies included descriptions of how John Harris and his wife beat and abused another couple while returning drunk from Mayday celebrations in Chelmsford.[4] Such examples suggest a higher level of violent behaviour than that indicted in the two courts which form the main object of this study.[5]

The most striking evidence of an undercurrent of actual or potential violence survives in quarter sessions recognizances for keeping the peace or being of good behaviour. Both Lambarde and Dalton devote lengthy sections of their respective handbooks to descriptions of the justices' powers in taking such bonds,[6] and the frequency with which Essex JPs had recourse to them justifies the writers' preoccupation. Lambarde described 'Surety of the Peace' as 'An acknowledging of a bond to the Prince, taken by a competent Judge of Record, for the keeping of the Peace',[7] usually taken after a complaint made by an individual or a group of persons, or sometimes on the justice's own initiative. The substance of the complaint had to include threats of violence to the person or to property, notably threatened arson; the accused was then bound over to answer at the next sessions, two others usually acting as surety for him. The power to bind over to be of good behaviour, although thought to be 'of great affinitive with that of the Peace',[8] was held to be more powerful. Accordingly, Lambarde advised that the justices should only commend it 'upon sufficient cause seene to themselves, or upon the Sute and complaint of divers, and the same very honest and credible persons'.[9] Dalton gives a list of malefactors who could be thus bound, from would-be perpetrators of violence to those that 'live idly, and fare well'.[10] Binding over for good behaviour was relatively uncommon at the county bench, although the Maldon sessions seem to have made full use of this weapon. In the years before the Civil Wars, the borough authorities employed it as a blanket safeguard against possible wrongdoers, with most of those bound over to answer at the sessions being also bound over to be of good behaviour.[11]

The county justices were much fonder of binding over to keep the peace, 1,688 examples being recorded in the surviving quarter sessions records of our period. Most of them were issued in the interest of individual complainants; a typical example is that of John Darcy, bound over in 1622 'by the complaynt of Tho. Browning the elder of Coggeshall carryer for stricking him with a payer of bellowes and indangering his life'.[12] Occasional petitions also survive from communities reporting violent behaviour on the

Table 9 *Treatment of persons accused of assault at Essex quarter sessions,*
1620–80

	Fine	Acquitted	*Ignoramus*	Pleaded not guilty	No details	Other	Total
Male subtotal	150	59	94	93	196	19	611
Females							
Widow	—	—	2	—	3	—	5
Spinster	2	1	1	—	3	—	7
Married	10	1	6	10	14	1	42
Female subtotal	12	2	9	10	20	1	54
Total	162	61	103	103	216	20	665

Notes: male styles, as given on indictments, were: gentleman, 82; yeoman, 114; husbandman, 82; craftsman or tradesman, 231; labourer, 81; no details, 21

part of one of their members in the hope of getting the offender bound over to keep the peace. Thus we find the parishioners of Great Horkesley complaining against Samuel Warner, 'the most dangerous bloudy villaine in the County', whose career of violence, they claimed, included killing a man at Boxted some twenty years previously, and being outlawed for an assault some ten years later. Now, in 1657, they felt compelled to 'request the gentlemen to ty him up as they use to deale w[i]th savage beasts'.[13] Binding over to keep the peace was, therefore, seen as a useful prophylactic against violence, and the frequency with which the device was used, even allowing for a few malicious complaints, is evidence of widespread acceptance of at least one aspect of the machinery of law and order.

Despite the practice of binding over, some 622 indictments for assault reached the assizes and quarter sessions, the social status and treatment of offenders being set out in tables 9 and 10. Assault was a misdemeanour, punishable by fining, and the accused, as was normal in trials for misdemeanour, was allowed to defend himself by traverse. The documents upon which the process following such a step would be recorded are largely missing for Essex, and it is therefore impossible to follow more than a handful of cases through to their conclusion. Perhaps the greatest difficulty in attempting to study assault, however, is the very loose definition it enjoyed in the period under consideration. Simply putting in fear or offering to strike a blow without actually striking constituted assault,[14] although the blanket legal phrases used on indictments preclude any analysis of the seriousness of individual cases. Conversely, crimes against the person had

Table 10 *Treatment of persons accused of assault at Essex assizes,*
1620–80

	Fine	Acquitted	*Ignoramus*	Pleaded not guilty	No details	Other	Total
Male subtotal	8	7	12	2	47	5	81
Females							
Widow	1	—	—	—	1	—	2
Spinster	—	—	—	—	1	—	1
Married	1	—	1	—	1	—	3
Female subtotal	2	—	1	—	3	—	6
Total	10	7	13	2	50	5	87

Notes: male styles, as given on indictments, were: gentleman, 12; yeoman, 11; husbandman, 7; craftsman or tradesman, 23; labourer, 26; no details, 2

not yet reached their modern level of legal differentiation,[15] and an assault indictment could cover much more serious offences, such as attempted murder or attempted rape. It seems inevitable that a large proportion of the ninety-one occasions on which men were accused of assaulting women were in fact attempted rapes, although the supporting evidence to justify such an hypothesis is only rarely forthcoming. One such case occurred in 1652, when the curate of Stambourne was indicted for assaulting a woman. Depositions show that he had attempted to rape her, and that she was saved when the barking of a dog attracted attention.[16]

The seriousness of the assault does not seem to have been reflected in the heaviness of the fine. Cutting off a thumb or injuring with a razor resulted in fines of 2/- and 3/4d respectively;[17] although details of this type are rarely given, it therefore seems likely that other considerations dictated fining policy. Legal opinion was in favour of adjusting fines in assault cases to the paying capacity of the guilty party,[18] and table 11 does suggest a rough correlation between the social status of offenders as given on indictments and the fines levied on them. The lowest fine levied, 4d, was on a labourer accused in 1638 of leaving his master before his time had expired and of assaulting him.[19] The most serious fine, on the other hand, was one of £20 for an assault on the constable of Stratford Langthorne in 1668.[20] Fining at this level was, however, exceptional; as table 11 indicates, fines for assault rarely amounted to more than 10/-.

Perhaps the most striking feature of assault indictments is the way in which they suggest that most social strata were willing to have recourse to

Table 11 *Relationship of social status of male offenders to amount fined in assault cases at Essex assizes and quarter sessions, 1620–80*

Status of offender	Amount fined					
	less than 1/-	1/1d to 5/-	5/1d to 10/-	10/1d to £1	£1/-/1d to £5	More than £5
Gentleman	—	5	1	—	6	1
Yeoman	—	3	8	4	2	—
Husbandman	—	6	5	2	2	—
Craftsman or tradesman	5	22	9	3	3	—
Labourer	5	11	9	3	3	—
Total indicted	10	47	34	13	18	1

Notes: Not all indictments record the amount of the fine imposed, hence the discrepancy between the figures for the numbers fined and the total number indicted

violence. Ninety-four men indicted at the assizes and quarter sessions for assault, or 13.5% of all males thus indicted, were described as gentlemen, and a further 125, or 18%, as yeomen. Violence at the bottom of the social scale is, of course, underrepresented in court indictments; the cost of litigation, here as elsewhere, prevented the very poor from taking a case to court. One Essex JP wrote to the clerk of the peace explaining that he had withdrawn a recognizance in an assault case since those involved were 'verie poore men and agreed among themselves',[21] and similar cases must have been numerous if unrecorded. Any desire to use assault cases as a barometer of violence must also be modified by an awareness that the actual amount of violence involved in an assault could be negligible, and that assault indictments could also be brought for reasons of malice, or as just one step in a legal battle of nerves. Even after allowing for all these considerations, the inescapable impression remains that, if major county families no longer regularly indulged in overt acts of violence, the lesser gentry and yeomanry were still prone to violent behaviour. Detailed parish studies confirm this impression: an investigation of crime in one Essex village has revealed that 'assault was very much an offence of the more prominent and wealthy villagers'.[22] Certainly violence was not yet the prerogative of the slum subculture which is regarded by modern criminologists as its most usual environment.[23]

Court records allow insights into certain key areas of potential interpersonal violence. The family is an obvious starting point. Modern studies have commented on the amount of violence that can be aroused in the family circle,[24] and it has been pointed out that 'aggression, like charity, begins at home'.[25] Seventeenth-century observers were aware of the dangers of children, servants, and wives being subjected to 'immoderate' correction, while William Gouge antedated Freud by almost three centuries in observing, in connection with family violence, that 'the nearer and dearere any persons be, the more violent will be that hatred which is fastened on them'.[26]

In contrast with the large numbers of murders within the family at this time,[27] only two indictments for assault within the nuclear family have been found in the Essex records of this period, one involving a gentleman assaulting his wife, the other a wife assaulting her husband, a yeoman.[28] This dearth of formal indictments must indicate an unwillingness to report violence within the family. To indict one's wife for assault would incur considerable derision, and husbands who submitted to such treatment from their spouses could be subjected to ritualised community satire.[29] Similarly, in an age which accepted male domination and in which divorce was difficult, indicting one's husband for assault was not something to be undertaken lightly, and might even have been regarded as intrinsically counter-productive.

If family violence rarely resulted in an indictment, there is widespread evidence of it among other court documents. Occasionally these afford insights into the unusual causes of domestic strife, as in the case of the tumultuous and anti-puritan Richard Bright, who threatened his wife that he would 'Drown her or burne her because she went to sermons'.[30] More typical, perhaps, was Thomas Holland of Stifford, whose wife complained of frequent beatings by him in 1676. According to one witness, Holland declared 'God dam him, he would stab his wife, and a short life and a merry one was better than a long and a sad one'.[31] The husband was not, however, the only perpetrator of family violence. The inhabitants of Rettendon complained in 1646 against Margaret Granfield, 'a verie contentious and troublesome woman', who controlled her husband, 'For she rules the roast'. Margaret had assaulted the parish officers and torn the clothes from their backs, and our sympathy must be extended to her husband John, even if she did protect him from paying taxes until the army was brought in![32] In-laws could be troublesome. In 1672 Thomas Person, a weaver aged seventy-five, informed the Colchester Bench that 'on Tuesday last in the Evening som discord happened betweene him and his wife uppon which for quietness sake he went out of the house unto the house of Goodwife hammond and set downe there complayning of his wife saying that his wife was a scold and her mother was a scold and so was her aunt.' His lamentation was interrupted by the arrival of his wife's brother, a neighbour of Hammond, who had overheard the conversation and now set upon him, threatened to kill him, threw him to the ground, and sprained his wrist.[33]

Similar pressures to those dissuading wives or children from taking their husbands and parents to court for assault probably explain the paucity of formal indictments levied by servants against their masters. The employer of domestic servants, like parents and schoolteachers, was entitled to use a degree of licensed violence over his subordinates, and it is perhaps significant that William Perkins thought it necessary to remind his readers that a master's powers of correction did not extend to power of life and death.[34] There is evidence that many masters exceeded even what the seventeenth century held to be reasonable chastisement, and a number of apprentices were released from their indentures by court order on grounds of ill-treatment.[35] Other complaints reached the bench. Eleanour Hawkins, a widow, had been beaten and ill-treated by the family with which she served, her master having added insult to injury by gaining £10 of hers and all her goods under pretence of marriage.[36] Ann Dickinson, accused of the theft of a ring from her employer's wife in 1638, confessed to the theft, later explaining to the examining justice that 'it was because her said Mrs had so cruelly whipt her, that she feared she would have killed her, for she had spent one rodd on her this examin[ant] and had another ready that if she would not have said she had it [i.e. the ring] she would have spent the other upon her'.[37]

Problems between master and servant were common. Complaints of refusals by masters to pay wages are scattered throughout the sessions records, and a number of ex-employees trying to obtain wages owed them were beaten.[38] Enforced apprenticeship under the Book of Orders and after probably worsened the problem, as in other countries,[39] and examples have been found of refusals to take parish apprentices.[40] Servants and apprentices could, of course, be very provocative, although it is impossible to say how often this was the result of maltreatment. A Felsted man complained in 1638 against a boy who had been bound apprentice to him, only to run away eleven times in his four years of service, returning on the last occasion 'all lowesry and devoid of all clothes'. His employer was so afraid of him that he dared not leave him alone in the house with his children for fear he might harm them, 'ffor truely he is of the kinde that there is noe Reformation'.[41] John Liveinge, the apprentice of Thomas Reynolds, reached the peak of a career of careless and churlish service in negligently burning down his master's workshop.[42] Christopher Wood, the servant of William Johnston, reproved for being in the alehouse when he should have been working, gave saucy answers, meanwhile 'Playinge with his fingers in waie of derision'. Johnston rapped him over his knuckles with a small cane, whereupon Wood assaulted him and his wife, and neighbours had to be called in from the street to protect them.[43] Despite the existence of such brave spirits, the impression remains that servants were more often the recipients than the offerers of violence.

Parish constables and other local government officers were especially at risk, eighty-three assaults against them being tried at the county quarter sessions, or some 14% of all assaults tried there. Most of these cases happened spontaneously as the officer went about his duties. A typical victim was Thomas Danckes, a watchman in Colchester, who reproved a man for swearing four oaths and reminded him that he should pay a shilling fine for each of them. At this, the object of reproof 'badd a turde in his teethe & laide handes upon him and tooke him by the throate'.[44] Occasionally, however, violence against a constable could be part of a more sophisticated feud. When William Mosse, a constable of Great Bromley, attempted to collect a 20/- fine owed by a certain Bromwell for unlicensed alehouse-keeping, Bromwell, in his capacity as bailiff of Tendring Hundred, promptly took out an action of debt against him, and laid a distraint of £24 on his goods. Mosse went to Mr Barnardiston, a local JP, and obtained a letter ordering the recovery of his property. On being shown this, Bromwell 'presented a pistoll at your petitioner and strack at him with it but it fired not & swore he would be his death'.[45] The willingness of constables to carry out a growing burden of duties in the face of resistance of this sort supports the contention that the contribution of these lesser officers to English local government has been consistently underrated.

Despite the delineation of these major areas of potential violence, it is difficult to discern a clear pattern of motivation in assault cases. Sometimes violence could follow the escalating tension of a long-standing dispute, as when it was complained that an assailant had been 'dogging' his victim for some time,[46] while there is occasional evidence of feuding in a parish continuing over several sessions,[47] and cross-accusations were sometimes brought for the same incident.[48] Drink often served as a means of loosening inhibitions against violence, as when two men began brawling after they 'fell to words about reckoning that was to pay for beere there druncke'.[49] Political differences could be extended into a fight. A royalist sympathiser tried to stab an ex-parliamentary soldier on Bardfield fair day in 1652,[50] and a Purleigh man, having wished 'a poxe on them' that had sequestered him, set about a woman who reproved him for his bad language.[51] There also exist cases of assault following threats of indictment for another offence, as when a Chelmsford alehouse-keeper assaulted the constable who had indicted him for keeping a disorderly house.[52] A more unusual case occurred on 5 November 1672 when Peter Barence set out with 'a company of Braintree men to oppose the townsmen of Bocking (according to an ancient custom)' and seriously injured a man with a club.[53]

These examples are interesting, but they do not permit the construction of a coherent pattern of assault cases in seventeenth-century Essex. Nevertheless, two important qualitative differences may be postulated between assault in seventeenth-century Essex and modern Britain. The first was the almost total absence of formal indictments arising from domestic violence; the second, the more inclusive social background of the persons accused. On this latter point, of course, allowance must be made for malicious prosecution and for indictment for assault of a technical nature. Even so, the evidence of petitions, depositions and recognizances emphasises that violence was common among all social strata. The habits of restraint had not penetrated very far among the minor gentry, yeomen, and artisans of Stuart Essex.

Whereas the study of assault is impeded both by underreporting and by the unsophisticated definition of the offence, the investigation of homicide is facilitated both by the presence of an officer (the coroner) whose duty it was to investigate suspicious deaths and by a relatively sophisticated body of law relating to the offence.[54] The courts were long used to differentiating between varying degrees of culpability in homicide cases, and such concepts as legally defined accidental death can be traced as far back as the twelfth century.[55] It was the late sixteenth century, however, that saw the emergence of a clear distinction between murder and manslaughter, the support of learned opinion thus being added to a reluctance by juries to convict for certain types of homicide that had been firmly established in the middle ages.[56] Murder was the most serious form of homicide, and was treated as felony without benefit of clergy, whereas those convicted of manslaughter could claim their clergy on the first offence. The vital element in assessing whether a homicide constituted murder lay in determining the degree of malice aforethought involved in the offence, murder being defined by Coke as 'when a man of sound memory, and of the age of discretion, unlawfully killeth within any County of the Realm any reasonable creature *in rerum natura* under the kings peace, with malice fore-thought'.[57]

A total of 195 accusations of homicide are known to have been tried at the Essex assizes between 1620 and 1680. No homicides were brought before the quarter sessions, but details of another six cases survive among the King's Bench Ancient Indictments, and a further thirteen in the Colchester sessions rolls. County assize records provide the bulk of the evidence, therefore, and attention in this chapter will be concentrated upon the 195 assize cases and the 310 persons tried in connection with them, details of whose social status and punishment are given in table 12.

As table 12 indicates, the attitude of the courts towards homicide accusations was a flexible one. Less than 30% of those named on indictments or coroner's inquisitions were found guilty, and of these over a third suffered the lesser penalty of being branded. Some 45% of the accused were acquitted, many of them on the grounds that the homicide in which they were involved was caused by accident (or misadventure) or by the more intangible agency of divine providence. Verdicts of accidental death seem usually to have been justified, arising when death was the outcome of

Table 12 Treatment of homicide suspects at Essex assizes, 1620–80

	Hanged	Read as a clerk, branded	Other punishment	Acquitted	Acquitted (divine providence)	Acquitted (accidental death)	Ignoramus	No details	At large	Other	Total
Male subtotal	41	34	4	63	31	17	11	25	14	21	261
Females											
Widow	2	1	2	2	1	1	—	—	—	—	9
Spinster	3	1	1	1	—	1	—	—	—	—	7
Married	1	—	1	16	7	—	1	2	—	3	31
No details	—	—	—	—	—	—	—	2	—	—	2
Female subtotal	6	2	4	19	8	2	1	4	—	3	49
Total	47	36	8	82	39	19	12	29	14	24	310

Notes: male styles, as given on indictments, were: gentleman, 18; yeoman, 27; husbandman, 23; craftsman or tradesman, 58; labourer, 115; no details, 20

such legitimate pursuits as horse-riding or tree-felling, the suspicion of foul play in these cases being only marginally greater than that in the numerous examples of accidental death that can be found in the King's Bench records. More equivocal are the returns of death by divine visitation, or divine providence, a definition not discussed by legal writers. It seems that this verdict was returned when an act of violence had taken place of which death could not reasonably be the expected outcome. Divine providence could therefore explain homicide cases where death resulted from an injury deliberately inflicted but not likely to occasion death. A good example of this occurred in 1656 when a man was struck by a brickbat and subsequently died. The death was attributed by the jury to 'a quinsey', and a verdict of divine providence returned.[58] Thus the most important function of the concept of divine providence, it would seem, lay in compensating for some of the defects of contemporary medical knowledge and treatment.

The readiness of juries to acquit homicide suspects, which provoked at least one writer to adverse comment late in the century,[59] indicates that the response to an accusation of homicide was not one of immediate horror. Even so, the exceptionally brutal crime could produce a sharp reaction from juries. The execution of persons convicted of specially heinous homicide might, indeed, be followed by the hanging in chains of the corpse of the murderer near to the location of the offence. Two such cases (one of which involved the beheading of the victim) survive in our sample, both of them from the 1630s.[60] It is also noteworthy that verdicts of self-defence were rarely brought, although this was the standard medieval ploy for avoiding conviction for murder.[61] Only four verdicts of self-defence were found, it being unclear whether these were treated as acquittals or returns of manslaughter; at least one of those accused who had his verdict reduced to self-defence was branded.[62]

Any attempt to derive any clear ideas about the predilection of various sections of society for violence based on details of the occupational status given on indictments is, of course, rendered invalid by the familiar problems surrounding the accuracy of a man's 'style' as given by assize clerks. Even so, further research would probably reveal that a number of those described as gentlemen or yeomen were, indeed, drawn from those social groups. One man accused of homicide in 1629, and described as a gentleman, was able to procure the help of friends in high places to secure a pardon, evidence, perhaps, that he was well-connected.[63] Occasionally persons accused of homicide can be readily connected with leading families, as, for example, when Augustine Petre, a member of a long-established aristocratic family, was accused of shooting a man.[64] Moreover, these more patrician killings often involved that unpremeditated, sudden violence which might be thought more appropriate to the lower orders; certainly northern depositions suggest that the gentry of that region were as willing to participate in brawls as were their social inferiors.[65] Such examples are again suggestive of a society in which a willingness to resort to violent behaviour was widely diffused among different social strata, and it is perhaps significant that no murderer described as a gentleman was executed. Table 12 also demonstrates a low conviction rate for females. This must be partially explicable by the tendency for women to be disproportionately represented in homicides within the family; twenty-four of the total of forty-nine females accused of homicide allegedly killed members of their family, as opposed to thirty-three out of two hundred and sixty-one men. It should also be noted that eleven of the females accused were indicted with their husbands.

The absence of assize depositions renders impossible a full understanding of homicide in Essex during this period,[66] although some deeper insights into the nature of the problem can be gained. Firstly, the family figures prominently in homicide cases. Thirty-one of the cases tried at the assizes involved relatives as victims and accused, and if the term 'family' is extended to include apprentices and servants the total rises to forty-two, over a fifth of all homicide accusations. This figure is probably an understatement; the wording of indictments and coroners' inquests does not reveal such relationships as step-child or step-parent (a relationship felt to be potentially difficult by at least one seventeenth-century writer),[67] cousin, or in-law,[68] and there are a number of cases in which the victim may have been a servant, although this cannot be proved. Those accused of killing servants or apprentices were perhaps the most likely group of suspected killers to escape conviction, only one such being found guilty.[69] Blackstone commented that misadventure was the proper verdict to bring when death resulted from the moderate correction of apprentices, offspring, or school-boys, 'for the act of correction was lawful'.[70] Such an attitude, presumably based on a conviction that if the masters and parents desisted from beating their charges for fear of killing them godly discipline would crumble away, probably explains the unwillingness of juries to convict those accused of killing their servants.[71] A pamphlet of 1680 suggests the reluctance with which such a verdict would be brought. Sarah Bell, arraigned for killing her twelve-year-old servant, recounted how she had thrown a knife at her in a fit of rage, 'the said girl having crossed her, in not performing a message she had sent her on'. The knife had struck the girl, causing a wound three inches deep, and death subsequently ensued. We are told that 'although the Prisoner pleaded innocence and that she intended no such cruelty, yet she having often threatened her before, she was brought Guilty of manslaughter, and she was burned in the hand accordingly'.[72] One cannot help feeling that Bell was fortunate.

Despite the apparent lenience with which such offences were treated at the assizes, local opinion was sometimes easily aroused in cases where the victim was an apprentice. An accusation in Elmstead in 1657 involved the unusually high number of nine witnesses, and one at East Hanningfield in 1658 six.[73] When a Colchester man returned to the town without his servant, whom he had received from the Chelmsford overseers of the poor together with ten shillings and clothing, an investigation was mounted, mainly, it seems, on the initiative of local women.[74] The disappearance of William Fuller, an apprentice of Great Bromley, provoked 'a rumour in the country that he hath been made away & buried on Warley Com[m]on',[75] and the death of a girl apprentice, Elizabeth Round, was suspicious enough to warrant investigation.[76] William Ashley, servant to a Tolleshunt Major man, died as a result of a blow received from his master when he returned home late from Maldon fair. His master had already once thrown a pitchfork at him in a burst of temper when Ashley had overturned a cart, and a local clergyman questioned the boy on his deathbed about the treatment he had received from his employer.[77] These manifestations of local concern must have conflicted with the attitudes of jurors. It is instructive that in Colchester, where the authorities and juries would have a more intimate knowledge of the circumstances surrounding such cases, four out of five indictments for killing apprentices resulted in hanging.[78]

Homicide within the family circle in the strict interpretation of the term provoked a more varied response from the assizes, although here too returns of death by divine providence or *ignoramus* were brought in dubious cases involving corporal punishment.[79] Eight capital convictions, one branding, and two verdicts of insanity were brought against those accused of family killings. Alleged victims were most commonly children (sixteen cases), and spouses (seven cases, two husbands and five wives). Others were fathers (two cases), brothers or sisters (three cases), granddaughters (two cases), and daughters-in-law (one case). Murder of a husband by his wife, like murder of a master, was treated as petty treason,[80] and persons convicted of such murders suffered the appropriate penalties. Only one woman, who aided the murderer of her husband in 1627, was burnt in this period, and there is one case of a servant being convicted for killing his master.[81] Of the two cases of parricide, one occurred when a man was poisoned by his daughter, the other when a son armed with a 'hedging beatle' killed his father. Both the accused were executed.[82]

The frequency of homicide within the family contrasts with the rarity of formal indictments for assault between relatives. This is doubtless a reflection of the seriousness with which killing was considered; non-homicidal violence might be tolerated by the neighbours and go unreported by the victim, but a murder was a serious matter and difficult to conceal. Nevertheless, even if 'family' is interpreted in the widest sense to include servants and apprentices, family killings account for only some 21% of all homicides tried at the assizes, compared with the 50% quoted in modern studies of British homicide.[83] Thus despite the presence of serious domestic

Table 13 *Method of killing in homicide cases, Essex assizes, 1620–80*

Method	Total	Within family	Verdict			
			Hanged	Read as a clerk, branded	Acquitted	*Ignoramus*
Hands/feet	45	10	8	7	24	1
Stick/staff	36	5	2	7	17	2
Other blunt instrument	18	2	2	3	7	1
Knife	13	1	6	—	1	—
Sword	8	—	—	2	2	1
Tools	23	1	7	3	4	2
Gun	22	2	—	2	15	1
Aggravated neglect	15	11	1	1	10	—
Poison	5	5	2	—	2	1
Other	10	1	—	2	6	—

Notes: all figures refer to accusations rather than to persons accused. Acquittals include verdicts of divine providence or accidental death

tensions (even Ralph Josselin was nearly killed in his infancy by a knife wielded by his sister, 'a wilde childe'),[84] violence outside the family accounted for a larger proportion of homicides in Stuart Essex than in modern England. The Stuart murder, then, was more likely to involve violence directed towards outsiders than its twentieth-century counterpart.

Further insights into the nature of homicide can be gained by considering the means by which homicide was carried out. Table 13 gives an analysis of the method of killing, together with details of the frequency with which the more important verdicts were applied to each category.[85] As these figures indicate, the most common methods of alleged killing were simple beating, whether by striking with the hand or by kicking or by the agency of readily available blunt instruments in the form of sticks, staves, cudgels, whips, or stakes, all of which are comprehended in the category 'stick/staff'. Other blunt instruments included stone pots, candlesticks, or even stones or pieces of hard earth. These three categories seem to form a unit. Indictments for killing by these methods were slightly more likely to result in an acquittal than a conviction, and a high proportion of convictions was brought for manslaughter, a reflection, perhaps, of the sudden and unpremeditated violence that must most often have formed the background to a homicide where these means were used.

Conversely, the number of homicides committed with knives or swords does not seem to have been very high. Accusations involving knives were few, and it is difficult to envisage why such weapons should be much less available than staves or cudgels. It is noticeable, however, that those accused of killing with knives were usually likely to be executed.[86] The use of the sword, despite that weapon usually being regarded as a gentleman's, shows a surprising lack of class bias. Only two of the homicides involving the use of the sword were allegedly committed by gentlemen, and there is no evidence of duelling in the county during this period in records consulted for the present work.[87] It is, moreover, difficult to relate the deaths due to shooting to an increase in criminal homicide resulting from weapon carrying. As table 13 indicates, a disproportionately high number of accusations of homicide by gunshot wounds ended in verdicts of acquittal, most of these being brought on grounds of accidental death. This tendency appears to have been an accurate reflection of the widespread failure to observe the elementary safety rules governing the use of firearms. One case occurred in 1648 when a group of troopers were examining a pistol in a Roydon alehouse when it fired and killed one of them, and another when a gun accidentally went off as a warrener climbed a fence.[88] After another, non-fatal, shooting, the victim petitioned the bench that she 'believeth that the man was ignorant of any wilful doing of her wrong', and did not know that the gun was loaded.[89]

The category of tools is to some extent an artificial one, as homicides allegedly committed with tools could be grouped with those allegedly caused by knives and swords or by blunt instruments. However, it was felt that since the implements involved in these cases were the normal tools of husbandry or rural industries – pitchforks, axes, shears, shovels, shoeing hammers – their employment lends weight to the suspicions that homicide in this period was essentially unplanned and sudden. The impression is that the alleged killer in these cases simply used what was nearest at hand when some sort of immediate provocation arose. Similarly, the methods of killing placed in the 'other' category do not demonstrate any great taste for the elaborate or the esoteric; they included throwing out of the window, burning on a fire, or casting into a tub of scalding beer wort.[90] Given the main methods of killing – with hands or feet, with the sticks or cudgels whose possession must have been widespread, or with common tools – an impression is created that the act of homicide was usually overt, spontaneous, and, in the short term, unpremeditated.

An exception must, of course, be made for accusations involving poisoning. It was the very degree of premeditation and stealth implicit in murder by poison that led Coke to comment that 'of all murder, murder by poysoning is the most detestable',[91] while one observer asserted that 'women have in all ages used poisoning more than men' because its clandestine nature gave it considerable appeal to the physically weaker sex.[92] In fact this method of killing was very uncommon in Essex during this period, and three of the six persons accused of using it were male. There is some evidence of suspicions of poisoning that failed to reach the stage of indictment, although these hardly suggest a widespread fear. John Polly of Hatfield Peverel, not content with beating his mother-in-law, inciting his wife to steal, and attempting to seduce her sister, was also thought to be planning to poison his stepson.[93] In another case, a girl sent to London with urine samples from her employer's sick son was thought to be mixing poison in the medicine with which she returned.[94] There was, however, only one dramatic example of poisoning, that involving Richard Skeete, tried by the Colchester borough sessions in 1639. Skeete, a 'cunning man' and doctor, poisoned his wife, four children fathered by him on a local girl, and a female witness. He was indicted for the murder of two of the children and the two women, and was hanged, together with Lydia Downes, his unfortunate mistress and accomplice.[95]

Perhaps the most significant feature of cases of poisoning was that all five of those recorded at the county assizes occurred within the family, although since the poison had to be administered in food or drink this is not surprising. Similarly, killing by what has been described as aggravated neglect was usually perforce a domestic form of killing; the term is used to describe the sometimes lengthy record of beating, undernourishment, and general maltreatment of apprentices and children that allegedly led to their death. Given that some sort of position of responsibility is assumed to have rested in the alleged killer in all these cases, it seems likely that all of them should be classed as 'family' killings in the wide sense of the term, although in four cases no definite relationship can be established. As table 13 indicates, convictions for this type of homicide were very infrequent.

Assize indictments and inquests suggest that murders were rarely carried out as a means to committing another crime. The absence of depositions for the Home circuit obscures this point,[96] but it seems unlikely that some mention of such added circumstances would not be given on coroners' inquests. One group of five men indicted for homicide in 1630 was also accused of highway robbery, and may have killed their victim while attempting to carry out an offence of this type.[97] The only concrete evidence of murder being used to facilitate a robbery is provided by a case committed in 1656 which remained untried until 1667. Thomas Kidderminster, a gentleman who had made some money from estate management in Cambridgeshire, was murdered by the landlord, landlady, and ostler of The White Horse in Chelmsford and the £500–£600 he carried with him taken. His body was buried in the yard of the inn, and lay undiscovered for a decade, until the owner of the next house discovered it while digging the foundations for a new wall. The coroner called to view the corpse, Talcott, placed an advertisement in the London newspapers asking anybody able to assist with enquiries to contact him. Kidderminster's widow saw the advertisement, and subsequent enquiries found the ostler, who was hanged, the landlord and landlady having died.[98] No other example of this sort has been found. There was, however, one case in which a man was accused of killing a woman he had raped.[99]

It seems likely, then, that Stuart homicides were characteristically unplanned acts of violence arising spontaneously from quarrels, being simple assaults that went too far in most cases. Piecemeal evidence from Essex and the more voluminous northern depositions would support such an assertion, but having made it, it is difficult to derive any clear pattern as to the nature of this violence. One striking fact is the frequency with which killing occurred after the consumption of alcohol. The example of William Purcas, who killed his mother while in his cups, has already been cited, and other cases are recorded in Essex sources.[100] Numerous cases can be found in the northern depositions: a corporal and sergeant fall out while drinking, and fight with swords in the back yard of an inn; a group of sailors fall out over the bill for the drink they had consumed; troops and civilians argue in an alehouse in York over a game of cards, and one of the former is described as 'a Welsh dogg or tyke'.[101] Overall, of the sixty-four homicides recorded in these depositions, no less than twenty-one occurred during or after drinking in an alehouse. Drink, therefore, obviously had an important part in releasing the Stuart Englishman from such inhibitions as he may have felt about the use of violence.

One exceptionally well-documented case from Essex might serve to illustrate this type of killing. In 1629 John Eve, Thomas Wood and Abraham Sawkins were sharing a room in The Blue Boar, at Maldon and asked James Remmington to join them in a 'game with shillings and testers called underhatt'. Remmington, after some reluctance, agreed to join them 'so far as a crowne would laste'. After some play, a dispute broke out over a shilling, a scuffle ensued, and Eve struck Remmington a fatal blow with a rapier. A barber-surgeon, Thomas Abs, was called, but Remmington died the following day. The case was removed to the King's Bench on a writ of *certiorari*, but no trace of it has been found in the ancient indictments. The state papers, however, reveal that Eve mobilised friends in high places to procure a pardon for him, and a stray reference in the Maldon archives shows that he was subsequently aquitted. This set of circumstances – the meeting in the alehouse, the falling out over a bill or a game of cards, or the imagining of a new insult or the remembering of an old one – seems to have formed the background to many homicides.[102]

Apart from the influence of drink, there appears to be no clear pattern behind indictments for this offence. A number of those accused were clearly mentally unwell. The indictment of a Boreham man accused of beating his son's brains out on some stones in 1641, for example, recorded that he was insane at the time.[103] In a northern case, local opinion was surprised when a man killed his servant, since it was held that the employee was a man 'he loved very well because they frequently tooke tobacco together'. The killer, however, suffered 'melancholy fitt[es]'.[104] Contemporaries would also probably have diagnosed melancholia as the basic problem of a woman who killed her daughter and subsequently explained that 'it was for her daughter's good to free her from sinn'.[105] Others displayed a degree of temper which verged on the unbalanced: the Yorkshireman John Borrowes attacked John Jones when he found the latter stealing wood from a close of his. He set about Jones with a 'watch bill or broome hooke', knocked him to the ground, and 'did cutt or hacke this throate with the same to make him lye still'. A witness deposed how he later found Borrowes hacking at some wood.[106]

The Essex and northern sources, however, suggest that the motives behind a killing could be infinitely varied. Robert Davye, according to one Essex coroner's jury, killed Robert Taylor after 'some wrangelinge speeches concerning wheat which the said Davye had bought of the said Taylor'.[107] Northern depositions record 'a former quarrel' as the background to one homicide, a suit between the victim and offender in another, a quarrel over a stolen halter in a third, and a dispute over a horse that had strayed into the offender's fields and eaten grass in a fourth.[108] In a Yorkshire case of 1666 a youth named William Knaggs went into the grounds of Mr Edward Ruddocke in the evening of 30 April to search for a young ash tree with which to make a maypole, and was shot by one of the gentleman's servants acting under instructions from him.[109] In an even more remarkable incident in Leeds in the following year William Swynyard killed a youth and a young woman when he fired a gun charged with buckshot into the crowd that was riding the stang outside his house.[110]

These cases serve to reinforce the hypothesis that the seventeenth century was a period in which tempers were characteristically short. Depositions relating to violence, like those relating to defamation, are suggestive of a society in which men and women of all social groups were quick to anger and ready to use violence, of a physical or verbal nature. Contemporary literary sources suggest that the moralists of the period were aware of the problem. Dod and Cleaver, for example, urged that 'hastie and unadvised anger, rash wrath and unjust' was to be shunned by all those wishing to keep the sixth commandment; they enjoined their readers to 'avoid the occasions that will provoke us to it [i.e. murder] as men will keep gunpowder and tow, or such drie stuffe from the fire: so let us be as wise to preserve our soules from those sparkes that would fire it with anger'.[111]

What is perhaps most significant is the degree to which anger was directed outwards. Suicide in early modern England has hardly been studied, and we will probably never be able to construct statistics which reach even the degree of reliability of those which emerge from studying homicide. However, what is perhaps the most striking difference between homicide in Stuart Essex and homicide in modern England is the virtual absence in the former of murder followed by suicide. In the early 1960s something like a third of murders committed in England and Wales were followed by suicide – that is, acts of violence in which aggression was directed both outwards and inwards more or less simultaneously.[112] In Essex no such cases were recorded at the assizes in the seventeenth century, and it has proved possible to discover only one case in the other records consulted relating to the present study. This occurred at Heydon in 1631, and resulted in a verdict of insanity.[113] This, it could be argued, indicates important differences between Stuart and modern Englishmen.

It lies outside the terms of the present study to embark upon a full-scale discussion of the social psychology of the early modern Englishman. However, as has been seen, studying homicide in this period suggests a society in which the psychological check against acts of violence seems to have been weaker than in modern England, and that the spontaneous, unplanned, and overt act of killing was characteristic of the homicide of the period. The dearth of murders followed by suicide supports this contention; the Stuart Englishman was very likely to externalise his frustrations and aggressions into acts of violence that could easily result in a fatality.

The hypothesis that most homicides committed outside the family were the results of unpremeditated brawls is not, of course, inconsistent with a long-term history of worsening relationships between the two parties involved in a homicide that must often have preceded the final, fatal, incident. The murder in Colchester in 1635, for example, by Martha Boram of her neighbour, Goodman Stephens, seems to have come at the end of a period of tension.[114] However, the problem of victim–offender relationships, upon which considerable weight has been placed by modern criminologists,[115] must remain intangible given the virtual absence of assize depositions. Certainly the phenomenon of what recent writers have described as 'victim precipitation' existed in the seventeenth century. It lies behind the whole concept of killing in self-defence and, at one or two removes, behind the idea of manslaughter constituting a lesser offence than premeditated murder. As the evidence of witnesses in seventeenth-century depositions indicates, it is rarely an easy matter to determine who exactly is responsible for starting a fight.

To attempt to assess homicide rates and long-term fluctuations reintroduces the familiar problems involved in quantifying seventeenth-century evidence. As table 14 indicates, homicide accusations were not given to dramatic fluctuations in terms of absolute totals, although within these totals the percentage of accusations resulting in a conviction tended to vary from 55% to 10%. It appears that the 1620s and 1630s were the years when a homicide suspect was most likely to be hanged, although the exceptionally

Table 14 *Variations in homicide rate and convictions for homicide at Essex assizes, 1620–80, by quinquennia*

	Indictments	Total accused	Hanged	Read as a clerk, branded	Other punishment	Total convicted	Percentage convicted
1620–4	6	9	3	1	—	4	45%
1625–9	24	37	8	3	1	12	30%
1630–4	13	29	14	2	—	16	55%
1635–9	7	11	1	2	—	3	27%
1640–4	18	38	2	3	—	5	13%
1645–9	12	12	4	—	—	4	33%
1650–4	16	20	4	2	—	6	30%
1655–9	32	49	2	3	—	5	10%
1660–4	20	24	2	3	2	7	29%
1665–9	18	35	3	7	4	14	40%
1670–4	15	22	1	4	—	5	22%
1675–9	17	23	3	4	—	7	30%

Notes: figures for indictments refer to those tried, rather than to those committed, in the given period

bad survival rate of assize documents from those decades obscures the point. There is no obvious reason for the rise in accusations in the late 1650s, especially as there was no corresponding increase in judicial severity towards the accused.

Any rate deduced from these figures must, perforce, be tentative. Taking the period 1645–79, when assize files survive in an almost unbroken series, we find a total of thirty-seven homicide indictments tried at the assizes which resulted in a verdict of guilty, or an average of just over one each year. If the county's population is estimated at about 110,000 during this period, and some allowance made for missing files, this gives a homicide rate running at about three times the level current in mid twentieth-century England.[116] This figure must, however, be an understatement. Firstly, there are the numerous acquittals through verdicts of divine providence, many of which were brought on what seem to have been very dubious grounds. Secondly, the numerous unqualified acquittals and cases where the accused is recorded as being at large presupposes the existence of a deceased party who died somehow, and may well have been murdered in some cases. This, of course, raises the whole problem of detection, which will continue to defy the historian of crime. It seems likely, however, that homicide was less easily concealed than other offences, and would provoke a sharper response than other forms of crime. However, any suggestion that the homicide rate was higher in Stuart than in modern Britain has to take into account the differences in medical knowledge between the two periods; one recent writer has postulated that the current stability of the English murder rate, which contrasts with the rise in other crimes of violence, owes much to medical advances.[117] Being stabbed, or even being hit on the head with a brick, was far more likely to prove fatal in the seventeenth century than in a modern society.

These considerations make it difficult to regard comparison of homicide rates in Stuart and modern England as anything more than an academic exercise, and attempts to make quantitative distinctions between the two little more than hypothetical. What has emerged from this discussion of homicide cases tried at the Essex assizes is the existence of three very marked qualitative features of early modern English homicide. Firstly, the social status of the persons accused provides yet more evidence that violent behaviour was more widespread among the upper social strata than in modern Britain. Secondly, given the relatively low level of homicide within the family, and the virtual non-existence of murder followed by suicide, the Stuart Englishman seems unusually ready to vent his frustrations on his fellow men in general. And thirdly, homicide in this period, among all social groups, was generally the outcome of a sudden and, in the short run at least, unpremeditated brawl.[118]

One subdivision of homicide, however, has sufficient peculiarities to warrant separate examination. This is infanticide, a crime as yet little studied,[119] but which will probably emerge as one of the most characteristic offences of the early modern period. It was certainly one of the most frequently prosecuted offences at the Essex assizes between 1620 and 1680; a total of eighty-three women were accused of killing their new-born children at that court during this period. It was also an offence marked by a high capital conviction rate, thirty of those accused, and one female accomplice, being hanged. The law relating to infanticide had been made more stringent by 21 Jac. I cap. 27, which made concealment of a stillbirth a capital offence ranking with infanticide, and a number of those tried for infanticide in this period must have come under this provision. Hence Ann Poulter was committed to the county gaol in 1669 'for having a bastard child (as she confesseth was still borne and afterwards conveyed away and buried privily)'.[120] Such details are rarely forthcoming, and those tried for infanticide, whose treatment is given in table 15, must be considered as a homogeneous group.

Table 15 seems to indicate a trend towards more lenient treatment of infanticide suspects as the century progressed. The sample is too small to allow any definite assertions on this point, but the high number of hangings in the 1630s is remarkable. This contrasts with a more lenient attitude later in the century, which may well have been attributable to the unpopularity of the 1624 statute in legal circles. The preamble of the Act of Repeal in 1803

Table 15 *Treatment of persons accused of infanticide at Essex assizes, 1620–80, by decades*

	Hanged	Pleaded pregnancy	At large	Acquitted	*Ignoramus*	Dead	No details	Other	Total
1620–9	5	—	—	3	—	—	2	—	10
1630–9	11	—	—	1	—	—	—	—	12
1640–9	1	—	—	7	1	—	5	2	16
1650–9	5	—	—	3	—	1	1	1	11
1660–9	5	—	—	9	—	1	2	—	17
1670–9	4	1	1	12	—	—	—	—	18
Total	31	1	1	35	1	2	10	3	84

suggested that it had been unenforceable for some time,[121] and Blackstone remarked that it was applied with lessening severity from the early eighteenth century, largely because the presumption of the guilt of the accused in the Jacobean statute was felt to be un-English.[122] This tendency, on the Essex evidence, was already well established by the late seventeenth century. Moreover, it is interesting that when the courts consulted midwives on the possibility of the death of the children in question having arisen from natural causes, their evidence was usually in support of such an opinion, or non-commital. A Maldon woman called to give evidence in such a case deposed that although she could not be certain 'she hath known children to be delivered dead in the same manner',[123] and in a Colchester case the midwife consulted was certain that the death of the child would have been averted if help had arrived in time.[124] Girls who suffered miscarriages could also be subjected to lengthy interrogation.[125]

The overwhelming majority of women accused of infanticide at the Essex assizes in this period were described as spinsters: of the eighty-four indicted, only seven were described as being married, three as widows, and one variously as being either a widow or a labourer's wife. As in the eighteenth century,[126] persons accused of infanticide were characteristically unmarried and young. Infanticide within marriage would, of course, have been difficult to detect, a consideration which suggests that the sample of infanticidal mothers tried at the assizes was probably a distorted one. Even so, an unwanted child born to married parents could be more effectively, and less obtrusively, got rid of by a period of deliberate neglect rather than by infanticide proper. This latter course would have a greater appeal to the unmarried mother anxious, in a period when considerable odium was laid upon pregnancy outside marriage, to dispose quickly of a source of shame and inconvenience.[127] It would also seem probable that in seventeenth-century Essex, as in both England and France in the following century, the young servant girl was especially likely to commit infanticide.[128] Once again, the point is obscured by the absence of assize depositions;[129] as we have seen, however, the servant girl of this period was very vulnerable to unmarried motherhood,[130] from which it might be inferred that she was correspondingly prone to infanticide.

It is difficult to assess the attitudes of contemporary society towards infanticide from the court records consulted for this study. One petition from an Essex parish, in which an infanticide was described as 'an unaturall and barbarous murther', suggests that local opinion could, on occasion, be aroused by the offence.[131] It is probable, however, that in a society where mechanical contraception was virtually unknown, and the penalties of unmarried motherhood, in moral and material terms, were so heavy, a high proportion of bastards were quietly killed at birth. A number of these deaths must have taken place with the compliance, if not the approval, of friends and relatives, although no Essex equivalent has been found for the infanticide factories that were apparently operating in London during this period.[132] The 'dark figure' of undetected infanticides must have been very great, and the attitudes of the more disorderly elements among the poor towards the offence were probably flexible. When Lydia Downes, the mistress of Richard Skeete, the Colchester poisoner, was delivered of her first bastard by him, she answered suggestions that the child should be killed by objecting that she 'was not so hard hearted as to make it awaie'; her reluctance was brushed aside by a maidservant, who replied 'tush, it was not the first that she had made awaie'.[133] Such attitudes, at least in the opinion of the present writer, were more common than the evidence suggests.

It is, perhaps, no accident that a discussion of violence in early modern England should end on such a tentative note. As has been obvious in the foregoing chapter, reconstructing the qualitative and quantitative aspects of violent behaviour in seventeenth-century England is a difficult process unlikely to meet with more than partial success. In particular, the nature of the documentation, the problem of the 'dark figure', and advances in medical techniques make it impossible to formulate any direct, statistical comparisons between criminal violence in seventeenth-century and twentieth-century society. There are, nevertheless, a number of conclusions which can be postulated, however cautiously. It would seem that seventeenth-century England was a more violent society than modern England. Extensive reading of court archives leaves the impression of a society where tempers were quick, and where violent behaviour was widespread through many different social strata. Nevertheless, it is the suspicion of the present writer that although society was more violent in the seventeenth century, the level and nature of this violence was not so high as to constitute a qualitative change. It was, perhaps, easier to get into a fight in Stuart England, but the way in which to do so (most commonly over drink in the alehouse) would not be particularly unfamiliar to the modern Englishman. Moreover, the relative absence of violence (and, in particular, of homicide) being used as a means to further another crime is striking, suggesting that even habitual criminals in this period were neither very brutal nor very violent.

Part Four

General themes and wider issues

9. Punishment

Any system of criminal law must, in the last resort, depend upon sanctions for its enforcement. Arguably, this assertion was truer when applied to early modern England than to most other contemporary European states. Despite the existence of informal methods of reaching an extra-judicial settlement of a criminal accusation (some of which will be discussed in the next chapter), the English criminal law, in its intentions at least, was punitive rather than restitutive in character, and had been for several centuries: the objectives of the king's court was to punish the criminal, not to effect or regulate a reconciliation between him and his victim. The theme of punishment, therefore, is of crucial importance to any study of the history of crime in England. Two other factors reinforce this importance when dealing with the early modern period: firstly, the sixteenth and seventeenth centuries are frequently portrayed as an important era of socio-economic change, and it might be expected that such change might well produce alterations in the types of punishment inflicted on convicted criminals.[1] Secondly, the harshness of punishment traditionally ascribed to the English criminal law during this period, and, more particularly, its apparent dependence upon capital punishment, are topics which demand close attention. Contemporary observers and later non-specialist historians both commented upon the frequency with which the death penalty was recommended in the English Statute Book, while this point has obviously impressed itself upon legal historians. When, for example, we find S. F. C. Milsom claiming that the medieval criminal law had 'done no more than systematise barbarity',[2] it is evident that the frequency with which the legal code recommended the death penalty was a major element in such barbarity as remained.

Most highly placed Stuart commentators would have welcomed this barbarity, for it is evident that the main objective of punishment was deterrence: there was no certainty that criminals would be caught, so potential criminals had to be terrified. As Beccaria was to point out in the next century, it is probably inevitable that the severity of the sanctions imposed by the criminal law should vary inversely with the uncertainty that offenders would be caught and thus subjected to those sanctions. In seventeenth-century England, therefore, the legal code depended heavily on the death penalty. Treason, murder, grand larceny, robbery, rape, mayhem and arson were all capital offences at common law, and statutory additions to this modest list of basic crimes brought the total of capital offences to about fifty by 1688.[3] Even before the dramatic increase in capital statutes which followed the Glorious Revolution, the English criminal risked death for a wide variety of offences.[4]

The means by which death was inflicted, setting aside the privilege of decapitation reserved under certain circumstances for peers, the barbarities reserved for traitors, and the use of the *peine forte et dure*,[5] was hanging. In contrast to the numerous accounts of hanging in London,[6] few descriptions of provincial executions seem to have survived from this period. It is probable that they were treated much as in London, as public spectacles in which both the inadvisability of breaking the king's laws and the majesty of the state were demonstrated. The criminal was permitted to make a farewell speech to the crowd, in which he invariably dwelt on the evil of his ways and the righteousness of his punishment. This was apparently a sixteenth-century innovation,[7] a humble equivalent of the custom of Tudor monarchs of turning treason trials into elaborate set pieces:[8] every public execution was, therefore, a spectacular reminder of the powers of the state, doubly effective because of its essentially local nature. The impact of these spectacles can be deduced from such accounts of provincial execution as do survive: in 1680, for example, a pamphlet was published describing the execution of John Marketman, sentenced to death at the Essex assizes. Marketman was a sea-surgeon who had murdered his wife on discovering that she had been overfamiliar with a neighbour while he had been at sea. On receiving his sentence, Marketman 'on his bended knees did beg as his last request of the Judge' that he might be executed at his native West Ham, where the crime had been committed. The event was attended by 'some Thousands of sorrowful spectators' who were treated to a good show. After a sermon, the prisoner was accompanied to the scaffold by his mother, 'who, poor soul, drowned in Sorrow when she came to the Gibbet, fell into a swoon, hardly to be recovered'. While standing on the ladder, the murderer made a speech that was a model of its kind, declaring:

That he had been very disobedient to his too indulgent Parents, and that he had spent his youthful days in Profanation of the Sabbath and licentious evils of Debaucheries beyond expression, and that he had been over penurious in his narrow observance of his wive's ways, desirous that all should pray to the Eternal God for his everlasting welfare, and with many pious expressions ended this mortal life.[9]

The delivery of such exhortations reinforced the benefits to be derived by the state from public execution, moral warning being added to the practical demonstration of the fruits of criminality.

At first sight it would seem that the frequency of executions afforded the authorities ample opportunity to impress these lessons upon the county's

Table 16 Capital punishments inflicted at Essex assizes, 1620–80, by quinquennia

	Homicide	Infanticide	Theft	Burglary/housebreaking	Highway robbery	Pickpocketing	Robbery	Sexual offences	Witchcraft	Coining	Counterfeit gipsy	Military desertion	Total
1620–4	3	1	10	7	1	—	1	2	—	—	—	—	25
1625–9	9	4	18	20	4	3	1	1	—	—	1	1	63
1630–4	14	7	28	44	6	—	—	1	—	—	1	—	100
1635–9	1	4	7	8	—	—	—	—	—	—	1	—	21
1640–4	2	—	2	3	3	—	—	—	—	—	—	—	10
1645–9	4	1	6	2	3	—	—	—	19	1	—	—	36
1650–4	4	2	12	17	3	2	—	—	—	—	—	—	40
1655–9	2	3	2	15	3	—	—	1	—	—	—	—	26
1660–4	2	3	7	16	6	—	—	2	—	—	—	—	36
1665–9	3	2	5	5	6	—	—	—	—	—	—	—	21
1670–4	1	1	3	21	1	—	—	1	—	3	—	—	31
1675–80	3	3	10	8	2	—	—	—	—	1	—	—	27
Total	48	31	110	166	38	5	2	8	20	6	1	1	436

Notes: counterfeit gipsy defined as felony without benefit of clergy by 1 & 2 Philip and Mary cap. 4, 5 Eliz. I cap. 20

populace. As table 16 shows, a total of 436 persons are known to have been executed after trial at the Essex assizes between 1620 and 1680. This figure is, of course, an underestimate, since many assize files are missing; if allowance is made for these, the total of executions at the assizes might be estimated at some 600, or an annual average of ten. Records of executions at other courts do little to modify this figure; four persons were hanged at the quarter sessions, all of them before 1634, and a further eleven are known to have been executed at Colchester borough sessions. It was at the assizes, then, that the overwhelming majority of executions in the county took place, and it is to table 16 that we must turn for details of capital punishment in the county.

The data in table 16 demonstrate the peculiarity of the late 1620s and the early 1630s.[10] Over a third of those known to have been executed were punished in those years, and, since several assize files are missing from this period, the proportion of those actually suffering the death penalty was probably much higher.[11] After 1645 the survival of files is more complete, and it may safely be argued that the second half of the century saw a lower level of capital convictions. On the evidence of table 16, the mid seventeenth century seems to have been something of a watershed in judicial attitudes to the use of capital punishment, representing a move away from the high conviction rate of the Elizabethan period[12] towards the lower levels of the eighteenth century.[13] The English law possessed many statutes enjoining capital punishment, and these were to become more numerous after 1688; students of the application of the criminal law in the eighteenth century have, however, discovered that the actual use of capital punishment in their period was becoming increasingly selective.[14] In a sense, the death penalty was used on what were felt to be appropriate occasions, or inflicted on what were felt to be appropriate criminals: the majority of those convicted for capital felonies were, in fact, escaping with lesser penalties. Essex assize records suggest that this trend, probably already well established, became more marked around the mid seventeenth century. From the late 1640s onwards far fewer people were executed for property offences than in the late Elizabethan or early Stuart periods, and even the decade of puritan ascendancy in the 1650s was not marked by a noticeable harshness to this type of offender. A similar process seems to have taken place with homicide, although the sample is too small to permit any very definite conclusions. The exact origins and implications of these changes will only become fully apparent in the light of comparative studies of assize records in other counties, and also of research into the attitudes of judges and the legal profession.

One element in this growing selectivity in the application of the death penalty must have been the awareness that a severe criminal code based on the frequent use of capital punishment could be counter-productive. As

Blackstone pointed out: 'The injured, through compassion, will sometimes forbear to prosecute: juries, through compassion, will sometimes forget their oaths, and either acquit the guilty or mitigate the nature of their offence: and judges, through compassion, will respite one half of the convicts, and recommend them to the royal mercy.'[15] This willingness on the part of the courts to soften the harshness of the law was, on the evidence of Essex court records, well established in the seventeenth century.

The most common means of avoiding capital punishment was through benefit of clergy.[16] This anomaly was praised by Blackstone: 'the wisdom of the English legislature having, in the course of a long and laborious process, extracted by a noble alchemy rich medicines out of poisonous ingredients; and converted, by gradual imitating, what was at first an unreasonable exemption of particular papist ecclesiastics, into a merciful mitigation of the general law, with respect to capital punishment'.[17] This 'merciful mitigation' saved the lives of several hundred criminals tried before the Essex courts between 1620 and 1680. Thus 34 murderers (or some 41% of those known to have suffered physical punishment) had their verdict commuted to one of manslaughter and were branded, 524 thieves (47% of those suffering physical punishment) enjoyed benefit of clergy, as did 115 burglars (43% of those suffering physical punishment).[18] Since the test of 'clerical' status was an ability to read, the historian must either revise his preconceptions about the literacy of the Stuart poor, or pursue a suspicion that the reading test was not applied very rigorously.

Although no direct evidence to support this suspicion has been discovered in Essex sources,[19] there is ample evidence that by the seventeenth century the reading test was little better than a 'pious perjury'. The test was abolished by statute in 1705, when benefit of clergy was extended automatically to all first offenders on clergyable charges,[20] which suggests that the courts had long since dispensed with a strict interpretation of the law on this point. The tradition that the opening verse of Psalm 51 should be employed as the set passage implies that the unlettered felon might escape through learning the relevant sentence by heart, and a seventeenth-century writer described how many 'prisoners indicted and convicted for lesser felonies' could 'say it by rote (as they say) and so do crave mercy, in desiring to be put to read this Psalme of mercy'.[21] Even those who had not taken this precaution did not need a high standard of literacy to survive. Sir Thomas Smith, writing in the mid sixteenth century, commented that many of those successful in claiming benefit of clergy read 'God knoweth sometime very slenderly',[22] and the situation had not altered greatly a century later; it was claimed in 1655 that, 'Were it not for the favour of the Court, not one in twenty could save their lives by reading'.[23] A petition to the House of Lords indicates how far the rules might ordinarily be bent in favour of the offender. The petitioner, maliciously indicted and subsequently convicted for stealing a buck by a John Farwell, a Somerset JP, 'desired to read the Psalm of Mercy, but Farwell so incensed the judge against him, that there was not only a clear bar made to prevent promptings, but the judge turned unto one of the hardest verses to read, which by God's grace he was enabled to do, and so escaped hanging, and was burnt in the hand'.[24] The dependence of a successful plea of clergy, to a large extent at least, upon the goodwill of the judge is illustrated by the case of a judge who, confronted by a prisoner who could not read, said: 'What, will not that obstinate knave reade indeede? Goe take him away and whip him.'[25] There were, of course, occasions when felons failed the reading test and were hanged, which suggests that the granting of benefit of clergy was not automatic.[26] Nevertheless, it remains clear that the procedure in claiming clergy was normally elastic, weighted in favour of the accused, and was widely accepted by judges as a means of mitigating a harsh legal code.

Another familiar expedient for avoiding verdicts of death was the undervaluing of goods allegedly stolen in grand larceny cases.[27] One writer was convinced that the practice was widespread, and implied that its use in individual cases depended upon the discretion of the court when he stated:

although *twelve pence* keeps not the old Rate, but the Modern, yet things are prized in trials of Life far below their worth, and no man loseth his life (in a single and simple Felony) but where the thing stoln riseth to more than many twelve pences (especially after the old estimate) but indeed the quality of the Offender, circumstances of the offence, and the times, are mainly considerable in our Law, where any man's life is taken away in such a Felony.[28]

It is impossible to calculate how often the value of goods as stated on indictments was an underestimate, but jury verdicts reveal that 165 thieves escaped conviction for grand larceny by the 'pious perjury' of the jury finding them guilty to less than a shilling, despite the value of the goods given on indictments. This total represents some 6% of all those convicted for theft, although the full importance of the practice becomes apparent when the figure is compared with the 110 felons hanged and 524 branded for grand larceny. Were it not for undervaluing, the total of those convicted for grand larceny would have increased by 20%. Combining the totals for those granted benefit of clergy and for those whose crimes were undervalued reveals that 86% of those charged with grand larceny and who were eventually convicted escaped the noose.[29] Further evidence of the willingness of the courts to mitigate the harshness of the law when dealing with theft is provided by the practice of adjusting details of the value of stolen goods to circumvent statutes. Hence the statute of 1623 which extended benefit of clergy to women stealing goods worth less than 10/- was followed by a number of indictments in which women accused of stealing goods worth more than this sum were found guilty for 9/- or less, and branded.[30]

Even if convicted for a capital offence, the criminal could still escape through pardon or reprieve. Preserved as a royal prerogative (although, in practice, judges' recommendations were followed),[31] the pardon as it was known in the period under review seems to have originated from the reign of Henry I.[32] The main defect of the medieval pardon was that those with money or power were better placed to obtain it, and it is possible that this situation still obtained in seventeenth-century Essex. John Eve, charged with murder in 1630 and eventually pardoned, had friends in high places,[33] while literary sources describe how, late in the century, a thief was saved from hanging at Chelmsford by the direct intervention of the sheriff, whose servant he had previously been.[34] Such examples suggest that the situation current in the eighteenth century, when convicted felons would regularly seek the intercession of the great on their behalf in hopes of obtaining a pardon,[35] already obtained in the seventeenth century. The offender might also escape through one of the general pardons which were issued to mark important occasions. These events were, of course, too uncommon to modify the overall severity of the law, and were usually hedged with exceptions including the more serious offences; the general pardon of 1660, for example, excluded murder, piracy, buggery, rape, bigamy and witch-craft.[36] Even so, minor offenders, notably thieves, were saved by these exercises in clemency.[37]

Pardon was more usually extended through the system of remands and reprieves. This to some extent made nonsense of trial by jury, in that the judge was empowered to ignore the decision of the jury, or could even (by remanding the prisoner before trial) remove him from court altogether. Blackstone wrote that a reprieve was granted

as where the judge is not satisfied with the verdict, or the evidence is suspicious, or the indictment is insufficient, or he is doubtful whether the offence be within clergy, or sometimes if it be a small felony, or any favourable circumstances appear in the criminal's character, in order to give room to apply to the crown for either an absolute or a conditional pardon.[38]

The system was apparently familiar in the seventeenth century,[39] and was instrumental in saving numerous convicted felons from execution. Most of those benefiting from it were property offenders, but on occasion reprieves were granted for bigamy, arson, infanticide, and witchcraft.[40] Additional impetus was given to the use of reprieves by increased recourse to transportation.[41] Originating from the medieval practice of regarding exile as the next worst thing to execution, transportation was a standard feature of English court procedure by the late seventeenth century, some 4,500 convicted felons being sent to the colonies between 1655 and 1699.[42] Access to transportation was through a derivation of the earlier use of pardon, the condemned criminal suing for a conditional pardon under the Great Seal. The system was regularised by the legislation of George I,[43] a successful request to be transported being presumably dependent upon the

Table 17 *Use of remands and transportation for property offences, Essex assizes, 1620–80, by quinquennia*

	Theft	Highway robbery	Burglary/housebreaking	Total remanded	Total transported
1620–4	1	—	—	1	—
1625–9	1	3	3	7	—
1630–4	2	—	—	2	—
1635–9	—	—	—	—	—
1640–4	1	—	—	1	—
1645–9	1	—	3	4	—
1650–4	3	2	1	6	—
1655–9	1	—	1	2	—
1660–4	2	—	4	6	—
1665–9	9	—	1	10	10
1670–4	6	—	1	7	7
1675–9	1	—	5	6	2

goodwill of judges during the seventeenth century. This was sufficiently forthcoming to provoke complaints from the colonies about the number of felons being sent to them in the 1670s.[44] As table 17 indicates, Essex assizes made their contribution to this situation. The possibility of transporting felons obviously made the whole idea of reprieves much more attractive: in a sense, as in the middle ages, exile could now be used as an alternative to execution.

The treatment of felons at the assizes in seventeenth-century Essex seems, therefore, to confirm what is emerging as the norm in such matters between the sixteenth and late eighteenth centuries. There was a draconian legal code with ample statutory provision for the infliction of the death penalty, and a large number of felons were hanged. Nevertheless, an overwhelming majority of those persons theoretically at risk of the noose evaded it, and did so through the regular application of practices designed to allow suspects or convicted persons to evade the full rigour of the law; benefit of clergy, undervaluing of goods in theft cases, other forms of tinkering with the wording of indictments, pardons, and reprieves. The nature of the records makes it difficult, of course, to discover exactly what happened in every case, although it is possible to obtain a fairly detailed impression of the processes at work in a few rare courts enjoying exceptionally rich documentation.[45] Such examples, and the more scattered evidence found in less favoured archives or in contemporary comment, make it evident that, generally speaking, persons who were hanged for felony in early modern England were either very unlucky or fairly atypical.

The unlucky offender was primarily the person who committed a property offence during a period of unusual sensitivity to law and order problems on the part of the courts. It is no accident that it was the 1620s and 1630s, decades of exceptional economic stress, which witnessed the greatest number of executions in the county; in the sixteenth century also, both the Essex assizes and the Colchester borough sessions had sent more felons to the gallows in times of bad harvest. The unlucky felon might also be the one who could find nobody to intercede for him. Such criminals, one suspects, would most usually be those atypical ones, the habitual or exceptionally heinous offenders; these felons were most likely to arouse the hostility of the court, and least likely to find anybody to speak for them. Even the fate of these unfortunates, however, demonstrates what was the underlying premise of contemporary sentencing policy: the punishment should, as far as possible, fit both the crime and the criminal.

The wealth of evidence on the treatment of the serious offender contrasts with the scarcity of references in the assize and quarter sessions records to what might be termed the more *folklorique*[46] punishments involving some form of public humiliation.[47] The Essex assize records, for example, afford only one example respectively of the use of the stocks[48] and of the pillory.[49] Even in the archives of the Essex boroughs, where such punishments might have been expected to have been more frequent, given their obvious applicability to the needs of smaller communities, details of such punishments are rare. Only one example of the use of the ducking stool has been found in the period covered by this study, at Saffron Walden in 1672, when it was employed to chastise an adulteress.[50] Similarly only one example of the practice of carting has been found, when a couple who were cohabiting without being married were taken round the streets of Colchester in a 'tumbrill'.[51] References to the use of the stocks are somewhat more frequent,[52] and they provide one of the more remarkable examples of the way in which punishment could be used to publicise the outcome of a particular offence. When a clothworker was found guilty of embezzling his master's wool at Colchester in 1667, it was ordered that he should be placed in the stocks 'and sitting there shall have a skayne of yard about his neck and a peese of paper pinned to his hatt or Capp upon which his offence shall be written in Capitall letters'.[53] In general, however, punishments of this type are only rarely referred to, and it is impossible to gain any insights into changing attitudes either to the appropriateness or to the effectiveness of their application.

One institution which might well have eroded habitual recourse to these traditional forms of public punishment was the house of correction, which constituted an excellent device for dealing with the petty offender. The English house of correction was, of course, merely the national variant of a remedy for disorder and petty crime that was applied over much of western

Europe from the mid sixteenth century onwards, the Amsterdam *Rasphuis* being perhaps the most famous product of this tendency. Such institutions were symptoms of a fumbling towards new thinking on crime, punishment, and related matters in the face of what were arguably new social problems. Although the connection should not be over-simplified, it remains undeniable that the emergence of the house of correction and its continental equivalents was essentially a response to the problems presented to national and local authorities by the massive increase in the number of the poor which attended the population increase of the period. For the poor were not only more numerous; in the eyes of authority, and probably in reality as well, they were also intrinsically disorderly and potentially criminous. Those among them unable to work had to be cared for; those willing to work but unable to find employment had to have employment found for them; and those unwilling to work and given to begging, vagrancy, or petty crime as an alternative had to be discouraged from their dissolute courses by a punishment which included a healthy dose of labour discipline. In England, the prototype of the house of correction was the London Bridewell, which from its inception in 1555 combined the attributes of a hospital, a workhouse, and a reformatory. Elizabethan legislation attempted to set up such institutions nationally,[54] although it was probably a statute of 1610 which finally established houses of correction throughout the realm.[55] Despite the confusion over its role, the idea that the house was the medium through which the offender might be reformed and changed into an honest and hardworking citizen rapidly assumed a central importance. When the Book of Orders was reissued in 1631, for example, it was recommended that prisoners awaiting trial should be set to work in the house of correction rather than being incarcerated in the county gaol, since 'they may learn honestly by labour, and not live idly and miserably long in prison, whereby they are made worse when they come out than they were when they went in'.[56]

In Essex, the setting up of houses of correction followed the national pattern of local experimentation and false starts within a framework of statutory demands and central government directions. The earliest mention of a house of correction comes in 1587, but continuous evidence of a house, at Chelmsford, dates from 1607.[57] Other houses of correction were set up in the period, notably that at Barking, in operation by 1609,[58] and Colchester.[59] The Chelmsford house has left us exceptionally good records of those who passed through it; apparently it was regularly delivered, much like a gaol, and the returns of those incarcerated which the keepers of the house regularly made to the quarter sessions provide important insights into the use of the house against minor offenders. This aspect of the house of correction's work is, of course, of central interest to the historian of crime; it should not be forgotten, however, that it still exercised its other functions.

Table 18 *Offenders at Chelmsford house of correction, 1620–80*

	Male	Female	Total
Vagrancy	143	56	199
Disorderly life	101	54	155
Living out of service	27	23	50
Deserter of family	38	5	43
Disorderly servant	6	2	8
Runaway servant	28	3	31
Bastardy	7	55	62
Poaching	7	—	7
Alehouse offences	8	2	10
Scold	—	1	1
Nightwalking	2	2	4
Hedgebreaking	4	—	4
Attempted rape	1	—	1
Lunacy	2	2	4
Cheating	4	—	4
Pilfering/Theft	3	1	4
Held pending trial	3	3	6
Other	3	5	8
Unspecified	179	66	245
Total	566	280	846

Notes: based on 117 surviving returns made by keeper of house of correction to the quarter sessions. The first surviving return for the post-1620 period was found in the Easter 1626 roll. There is an almost unbroken series of returns for the period 1649–69

An inventory of the Chelmsford house's equipment, compiled in 1651, included not only legirons, handcuffs and a pillory, but also spinning wheels and a loom,[60] while it was part of the contract of a new keeper appointed in 1661 that he should provide relief for sick persons in his custody from his salary of £50.[61]

The records of the Chelmsford house, however, suggest that its main *raison d'être* was the punishment, and perhaps the reform, of petty offenders. As table 18 indicates, most of those committed to the house were either vagrants, or resident nuisances, who had behaved badly enough to be felt worthy of correction for living a disorderly life. Many of this latter group were persons given to the general disruption of their community whose actions could cause considerable local annoyance, but were not serious (or perhaps coherent) enough to provide grounds for an indictment. Petitions against such nuisances sometimes contained requests that they be sent to the house of correction,[62] and the keepers' calendars record the incarceration of persons of 'ill fame', or of 'ill repute or lewd behaviour', or who refused to follow 'any good way of life', or who followed a disorderly life, pilfered, or had no calling.[63] Other sources provide further evidence of how the house acted as a general depository for the disorderly petty offender; Ralph Josselin noted in his diary how one of his parishioners, 'a quaker, a rude fellow, disobedient to his mother', was 'sent to ye house of correction' in 1675.[64] The Chelmsford house was also used to supplement the resources of the county gaol. As table 18 suggests, a number of serious offenders were held in the house pending trial. In addition, a few convicted felons were sent to the house after being branded, presumably for a more lengthy reminder of the wickedness of their ways than that provided by the hot iron.[65] Even more instructive is the example of other persons tried at the assizes who had been acquitted. It seems probable that some presumption of guilt rested upon them, or that it was felt that, even if they had evaded punishment for a specific offence, their general way of life was disorderly enough to warrant reform.[66] The use of the house of correction, therefore, offers a parallel in the treatment of petty offenders to the flexibility shown by the courts towards the more serious felon. One may doubt the efficiency of the house of correction in doing much to reform those placed in it; even so, it offered individuals or communities and the county authorities alike a means of doing at least something to curb the delinquencies of a wide range of nuisance offenders.

   This study of punishment, based mainly on the assizes and quarter sessions of one county, can hardly hope to provide a comprehensive review of the theory and practice of the subject in its Stuart context. In particular, contemporary opinion on punishment is a subject which cries out for serious analysis. On the other hand, certain generalisations can be made on the basis of the evidence presented in this chapter. It would appear that punishment was in a transitional (insofar as the word has any real meaning) phase. In one sense, the seventeenth century saw the retention of traditional practices; the most notable of these, perhaps, was the continued importance laid on the publicity of punishment, whether public execution, public whipping, the pillory, carting, or that public penance in a white sheet which was the standard penalty inflicted by the ecclesiastical courts. The objectives and end product of these public punishments, in both the official and the popular mind, warrant further investigation; for the present, it seems that they offered a mixture of satisfaction for the community that it was being visibly revenged, humiliation for the offender, and deterrence for those likely to emulate him. Conversely, the house of correction arguably represents early experimentation with the 'modern' idea that the offender is capable of amendment, and ought to be reformed by society as well as punished. Altogether, despite the contradictory elements present within it, the system was probably adequately suited to contemporary expectations of what the law and order machine should offer by way of punishment. Not least, it was extremely flexible, able to adapt itself to an almost infinite range of individual cases. Study of the system in operation, however, and even the most partial knowledge of the thinking that lay behind it, suggests that its aims were confused: the Stuarts were uncertain as to whether punishment of criminals should be motivated by revenge, deterrence, or a desire to reform. It is a sobering thought that as these words are written, exactly three centuries after the terminal date of the period covered by this book, public opinion is still unable to untangle this confusion.

10. Crime and the local community

The social context within which crime took place is of crucial importance, on account of the dependence of the law enforcement system in this period on the reporting and prosecution of crime by members of the population at large. The presentment or indictment of an offender was usually the outcome of decisions made either by the individual offended against or by unpaid amateur officials. The student of seventeenth-century crime must, therefore, attempt to attain some understanding of the processes that usually lay behind the decision to take a case to court, and to obtain a deeper knowledge of the offenders and victims of the period than that provided in formal court records. Obviously enough, the ideal way of so doing is through the microscopic village study, and such studies as have been undertaken of Essex parishes have provided ample support for the premise that a detailed examination of crime and control in individual communities constitutes one of the most fruitful approaches to the history of crime.[1] If based on sufficient documentation, the village study is an essential means towards gaining as comprehensive a view as possible of offenders, their victims, and the power structure within the village. These matters are of manifest significance for the historian of crime.

There is, moreover, a second consideration which renders the study of crime in its local context essential, namely, the presence of a number of offences which can only be understood in the context of the pre-industrial village. There existed a variety of crimes which, whatever the origins of their legal definition or the seriousness of the penalties attached to them, can be treated together because their existence depended upon the persons accused of committing them being part of a community of that type. They comprehended a whole spectrum of illegal behaviour, and, indeed, provide a powerful reminder of the multi-faceted nature of 'crime' in the early modern period. They included a number of felonies, such as witchcraft or arson; common nuisances, including such mundane matters as failing to clean ditches or leaving dungheaps on the street; the enforcement of certain obligations placed upon the parish or upon individuals within it; breaches of community norms; and (as might be expected in an age when the courts were still used to resolve interpersonal conflicts) the articulation of neighbourly tensions. It is to this broad category of crime, much of it

154

essentially petty in nature but all of it characteristic of law enforcement in the pre-industrial world, that we will turn our immediate attention.

Perhaps the most numerically important subdivision within this type of offence was that constituted by the prosecution of those failing to meet their obligations towards the upkeep of the highways. There were 3,230 presentments at quarter sessions against those who did not meet the statutory requirements which enjoined the more substantial villagers to provide carts and draught animals, and the poor their labour, for the repair of the highway.[2] Some 60 persons were felt to be persistent enough in their negligence to be indicted for such infringements, while a further 189 indictments were brought against individuals or parishes for failing to repair stretches of highway, road, or footpath for which they were held responsible. To these offenders guilty of omission might be added ninety-three persons indicted for obstructing, blocking, or damaging the highway.[3] Despite this constant stream of presentments and indictments, the problem of enforcing the laws relating to the upkeep of the highways proved intractable. Bad or obstructed roads were a nuisance, but it proved impossible to inculcate the public at large with a sense of responsibility towards the king's highway, and by the end of the seventeenth century the first turnpikes had appeared in Essex.[4] The report of Humphrey Harvey, surveyor of the highways for Great Holland in 1658, epitomises the difficulties involved in this area of local government: his presentment of those parishioners who had failed to do their statutory road repairs began with his 'partener', the other surveyor, who had neglected his office.[5]

The upkeep of bridges constituted a similar problem. Seven hundred and fifty-two presentments and one hundred and twenty indictments were brought in hopes of compelling individuals or parishes to repair bridges for which they were responsible, or to bring to notice the need for the repair of such bridges as it was the county's duty to maintain.[6] Ruinous bridges were as great an obstruction to travel as were bad roads, and on at least one occasion it was reported that two men had drowned while trying to cross an unrepaired bridge.[7] However, as with road repair, there is little evidence of any improvement during the century, and very little proof that repeated presentment or indictment of those responsible for decayed bridges brought any improvement.

Bad roads and ruinous bridges were just two of the more obvious nuisances that a community might seek to overcome by indictment: there was also a very wide variety of petty irritations that might be brought to the attention of the courts. Uncleaned ditches might cause as much inconvenience as bad roads or broken bridges.[8] Various industrial practices could cause a nuisance. In 1620 the owners of eight starch houses in West Ham were indicted at the King's Bench for polluting the atmosphere of the area with fumes; rivers and streams were occasionally reported as being polluted; and one presentment told how a common pond had been made 'Unwholesome with foule sudds and cloathes'.[9] Yet more evidence of the variegated nature of nuisance offences is provided by references to dangerous dogs. No parallel has been found for the Elizabethan case of a girl being killed by two mastiffs who slipped their chains,[10] but odd references suggest that neighbours who failed to control their dogs might cause problems. Several reports reached the bench of these animals attacking passers-by, one man was reported for failing to hang a dangerous mastiff after being ordered to do so by the bench, and another was ordered to contribute to the maintenance of a man who had been crippled by a dog of his.[11] Well might Josselin comment, after losing a hog that had been bitten by a mad dog, 'blessed bee God it was not a child'.[12]

The tranquility of the parish was, however, more likely to be disrupted by its human residents than by troublesome dogs. As we have seen, failure to meet obligations might lead to prosecution: there were also a number of more active methods by which an individual might disrupt the life of his or her community. It is probable, for example, that a largely illiterate or semi-literate society will place special emphasis on the power of the spoken word, and as prosecution for swearing indicates, strong language could provoke a hostile response. Likewise scolding must have constituted a real threat to public peace in a face-to-face society, and court records reveal a constant undercurrent of harsh words among neighbours. Scolding could be associated with other offences. One woman was presented for 'rayling and scoulding at her neighbours and for living incontinently, as the common fame and report goeth',[13] and witches might also be accused of being scolds. Mary Cutford of Rainham, presented before the Archdeacon of Essex for wishing herself to be a witch so that she could be revenged on Ann Dawdrey, had already been presented with her proposed victim for 'scoldeing, brawlinge, and fightinge to the disturbance of their neighbours'. The two women had indulged in a stand-up fight in the street during which they had thrown crockery at each other.[14] Such cases suggest that scolding might best be seen in the context of more general disorderly behaviour likely to upset the tranquility of the community. Even so, the determined scold could constitute a serious threat to the peace of a neighbourhood, as is suggested by the formidable Maldon couple presented to the leet for 'anoince of the holl p[a]rish with ther tonges'.[15]

Further evidence of the importance attached to the spoken word is provided by defamation cases. England, for reasons that have yet to be fully investigated, experienced a massive upsurge in litigation over words from the mid sixteenth century onwards, and one writer has gone so far as to claim that 'the amount of litigation aroused by slander was a phenomenon of the age'.[16] This rise in litigation was accompanied by an increase in the complexity of the law relating to defamation.[17] In the late middle ages, slander had been a matter either for the ecclesiastical courts or for manorial or borough jurisdictions. From about 1500 onwards, however, the common law courts began to take an interest in suits over words, and had soon encroached fairly heavily on the church courts' competence in such matters. Briefly, by about 1620, the common law courts were dealing with defamations imputing conduct which might be prosecuted at the criminal courts, or with imputations which might lead to a loss of trade or other material disadvantages. Conversely, the ecclesiastical courts heard suits in which the words spoken alleged conduct which might lead to presentment before them. The common law courts normally awarded damages against unsuccessful defendants in defamation suits, while the ecclesiastical courts imposed penance.

Defamation, as well as being the basis for a suit at common or ecclesiastical law, might also be indicted as a criminal offence, because of what Blackstone described as 'the tendency which all libels have to create animosities, and to disturb the public peace'.[18]

Given the remedies available in other courts, it is hardly surprising that only twenty-two cases of defamation were indicted at the assizes or quarter sessions. Analysis of these and other Essex cases gives an impression of a society which was sensitive to a wide range of slights. Twelfth Night celebrations at Colchester in 1623 were enlivened when a libel was circulated showing various of the town's clergymen taking tobacco with the devil;[19] a Boreham gentleman was indicted for defamation after complaining that a neighbour was trying to turn his servants against him;[20] while a more serious case occurred in 1677 when Sir John Bramston was the subject of a libel circulated in Chelmsford accusing him of popery, this being just one incident in his long struggle with the Mildmay faction.[21]

Despite such cases, it seems that most defamations indicted at the assizes or quarter sessions, like those with which the church courts concerned themselves,[22] involved allegations of sexual misconduct on the part of the complainant. Thus we find an Ingrave husbandman being bound over for calling the wife of one of the local gentry a 'pocky tayle queane', and another example involved a couple who declared that a woman was a whore, adding that her mother was one too.[23] Even the gentry were involved in defamation cases. John Sarton of Epping, described as a gentleman, was indicted in 1645 for composing a lengthy piece of verse concerning the amatory adventures of one of his co-parishioners, Martin Masters. Four lines will suffice to convey the flavour of the piece:

I prethy little Martyn amend they lewd life;
And ly no more with the constable's wife;
Thou[gh] she want more of her sight as we know;
Yet she hath feeling truly below;[24]

A fine example of defamation among the gentry is provided by the case of

Thomas Glascock, who was accused of saying to Bridget, the wife of Robert Audley: 'You are a damned whore, you have bin ridd above twentie times by severall persons before you againe came to this country (meaninge the county of Essex), you are a bawdy bitch and came out of a bawdy house, and you are a dounghilly whore.'[25] Such defamation could be very damaging to an individual's standing within the community: one senses that it was not purely a legal fiction which led Joan Swifte, a butcher's wife of Stratford, to complain to the King's Bench that since being defamed as an adulteress she was 'brought into very much scandal and disgrace amongst her neighbo[u]rs liveing thereabouts'.[26]

Another source of communal strife was barratry. The offence was evidently a widely defined one. Dalton described the barrator as any sort of disturber of the peace, a taker by force or stealth of other men's goods, an inventor or sower of false reports, 'he who is a common mover and stirrer up (or Maintainer) of Suits in Law in any Court, or else of Quarrels or parties in the Country', or, more generally, 'a Common Wrangler that setteth men at odds, and is himself never quiet, but at Braul with one or other'.[27] The existence of a blanket offence of this type was of obvious utility to a community attempting to restrain one of its more turbulent members, and it is interesting to note that one barratry indictment was witnessed on behalf of a whole parish.[28] Thirty-nine persons were indicted for this offence at the assizes and quarter sessions, and a further two at the King's Bench.[29] Dalton recommended that a convicted barrator should be bound over to keep the peace,[30] while Blackstone suggested fine and imprisonment.[31] No details are found of punishment on indictments, although a quarter sessions order book mentions a fine of £500 on Thomas Cudmore, a Kelvedon gentleman and assize grand juror, in 1679. The high fine is attributed to 'the heynousness of his offence', but no further details are given, and it must be surmised that Cudmore was using his position of responsibility to trouble his neighbours. Certainly he ceased to be a grand juror at about this time.[32]

As might be expected, investigation of those accused of barratry can reveal a history of contact with the law in which a barratry indictment forms only one episode. Thomas Briggs, a labourer of Little Baddow indicted at the assizes for barratry, had been bound over three times at the quarter sessions, twice to answer for unspecified matters, once to keep the peace to his wife.[33] Edward Constable of Aveley, indicted for barratry in 1651, appeared on a riot charge three years later, was twice involved in bindings-over to keep the peace, and was bound over to keep the peace to his wife, herself indicted for barratry in 1639.[34] Alice, the wife of William Harrington, a Sible Hedingham gentleman, was apparently incapable of getting on with her relatives. Two people sharing her surname were bound over to keep the peace to her, and she attempted to prosecute another for rape. The indictment in this case was found *ignoramus*, indicating that the accusation was not a very well-founded one. Alice was herself indicted for barratry in 1646.[35]

It is evident from these case histories that the barrator could act as a constant irritant to his or her neighbours, but analysis of those indicted for barratry indicates that the barrator differed from other nuisance offenders. Firstly, whereas the archetypal scold or witch was female, the barrator was usually a man; only six of the forty-one accused were women. Secondly, the barrator was not drawn from the poorest members of the parish. Three were described as gentlemen (and one as a gentleman's wife), two as clerks, eight as yeomen, four as husbandmen, and fifteen as either tradesmen or artisans or as their wives, as opposed to only five classed as labourers. Again allowance must be made for the problems of accepting a man's style as given on an indictment; nevertheless, indictment for barratry, on those occasions when it was a manifestation of community feeling, seems to have been the method used for dealing with the better off, more self-confident local nuisance. The poor incurring the displeasure of parochial opinion were probably more easily cowed by other means, including perhaps informal admonition from the parish officers, or a spell in the house of correction.

Another phenomenon which is perhaps best understood in the context of tensions within the community is witchcraft.[36] By 1620 witchcraft prosecutions were becoming increasingly rare in Essex, and had it not been for the outbreak of a serious local witch craze in the closing stages of the First Civil War[37] the offence would have been extremely uncommon in the period covered by this book. As it was, a total of 101 indictments were tried at the assizes between 1620 and 1680. Of these, however, fifty were tried at the Trinity assizes of 1645,[38] and were directly attributable to the activities of Matthew Hopkins, while a further fourteen were tried in the immediate aftermath of these mass trials. Hence nearly two thirds of these cases occurred in the exceptional circumstances of the 1640s and early 1650s, and a geographical concentration might be added to this chronological one. The cases tried in 1645 were unusually localised, and are largely responsible for Tendring Hundred's exceptionally high share of witchcraft cases (forty-three of the total).[39] The 1645 trials were also unusual in producing a large number of convictions; nineteen of those accused in that year were executed, only one other alleged Essex witch being hanged in our period.[40] Witchcraft is, of course, a subject which has attracted considerable attention from historians and others, and about which a good deal of nonsense has been written. On the evidence of Essex court materials used in this present study, however, it must be concluded that it was (except in the Hopkins era) an offence that was neither particularly frequently prosecuted nor usually likely to result in conviction.

On the other hand, Macfarlane's interpretation of accusations of witchcraft in Essex does raise some very pertinent points about other types of crime and about wider problems concerning the relationship between social change and social conflict. His thesis is a complex one, but central to it is the theme of deteriorating relationships between rich and poor villagers in a period of steady socio-economic change. Population increase, accentuated social stratification, and advancing agrarian capitalism in the late sixteenth century not only created a large body of rural poor but also created confusion towards this group in the minds of the more substantial villagers. In such a situation, it is easy to see how this more prosperous group might feel that the weak and dispossessed (it is no accident that the stereotype of a witch was a poor and elderly woman) would attempt to redress the changing balance of society through *maleficium*. Indeed, the fact that accusations of witchcraft were beginning to slacken in their intensity by 1620 might be evidence that the developments central to Macfarlane's interpretation were working themselves out by that date: attitudes were adjusting to rural capitalism, the countryside was less close to a subsistence crisis than it had been at various points in the late sixteenth century, and the poor law was beginning to institutionalise the problem of poverty. Even so, a study of the background to accusations of witchcraft does raise a number of interesting problems. Firstly, the rarity with which gentry were involved, either as the victims or as the accused,[41] might be taken as evidence of the limits of that group's involvement in village life: villagers were obviously able to experience and resolve disputes independently of their social superiors. Secondly, the antecedents to formal prosecution, the growing suspicions and attempts at informal counteraction that so often preceded indictment for witchcraft, were, as we shall see, by no means unique to this offence. Treating witchcraft as a 'normal' crime does have its problems;[42] conversely, the social context of Essex witchcraft so richly portrayed by Macfarlane is very relevant to the study of other types of crime.

One such was arson, which has recently been interpreted as arising from tensions within the community, and particularly tensions between rich and poor. Defined as the malicious and voluntary burning of a house or outhouses, arson was felony without benefit of clergy.[43] Fire was a continual source of danger during this period,[44] and an awareness of the problem caused many local authorities to take fire precautions; Chelmsford leet, for example, ordered the annual sweeping of chimneys within the town on pain of a 10/- fine.[45] Buildings were evidently very vulnerable to fire, and arson must have been a very easy offence to carry out. It has, indeed, been argued that fire-raising, now identified as a major form of social protest in early nineteenth-century England,[46] was also a means by which the weak might seek revenge for real or imagined wrongs in the early modern period.[47]

Such a view may be qualitatively correct – lack of assize depositions makes close investigation of cases impossible – but the offence was very unimportant in quantitative terms. Only nine indictments for arson survive. All of them were tried at the assizes, and involved eight accused, including one married couple. Of these, only one is known to have been found guilty, an Ashton labourer indicted twice at the Trinity 1645 assizes.[48] To this list can be added one indictment for attempted arson[49] and a handful of bindings-over to answer for the offence, some of which correspond with indictments. There is little evidence of widespread suspicion of arson. When Colchester pest-house was burned down in 1631, arson was suspected,[50] but fires were just as likely to be attributed to accidental causes.[51] A number of cases in which generally disorderly members of the community added threats of arson to a general outburst of spleen exists, as when William Osbourne of Leigh 'Threatened to sett on fire a house at Leigh and to make the said town of Leigh a bloudy towne',[52] but it is difficult to represent such violent speeches as evidence of deep-laid plans for revenge against a community. It is difficult to depict arson as widespread during this period, despite the ease with which it could be carried out. The lack of evidence of widespread suspicions of fire-raising, and the lenient attitude of the courts to such indictments as were brought, do not suggest that the arsonist was a major source of anxiety to the property-owners of the period.

There is even less evidence of an analogous method of clandestine revenge, the maiming or killing of cattle, a striking contrast to the frequency with which alleged attacks on animals figured in witchcraft indictments.[53] A woman from Bocking was bound over for stabbing a co-parishioner's cow and threatening to kill the rest of his cattle, and Thomas Turnor of West Hanningfield was bound over to answer a local yeoman for reviling him 'with all the foule languadge that maie be' and threatening 'to mischiefe and kill his cattell'.[54] The conclusion reached by two recent writers from nineteenth-century-evidence, that cattle-maiming 'never played a significant part in England and is probably best neglected',[55] seems to have been equally valid in the seventeenth century. On the evidence of Essex court records, Stuart Englishmen and women at odds with their neighbours would resort to physical or verbal violence rather than indirect attacks on property.

There were, then, a number of offences which are only comprehensible in the limited, face-to-face world of the early modern village. In this world, individuals might be coerced into performing their obligations to the community or to the state, or disruptive villagers curbed, through recourse to the courts. With witchcraft, arson, and cattle-maiming, however, we are entering a set of problems which cannot be explained by simply invoking interpersonal tensions or community action against the deviant. The major complication is that although tension undoubtedly existed between those accused of such offences and their accusers, it was the expression not merely of conflict between persons, but also most often of conflict between persons of different socio-economic strata; witchcraft, arson and cattle-maiming have all been regarded by historians, and by some contemporaries, as means by which the weak of the parish might retaliate against the powerful. The late sixteenth and seventeenth centuries were a period of marked economic and social change, not least in Essex with its increasingly market-oriented agriculture and its highly capitalised textile industry. One outcome of this period of change was an intensification of social stratification, and, in particular, of the emergence of a body of poor which was not only very numerous but also potentially disorderly. Interpersonal conflict in Essex villages and small towns did not occur only between equals; it also formed part of a larger conflict between rich and poor, the powerful and the dispossessed, within the community. The process took place against a wider, indeed European, context, which led to the 'criminalisation' of the poor.[56] Those who had been regarded in the middle ages as God's poor were increasingly being regarded as the devil's: as we shall see, the Essex poor presented their governors with a number of difficulties which went far beyond the simple relief of poverty.

The problem is, of course, complicated by evidence of continued criminality on the part of gentry, yeomanry, and other members of the parochial elite. Such persons were regularly accused of the more common community nuisance offences – failing to clean ditches, blocking roads and footpaths, defamation, barratry and so on – and were also accused of more serious offences, notably crimes of violence. As I have argued elsewhere, the presence of this type of petty crime by the 'middling sort' should not be lost sight of; indeed it forms an important sub-category of disorder in the sixteenth and seventeenth centuries.[57] Inhabitants of parishes afflicted by a troublesome family drawn from the gentry or the middling sort would doubtless have found the argument that the poor of the period were uniquely disorderly a very unconvincing proposition. Consider, for example, the Cawood family of South Weald. When Gabriel Cawood was bound over to keep the peace to his mother and sister in 1643 it was noted on the recognizance that: 'This Gabriel hath heretofore been corrected and imprisoned uppon his mother's complaint, but in truth they are both faulty and esteemed crazy headed.' The history of the family over the previous thirty years was punctuated by assaults and bindings-over to keep the peace, while Gabriel had been committed to the house of correction for disobeying his parents. The feud with his relatives was perpetuated after his death. His will divided his estate between a 'loving friend' and a 'Loving Kinsman', leaving only 'one shilling to be paid within one month next after my decease' to his wife. His mother's will was equally insistent that her estate went to her daughter.[58] Another family to figure prominently in court records were the Osbournes of Leigh. The Osbournes were not gentry, but their status as fishermen put them above the very poorest, and over a forty-year period members of the family were indicted or presented for a variety of offences including assault, forestalling, unlicensed higgling, drunkenness, theft, failing to do statutory work on the highways, and assaulting a hearth tax officer, as well as being bound over to keep the peace or answer for various unspecified misdemeanours.[59]

The criminality of the middling sort was, therefore, a distinctive feature of the problem of law and order of the period. Analysis of it is, however, obscured by the contemporary taste for vexatious or malicious litigation. The litigiousness of the aristocracy and gentry in early modern England is a familiar theme,[60] but the desire to 'wage law' was by no means restricted to the upper reaches of society,[61] and prosecutions in criminal cases, like suits at civil law, were doubtless on occasion founded on very slight grounds. The impact of this phenomenon was probably greater in other courts than those whose work forms the basis of the present study, but the records of the Essex assizes and quarter sessions do furnish occasional complaints of malicious prosecution. In 1637, for example, George Smith of Great Oakley complained that the minister of the parish was attempting to close down his alehouse, and 'by vexatious suites & threates' had 'p[ro]cured diverse handes against y[ou]r petit[i]on[er]'.[62] In 1651 Stephen Brockwell wrote to the bench complaining that he had been bound over falsely by 'a woman of a virulent & mallitious spirit'.[63] In 1679 a petition reached the bench from the inhabitants of Springfield, who claimed that a servant girl had been committed to gaol maliciously 'for some p[re]tended misdemeanour' by her master.[64] Such examples indicate that the problem existed, but they are hardly numerous enough to suggest that it was a very major concern, and they suggest that in Essex, as in seventeenth-century Wiltshire, vexatious and malicious prosecution was more likely to be a feature of misdemeanour than of felony cases.[65]

The problems involved in studying litigation are therefore of great interest, and serve to remind us that it is dangerous to take an over-simplified view of Stuart lawbreakers. Nevertheless, a detailed study of Essex villages of the seventeenth century indicates that those accused of criminal or disorderly behaviour were drawn with increasing rarity from the village elite. In Earls Colne, substantial parishioners were much less likely to be involved in sexual misbehaviour in the late seventeenth century than in the late sixteenth century.[66] In Terling, the last member of the village notables to be presented for drunkenness saw fit to make a public declaration of his shame at the offence, and to promise future amendment.[67] In Kelvedon, although the issue was perhaps less clear-cut, it would seem that offenders from the middling sort were rarely in trouble for anything more serious than a petty nuisance.[68] It was, therefore, the criminal poor who constituted the gravest threat to law and order in seventeenth-century

Essex: it is their delinquencies, and the ways in which they were combated, which will form the central theme of the remainder of this chapter.

To the general historian, the most familiar member of the disorderly poor is that great source of anxiety to early modern authority, the vagrant. The vagrant as an enemy of society was essentially a creation of Tudor legislation,[69] and the Elizabethan vagrant, as described in the popular literature of the period, has passed into the textbooks as *the* criminal stereotype of the age. Only recently has doubt been cast on the uncritical acceptance of the views of the Elizabethan pamphleteers,[70] and the vagrant emerges from Essex court records as a much less terrifying figure than that portrayed in contemporary popular literature. Groups of vagrants tended to be formed by or around a family, and rarely exceeded half-a-dozen in number. It would seem, therefore, that the archetypal vagrant was not a member of an ambulatory subculture, but rather a displaced member of the poor, or even simply a migratory worker. The distinction between the poor on the road in search of work and the vagrant proper is, however, a difficult one to draw: there must have been many like Edward Miller, described as 'a wandringe fellow who sometimes begged & sometimes wrought', who was found dead in a barn in 1655.[71]

It is impossible to calculate the number of vagrants on the roads in this period. The calendars of Chelmsford house of correction record that vagrants passed through that institution, but they do not run in an unbroken series and probably only record those vagrants dealt with immediately before a sessions. Colchester records mention 237 vagrants between 1630 and 1664 who were passed back to their place of last settlement, but this is probably an understatement.[72] Divisional returns from justices under the Book of Orders give a more immediate impression of the number of vagrants punished, 87 being apprehended in the South-Eastern Division in 1636, and 203 in the following years.[73] The place of last settlement of vagrants, as revealed on map 4, was most usually in Essex itself, the London area, or East Anglia, which might support the view that vagrants were characteristically the displaced poor rather than professional rogues. Despite this trend, almost every English county contributed to vagrants picked up in Essex, and their numbers also included Scots, Irish, a man speaking an unknown tongue thought to be French,[74] and a woman from Barbados.[75]

If these travellers were not the organised rogues of the pamphlets, they could still constitute a social problem. The migrant worker was very much a marginal figure in society, and theft depositions reveal that the migratory worker or lone vagrant had an opportunistic attitude to stealing.[76] Robert Richardson, examined on suspicion of theft at Maldon in 1624, described how he had spent the last few months in a variety of agricultural pursuits. He had worked 'in husbandry' at Bocking, had spent the winter months threshing for his uncle, and had then worked at weeding at St Lawrence and

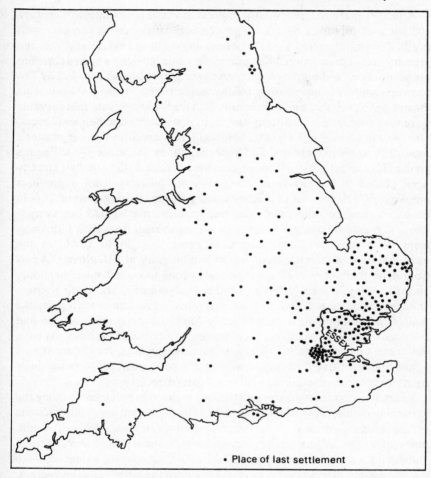

• Place of last settlement

Map 4 Place of last settlement of vagrants passing through Chelmsford and Colchester houses of correction, 1620–80

North Fambridge. Finding no further employment in the area, he had lived rough in the marshes, eventually stealing the four sheepskins for which he was apprehended.[77] Richardson and his petty crime were probably more typical of vagrant criminality than the depredations of the professional rogue, although the latter did exist. Reference has already been made to vagrant pickpockets, and evidence of vagabond fortune-tellers suggests the presence of rogues living off their wits.[78] Such exceptions do not, however modify the conclusion that the Essex vagrant was not a very terrifying figure; but this is not to deny that he was a continual nuisance.

A further marginal, potentially rootless element in seventeenth-century society was provided by the large numbers of domestic servants who fulfilled a vital function in an economy in which the household was the primary unit of production. Disciplining servants must have been a constant preoccupation, and employees like the young man bound over in 1623 to answer a number of unspecified 'misdemeanours and cozenages' against his master were probably all too numerous.[79] Depositions reveal that servants were very susceptible to the temptations of petty theft from their employers. One girl, in service at Cressing, habitually lent quantities of her master's foodstuffs to his neighbours, and kept the money she made by selling his goods. The investigation of these activities revealed that she had already been placed in the house of correction for pilfering from a previous employer.[80] The servant of a Brentwood yeoman, finding himself 26/- in debt to a tobacco seller, stole clothing from his master and ran away.[81] Other servants showed themselves as willing to steal from their fellows as from their employer; one such case came to light in 1621, in the examination of a man accused of theft and burglary at Elsenham.[82] Apart from petty theft, servants were especially prone to sexual misdemeanours and, as we have seen, a large proportion of the mothers of illegitimate children in this period were domestic servants.[83] The fate of such girls, like that of the pilfering servant, was likely to be dismissal from service and eventual entry into the ranks of the hard core of criminal vagrants. At best, the presence of a large number of household servants, for the most part young and essentially rootless, constituted a permanent problem for those trying to attain a disciplined and well-ordered society.

Vagrants, migrant workers, and the less respectable elements among the extremely mobile army of servants therefore constituted important sections of the criminal orders of seventeenth-century Essex. Without doubt, however, as the century progressed, the most frequent perpetrators of crime and disorder were the resident poor. It is, of course, to some extent otiose to make clear-cut distinctions between the poor of the parish and the vagrant: this was a period of high geographical mobility, and the poor were constantly on the move. They were extremely vulnerable to economic pressures or other adverse circumstances, and if one place of residence proved unsuitable, they had little compunction in moving on in search of something better. One parish's resident poor delinquent might easily become another's vagrant or troublesome servant. Despite these reservations, and notwithstanding the attention lavished by Elizabethans and later historians upon the vagrant, there is considerable evidence that it was in fact the resident poor of the parish who were given to a wide range of disorderly and criminal behaviour.

Certainly a number of contemporaries thought so. Dalton, for example, in his enumeration of the grounds upon which suspicion might be fastened on individuals after a felony had been detected, gives the practical working justice's portrayal of the characteristics of the country malefactor. The investigation should take into account the suspect's family background, to see if his relatives 'were wicked, and given to the same kind of fault'; his education and upbringing, whether 'idely, or in any honest Occupation'; 'his means, if he hath whereon to live or not'; and his physical ability and mental predisposition for the crime being investigated. The justice was also to consider the suspect's course of life, 'if a common Ale-house haunter, or riotous in Diet, Play, or Apparel', his local reputation, his previous record, and the company he kept.[84] Dalton, it would seem, had a well-defined criminal stereotype in mind when advising his readers on how to investigate felony.

Archival materials support the view, implicit in Dalton's opinions, that there existed a body of petty criminals given to an almost infinitely varied repertoire of delinquency.[85] Perhaps the most striking evidence of the existence of the petty offender comes in the numerous petitions to the bench in which parishioners complained, at times graphically, about the misdeeds of certain of their neighbours. Typical of these 'articles of complaint' were those exhibited in 1621 against Robert Godfrey, an alehouse-keeper of Blackmore. The list of evil-doing attributed to him is impressive. He was a blasphemer, 'dycer', quarreller, and had broken the peace; he was suspected of felony, of receiving stolen goods, and of harbouring suspicious persons; he had seldom attended church in the previous year, and was suspected of being father to his maidservant's bastard, suspicion against him on this count having first been levelled by his wife; he had, moreover, kept a disorderly alehouse that had been suppressed three times, was wont to carry beer out of his house to various of the ill-affected of the parish, had entertained on the sabbath, and had on one recent occasion been found dead drunk by the constables after an alleged twenty-four hours of solid drinking.[86] Another portrait of the local petty offender survives from 1664 when a petition was received from South Ockendon against two men who were 'generally knowne to be constant nightwalkers, Deare Stealers, Sheepe-stealers, Geese-stealers, Counter-fiters of ye officers hand[es] of the parish, cheat[es], Idle and Lazei fellows, seldom or never doeing any work; & in fine, given to all Cunning & Craft Villanie whatsoever'. The petitioners urged the justices to 'dispose of them as may seems best, for ye preservation of ye peace & safetie of our good[es]'.[87]

From these petitions a composite picture of the minor delinquent can be constructed, and of the conduct with which he or she scandalised the parish: violence, physical or verbal, petty theft and damage to property, poaching, drunkenness, failing to follow a calling, and perhaps sexual immorality. It was probably this type of behaviour that lay behind the 114 presentments for following a disorderly life that were brought before the quarter sessions in the years 1620–80. Even these petitions, however, could contain details of behaviour that fall outside the strictly criminal. The most bizarre example of these complaints involved Edward Mayer of Wivenhoe, described in 1641 as 'An obstenate and refractorie fellow who will not live in ranke or order amongst his neighbours in a house; But will live in a boate drawen up on dry land', to which was appended a chimney which local opinion thought to be a fire risk.[88]

As this last case suggests, the variety of disorders of the petty criminals of the period could be very varied. On the other hand, it is possible to trace a number of offences to which they were especially prone. Among the more obvious of these was poaching, a familiar enough subject to students of crime and social tension in the eighteenth and early nineteenth centuries. Detailed study of small-scale poaching in our period is, unfortunately, precluded by the absence of summary convictions, but it is obvious from other sources that the offence was common enough. Certainly the legal history of the offence indicates that the crime had long been familiar nationally. Gradual evolution of the Norman forest laws had resulted in the first real game law in 1390,[89] and similar legislation followed. By the seventeenth century the law on poaching was confused, and was to become more so in the eighteenth century. Whatever the provisions of individual statutes, however, the class basis of the game laws was obvious. Blackstone, after commenting unhappily on the complexity of the laws against poaching, added that 'the only rational footing, upon which we can consider it a crime is, that in low and indigent persons, it promotes idleness, and takes them away from their proper employments and callings'.[90] A century and a half before these comments, the first Jacobean game statute was specifically directed against 'the vulgar sort, and Men of small worth',[91] while it was the famous game law of 1671 which, in the graphic words of J. P. Kenyon, finally distinguished between 'the God-given race of landowners and the rest'.[92] By the seventeenth century, despite the occasional indictment of persons described as gentry or yeomanry, poaching was beginning to be regarded as one of the characteristic activities of the disorderly rural poor.

Indictment at the assizes and quarter sessions was a sanction rarely brought against the poacher, who was more commonly dealt with by summary conviction or by the petty sessions.[93] The 139 indictments against poachers brought in the county between 1620 and 1680, therefore, must be a serious underrepresentation of the full extent of the offence. These fall into no clear chronological pattern,[94] apart from an inflation of prosecutions following attacks on royal deer parks in 1642,[95] Similarly, there is little clear-cut pattern of geographical distribution. Poachers were predictably troublesome in Waltham Forest and the wooded areas adjacent to London, their activities doubtlessly being encouraged by the constantly expanding market in the capital for poached game.[96] Other evidence confirms the attraction of these areas for those bent on illicit hunting. William Holcroft, in his dual capacities as justice and verderer of Waltham Forest, recorded numerous references to poachers in his notebook,[97] while it is worth recalling that the licences of alehouse-keepers in the forest contained a clause forbidding them from harbouring deer-stealers or persons suspected of such.[98] There was also, however, a cluster of cases around the Petre estates in the centre of the county, although it is unclear whether this was the outcome of an unusual readiness to prosecute on the part of that family or of the peculiar attractiveness of recusant deer to the poacher.

Many of the indictments, particularly those referring to the poaching of royal or aristocratic game, described descents by groups of offenders on deer-parks, which at times led to violent conflict with the servants of the landowner. Fighting broke out between Lord Petre's servants and poachers on that nobleman's estate in 1643, and poachers and keepers snapped firelocks at each other on the same ground some two decades later.[99] In 1641 another battle took place when the Earl of Middlesex's men fought poachers.[100] At least two poachers were killed in such incidents, one in 1641, and another in 1669 in the course of yet another attack on Petre property.[101]

Against these dramatic incidents must be set constant small-scale poaching, which was another facet of the activities of the petty criminal. There were many men like George Deersley of Hockley, described as 'a common poacher huntinge downe many hares with beagles, and then taking them up with grey-hounds', or John Webb and John Allen, presented for habitually going out with snares and 'engines' after pheasants and part-ridges.[102] Although the personnel involved in the two activities frequently overlapped, this type of poaching was different from the large-scale and often well-planned attacks on parks. Underlying petty poaching was a more casual attitude which was more akin to the outlook of the casual nuisance offender than that of the organised criminal. As one poacher remarked when apprehended, it was no great offence to take a rabbit or two in the snow.[103] As this statement suggests, many of the rural poor must have regarded poaching as a very venial offence; their attitudes to rights over game were, even at this date, at odds with those of the landed orders.

Poaching is familiar enough to the historian. There were, however, other offences characteristic of early modern rural society, which, although analogous to poaching in that they might arise out of the different definitions of property rights made by the poor and by the landowner, have received less attention. One such was gleaning, which formed the background to many accusations of grain-theft at harvest time. Gleaning played an important part in getting the poor through the winter,[104] but as rural capitalism progressed in the sixteenth and seventeenth centuries there was less willingness on the part of landholders to follow the advice of

traditionalists and 'let gleaners glean, the poore & meane'.[105] Some
landholders were willing to take the law into their own hands. A Witham
woman complained to the bench of being beaten by the owner of a field
where she had been gleaning 'according to the Custome in harvest tyme'.[106]
Woodstealing generated similar tensions; one allegedly habitual wood-
thief, the widow Margaret More of Southminster, died as a result of a
beating inflicted on her by a landholder who found her gathering wood.[107]
Woodstealing was probably one of the most characteristic crimes of the
period, although the low value of the few bundles of faggots usually stolen
meant that it was rarely thought worth indicting.[108] The rarity with which the
offence figures in indictments, however, is more than offset by the frequency
with which it is referred to in other sources. Chelmsford house of correction,
Colchester house of correction, Saffron Walden quarter sessions, Finchingfield town authorities, and court leets of various manors were all concerned
with wood-thieves at one time or another in the period under review.[109]
Theft of firewood was, therefore, a sensitive matter in Stuart Essex, but one
to which the poor, ever desirous for fuel, were necessarily addicted.

An accusation of grain-theft following gleaning, or of wood-theft, might
be levelled against members of the poor who thought they were merely
exercising a customary right in gleaning land that was, or had been until
recently, common. The labouring poor were also, however, given to theft
proper. Most of their thieving was, of course, on a very small scale, and was
therefore seriously underrepresented by indictment for theft. There must
have been many families in Essex like the Wenlockes of Myddle in
Shropshire, who 'never stole any considerable goods, but were night
walkers, and robbed oarchyards and gardens, and stole hey out of meadows,
and corn when it was cutt, in the fields, and any small things that persons by
carelessness had left out of doors'.[110] Only very rarely would such thefts be
irritating enough to provoke an indictment. Woodstealing, gleaning and
other forms of petty theft – pulling wool off sheeps' backs,[111] or milking
other men's cattle clandestinely[112] – all appear in court records but
comparatively rarely, and were manifestly the work of the less terrifying
criminal elements. Only a few of these offenders have left easily accessible
records of a criminal career, and the precise nature of their delinquencies
will remain shadowy until detailed parish studies which will permit the
reconstruction of criminal biographies have been completed. The presence
of the petty thief is, however, incontrovertible; certainly the gentry in
parliament were convinced on this point, and a statute of 1601, intended to
'avoid and prevent divers misdemeanours in lewd and idle persons', gives a
portrayal of petty theft which is broadly similar to that given by court
records. The 'lewd and idle persons' were given, among other things, to the
'unlawful cutting or taking away of corn and grain growing, robbing of
orchards and gardens, digging up or taking away fruit trees, breaking of

hedges, pales or other fences, cutting or spoiling of woods or under-woods standing and growing, and such like offences'.[113] The statute remarked that such petty crime acted as an encouragement to the maintaining of idleness among 'lewd and mean persons'. These were obviously seen by the legislators as being drawn from among the very poor; the perpetrators of these offences, the Act claimed, were not usually able to 'make recompense or satisfaction' for their misdeeds, and were therefore to be punished by a whipping after summary conviction by a JP or equivalent officer.

The presence of the 'lewd and idle' poor would thus seem to be an established feature in Elizabethan and Stuart England. It remains to be seen, however, how far their impact varied between different areas of England, or even between different parishes. Like so many other aspects of the social history of this period, this problem will only be illuminated when more studies of individual parishes have been completed. The Essex evidence does, however, suggest that one element of the current conventional wisdom about regional variations in lawlessness might be in need of modification. In particular, it has been claimed that a sharp distinction existed in this period between nucleated villages in arable areas, with a hierarchical social structure and a resultant firm control over the lower orders, and the more scattered settlements in forests, heaths, and woodlands. A. E. Everitt has argued, in a very persuasive piece of writing[114] which is rapidly acquiring the status of a new orthodoxy,[115] that these latter areas experienced a new wave of immigrants during the population rise of the late sixteenth and early seventeenth centuries. These newcomers are seen as forming a disorderly component of rural society, outside the normal control of parson, landlord or constable. Living in the outlying parts of scattered settlements, the new arrivals, rootless and lawless, constituted a greater threat to order than the 'relatively stable and docile populations' of the arable areas.[116]

Essex, with its settlement pattern of scattered hamlets, enclosures and dispersed farms traditionally associated with areas colonised from woodland, was an area which might, at first sight, seem attractive to Everitt's lawless squatters. Certainly there is evidence of the presence of squatters in the county, and of steady encroachment on woodland and forest. The 200 new dwellings built on freshly cleared land in Waltham Forest between 1568 and 1630[117] argue the existence of both squatters and encroachments; it is unlikely, however, that the phenomenon was limited to the woodlands and heaths of the county. The years 1574 to 1594 witnessed the construction of thirty-one new dwellings on the wasteland of Barking manor, hardly an isolated and virgin woodland site even in this period.[118] The geographical distribution of prosecutions against the erection of illegal cottages, one index of official sensitivity over the arrival of new elements in Essex parishes, suggests that the problem was greater in the clothing hundreds and the mixed-farming area around Chelmsford than what might properly be described as forest areas. The most heavily wooded area, Waltham Hundred, was not remarkable for a high number of prosecutions of this offence, or, for that matter, of any other.[119]

There can be little doubt that squatters were seen as a problem by the authorities, but their peculiar affinity for any particular type of settlement remains, in Essex at least, unproven, while non-forest areas suffered problems from newcomers even when these were not squatting in isolated parts of the parish. Such references as those to the disorder caused by recently arrived settlers on Tiptree Heath[120] fit neatly into the pattern described by Everitt; however, the most eloquent description of the trouble caused by disorderly newcomers into a community comes from Aveley, a nucleated village on the prosperous southern marshlands.[121] Here the problem was inmates in existing buildings; in a review of manorial records drawn up in the early seventeenth century many of these were described as 'being of the lewd sort as whores, scolds, lazye and Idle people [who] have brought horrible and not to be named syns and wickedness into the towne insomuch as . . . perpetuall drunkeness, Frayes and bloodshed'. Here we have something like the personnel of Everitt's thesis without the topography. It should, moreover, be noted that trouble in the manor was not restricted to these newcomers. The misdeeds of the inmates were matched by those of the tenants of the manor, who were presented 'for suffering in there howses things not to be spoken of nor tolerated', and who also had a taste for woodstealing and hedgebreaking.[122]

The idea that the inhabitants of heathland and forest areas were uniquely criminal is therefore in need of further testing, and it is interesting to note that the first detailed study of a village in such an area, Myddle in Shropshire, comments that it 'was far from being an idle and lawless woodland community such as Norden and other contemporary writers judged the type to be'.[123] Certainly those seeking an easy and universally applicable key to the understanding of crime distribution in seventeenth-century Essex will not find it in the shape of squatters moving into heathland or wooded areas. Doubtless something of this sort caused problems in some parts of the county, but the forest areas did not contribute disproportionately to the patterns of crime as revealed by assize and quarter sessions indictments. On the evidence of these,[124] the sections of the county suffering the heaviest crime rates were Chelmsford Hundred, a well-cleared and long-enclosed area, and the textile-producing hundreds. The clothing region has been described as a classic example of an area where stock raising was combined with domestic industry.[125] However, the stratum of society which was thought of as especially dangerous when depression hit the new draperies was the poor weavers who, it was reported in 1629, could not subsist without a weekly wage,[126] or the textile workers who were described as living four families to a tenement in 1641.[127] These have the appearance of an industrial proletariat, rather than an agglomeration of squatters or cattle-raising smallholders.[128] The squatter did constitute a problem in the county, but only as one element in a larger body of rootless or near-rootless poor.

From the closing decades of the sixteenth century onwards, controlling the poor became one of the main objectives of both legislators at Westminster and local government officers in the counties. One aspect of this was, of course, the emergence of a very durable system of poor relief in the closing years of Elizabeth's reign; another was increased activity on the part of the machinery of law and order. One result of this increased activity, the greater burden placed upon the justice of the peace, is familiar, and has already been referred to. The justice's function in the maintenance of law and order was obviously crucial; it is easy to understand, for example, the sense of reassurance that Ralph Josselin evidently felt when he noted in 1649 that three justices lived near Earls Colne, at a time when there were 'but few in ye countie'.[129] However, it should be remembered that offenders were normally prosecuted at the initiative of persons offended against or of parish officers: the criminal would rarely find himself in court through the direct intervention of the justice. The justice's role was important, but it was in a sense a passive one: the magistracy might, on occasion, initiate drives against offenders, but it was more often, like the courts, something to which people had recourse when they thought it necessary. In suppressing crime and disorder, the JP was largely dependent upon the co-operation of inferior officers and, in the last resort, what might be described (at the risk of committing an anachronism) as the general public.

This point has been well made by the editor of the sessions rolls of another county:

The strength of the system lay in the fact that justices were not administering a policy of repression; rather, they were to control and encourage self-expression on the part of the humbler subjects, who assumed responsibility within the parish at frequent intervals as constable, overseer, or supervisor of the highways, more or less under magisterial control. This, together with the constant call on their services on inquests, or as sureties, made men aware that they were not outside the machinery of government: on the contrary, they were part and parcel of it, small cogs no doubt, but indispensable.[130]

Godfrey Goodman, vicar of Stapleford Abbots 1606–20, had this view of the minor officeholders of the period:

For here in the countrey with us, if a man's stock of a few beasts be his own, and that he lives out of debt, and paies his rent duly and quarterly, we hold him a very rich and sufficient man; one that is able to doe the King and countrey good service; we make him a constable, a Sidesman, a Head-borough, and at length a Church-Warden; thus we raise him by degrees, we prolong his ambitious hopes, and at last we heape all our honours upon him. Here is the great governor amongst us.[131]

Hence the repression of crime in Stuart England was the business not merely of the justices, but also of minor property-owners, yeomen, tradesmen, and the more prosperous artisans.

If the broad socio-economic changes of the half century before 1620 had created a large body of disorderly poor in Essex, they had also initiated changes among the village elite. A more marked social stratification had produced a more distinct class of village notables: detailed work on Essex communities confirms Goodman's assertion that it was from these comparatively 'rich and sufficient' men that officeholders were drawn. These notables (again as Goodman suggests) tended to serve in a variety of capacities, as manorial court jurors, manorial officials, constables, sidesmen, churchwardens, overseers of the poor, and so on. The net result was the creation of what might be described as oligarchic rule within the parish: local offices were held, and local power exercised, by the richer members of the community.[132] The difference between the officeholders and those they ruled was not, however, merely one of wealth. As the seventeenth century progressed, it has been argued,[133] the village notables became distinguished from the poor not only by their relative affluence, but also by their adoption of what were, in many respects, some of the values of a different culture. By the late seventeenth century the divergence between rich and poor was paralleled by a divergence between 'respectable' and 'rough' values: the petty gentry, yeomanry, and richer artisans were separated from the labourers not only by wealth, but also by officeholding, educational attainment, greater involvement in formal religion, and perhaps even by dress and diet. The first steps had been taken towards that alliance between landlord and tenant farmer against the agricultural labourer that was such a feature of the English countryside in the nineteenth century: for one of the most significant developments of the period was the partial acceptance by the upper strata of village society of many of the values and attitudes of their social superiors.

It must be reiterated, however, that in our period this acceptance was partial. It has been argued[134] that the parish elite in their capacity of parish officeholders saw themselves in an essentially intermediary position between the desires of county and central government and the needs of their fellow villagers: they were, moreover, acutely aware that holding local office was very much an exercise in the art of the possible.

To such men court action was a fairly remote sanction against the petty offender. It was implicit in the system of parish officers that the peace should be kept with minimal recourse to exterior agencies. The ethos which, it is still claimed, pervades the modern English country police, with its emphasis on a 'quiet patch' and on the absence of official reports as 'the hallmark of good policing',[135] would have been entirely comprehensible to the seventeenth-century parish constable. Something very like it is encapsulated in the advice offered to parish officers confronted with a moral offence by the Clerk of the Peace of the County Palatine of Lancaster:

> Use all meanes possible for to prevent it
> And if you cannot, faile not to present it.[136]

It is interesting that, in this context, taking the case to court was regarded as a second best.

These considerations must be remembered when attempting to assess the efficiency of the parish constables. Much of the criticism directed against them has been coloured by a failure to realise that using the modern police force as a yardstick against which to measure the Stuart parish officer is to attempt to compare two very different concepts of law enforcement. Numerous examples could, of course, be cited of failings on the part of constables: over a hundred indictments were brought against constables on one count or another. These cases are too numerous to catalogue, but two broad conclusions emerge from studying them. Firstly, the delinquent constable was more usually guilty of a sin of omission than commission, of having failed to attend the hundred constable, or of having failed to keep watch, rather than of actively having interfered in the course of justice. Secondly, when the course of justice was interfered with, it was usually in favour of the offender rather than the system of law enforcement.

This tendency was strongest, perhaps, in attempts to prosecute religious nonconformists. One constable, on receiving a letter from the justices in 1663 demanding more strenuous action against nonconformists, remarked that it would be more sensible to send out orders against swearing, whoring, and drunkenness; and another constable, charged in 1677 with failing to serve a writ on 'fenaticks', replied that he thought it a pity to prosecute such harmless people.[137] Examples of similar obstruction when the offender was a criminal in the strict sense are not forthcoming in such explicit terms, but probably lie behind a number of the cases in which constables were accused of negligently allowing escapes. Such failings might provoke the disapproval of the modern observer, but it is salutary to compare the delinquencies of the parish constables with the depredations inflicted on the inhabitants of the county by the nearest equivalent to a body of full-time law-enforcement officers, the sheriff's bailiffs. A system depending on parish constables may have had its drawbacks, but was probably adequate to meet the needs of rural society during this period. Given contemporary standards of public morality, and the common attitude to officeholding, the existence of a professional police force in seventeenth-century England would have been little more than a horrifying anachronism.

The flexibility inherent in the better aspects of dependence on an unpaid amateur police force was reflected in attitudes to certain types of offender. It seems that many persons were only indicted or presented after a lengthy period during which informal coercion was attempted. Daniel Finch of Great Burstead, who habitually came home drunk and abused his wife and children, had been admonished on several occasions by the constables and other 'honest neighbours' before being presented at the quarter sessions.[138] Similarly, the keeper of a disorderly house at Roxwell, presented before the same court in 1643, had 'lately received a friendly admonition by a minister'. His response, the presentment recorded, was not only to fail to mend his ways, but also to voice some unfriendly comments about the clergy and the parliamentary regime.[139]

On a more strictly criminal level, there is evidence that small-scale pilfering would sometimes be tolerated until the theft of some unusually large item exhausted the patience of the victim. A householder burgled in 1621 brought a successful prosecution against two men who were 'p[er]sons that lived ydlie and had in times past done many pilferings and come into his house in the night tyme and stolen a pott of flower, a loyne of veall and a fatt pullett',[140] while after a theft in 1622 a Finchingfield man could readily bring to mind 'divers ill-disposed persons in the parishes adjacent' as likely thieves.[141] Depositions reveal tolerance for several months[142] or a year[143] before any attempt to prosecute. In other cases suspicion after a theft would fall on somebody with a local reputation for thieving, like the Chrishall labourer who 'had beene formerly called into question for such like thinges', or the Springfield man accused of poultry-theft because he 'hath been accused formerly for stealing hens'.[144]

A variety of considerations might affect a decision not to take a case to court. Edward Hext, a Somerset justice, described in the 1590s how many thieves escaped because the common countryfolk 'wold not procure a man's death for all the goods in the world'. No evidence of this reluctance has been found in Essex, although there is some to support his assertion that the 'troble and chardge' involved in bringing a prosecution acted as a disincentive for taking a case to court.[145] When two women were reported in 1652 for slander, an interested party wrote to the bench that one of them, formerly his servant, had stolen a spoon from him, but he 'being att that time full of business, had not leysure to convent hir before ye maiestrate'.[146] Another victim of a theft wrote to the Maldon bench that the stolen goods in fact belonged to his 'partner', gave a favourable character reference for the alleged thief, and stated that he had 'no Reson to folow the law for Another man's goods'.[147] In another case, the victim of a petty theft wrote to the Colchester authorities that he was in London on business, expressed an unwillingness to have the accused hanged, and urged the justices to 'devise som shorter punishment for hym as also esing me of my travell and charg[es]'.[148] Evidence of this type proves that the punishment of thieves was not necessarily high on the priorities of Essex property-owners during this period, especially if they were under the pressure of other business.[149]

A further disincentive to prosecution was provided by the costs involved in taking a case to court. The clerical staffs of both the assizes and the quarter sessions depended upon fees for their living.[150] Accordingly, a fee was charged at every stage in a trial, and, for a man of moderate means, the expenses involved in prosecuting an offence could be substantial. It is difficult to calculate the precise costs involved in bringing a felony to trial, or to determine the extent to which the fees charged by the clerk were divided between the accuser and the accused. Isolated examples of charges included the 2/- demanded by the clerk of the peace for accepting a presentment,[151] and the 5/- normally required for accepting a recognizance.[152] Some idea of the overall expense of prosecuting a crime might be gauged from the calculation that a defended misdemeanour action, including legal advice, might cost between £1/14/- and £4.[153] It should be noted, however, that such an expense was not, by contemporary standards, excessive.[154] Indeed, the fees charged by the assizes at least appear to have been static throughout the period under review; one assize clerk was able, in the 1630s, to demonstrate that the fees charged by the court had not risen for forty years,[155] and they were to remain at roughly the same level until well into the eighteenth century.[156] Moreover, at the Essex quarter sessions, fees were halved for widows and paupers.[157] Even so, the costs of prosecution, by constituting a deterrent against taking an offender to court, reinforce the impression that those offenders who did find themselves on trial in the seventeenth century did so because of a conscious decision on the part of those prosecuting them.

Incidents which might have led to criminal prosecution were often settled out of court. One pamphleteer commented on how cases of theft were often 'made up' between the victim and the offender if the former could recover his goods,[158] and a number of unsuccessful attempts by thieves to follow this course were reported to the Essex bench.[159] A Colchester case of 1670 depicts the reluctance with which an indictment might be brought. The complainant, reporting a theft by a neighbour, Susan Walker, which had been committed some weeks previously, was asked why she had not already reported the offence. She replied 'she was in Hopes by fayer meanes to have p[er]swaded the said Susan Walker to make her satisfaction & did try the mediations of friends to attayne the same'.[160] It is significant that immediate recourse to court action was not regarded as 'fayer meanes' in this context.

Moreover, it should be remembered that the community had a number of informal sanctions besides the law at its disposal when dealing with the petty malefactor. Employers had considerable powers of discipline over workers living-in or over apprentices, and many petty thefts must have been punished by correction from the master. Similarly, many continually delinquent servants were simply dismissed, an antecedent of the habit of employers, noted by modern observers, of regarding dismissal as an alternative to prosecution when dealing with pilfering among employees.[161] Landlords, especially those belonging to powerful county families, must have enjoyed considerable powers of informal control over their poorer tenants. Little direct evidence of this survives, a rare example being provided by a note of an incident in which Sir John Barrington caught George Hawkins of Takeley stealing wood on his land in 1674. Hawkins was made to set his mark to a paper in which he admitted his fault, expressed his sorrow, and promised never to do the like again.[162] Similarly, clergymen might take an active interest in disciplining their flock. The importance of an energetic parson for the maintenance of local order may be deduced from a petition from Great Burstead of 1639 complaining that since the death of 'the late Reverend and painfull pastor', William Pease, who 'in his life was a great instrument of godoes glories: and was verie Careful of the peaceable and good order of the town', the number of unlicensed alehouses in the parish had multiplied.[163] The minister was, of course, at his most powerful in alliance with the 'well affected' of the parish. Stephen Vassall, rector of Rayleigh from 1609 to 1644, seems to have enjoyed this sort of support. In the late 1630s and early 1640s he drafted a number of petitions to the bench against nuisance offenders, these being endorsed by a group of witnesses who turned up regularly as court leet jurors and minor officeholders.[164]

Such examples remind us of the importance of the small property-owner in the law-enforcement system, and introduce an important aspect of the cultural divergence between the rich and poor villager alluded to earlier. The presence of the godly minister, like Vassall at Rayleigh or Anthony Sammes at Burnham,[165] could be crucial in reinforcing puritan ideas among the rural middling sort. As Wrightson has commented: 'It is probable that some kind of differentiation between the behaviour of rough and respectable parishioners had long existed, but one finds it not only becoming articulate and active within our period, but becoming so in a manner which bears the stamp of puritan influence.'[166] The impact of puritan ideas about godly discipline, allied to the more marked social stratification of the period, must have given many parish officers an ideological rationale for doing what they had to do anyway; the result was that, in at least some villages, they did it more efficiently. As we have agreed, the acceptance by the village elite of certain of the attitudes of central government and the local gentry was crucial to the successful running of the system of law and order. Nowhere was this more evident than in the encouragement that widespread puritanism among the middling sort gave to the prosecution of regulative offenders. The ungodly poor, given to idleness, drunkenness, swearing, bastard-getting and petty theft, must have fitted readily into the conceptual framework of the parish officer coming fresh from a puritan sermon or tract which pondered the basic sinfulness of unregenerate mankind.

Puritanism might well have been a spent force by 1660, but the reality of social differentiation within the parish remained, and indeed became more marked. By the late seventeenth century the resident poor were seen as a national problem, a problem from which Essex was by no means exempt: in Terling, for example, a parish of 600 souls, some 60 ratepayers were taxed between £130 and £170 annually for poor relief in the 1690s. The poor rates might be burdensome, but it has been claimed that by this date the poor law was providing the village elite with a handy means of disciplining the disorderly poor. Arguing from his work on Terling, Wrightson has claimed that: 'The Parish vestry alone in the later seventeenth and in the eighteenth centuries exercised through the poor law which it administered and the economic and social ascendancy of its members, a far more subtle control of the behaviour of the labouring population than could possibly be achieved by court prosecution.'[167] The development and implications of this tendency could form a useful basis for another detailed study; vestiges of it in the Essex assize and quarter sessions records are infrequent, although cases such as that in 1655, when the bench was petitioned that John Ginner of White Colne should cease to receive poor relief because he had 'notoriously many waies misdemeaned himself', are suggestive.[168] Socio-economic change in England in the sixteenth and seventeenth centuries produced a large body of poor whom contemporaries, correctly, saw as the social stratum most likely to indulge in crime and disorder. However, the growth of an efficient poor relief system with its concomitant potentialities for enforcing social discipline rendered court action against their delinquencies increasingly redundant.

The undoubted existence of a large body of poor, and their undoubted attachment to certain forms of crime and disorder, raises the problem of the existence of a 'criminal class' in the seventeenth century.[169] If, in its most limited sense, a 'crime' is defined as any act which breaks a law, it would seem logical to define a criminal simply as a person committing such an act. In its current usage, however, the term 'criminal' has acquired connotations which have given it a more complex meaning. This is largely the outcome of the nineteenth-century debate on crime, which was coloured by the conviction that at the root of the problem lay the existence of a separate 'criminal class'.[170] This attitude, founded on observation of the social consequences of urbanisation and industrialisation between 1815 and 1850, produced the stereotyped image of the criminal as an urban slum-dweller habitually involved in crime. This idea of the 'criminal classes', modernised into the concept of the 'criminal subculture', still forms the starting point for most current debate on crime,[171] and its applicability to the early modern period must now be considered.

Certainly something like the nineteenth-century 'criminal classes' existed in London in the Elizabethan and Stuart periods. Pamphlet literature suggests the existence of a well-defined criminal subculture, while the

Middlesex sessions records reveal the existence of organised prostitution and the large-scale receiving of stolen goods, two useful indicators of the presence of professional crime.[172] One criminologist, indeed, has claimed that metropolitan crime in the seventeenth century might be defined as 'craft' criminality, related to the contemporary economic system based on the rural and artisanal small producer.[173] Outside the capital, however, the picture is more obscure. Future research might well prove that provincial towns were afflicted by a less developed version of the London criminal orders, but there is little evidence of organised professional crime in the countryside. In Essex, as we have seen, there is only limited evidence of the presence of the professional criminal. The hard core of criminal vagrants and full-time rogues was seemingly more limited in reality than in contemporary pamphlet literature; there is little evidence of organised prostitution; receiving of stolen goods, although obviously widespread, was apparently organised very much on an *ad hoc* basis; and even highwaymen were often amateur rather than professional criminals. There are certainly some vestiges of organised crime, and if assize depositions survived, they would probably echo those of the Northern circuit in providing evidence of horse-dealers and coin-clippers regularly given to crime;[174] on the other hand, the impression is very much that such individuals were the exception.

Conversely, even though organisation may have been absent, certain forms of crime must have been very attractive to the broad mass of Essex's agricultural workers and clothworkers. Peter Clark, studying the lowest class of immigrant into Kentish towns in this period, has claimed that 'few honest poor can have survived'.[175] The accuracy of this striking statement needs to be tested in the light of detailed local studies; at present, however, it seems to have much to commend it. In good times the position of the poor was bad enough; students of the economic history of the county find it impossible to discover how the agricultural labourer got through the year,[176] and at best all he could hope for was a bare subsistence. In times of crisis, with a harvest failure, or a stop in the cloth trade, the existence of the poor passed from the precarious to the desperate. Under such circumstances, the rabbit poached from the local landowner, the wood stolen from the hedges and fences of yeomen, or the shirt stolen from a hedge as the poor labourer tramped the road in search of employment might become essential for survival. At the same time, the poor became increasingly the subject of regulative legislation. They were seen as being idle, drunken, and unchaste, a shiftless and potentially disorderly element in the body politic. There may not have been an organised 'criminal class' in the English countryside, but contemporaries certainly thought of the poor *en masse* as a 'dangerous class',[177] very much in the way early nineteenth-century observers were to think of the burgeoning urban proletariat. To a large extent, court archives suggest that these fears were far from groundless. It is, of course, worth considering whether it was possible to hold any other opinion of the labouring population when the socio-economic system relegated the bulk of them to the status of 'the poor'; a social group whose members, we are told, could look forward to no better future than an almshouse and a badged coat, and that only if they trod carefully in their dealings with their social betters.[178]

It must be reiterated, however, that the methods of dealing with crime in the seventeenth century were both infinitely varied and very flexible. This suggests that criminal statistics derived from indictments for this period (and, one suspects, most others) are very suspect. They reflect not so much the incidence of crime, but rather the incidence of a willingness to prosecute, and such a willingness often only developed after a lengthy period in which expedients other than prosecution were tried. The problem has, of course, been a recurrent theme of this book, but needs restatement here. Lurking behind the attempts to avoid formal prosecution was the knowledge that indictment at the assizes or quarter sessions was a fairly extreme sanction to bring against an offender, and likely to cause trouble and loss of time and money to the prosecutor. Faced with anything less than a serious crime, or with a persistent offender who might be thought to have gone too far, the remedy would be sought most commonly in the battery of alternatives to indictment: using the local manor or archdeacon's court, binding over to keep the peace, sending the offender to the house of correction, or a whole repertoire of informal sanctions. Two general propositions emerge: firstly, that petty crime is more representative of a society's criminality than the serious offence, and this petty crime was very unlikely to be recorded in indictments; and secondly, given the alternatives and the obvious predilection for using them, such offenders as *were* indicted may well have been atypical, either persistent offenders or outsiders who attracted an unusually hostile response. Such conclusions remind us of the limitations of the quantitative analysis of indictments; it is to this problem, however, that we must turn next.

11. Overall patterns of crime in Essex, 1620–1680

The study of general trends in the recorded crime of this period, resting as it must on quantification, is beset by a number of difficulties. Any attempt to derive statistically based conclusions from early modern archival materials is a risky enterprise, and the problem is compounded for the historian of crime by the inherent difficulties of interpreting any set of criminal statistics. These can only reflect reported (or, in our period, recorded) crime. Any conjecture about the 'dark figure' of unrecorded crime can amount to little more than guesswork, and, as we shall argue, fluctuations in such offences as were recorded were not necessarily the product of real changes in crime rates. Moreover, our task is further complicated by the exigencies of record survival. The only years enjoying anything like a complete run of assize and quarter sessions indictments are 1645–69, and although acceptable conclusions about the patterns of recorded crime can be formed from some of the surviving evidence that lies outside these years, they must depend upon unusually sensitive handling of the available materials. Whatever the difficulties, an attempt must be made at tracing and explaining the fluctuations in the recorded crime of the county. As the following chapter will demonstrate, this is a very useful exercise.

As an initial step, all surviving King's Bench, assize, and quarter sessions indictments were counted, the results of this computation being set out in tables 19–21. Two units of measurement were used, one geographical, the other chronological. It was felt that to present figures for each parish would be too complex, and would be invalidated since few Essex parishes were the location of a sufficient number of indicted offences to allow the analysis of long-term trends. It was therefore decided to take the hundred as the initial unit of study, a decision which introduces its own problems. Firstly, Essex hundreds (see map 5) were not uniform in size or social structure, although enough is known about these differences to make possible informed comparisons. Secondly, difficulties arise from the boroughs enjoying their own rights of criminal jurisdiction. The archives of Colchester, Maldon, Harwich and Saffron Walden all contain criminal records, but they are too fragmentary for statistical manipulation either in the general total or as a basis for separate consideration. For the purposes of this chapter, therefore, indictments tried at the independent borough courts have been ignored. On

quinquennia	Larceny	Burglary	Breaking and entering	Pickpocketing	Highway robbery	Homicide	Infanticide	Assault	Riot	Forcible disseisin	Closebreaking	Witchcraft	Sexual offences	Unlicensed alehouse-keeping	Disorderly alehouse-keeping	Drunkenness	Other drink offences	Road repair	Highway default	Bridge repair	Keeping inmates	Cottage building	Forestalling	Unapprenticed trading	Other economic offences	Moral offences	Community offence: commission	Community offence: omission	Poaching	Negligent/delinquent constable	Negligent/delinquent bailiff	Miscellaneous	Total	Percent of all recorded offences, 1620–80
1620–4	183	13	9	—	2	9	9	31	12	9	9	5	9	22	8	4	1	1	—	1	6	16	—	4	4	1	2	2	9	3	2	35	408	4.75%
1625–9	364	53	9	4	8	23	7	41	12	11	6	11	10	41	5	8	3	—	—	—	6	23	1	15	1	—	5	4	5	7	3	22	714	8.25%
1630–4	340	56	28	3	8	17	8	35	6	10	4	2	6	33	10	1	3	3	3	5	11	26	8	6	6	1	3	3	5	8	2	42	704	8.25%
1635–9	294	15	1	1	1	8	4	60	17	13	6	6	1	64	5	6	2	13	2	11	13	42	2	15	2	7	7	4	4	8	3	40	622	7.25%
1640–4	160	18	10	—	10	17	8	61	21	15	7	1	35	35	25	10	1	27	4	9	9	19	9	21	7	—	6	8	41	6	3	45	690	8%
1645–9	262	26	13	3	6	11	11	49	21	21	2	34	3	64	13	12	6	25	1	13	29	31	8	10	3	3	6	11	6	15	7	26	869	10.25%
1650–4	287	43	17	2	6	15	2	66	11	33	3	3	23	202	8	17	3	19	6	18	50	39	14	13	10	18	5	8	6	6	6	58	951	11.25%
1655–9	163	26	17	—	12	32	11	84	4	10	2	19	11	128	13	12	7	9	5	13	22	20	5	9	16	24	8	10	6	12	6	48	705	8.25%
1660–4	179	34	19	1	9	21	6	65	14	7	2	4	4	86	6	5	4	25	15	17	14	23	1	66	2	16	16	5	6	13	9	103	755	8.75%
1665–9	152	8	14	1	4	24	8	76	11	6	3	4	6	53	12	5	4	14	1	6	12	16	6	18	22	4	2	18	10	13	10	63	571	6.75%
1670–4	99	11	12	—	8	15	3	30	8	3	2	1	4	141	22	4	5	22	1	15	19	5	4	15	2	1	11	11	7	20	5	241	739	8.5%
1675–80	141	15	16	3	8	17	6	54	21	9	3	—	3	58	37	1	24	25	24	8	30	9	—	12	39	2	7	16	19	20	5	218	829	9.75%
Total	2624	318	165	18	81	209	83	652	139	147	42	101	89	878	164	88	52	189	60	120	221	270	68	204	96	27	85	100	139	119	68	941	8557	

Notes: highway default represents the failure to perform statutory work on the highway. Keeping inmates, i.e. subtenants, was contrary to poor law regulations. Cottage building represents contravention of 31 Eliz I cap. 7. Unapprenticed trading represents the exercise of a trade without having undergone the required seven-year apprenticeship. Barratry is an example of a community offence of commission; the failure to clean a ditch an example of omission. The total columns refer to indicted offences committed in the relevant quinquennium, but not to those tried

Table 20 Offences indicted at Essex assizes and quarter sessions, with Essex King's Bench indictments, 1620–80, by hundreds

	Larceny	Burglary	Breaking and entering	Pickpocketing	Highway robbery	Homicide	Infanticide	Assault	Riot	Forcible disseisin	Closebreaking	Witchcraft	Sexual offences	Unlicensed alehouse-keeping	Disorderly alehouse-keeping	Drunkenness	Other drink offences	Road repair	Highway default	Bridge repair	Keeping inmates	Cottage building	Forestalling	Unapprenticed trading	Other economic offences	Moral offences	Community offences: commission	Community offences: omission	Poaching	Negligent/delinquent constable	Negligent/delinquent bailiff	Miscellaneous	Total	Percent of all recorded offences, 1620–80
Witham	113	12	12	—	3	3	5	26	3	6	1	—	2	62	8	5	1	7	7	13	31	20	—	20	1	2	2	4	6	3	2	32	412	4.75%
Lexden	233	47	12	—	11	11	5	63	17	17	8	6	8	162	7	15	9	29	9	19	22	32	—	25	8	3	5	15	4	12	9	128	952	11%
Hinckford	411	54	18	6	5	32	9	92	28	27	2	15	14	98	14	21	8	8	—	9	51	41	1	46	7	3	12	14	8	14	11	197	1276	15%
Dunmow	80	11	6	—	—	6	5	18	6	5	2	2	1	57	7	3	—	3	3	6	2	13	—	4	1	13	4	—	8	5	10	30	310	3.5%
Harlow	94	14	2	—	5	6	3	12	2	4	3	2	4	21	4	—	—	3	3	3	9	14	—	9	—	—	—	2	3	4	—	16	242	2.75%
Freshwell	81	5	6	1	3	3	2	16	3	3	2	—	4	21	—	2	2	1	1	1	4	6	—	2	—	3	3	4	3	4	—	47	217	2.5%
Uttlesford	134	21	11	1	3	5	6	24	3	3	4	—	6	36	22	5	3	16	6	2	3	13	—	4	—	—	5	4	3	5	5	46	400	4.75%
Clavering	19	3	4	—	1	—	1	5	3	—	1	—	3	—	—	—	—	4	11	1	8	7	—	—	—	—	—	1	—	1	1	8	78	1%
Becontree	223	23	14	—	25	28	6	54	8	10	2	5	9	57	8	2	2	14	1	10	18	—	3	14	13	—	11	7	20	5	1	57	657	7.75%
Waltham	66	6	1	1	2	6	2	—	1	2	1	—	4	19	2	1	3	5	—	3	3	7	1	9	—	—	1	1	16	2	—	13	198	2.25%
Havering	35	10	4	2	2	—	—	10	2	—	1	—	1	—	—	3	—	—	—	—	—	1	2	3	—	—	1	1	1	—	—	9	83	1%
Chafford	101	10	3	—	3	15	4	41	8	7	1	3	3	48	12	1	6	6	2	5	4	9	6	3	1	—	7	3	12	9	6	35	377	4.5%
Ongar	161	20	9	—	5	12	7	27	3	10	2	2	5	23	4	2	1	23	2	—	5	14	2	11	2	1	2	4	3	11	5	47	439	5.25%
Barstable	147	16	13	2	8	12	6	38	5	11	2	5	9	16	19	5	7	11	15	14	12	10	10	9	3	2	5	11	15	7	2	45	478	5.5%
Rochford	93	12	12	1	—	9	9	35	5	3	1	3	6	12	12	5	1	6	2	5	1	6	18	5	18	—	5	3	6	2	—	19	313	3.75%

Dengie	115	15	7	—	8	4	17	6	3	2	—	2	39	10	5	1	7	—	7	14	2	1	2	—	7	1	8	10	5	23		321	3.75%
Thurstable	74	8	5	—	9	3	14	5	2	—	1	3	18	4	2	1	1	—	2	10	18	—	2	—	—	3	3	2	1	1	47		239	2.75%
Winstree	41	6	4	—	4	—	11	1	—	—	—	1	29	5	3	—	9	—	9	3	—	1	—	—	1	4	—	7	1	6		145	1.75%
Tendring	122	9	8	—	19	4	18	15	10	1	43	2	30	11	4	5	6	1	—	12	4	2	5	2	1	3	7	3	12	4	23		386	4.5%
Chelmsford	281	19	12	5	5	19	2	122	17	21	6	5	6	130	15	7	7	26	—	15	22	37	10	35	38	1	12	15	18	8	5	113	1034	12%
Total	2624	318	165	18	81	209	83	652	139	147	42	101	89	878	164	88	52	189	60	120	221	270	68	204	96	27	85	100	139	119	68	941	8557	

Notes: as table 19

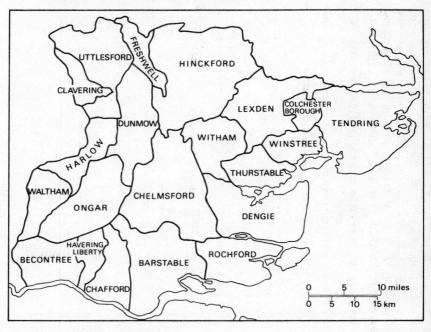

Map 5 The Essex hundreds

the other hand, offences committed in these boroughs but tried at the King's
Bench, assizes, or quarter sessions have been included in the calculations.
Offences committed at Colchester and tried at one of the three superior
courts have been included in the figures for Lexden Hundred, those for
Maldon in the figures for Dengie Hundred, those for Saffron Walden in
Uttlesford Hundred, and those for Harwich in Tendring Hundred. Havering
Liberty, like the larger boroughs, enjoyed its own court of sessions, but none
of its records survive. Offences committed in Havering and tried at the three
courts under consideration have, however, been totalled.

Just as the parish, in the context of this study, generally constitutes too
small a unit for study, so annual figures of recorded crime are too small and
fluctuate too wildly for the purposes of an initial analysis. As a starting
point, indictments were counted on a quinquennial basis. Table 19 shows
the results of this computation, and serves as a background to other
calculations. Table 21 shows the contribution of each hundred to the
indictments by quinquennia, and serves as a basis for a consideration of the
geographical distribution of recorded crime. The figures given in tables 19–
21 thus provide a starting point for the investigation of shifts in crime during
the period.

Table 21 Essex assize quarter sessions, and King's Bench indictments, 1620–80, by quinquennia and hundreds

	1620–4	1625–9	1630–4	1635–9	1640–4	1645–9	1650–4	1655–9	1660–4	1665–9	1670–4	1675–80	Total
Witham	33	51	25	18	23	46	79	31	32	19	38	17	412
Lexden	53	67	62	60	61	86	124	107	141	43	57	91	952
Hinckford	60	143	113	86	84	137	140	92	92	58	181	90	1276
Dunmow	11	20	30	15	19	31	46	31	23	14	33	37	310
Harlow	13	16	27	31	32	15	25	20	16	10	14	23	242
Freshwell	10	17	22	23	20	9	23	23	11	10	33	27	217
Uttlesford	23	32	41	30	37	54	41	5	21	27	33	29	400
Clavering	4	4	10			10	7				6		78
Becontree	33	30	50	36	51	66	52	71	60	43	19	87	657
Waltham	3	12	13	10	31	16	25	14	20	19	19	16	198
Havering	6	7	3		6	2	15	10	4			18	83
Chafford	10	31	26	35	28	43	60	31	34	19	17	43	377
Ongar	18	31	46	43	35	35	59	26	45	34	22	45	439
Barstable	26	39	50	38	37	35	43	26	41	41	24	78	478
Rochford	15	18	33	16	39	31	23	16	41	25	12	44	313
Dengie	16	32	31	29	23	50	22	22	24	18	30	28	321
Thurstable	14	26	13	23	14	7	51	17	17	21	17	18	239
Winstree	6	21	21	12	14	10	34	5	11	5	10	3	145
Tending	8	29	26	26	50	37	38	34	22	69	28	19	386
Chelmsford	46	88	73	81	81	145	68	81	81	89	87	114	1034
Total	408	714	704	622	690	869	951	705	755	571	739	829	8557

Since Essex was not a homogeneous economic or social entity, the relationship between crime and the various economic sub-regions within the county demands attention. A study of tables 19 and 20 makes it obvious that grand totals in themselves are too crude an indicator. To allow for more sophisticated insights into these fluctuations, the offences indicted were set out under thirty-two headings. These figures, although interesting, were felt to need simplification before analysis, and were accordingly divided into broader categories. Attention was focused on five main groups of indictments: those involving property offences (larceny, burglary, breaking and entering, pickpocketing and highway robbery); those involving violent offences (homicide, assault, forcible disseisin, riot, and closebreaking); drink offences (unlicensed alehouse-keeping, disorderly alehouse-keeping, drunkenness, and other drink offences); economic offences (forestalling, engrossing, regrating, following a trade without having served due apprenticeship, and other economic offences); and those concerned with a wide spectrum of wrongdoing which can only be classed as 'miscellaneous'. Economic offences were found to be surprisingly few, and it was decided to forgo further discussion of them.

The percentage contribution of each of these broad subdivisions to the total of recorded offences is set out in figure 2. Perhaps the most striking conclusion to be drawn from this evidence is that property offences underwent a decline in importance relative to other indicted offences, as well as the absolute decline demonstrated in table 20. In interpreting figure 2, it must be borne in mind that assize files enjoyed only about a 50% survival rate before 1644, and that *ignoramus* indictments are largely missing before that date.[1] It appears, then, that if due allowance is made for record loss, property offences were at least three times more common in the years 1625–34 than they were in the 1660s. This conclusion, especially when taken with the increased unwillingness of the courts to bring capital convictions for larceny in the second half of the period under review,[2] serves as a corrective to the historical folklore which teaches that attitudes to property offences were hardening in the seventeenth century. The period which, it has has been claimed, witnessed the arrival of the moneyed interest as a political and social force on a national level, with a concomitant emphasis on the importance of property, was not marked by any hardening of attitudes towards thieves, burglars, and robbers in Essex. The much-quoted increase in capital statutes for crimes against property which followed 1688[3] does not seem to have been preceded by any long-term increase in either the level of indictments or the severity of the treatment of these offenders in the county.

Violent offences were not subject to the same sort of fluctuation shown by other offences. It is, perhaps, possible to trace an upward trend in 1644–69, the period of full record survival, but analysis of specific offences within the

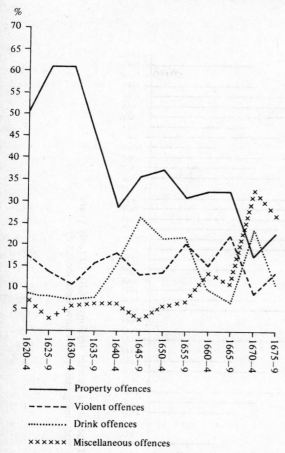

Fig. 2 Broad trends in indicted crime in Essex, 1620–80: showing the percentage of individual types of offence from all indictments in each quinquennium

broad category suggests a more complex situation. The study of homicide accusations is hampered by their relative paucity and the poor survival of assize files before 1645; it would seem, however, that after a rise in the 1650s and 1660s, they returned by the end of our period to roughly the same level as at the beginning.[4] Something more like a definite trend can be traced when dealing with assault indictments. Figure 3, based on quarter sessions records, which dealt with some 88% of known assault cases, shows that these cases increased steadily although gently throughout the period. Two main conclusions, therefore, emerge when violent offences are compared with property offences. Firstly, the contrast between the large-scale

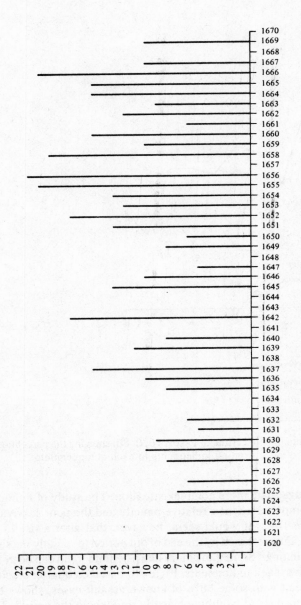

Fig. 3 Assault indictments at the Essex quarter sessions, 1620–70 (only years enjoying survival of four rolls containing indictments have been included)

fluctuations in property offences and the comparative stability of crimes of violence reminds us that 'crime' is essentially an umbrella concept, and that a wide variety of different types of behaviour shelter beneath it: the violent offender was a different type of 'criminal' from the perpetrator of crimes against property, and subject to different pressures and motivations. This is only to be expected, if, as we have suggested, violent offenders were drawn from a wider social spectrum than thieves or burglars. Secondly, those seeking to trace in the early modern period a transition from 'feudal' crimes, based primarily on interpersonal violence, to more modern forms of crime typified by property offences, will derive little comfort from these Essex figures. Such a transition may have occurred, but if so, it came after 1680.[5]

Both the multifarious nature of crime, and the problem of isolating what species of crime was 'typical' of the early modern period, become more apparent when drink offences are considered. These underwent considerable fluctuations in our period, although it must be remembered that other indices of official action against this type of offence, notably presentment, modify the impression given by indictments alone.[6] It is with drink offences, however, that we first encounter the problem of the impact of variations in the aims and energies of law-enforcement agencies upon criminal statistics. The enforcement of the drink laws, and of all other forms of regulative legislation, demonstrates the distinction between what might be called 'created' criminality, and 'real' crime. This division arises from the basic concept that whereas some acts are illegal because they are wicked, others are wicked because they are illegal. The importance of this distinction between 'real' and 'created' crime can, for our immediate purposes, best be demonstrated by the different ways in which those accused of these two classes of crime might find themselves in court.

'Real' crime, in this period, was essentially prosecuted through the energy of the victim. A characteristic pattern of the events preceding indictment for theft demonstrates this point. On discovering the theft, for example of a sheep, the owner. for a variety of reasons (long-held suspicions, gossip among his neighbours, or the disrepute in which the supposed malefactor was held), would eventually form strong suspicions against one of his fellow villagers. If sufficient evidence were found, the suspect would be taken before a magistrate, to whom fell the task of examining the accused, and noting the evidence of the supposed victim, the constable, and anyone else able or willing to give evidence. The accused would then be bound over to appear at the assizes or quarter sessions or, if a not very trustworthy character, committed to gaol. Hence the accused came to trial as a result of a specific complaint laid before the authorities by an aggrieved party.

From the mid sixteenth century onwards, however, governmental attempts at enforcing a body of regulatory laws superimposed a new background to prosecution upon this intensely personal system. The outcome of these attempts was the indictment of a large number of offences, among them those connected with the drink trade, which were essentially 'created' crimes. In its classic form 'created' crime was the outcome of a process involving the whole chain of government. The central authority would periodically decide to encourage the rulers of the localities to take more strenuous action against disorderly elements in the areas they controlled. Consequently the Privy Council (or its Interregnum equivalents) would send out instructions on the lines of the Book of Orders which eventually would be disseminated down to a parish level in the form of a set of articles upon which parish constables were required to frame presentments against petty offenders. This would inject a mood of greater urgency into the standard system of hundred presentments which operated in Essex during the period. Aware of pressure from above, the constables would then present a number of minor malefactors who, in normal circumstances, would not have been thought worth disturbing or who might have been dealt with informally. If such governmental activity resulted in formal prosecutions in the form of indictments, it could produce a considerable impact on the type of criminal statistics under consideration here. Variations in the energy or objectives of the personnel of central and local government could thus produce fluctuations in the recorded levels of certain offences, notably those involving drink and the regulative, administrative and nuisance offences categorised for our immediate purposes as 'miscellaneous'. Such variations would also be manifested in the number of recognizances taken by justices and the length of the hundred jury presentments received at the quarter sessions.

Exploitation of these sources provides the necessary statistics upon which to base comparisons of the vigour with which various regimes set about the task of maintaining order in Essex. The importance of the problem is patent. As we have seen, a distinctive feature of law enforcement in the period was the impact of increased social stratification at parish level, and the attachment of village elites to 'respectable' values. Arguably it was the desire of government to enforce these values which created one of the distinctive features of crime in the early modern period. It is, of course, a nonsense to suggest that nobody in central or county government before 1550 worried about drunkenness, bastard-getting, work discipline or church attendance; it is undeniable, however, that after this date the enforcement of the laws regulating these and related forms of misconduct loomed increasingly large both in the writings of moralists and legislators and in the activities of local government. Moreover, the study of fluctuations in the prosecution of regulative offences provides a handy yardstick with which to measure the impact on localities of change at the centre of affairs. The years 1620–80 were marked by a number of distinct episodes in the fortunes of local government: the years of 'Thorough' in the 1630s; the Interregnum, with its intensification of the discussion of the reformation of manners[7] and the introduction of the major-generals; and the post-Restoration period, supposedly marked by a loss of interest in local government on the part of Westminster,[8] and a consequent slackening of administrative energies in the localities. Evidence from Essex suggests that this 'conventional wisdom' about English local government in the seventeenth century, still part of the stock-in-trade of many historians, is in need of re-examination.

Although most quarter sessions recognizances and hundred jury presentments are missing from the 1630s and 1670s, sufficient survive for the remainder of the period to allow comparison. Totals of recognizances, given in figure 4, support two of the major preconceptions about the period: the relatively high level of activity on the part of Interregnum justices, and the slackening of magisterial efforts in the years which followed the Restoration. Unfortunately, poor record survival precludes the forming of any conclusions about the years of Thorough. On the evidence of the number of recognizances taken by the Essex justices in 1637, however, it would seem that a high level of local government activity was maintained long after the initial impulse from the central government was past.[9] Hundred presentments at the quarter sessions show a rather different picture, mainly because they were subject to short-term aberrations. In 1629 the total was pushed up by the presentment of an unusually high total of 216 individuals for failing to carry out their obligations to repair the highways, while presentments for all years before 1640 were bolstered by the inclusion of numerous religious offenders, who figured more and more rarely in this type of document after that date. Even allowing for these difficulties, examination of hundred presentments given in figure 5 produces some rather unexpected results. If religious offenders are ignored,[10] an average of 187 individuals was presented each year between 1650 and 1656, and an average of 250 each year between 1661 and 1664. On this index, the Restoration witnessed a more active campaign against the local nuisance offender than did the period of puritan ascendancy. The totals for both recognizances and presentments demonstrate a high level of activity in the 1620s, and the latter bear ample witness to the county government's response to the crisis of 1629–31.

Apart from isolated groups of presentments of specific types of offenders – obviously the result of some short-lived and often very localised initiative – there is little evidence of qualitative changes in the matters dealt with by presentment during the period. In particular, the desire for a reformation of manners in the 1640s and 1650s does not seem to have manifested itself in any great wave of presentments against moral offenders. There was, perhaps, more interest in bastardy at the quarter sessions, but this was

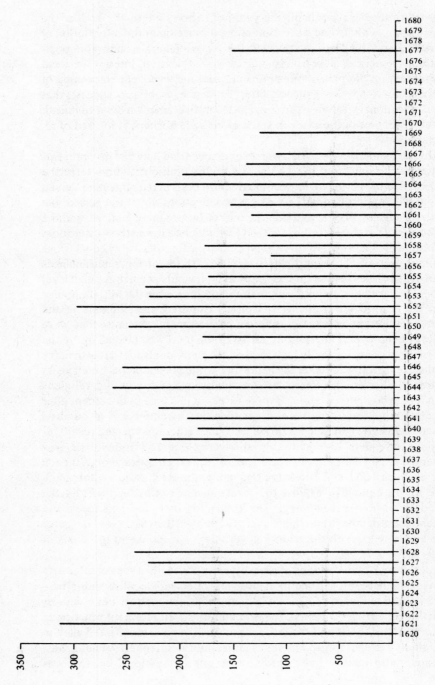

Fig. 4 Recognizances on Essex quarter sessions rolls, 1620–80 (only years enjoying survival of four rolls containing recognizances have been included)

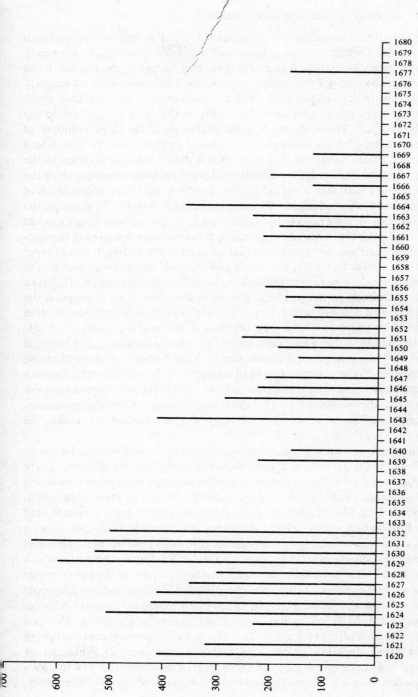

Fig. 5 Presentments on Essex quarter sessions rolls, 1620–80 (only years enjoying survival of four rolls containing presentments have been included)

probably little more than the consequence of the demise of those church courts which would previously have dealt with sexual immorality. Certainly presentments of that most constant source of danger to the morals of the seventeenth-century Englishman, the unlicensed alehouse, were not uniquely numerous in the 1640s and 1650s.[11] Indictments indicate that drink offences were prosecuted more frequently in the early 1670s than in the early 1650s.[12] These figures suggest that even if the large numbers of prosecutions of drink offences in the period 1645–54 can be linked to a 'puritan' desire to reform manners, such a desire was not peculiar to the Interregnum. The figures for indictments are especially surprising since the mid century was also a period of dearth, when regulative prosecution of unlicensed alehouses might have been expected.[13] As table 22 suggests, the years of dearth were marked by an increase in the presence of the unlicensed alehouse-keepers; it also demonstrates, however, that the level of presentment reached was no higher than that attained in the 1620s. It would seem that what might be loosely described as a 'puritan' attitude was common to all early modern governments seeking well-disciplined subjects. In Essex such an attitude permeated local government continuously throughout the period, and it is possible that the same sort of continuity was present in other areas. The years 1647–52, like the mid 1590s and the years 1629–31, comprehended a run of bad harvests and a trade depression.[14] On a national level, this last crisis was, it seems, met by local authorities along tried and tested lines.[15] The concrete reality of economic dislocation provided a more potent spur to exertion among the personnel of local government than did moralists' abstractions about a reformation of manners. Once the immediacy of crisis had gone, a 'puritan' ideology was not enough to sustain the diligence previously aroused.

The numerous indictments of drink offences in the 1670s must, however, be linked to the expansion of indictments of miscellaneous offences. There exists, from the 1630s, an almost unbroken series of assize files containing misdemeanour indictments and *ignoramus* felony. The number of indictments in these files of misdemeanour offences remains fairly constant until the Restoration, after which they increase rapidly. This increase is connected with constables' presentments, obviously (and at times explicitly) framed in response to set 'articles of enquiry'.[16] It is largely these files which keep the totals of indicted crime in the last two decades of the period under review so high, although the crimes being indicted changed drastically from those prior to the Restoration. In 1625–9, for example, property offences account for 61% of indictments, drink offences for some 8% and miscellaneous offences for 3%. In 1670–4 the respective contribution of these three categories is 17%, 23% and 32% (see figure 2). Although the two periods enjoyed roughly the same total of indictments – 714 to 739 – they were obviously afflicted by rather different types of recorded criminality.

Table 22 *Presentment of unlicensed alehouse-keepers at Essex quarter sessions, 1620–80, by quinquennia*

	Number of presentments	Percentage of total presentments
1620–4	266	18
1625–9	277	14
1630–4	198	9
1635–9	93	10
1640–4	124	10
1645–9	140	14
1650–4	260	34
1655–9	149	16
1660–4	81	8
1665–9	52	8
1670–4	27	6
1675–80	15	3

Notes: the special return under E.R.O., Q/SBa 2/6, have not been included here

Offences classed as 'miscellaneous' bear closer examination. Among the 241 indictments against offences of this type recorded for 1670–4 there exist many prosecutions of familiar petty delinquencies: false arrest, obstruction of the highway, bribery of a coroner, negligence by an overseer of the poor. Some 200 of these indictments, however, were brought against persons refusing to work.[17] This was a category of minor offender rarely indicted before the Restoration, but by the 1670s the general files of the Home circuit regularly contain indictments against persons who refused to work or who lived idly. Thus the most distinctive trend in indictments in the 1670s is the enforcement of labour discipline through the assizes. The precise background of this phenomenon remains elusive, but it must be linked to the growing sensitivity over the problem of the poor which has been traced in the second half of the seventeenth century.[18] What is striking is that these indictments were levelled against the resident poor. This situation shows a marked change from that obtaining in the late sixteenth century, when numerous indictments were brought at the assizes against vagrants.[19] The virtual discontinuation of the prosecution of this offence at the assizes by 1620[20] might be taken as evidence to support the opinion that governmental fears of vagrancy, and perhaps even vagrancy itself, were at their strongest in the late Tudor period.[21] On the evidence of these indictments, local governors in the late seventeenth century felt that the disciplining of the permanent parochial poor was a more important objective than the control of vagrancy. Another point to arise from these indictments, especially if they are taken in conjunction with the rise in the prosecution of drink offences, is that they indicate that the assizes were still very active in their task of co-ordinating local government.[22]

Although the offences of recusancy and failing to attend church have been excluded from this study, it is apposite to comment upon overall fluctuations in these offences at this juncture. Here, as elsewhere, variations in official approaches to the offender make it difficult to draw general conclusions. Despite occasional mass indictment of persons accused of these offences at the assizes in the years before the Civil Wars,[23] they were more usually dealt with prior to 1640 by presentment at the quarter sessions. Such presentments were common in the 1620s. There were, for example, 223 in 1625,[24] 182 in 1626,[25] and 184 in 1629.[26] The poor survival of documents in the 1630s then obscures the picture, but it is evident that the Interregnum witnessed a fall in these presentments. In the period 1650–6, for which a full complement of rolls survives, only eighty-two presentments of this type were made at the quarter sessions, and there is little evidence of their being prosecuted at the assizes.[27] Presentments at quarter sessions remained at a low level after the Restoration, none being made in the years 1661–3, and only five in 1664.[28] From about this point, however, recusants, Quakers, and persons refusing to attend church were indicted with increasing frequency at the assizes. These indictments, like those for drink offences or refusing to work, were largely drawn up from constables' presentments, and by the 1670s were reaching the level of the quarter sessions presentments of the 1620s. As might be expected, then, the prosecution of these offenders varied in intensity in accordance with the anxieties of the central government. The subject is, of course, one which merits extensive study in itself. One impression that does emerge from these prosecutions, however, is that court action rarely deterred those prosecuted; the same individuals were presented or indicted almost annually with little sign of amendment.

Variations in the level of crime did not result only from changes in the efficiency or ambitiousness of central or local government. Although the role of the administration in 'creating' crime was an important one, certain forms of crime were intimately linked to changes in the economic fortunes of the county. At the best of times there existed in Essex a large body of poor for whom the temptations for petty theft and other forms of property offence were strong;[29] when a bad harvest or a stop of trade occurred, the endemic poverty (and hence endemic criminality) of those living on or just above the subsistence line became dramatically, and often almost immediately, sharpened. Figure 6, plotting the wheat prices provided by W. G. Hoskins[30]

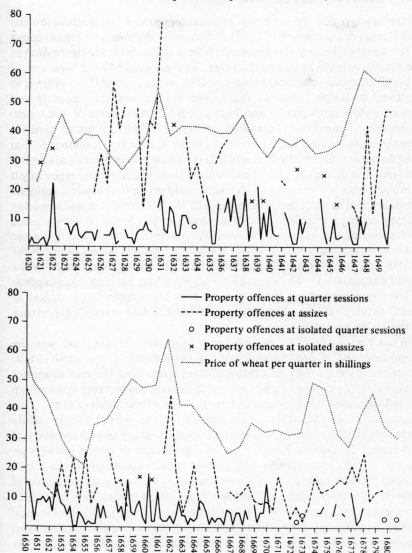

Fig. 6 Property offences at Essex assizes and quarter sessions, 1620–80, and wheat prices

against property offences indicted at the assizes and quarter sessions, demonstrates how direct the link between grain prices and property offences could be.

The three periods of the sharpest rise in wheat prices were all marked by a corresponding rise in property offences. Figure 6 re-emphasises the seriousness of the crisis of 1629–31, when one of the most troubled decades of the county's history was rounded off by a combination of depression in the textile industry and bad harvests. The period 1647–52 was one of national hardship, and local evidence of the grim nature of these years is to be found in Ralph Josselin's diary, with its frequent references to wet summers, low crop yields, and high prices.[31] The harvest of 1661 also prompted comment from Josselin,[32] while that of 1662, although hardly a bumper crop, was a source of obvious relief to him: in September of that year he wrote: 'Corn falleth much, a good wheat for 5s 6d. mislain 4s 8d; God make us thankful'.[33] Until mid century then, bad harvests, especially if combined with a stop in the cloth trade, could precipitate crisis conditions reminiscent of those of the terrible years 1596–8.[34] Even so, it is noteworthy that the county was able to absorb two bad harvests in the 1670s without a corresponding rise in the prosecution of property offences. Despite the bad years in mid century and in 1661, it would seem that the economy of the county enjoyed an agricultural base which grew steadily stronger as the century progressed.[35] The years 1647–52 were bad, but they do not appear to have provoked either the threat of social breakdown or the degree of administrative anxiety which were such a feature of the county's experience of the 1629–31 crisis.

What had made these earlier years especially troublesome was the coincidence of a bad harvest with a depression in the cloth trade. Throughout the century any dislocation of exports of the new draperies immediately threw out of employment the masses of workers upon whom the industry depended for cheap labour. Given their vulnerability to the international warfare which was endemic in the period,[36] it is hardly surprising that the history of the seventeenth-century new draperies was punctuated by slumps. Because of the dependence of textile workers on regular wages, such slumps had violent repercussions upon the social stability of the clothing areas. The years 1629–31 witnessed the period of greatest tension, but most of the other depressions in the clothing trade in the period dealt with by this study were the occasion of governmental anxiety and popular restlessness. The early 1620s was a period of national depression for the clothing trade. The areas producing the old draperies suffered most, but the Essex new draperies also experienced a short but sharp depression in 1622–3.[37] There were disturbances among unemployed clothworkers in the county, and clothowners, under pressure from the Privy Council, made their familiar plea that they were unable to set the poor on work because of their inability to sell the cloths they already possessed.[38] The period 1640–2, when an economic depression was accentuated by a political crisis, was another bad time for the cloth trade. A petition from Coggeshall in mid 1641 complained that the cloth trade had been depressed for six months, with a resultant trebling of the poor rates.[39] Such an experience was not atypical, and it was this background of economic troubles which explains the overtones of class hatred shown in some of the rioting in the Stour valley in the summer of 1642.[40]

The Civil Wars inevitably involved a dislocation of commerce, which was intensified for Essex in 1648 when the county's cloth trade suffered a crippling setback with the siege and partial destruction of Colchester. On a national level, clothing underwent a depression until 1653, this coinciding with the bad harvests of the mid century. By 1651 requests for aid with poor relief had reached Westminster from Bocking.[41] Recovery was impeded by the onset of the First Dutch War of 1652.[42] Further depressions affected the industry during 1658–63, during the aftermath of the plague of 1665–6, and during 1676–81.[43] In general these latter depressions do not seem to have produced disruptions as serious as those which occurred before the mid century. Although clothworkers rioted in 1674 and 1675,[44] their disturbances did not arouse the same fears of imminent social breakdown current during 1629–31 and perhaps during 1647–53. Moreover, as we have seen, the 1670s did not witness the massive upsurge in property offences which had accompanied these earlier crises and the bad years of the 1590s. Nevertheless, it is doubtful if this easier situation in the second half of the century stopped worry over social order in the clothing areas from being the main concern of the county's governors in times of economic depression.

Such a conjecture necessarily raises the problem of the geographical spread of crime in the county. Table 20 gives the overall pattern, but for the sake of clarity more detailed attention will be focused on a smaller number of hundreds. Firstly, the four most criminous hundreds were taken. These were Hinckford and Lexden, both of them clothing areas, the mixed-farming hundred of Chelmsford, and the 'suburban' hundred of Becontree, on the peripheries of London. To these were added two other hundreds with distinctive features, Uttlesford Hundred, which lay in the open-field area in the north-west of the county, and Tendring Hundred, the most remote and arguably the worst-governed part of Essex. Using the broad categories of offence outlined above, the criminality of these hundreds was as shown in table 23.

These figures demonstrate a greater degree of uniformity than might have been expected. Even though Tendring Hundred had only a low proportion of 'created' crime (in the form of miscellaneous offences), which might be expected given its relative remoteness, the close correspondence between the proportion of drink offences in that hundred and the county figure suggests that it was not so isolated from county government as might have been thought. The variations between the hundreds of Hinckford and Lexden, adjacent clothing areas which might have been expected to demonstrate the same trends, point to the difficulties involved in comparisons

Table 23 *Broad categories of indicted offences in six selected Essex hundreds, 1620–80*

	Total offences	Property offences		Violent offences		Drink offences		Miscellaneous offences	
Hinckford	1,276	494	39%	190	15%	141	11%	197	15%
Lexden	952	303	32%	119	12%	194	20%	128	13%
Chelmsford	1,034	322	31%	187	18%	159	15%	113	11%
Becontree	657	285	43%	108	16%	69	10%	57	19%
Tendring	386	139	36%	67	17%	50	13%	23	6%
Uttlesford	400	170	42%	45	11%	63	16%	46	11%
Essex total	8,557	3,206	37%	1,272	15%	1,182	14%	941	11%

of this type; it should be noted, however, that Lexden Hundred contained Colchester, whose independent jurisdiction obscures the pattern of indictment within the hundred. Perhaps the most consistent offences were crimes of violence, which seem to have been more evenly distributed throughout the county than any other of these broad categories of offences.

Examination of the fluctuations of specific types of offence within the hundreds leads to similarly inconclusive results. In view of the growth of London during the period, it was anticipated that there would be a shift in criminality towards Becontree Hundred. Accordingly, the chronology of property offences – the most numerous 'real' offences – was plotted in the four most criminous hundreds. The results of this process are set out in figure 7, which shows the percentage share of property offences in the hundreds in question by quinquennia. From this evidence, it would seem that the only conclusive change was a decline in the importance of property offences in Hinckford Hundred. Since those for Lexden (apart from a drop in 1670–4) remained relatively stable, it is difficult to relate this trend to any changes in the textile industry. Property offences were likewise stable in their contribution to recorded crime in Chelmsford Hundred, whereas the proportion of such offences in Becontree Hundred fluctuated wildly. Hence, although it is possible to trace an upward movement in the importance of property offences in Becontree Hundred, this was not a steady or indisputable trend.[45] It is very difficult, on this evidence, to delineate any major shifts in the geographical distribution of crime within the county in the period under consideration.

Similarly, there are few clear conclusions to be drawn from an examination of the connection between recorded crime and population density. Assessing seventeenth-century populations is an exercise only marginally safer than quantifying seventeenth-century crime, but previous research[46] has provided

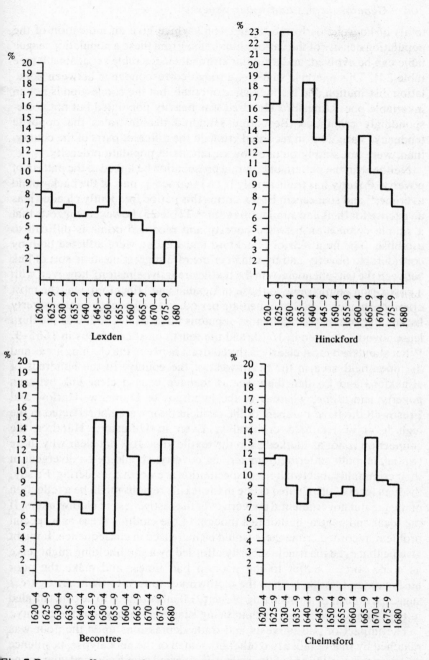

Fig. 7 Property offences in four selected hundreds: showing the percentage of the total of property offences indicted in Essex occurring in the respective hundreds, by quinquennia

totals of households for 1638 and 1662 which give an indication of the population density of the various hundreds. From these a population league table can be evolved, and a similar criminal league table set against it (see table 24). This exercise suggests a rough correspondence between population distribution and the incidence of crime, but the connection is not an invariable one. Uttlesford Hundred was heavily populated but not correspondingly criminous; Becontree Hundred demonstrates the opposite tendency. Variations in recorded crime in the different parts of the county, then, were not simply dictated by variations in population density.

Neither can the pattern of criminal prosecution be linked to the pattern of poverty. Poverty has traditionally been regarded as part of the background to crime,[47] and suspects in Essex during this period frequently pleaded it as an excuse for theft and similar offences.[48] Table 25, however, suggests that a simple connection between poverty and recorded crime is difficult to establish. The hundreds of Hinckford and Lexden were afflicted both by considerable poverty and by a high crime rate suggesting some sort of link between the two phenomena in the textile areas. Chelmsford, however, with a population comparable to those of Lexden and Hinckford, was the most criminous hundred in the immediate period, yet only eighth on the poverty listing. Becontree, the ninth most populous hundred in 1662, was the third least poverty-stricken in 1670, and the fourth most criminous in 1665–9. What stands out most clearly is the contrast between the clothing areas and the open-field area in the north-west of the county. In the hundreds of Hinckford and Lexden there seems to have been a clear link between poverty and crime, whereas in the hundreds of Dunmow, Harlow and Freshwell the large numbers of the resident poor were not reflected in the high level of recorded criminality. Even in Uttlesford Hundred the connection is not as marked as in the textile area. It is not clear why these two areas, both suffering from serious poverty, should be so divergent in their criminality, but two lines of speculation are worth considering. Firstly, the high level of prosecuted crime in the textile regions might be a reflection of the greater governmental concern over the restiveness of clothworkers. If the local and central authorities thought of the clothing areas as a special problem, recorded crime there would be increased in consequence. It might also be that even the fragile security afforded by a smallholding might serve as some sort of buffer to the poor in bad times, and make the poor husbandman less likely than the clothworker to turn to theft. As figure 7 suggests, even in times of dearth, property offences tended to be concentrated in the clothing areas, rather than being scattered throughout the county.

The impact of bad harvests and trade depressions upon the poor was matched by that of those two other horsemen of the apocalypse, pestilence and warfare. Visitations of the plague, in a period which counted quarantine as one of its few effective defences against pestilence, necessarily implied a

Table 24 *Overall criminality and population in Essex hundreds in selected periods*

	'Population League' 1638	'Criminal League' 1635–9	'Population League' 1662	'Criminal League' 1660–4
Hinckford	1	1	2	3
Chelmsford	2	2	3	2
Lexden	3	3	1	1
Uttlesford	4	9	7	13
Tendring	5	11	4	=14
Barstable	6	=6	5	=6
Ongar	7	4	6	5
Rochford	8	=15	8	=6
Dunmow	9	=15	10	11
Becontree	10	5	9	4
Chafford	11	=6	14	=8
Harlow	12	8	11	16
Witham	13	14	13	=8
Dengie	14	10	12	10
Freshwell	15	=12	16	20
Waltham	16	18	15	12
Havering	17	=19	17	19
Winstree	18	17	19	18
Thurstable	19	=12	18	14
Clavering	20	=19	20	17

Notes: sources for 'Population League' as chapter 11, n. 46 below; for 'Criminal League', see above, table 21

stop of trade. Seventeenth-century outbreaks of plague in the capital therefore had serious repercussions for Essex, a county whose economic life was geared to conditions in London. In 1625 a serious attack in London, with a corresponding breakdown in commercial intercourse between the metropolis and Essex, engendered considerable hardship in the county,[49] and it was probably this which prompted the sharp rise in property offences at the Hilary assizes of 1626 (see figure 6). The spread of plague into the county aggravated the problems of poor relief engendered by the economic disruption. In 1641–2 attempts to collect money from other parishes to relieve victims at Witham provoked unsympathetic responses from a number of communities unwilling to countenance such an extension of organised charity.[50] These earlier visitations of the plague, however, pall into insignificance when compared with the impact upon Essex of the Great Plague of 1665. The catastrophe in London in 1665 was accompanied, despite the usual attempts at quarantine, by heavy mortality in Becontree

Table 25 *Overall criminality and poverty in Essex hundreds, 1665–9*

	'Poverty League'	'Criminal League'
Hinckford	1	3
Dunmow	2	15
Lexden	3	=4
Harlow	4	=16
Uttlesford	5	8
Freshwell	6	=16
Witham	7	=10
Chelmsford	8	1
Waltham	9	=10
Winstree	10	18
Thurstable	11	=10
Clavering	12	20
Ongar	13	7
Tendring	14	2
Rochford	15	9
Dengie	16	14
Chafford	17	=10
Becontree	18	=4
Barstable	19	6
Havering	20	19

Notes: sources for 'Poverty League' in Burley, 'Economic development of Essex', p. 337; for 'Criminal League', see above, table 21

Hundred,[51] and in the following year the pestilence spread over the remainder of the county. In that year Braintree suffered some 1,500 plague deaths, as high a proportionate loss, according to one authority, as that sustained by any British town between 1348 and 1667.[52] Colchester lost perhaps 5,000 from a population of 10,000–12,000.[53] This last visitation, despite the commercial disruption it caused,[54] had surprisingly little impact on criminal statistics. It is difficult to see exactly why this should be so. Possibly the sheer immensity of the problems of the relief of the victims left the authorities no time or energy for dealing with any criminal activity. On the other hand, it might again be argued that the social structure was less vulnerable to natural disaster in the post-Restoration period than it had been in the 1620s, either through the increased soundness of its economic base, or as a result of better-organised poor relief. Certainly the recovery of Colchester after 1666[55] points to a great resilience in the society of the county.

Like the plague of 1665–6, the Civil Wars seem to have made little impact upon recorded crime in Essex.[56] The county was fortunate in that it was not the scene of any real fighting, the summer of 1648 excepted,[57] while for the duration of the First Civil War at least, an unusual degree of unity among the county's ruling elite[58] prevented any major breakdown of county administration. Although no regular assizes were held in England for three years from the summer of 1642,[59] and despite a year and a quarter's break in the holding of quarter sessions,[60] good order in the county was not, apparently, placed under any intolerable strain. Essex did, of course, undergo the stresses of economic disruption and heavy taxation, but these were manifestly less troublesome than armed conflicts or serious civilian divisions within the county.[61] The witch trials of 1645 must, of course, be seen in the context of the disruption, both psychological and administrative, engendered by the war;[62] but the stresses of the conflict do not seem to have caused any great rise in other kinds of recorded crime, and when such a rise did occur in the late 1640s it was the outcome of the familiar problems of harvest failure and economic depression.

Concentration on recorded crime might, of course, present a distorted picture of the impact of the wars. The organisation of armies and the need to supervise taxation may well have diverted the energies of the local administration away from the apprehension and prosecution of criminals. Moreover, an actual outbreak of fighting in an area would necessitate a disruption of the normal processes of law and order, with a consequent slackening in the number of cases brought to court despite a possible increase in the amount of crime actually committed. Such a situation seems to have arisen in the summer of 1648. The drop in the number of property offences tried at the summer assizes that year (see figure 6), a reversal of the general upward trend in such offences during the late 1640s, must be attributed to the disruption caused by the Second Civil War. There is, however, little direct evidence to suggest that the wars caused any great lawlessness in Essex which escaped formal prosecution. There were, of course, a number of generalised complaints about the erosion of law and order in the county. In the winter of 1642–3 a petition from Barking referred to 'sundry great robberies there lately committed'.[63] Later in the same decade Josselin bemoaned the prevalence of burglars and highway robbers,[64] and at about the same time the activities of this latter class of malefactors prompted a call from the Council of State for greater vigilance in various towns on the environs of London, among them Epping and Romford.[65] Even so, there is very little concrete evidence of any connection between the wars and the perpetrators of crime during this period. Examples of lawless soldiers or ex-soldiers are few, and even Josselin found the actual presence of troops less troublesome than he had anticipated.[66] The soldier who in 1652 encouraged a Walthamstow man to join the army, on the grounds of 'there being yet good plunder to be had', and offering the added inducement of a trip to Whitechapel, 'where he would show him neat wenches', is the nearest approximation that the quarter sessions records afford us of a brutal and licentious soldiery.[67] Even in 1648, when the presence of two rival armies at Colchester caused such a dearth of provisions that fears were expressed of a general rising of the poor,[68] the county showed a surprising resilience. Crime in Essex seems to have been affected less by the years of warfare than by the period of harvest failure and trade depression which followed them.

Two conclusions, then, emerge from this consideration of the chronological and geographical distribution of recorded crime in Essex between 1620 and 1680. Firstly, that it was the inhabitants of the textile-producing parts of the county who presented the greatest threat to law and order. Although the population density and level of poverty in the open-field area in the north-west of the county approached those of the clothing districts, its inhabitants were never to prove so troublesome. The rural proletariat[69] of the open fields never reacted as violently to an intensification of their poverty as did the textileworkers of Hinckford and Lexden hundreds, where economic dislocation was usually followed by a rise in property offences and public disturbances. The north-west of the county, it has been suggested recently, was an area 'of stable poverty where popular attitudes were characterised by stoic endurance'.[70] The 'stoic endurance' of the smallholder peasants in open-field Essex should not, perhaps, be overstated, but the inhabitants of that region, *en masse*, certainly seem to have been less volatile than the clothworkers. The contrast must be connected with different social structures and economic relationships in the two areas, or, perhaps more importantly, with different perceptions of those structures and relationships. In the textile areas the stable poverty of daily hardship was on occasion intensified by terrible bouts of unstable poverty. Here bad harvests hit harder than in the corn-growing north-west, while the stops in trade that punctuated the century had more dramatic effects upon the pool of underpaid labour which constituted the textile industry's workforce than even the worst harvest. Such crises were all the more serious given that among textileworkers there existed a nascent class-consciousness that had little to do with stoic endurance. The weaver who predicted a rising of the lower orders in 1624, commenting that 'their be more pore then riche';[71] the unemployed poor of Bocking who, it was feared, would make it unsafe for their social superiors to live among them in 1629;[72] the inhabitants of the Stour valley whose rioting in 1642 showed ugly signs of developing from an attack on leading royalists to an attack on their social superiors in general;[73] and the Colchester weavers who in 1675 organised a demonstration against wage cuts[74] – all of these, perhaps, had a more immediate idea of their relationship to other social groups than did their equivalents of the open-field areas. It is probably this ready erosion of deference in bad times, coupled with an objectively more miserable poverty, which accounts for the high level of property offences in the textile districts. Certainly contemporaries regarded inhabitants of such areas as something of a 'dangerous class'. One late sixteenth-century observer remarked on how, as a consequence of adverse economic conditions,

infinite nombers of Spynners, Carders, Pickers of woll are turned to begging with no smale store of pore children, who driven with necessitie (that hath no lawe) hath come idelie about to begg to the oppression of the poore husbandman, And robbe their hedges of lynnen, stele pig, gose, and capon . . . steale fruit and corne in the harvest tyme, and robb barnes in the winter tyme, and cawse pore maydes and servants to purloyne and robbe their masters, which the foresayd spynners etc. receve.[75]

Evidence from Essex criminal records confirms such impressionistic comment: a large and poor industrial workforce, dependent upon wage-labour and bereft of the dignity and sense of stability which even holding a few acres might provide, must have included many individuals who were ready to turn occasional thief.

Secondly, despite the existence of a significant crisis between 1647 and 1652, it was the 1620s which witnessed the highest level of serious crime in the period covered by this study. Two factors combined to produce this effect. On the one hand, conditions were bad for the lower orders of society. Wheat prices, although not reaching crisis levels until 1631, were never low (see figure 6). The cloth trade suffered an endemic depression which culminated in a total stop in trade in 1630.[76] The commercial life of the county was further disrupted by the plague of 1625, with its crippling effects on Essex's trading links with the capital. These economic troubles were worsened by troop movements in the middle years of the decade. Billeting and the normal depredations of the soldiery were added to problems faced by the inhabitants of the county. It is noteworthy that the presence of troops in the county seems to have caused more trouble in the 1620s than in the First Civil War.[77] These circumstances combined to produce a high level of crime; on the other hand, the knowledge of them provoked an unusual degree of vigour on the part of the county's local governors, and hence a high level of reported crime. During this troubled decade, despite occasional obstruction of the central government's aims and the first rumblings of political opposition, the Essex gentry, as justices and militia officers, evinced exemplary standards of efficiency and diligence, usually in close co-operation with the Privy Council.[78] The threat of crime and disorder never loomed so large as in the years 1620–31, and was never countered by a more resolute response from the forces of control.

That it is possible to make such an assertion does at least demonstrate how analysis of overall totals of indictments allows the delineation of certain patterns which can then be utilised to further our understanding of the nature and incidence of crime in early modern England. As we have seen, perhaps the greatest contribution of these patterns lies in their refusal to conform to any preconceptions. The decline in property offences over our period was contrary to expectations. Regulative offences were not at their highest during the 'Puritan Ascendancy' of the 1650s, and showed a surprising increase in the 1670s. The geographical distribution of offences, with their tendency to cluster in the clothing areas rather than the peripheries of London, was similarly unexpected. On the other hand, perhaps such findings should not surprise us: after all, the history of crime is still a relatively new discipline, constantly modifying our perceptions of past society. Two general themes do, however, emerge from the preceding chapter. Firstly, the study of overall patterns of recorded offences re-emphasises the assertion that 'crime' is a necessarily imprecise term. Throughout this book stress has been laid on the way in which the willingness to commit and report crimes could vary, both between various types of crime and between different periods. The total figures for indictments illustrate this point further: crimes of violence, crimes against property, and regulative offences all fluctuated to a different chronological pattern, evidence that they are different types of behaviour, each likely to have its own motivations, to provoke its own response among society at large, and to be committed by different types of person. Secondly, and especially relevant to fluctuations in regulative offences, is the problem of fluctuations in the desire to enforce the law: indeed, it is tempting to suggest that the historian should study at least some types of crime in the past in terms of 'enforcement waves' rather than 'crime waves'.[79] At any rate, factors affecting variations in enforcement are at least as worthy of study as those affecting real fluctuations in crime. Such considerations lead us towards those larger issues which will be discussed in the final chapter.

12. Concluding observations

The foregoing chapters have described the offences tried before two courts in one English county over a sixty-year period in the seventeenth century, and have offered some generalisations, both quantitative and qualitative, about the nature of those offences and of the persons accused of committing them. The pursuit of such a description, however, has necessarily involved touching upon a number of other types of evidence relating to the history of crime, and has introduced a number of themes whose connection with the analysis of court records in Stuart Essex is at times very indirect. It is, of course, inherent in the very nature of the subject that any study of the history of crime should be to some extent centrifugal: as has been hinted at various points in this book, the very term 'crime' is a loose description rather than a strict definition, and this looseness has doubtless been emphasised by the approach favoured here, an analysis based on different types of offence. As was pointed out in the introduction to this book, such a methodology is only one of a number of different ways in which crime in the past might be studied, each of which has its distinctive strengths and weaknesses. Writing the history of crime through the intensive examination of court archives dealing with a limited area and period has its problems and limitations: it also has its distinctive strengths.[1] Not least, it provides an alternative perspective on the subject to that offered by earlier writing, which has depended heavily on anecdotal evidence culled from literary sources, or from legal texts whose relevance to the actual practice of the courts was often very limited. The county study does show which offences and which offenders were prosecuted, and what punishments were inflicted: until such matters have been examined, debate on the history of crime is fairly meaningless.

Nevertheless, any historical approach, however fundamental its importance, should be amenable to being placed in the context of developing research and historical debate.[2] It is to such issues that we shall turn in this brief conclusion. Our objectives are twofold: firstly, to reiterate some of the major findings which have emerged from this study of the Essex archives, and to place them in some sort of more general framework; and secondly, to suggest some of the wider themes which the study of crime in early modern England touches upon.

There was, of course, no such thing as a 'typical' English county. It would therefore be idle to suppose that Essex, with its large and volatile textile workforce, its capitalist agriculture, and its proximity to London, should share the characteristics of a purely agrarian shire in the midlands, or one located in the wilder parts of the extreme north or west.[3] Moreover, it should be remembered that the county was essentially an administratively defined entity, and that crime, in its very essence, pays scant respect to administrators: the poor vagrant offender and the mobile professional thief operated across county lines, and a study based on the archives of any one county might well fail to give sufficient weight to such individuals. On the other hand, the county study does discipline the historian of crime by giving him a defined area of study and, more generally, a context within which to place his findings. As we have seen, patterns in the reporting and prosecution of crime in Essex were affected by changes in the personnel and ethos of county government, responded to economic crisis, and varied between the economic subdivisions of the county. Our understanding of many individual offences has been deepened by a knowledge, however partial, of the local context in which they occurred, and proponents of the microscopic village study might claim that use of such knowledge has been neither frequent nor deep enough: however, short of embarking on microscopic studies of the four hundred and fifty parishes within the county, or of the doings of the thirty or so justices who were active on its bench at any one time, it is hard to see how these objections can be met. Given the present level of writing on the history of crime in the early modern period, a study based on the county would seem to offer the most likely means of meeting both the demand for productive generalisation and the necessities of detailed context.

Even so, there remain some issues which demand more detailed attention. Perhaps the most significant of these is the need to understand the processes which lay behind prosecution.[4] Indictment, as has been argued at various points, was often an episode in a lengthy period of deteriorating relationships between the accuser and the accused, during which a number of solutions to the problems at issue may have been attempted: arbitration, other forms of settlement out of court, one of a number of informal sanctions, or such formal alternatives to indictment as binding over or committal to the house of correction. Behind every indictment there lay a story, but it is improbable that we will ever be able to uncover the details of such stories except in isolated cases. Clearly, depositions provide impressionistic evidence, and are often vital in giving fragmentary glimpses of what must have been normal patterns. Arguably, however, the most effective way of resolving this difficulty, and thus deepening our understanding of the background to court action, is the detailed village study. This, through the use of a variety of archival sources, allows the historian to place both the victim and offender in their social context, and thus to make more informed guesses about the social interactions which preceded prosecution.

Nevertheless, despite the alternatives available, and whatever the nature of the social processes involved, indictments *were* brought, and individuals *were* prosecuted before the Essex assizes and quarter sessions. As the previous chapter has demonstrated, it is possible to advance a variety of arguments about the reasons for fluctuations both in these indictments and in the punishment inflicted on those successfully prosecuted. On the other hand, the numerous occasions on which criminal statistics show an obdurate unwillingness to conform to any expected pattern should be remembered. Chronologically, this tendency is evident when the historian is faced by the surprising rarity of prosecution of engrossers and similar offenders in times of dearth, or by the phenomenon of regulative offences being more frequently indicted in the 'slack' 1670s rather than the puritan-dominated 1650s. Geographically, this obduracy is equally marked: the location of burglaries bearing no relationship to trade routes or concentrations of population; sheep-thefts being scattered throughout the country, rather than restricted to grazing areas; and even cases of poaching showing little correspondence to what, given the existence of extensive forest areas in the county, might have been their expected distribution. At times, of course, indicted offences do follow anticipated patterns: thus we find property offences rising in response to economic crises during 1629–31, or 1648–52, and horse-thefts and highway robberies being concentrated on main roads. In general, however, the study of indictments in seventeenth-century Essex demonstrates the unwisdom of presupposing any direct correlation between criminal statistics and economic or political phenomena. Work on the background to prosecution has suggested that the factors affecting the decision to bring an individual indictment were sometimes extremely complex: awareness of this should make the historian unusually cautious in his treatment of indictments *en masse*.

Moreover, it should be borne in mind that the discussion of trends in indicted crime often revolves around very small numbers of recorded offences, and that any slight increase in these numbers can lead to disproportionately large relative fluctuations. Indicted crime was the tip of a sizeable iceberg of indictable behaviour, and it is probable, for most offences, that even in periods when the willingness to prosecute was apparently strong, prosecutions represented only a small proportion of offences actually committed. This relative paucity of indictments should not, however, cause historians to despair of ever gaining a fully rounded picture of crime in this period: numerous other court archives, notably those of ecclesiastical and manorial institutions, exist to give us a more comprehensive impression of delinquent behaviour. As Wrightson and Levine have shown,[5] the study of fluctuations and changes in the nature of this less serious crime can tell us more about crime and the criminal in the past than any simplistic analysis of assize and quarter sessions indictments. Despite the significance of such work, we must reiterate that its peculiarly detailed nature precludes the adoption of this approach on a county level.

It is, therefore, to the analysis of crime indicted in Essex between 1620 and 1680 that we must return, and it is this phenomenon which we must attempt to place in a wider context. Firstly, it is striking that the serious crime recorded in our sample seems to fit very well into what seems to be emerging as the standard pattern in late medieval and early modern England: a preponderance of property offences, with homicide running as a poor second, and other felonies (rape, arson, and so on) negligible in number.[6] The ratio of property offences to homicide might have been higher in Essex than in some other contemporary or late medieval shires, but the basic pattern remains clear, suggesting that the transition from 'violence-dominated' crime to 'property-dominated' crime which some French historians have claimed took place between the fifteenth and eighteenth centuries simply does not exist for lowland England.[7] The fluctuations delineated in the study do, however, fit well with what seems to have been the broad shifts in serious crime, at least in southern England, between the mid sixteenth and mid eighteenth centuries. Firstly, it would seem that John Beattie's suggestion that homicide was decreasing steadily as the period progressed[8] is borne out by the Essex figures. Beattie's conclusions, based on Surrey and Sussex materials for 1660–1800, suggest a steady decline in homicide which amounted to a halving of the rate over that period. The poor survival of records obscures the point, but comparison of the rates obtaining in the years 1620–80 with those of the Elizabethan period suggests that the trend discovered by Beattie was part of a much longer development, perhaps beginning in the early sixteenth century.[9] Secondly, property offences (despite upswings in years of economic adversity) seem to have shown a steady decline from the late sixteenth century. In 1598, a hundred and seventy-one property offences were tried at one assize;[10] in 1631, the worst year for property offences in the period covered by this book, the figure was less than half this total, and by the 1670s the assizes were regularly trying twenty or less such cases at each session, a level roughly similar to that discovered by Beattie for Sussex in the late seventeenth century.[11] Despite a number of other partial explanations for this phenomenon, it is difficult not to interpret it as symptomatic of a basic socio-economic change in English society: the position of the rural poor, and hence perhaps of social relations in general, was less precarious in the late seventeenth than in the late sixteenth century.

The hypothesis that such a change took place is given considerable support from a change in the levels of executions. If as many felons were hanged in Essex in Elizabeth's reign as on the whole of the Home circuit in the mid eighteenth century, and if it is accepted that the level of executions in a society is somehow indicative of wider social attitudes or social relationships within that society, it is evident that something important had happened in the English judicial and law-enforcement systems between those two periods. Our Essex evidence suggests that the crucial point was the mid seventeenth century. In the late 1620s and 1630s every assize in Essex was followed by numerous executions as the authorities confronted the consequences of the worst economic crisis to afflict the county since the 1590s: from the 1650s onwards, however, hangings became rarer, and the way seemed paved for the more measured, even ritualistic, situation obtaining in the eighteenth century.[12] The precise reasons for this trend await further investigation: obviously, it must be connected to the increased soundness of the English economy, although it probably owed more to changes in the attitudes of the judiciary, and perhaps of the ruling strata in general. It is tempting, however, to see this development as being somehow connected to the ideas of a 'judicial revolution' which are beginning to attract scholars working on continental court archives,[13] and which is beginning to see a general growth in leniency by judges throughout Europe and a switch in their attention to new types of offences as the preoccupations of the state shifted. It is possible that the 'general crisis' debate will soon assume a legal and judicial dimension.

Whatever the accuracy of these suggestions about continental trends, it would seem that the years 1620–80 lie in a trough between two periods of what might be described as 'law and order consciousness' in England. The second of these, of which the best-known aspect is the proliferation of capital statutes for property offences which followed the Glorious Revolution, is the more familiar.[14] The earlier awaits investigation, although certain aspects of it are evident enough: the gradual exclusion of a number of offences from benefit of clergy[15] which was a persistent theme of mid Tudor statutes; the continual legislation against vagrancy and idleness;[16] and, above all, the emergence of the rogue literature of the Elizabethan period, which provided England with its first criminal stereotype. This first period of 'law and order consciousness' saw an increased interest in the efficient prosecution of crime from the middle years of the sixteenth century,[17] and was to persist into the reign of James I. The Jacobean era was marked by harsh legislation against such offences as bigamy and infanticide, and a continued burgeoning of regulatory statutes, of which those directed against drunkenness and abuses in the drink trade were the most numerous.[18] The closing years of Elizabeth's rule and the reign of James I also saw the emergence of the propagandists for the puritan reformation of manners, whose hostility to the 'common country disorders' of the mass of the rural population is of obvious importance to the historian of crime.[19] It was probably not until the middle of the eighteenth century that anything like the

Elizabethan and early Stuart worry about law and order, whether expressed in statutes, popular literature, or the works of social commentators, reappeared.

The problem is a vast one, and it is, perhaps, incautious to introduce it in a work which is based neither on literary evidence nor on a study of the attitudes and activities of the central administration. It is striking, however, that the seventeenth century lacked a clear criminal stereotype. Contemporaries inveighed against the unruliness of the 'meaner sort', of course; they had no concept of the dangerous elements in society as clear as that which the vagrant had provided in the late sixteenth century and which the member of the urban mob was to provide in the eighteenth. At the risk of over-simplification, it might be argued that, in the seventeenth century constitutional struggle, religious strife and civil warfare gave the rulers of England and the popular press a more immediate set of preoccupations. It could almost be claimed that excessive worry about crime, and the emergence of the criminal as an object of fascination in the popular press, might well be luxuries in which a society can indulge after it has reached a certain level of stability and cohesion.

Certainly there is little in the materials upon which this book is based to suggest that contemporaries were worried enough about crime to do much to alter the basic structure of the criminal law, or the basic preconceptions which underlay it.[20] Legal historians have found little to excite either interest or approbation in the criminal law of the early modern period. One, indeed, has claimed that before the Age of Reform, as far as the criminal law was involved, 'nothing worth-while was created. There is no achievement to trace', and has opined that the law in criminal matters 'had done no more than systematise barbarity'.[21] Lawyers were uninterested in the criminal law (partly because the accused in felony cases was not normally allowed counsel), while even those involved in assize work much preferred the *nisi prius* to the crown side, as the latter gave them less profit and little opportunity to demonstrate their skill and learning. This lack of interest must help explain the disregard for the letter of the law which is so often manifest when proceedings at the assizes and quarter sessions are studied. The most remarkable, and puzzling, aspect of this is the presence of innumerable, and (so far as can be seen) unchallenged, inaccuracies of fact on indictments. The regular extension of the benefit of clergy to illiterate prisoners, the undervaluing of stolen goods to bring the offender into the category of petty larceny, and the tinkering with the wording of burglary indictments are three other remarkable aspects. The archives of the Essex assizes and quarter sessions show how, in the lower levels of its operation, the English criminal law was obviously being regularly adjusted to meet particular circumstances, evidence perhaps that the problem of 'crime' was felt to be serious enough to warrant only piecemeal solutions. Even the proliferation of capital statutes in the eighteenth century, although obviously taking place in a general context of worry about the criminal as an enemy of property, cannot be interpreted in any simplistic way as evidence of a fear of crime. Study of eighteenth-century assizes suggest that these new laws were rarely used, and that most of those executed for property offences suffered under the statute or common law as it had existed in the reign of Elizabeth.[22] Moreover, the very enactment of these statutes seems to have owed more to isolated initiatives than to any consistent policy: as Radzinowicz has commented, 'practically all capital offences were created more or less as a matter of course by a placid and uninterested parliament'.[23]

Many of the basic assumptions of the legal thinking of early modern England are, therefore, unfamiliar and even perplexing to the modern student. This should not obscure the fact that the machinery of enforcing the criminal law, despite occasional critics, seems to have functioned to the satisfaction of most of those contemporaries whose opinions have come down to us. As has been apparent throughout this book, seventeenth-century Englishmen had rather different ideas on what the criminal law was for, and rather different assumptions about the law in general, from those current in modern British society. This issue is, of course, one aspect of the much wider problem of popular attitudes to the law in past centuries, a problem which has so far attracted more attention from historians of the eighteenth century than from those working in the Stuart era.[24] At the root of the problem lies the basic premise that the law was something which people used, whether the people in question were judges attempting to maintain the contemporary hierarchy by sentencing property offenders to death, an Essex yeoman binding a troublesome neighbour over to keep the peace, or members of a leet jury trying to dissuade another tenant on their home manor from impeding their progress along the village street with his dunghill. On different levels and for different purposes, the law ultimately owed its functioning to its acceptance by a broad spectrum of English society. The frequency with which the English were willing to resolve their conflicts or settle their disputes by recourse to the law is striking testimony to its success in achieving a type of acceptability.

To most contemporaries, the great virtue of the criminal law must have been its flexibility. To the modern observer, the early modern criminal law may seem to be a mixture of the arbitrary, the unpredictable, the irrational and the brutal. The fact that it functioned so long without reform suggests, in part at least, that it made rather more sense to contemporaries. For the serious offender, standing trial for his life at the assizes, the importance of this flexibility is evident enough; Douglas Hay has stressed its importance in reinforcing the potency of contemporary myths about the law in the eighteenth century,[25] and Essex court materials suggest that much the same situation was operating in the seventeenth century. The flexibility provided by the existence of ecclesiastical and manorial courts, of the house of correction, of petty sessions and of binding over gave offended parties a whole battery of means by which they could combat the petty offender. Even the much-maligned dependence upon amateur parish officers becomes more comprehensible once it is accepted that such a system was well-enough adjusted to the needs of the villages and small towns of pre-industrial England. The capacity of the parish officers to warn or admonish offenders before prosecution is, therefore, just one more aspect of the flexibility which characterised the law enforcement of the period. Such policing may not be appropriate to the modern industrial city, but as the examination of Essex villages has shown, it did possess a certain rationale in the seventeenth-century countryside.

Our final conclusion must be, therefore, that crime as an historical problem can only be understood by placing it firmly in its context. This book has been based on court archives, and it is the author's contention that the use of such materials provides one of the best avenues into the understanding of crime in the past; it should be remembered, however, that behind the abbreviated Latin of the indictments, and the colloquial English of the depositions, there lies the whole problem of attitudes to, and definitions of, crime, whether held by the ruling elite, by parish officers, or by the criminals themselves. It is not entirely irrelevant to turn to the opinions of a writer brought up in the country in the earlier part of the present century:

> As for us boys, it is certain that most of us, at some stage or other of our growth, would have been rounded up under present law, and quite a few shoved into reform school. Instead we emerged – culpable it's true – but unclassified in criminal record. No wilder than Battersea boys, we were less ensnared by by-laws. If caught in the act, we got a quick bashing; and the fist of the farmer we'd robbed of apples or eggs seemed more natural and just than any cold-mouthed copper adding one more statistic for the book. It is not crime that has increased but its definition. The modern city, for youth, is a police trap.[26]

The crimes a society experiences, and the processes that lead to their prosecution, are infinitely varied. They depend upon the level of economic development of that society, and upon its economic and social structure; upon the nature of its legal code, and upon the ability and willingness of the law-enforcement agencies to prosecute those who contravene it. They are also affected by the attitudes of the populace at large to different types of crime, and their readiness to report them. All of these are fit subjects of study for the student of the history of crime, and in the next few years much time will be spent exploring them. It is hoped that this book will contribute at least something to this growing area of historical investigation.

Notes

Abbreviations and conventions

Acts P.C.	*Acts of the Privy Council of England*
Ag. hist. rev.	*The Agricultural history review*
Am. hist. rev.	*The American historical review*
Annales E.S.C.	*Annales, économies, sociétés, civilisations*
Blackstone, *Commentaries*	William Blackstone, *Commentaries on the laws of England*, 4th edn (4 vols., 1771)
Cal. Com. Comp.	*Calendar of the proceedings of the Committee for Compounding &c. preserved in the State Paper Department of Her Majesty's Public Record Office*, 5 vols. (1889–92)
Cal. S.P. Dom.	*Calendar of State Papers, Domestic*
Coke, *Third institute*	Sir Edward Coke, *The Third part of the institutes of the laws of England: concerning high treason, and other pleas of the crown, and criminal causes* (1644)
Dalton, *Countrey justice*	Michael Dalton, *The countrey justice: containing the practice of the justices of the peace out of their sessions: gathered for the better help of such justices of peace, as have not been much conversant in the study of the laws of this realm*, 10th edn (1677)
D.N.B.	*Dictionary of national biography*
Econ. hist. rev.	*The Economic history review*
Eng. hist. rev.	*The English historical review*
E.R.O.	Essex Record Office
Hale, *Pleas of the crown*	Sir Matthew Hale, *Pleas of the crown, or a brief, but full account of whatsoever can be found relating to that subject* (1678). T. Dogherty's edition (2 vols., 1800) has been used
Holdsworth, *History of English law*	W. S. Holdsworth, *A History of English law*, ed. A. L. Goodhart and H. G. Hanbury (17 vols., 1903–72)
Josselin, *Diary*	*The diary of Ralph Josselin, 1616–1683*, ed. Alan Macfarlane (Records of social and economic history, new ser., 3, 1976)
Lambarde, *Eirenarcha*	William Lambarde, *Eirenarcha: or of the office of the justices of peace in foure bookes, gathered 1579: first published 1581: and now secondly revised, corrected and enlarged agreeably to the reformed commission of the peace*, 7th edn (1592)

Morant, *Essex*   Philip Morant, *The history and antiquities of the county of Essex* (2 vols., 1816)
P.R.O.   Public Record Office
Radzinowicz, *History of   Leon Radzinowicz, *A history of English criminal
English criminal law*   law and its administration from 1750* (4 vols., 1948–68)
Stephen, *History of the   J. F. Stephen, *A history of the criminal law of
criminal law*   England* (3 vols., 1883)
Trans. Royal Hist. Soc.   *Transactions of the Royal Historical Society*
V.C.H. Essex   *The Victoria history of the counties of England: a history of Essex* (6 vols., in progress, 1903–   )

The place of publication of books and pamphlets is London unless otherwise stated

1 Problems, sources and methods

1 L. O. Pike, *A history of crime in England* (2 vols., 1873–6), vol. 1, p. 5.
2 An example is provided by the relevant volume of that epitome of the textbook, the *Oxford History of England* series. Following the references to 'the criminal' given in the index, the reader finds discussions of the poor law, debtors, prisons, vagrancy, cheats, and transportation to the colonies. See G. Davies, *The early Stuarts*, 2nd edn (Oxford, 1959), pp. 301–4, 321, 449.
3 Radzinowicz, *History of English criminal law.*
4 See, for example, Baker's 'Introduction' to vol. 2 of *The reports of Sir John Spelman* (Selden Society, 94, 1978).
5 *Prosecuting crime in the Renaissance: England, Germany, France* (Cambridge, Mass., 1974); and *Torture and the law of proof: Europe and England in the ancien régime* (Chicago and London, 1977).
6 *History of crime in England.*
7 *Crime and public order in England in the later middle ages* (1973).
8 *Crime and industrial society in the nineteenth century* (1967).
9 *Crime and punishment in early modern Europe* (Hassocks, Sussex, 1979).
10 Alan Macfarlane, *Witchcraft in Tudor and Stuart England* (1970), p. 9.
11 *Albion's fatal tree: crime and society in eighteenth-century England*, ed. Douglas Hay, Peter Linebaugh, John G. Rule, E. P. Thompson and Cal Winslow (1975); E. P. Thompson, *Whigs and hunters: the origin of the Black Act* (1975); John G. Rule, 'Social crime in the rural south in the eighteenth and early nineteenth centuries', *Southern history*, 1 (1979), 135–53.
12 'Preface', *Albion's fatal tree*, ed. Hay et al., p. 14.
13 *Ibid.*
14 Such collections, apart from *Albion's fatal tree*, include *Crime in England 1550–1800*, ed. J. S. Cockburn (1977); *An ungovernable people: the English and their law in the seventeenth and eighteenth centuries*, ed. John Brewer and John Styles (1980); *Crime and the law: the social history of crime in western Europe since 1500*, ed. V. A. C. Gatrell, Bruce Lenman and Geoffrey Parker (1980); and *The journal of social history*, 8, no. 4 (Summer, 1975), which is devoted entirely to articles on the history of crime, most of them dealing with late medieval and early modern England.
15 For an example of the value of such a study see R. W. Malcolmson, 'Infanticide in the eighteenth century', *Crime in England 1550–1800*, ed. J. S. Cockburn (1977).

16 So far, little on this subject has appeared in print. For a stimulating examination of one of the more relevant aspects of the problem, see Keith Wrightson, 'The puritan reformation of manners, with special reference to the counties of Lancashire and Essex, 1640–1660' (Cambridge University Ph.D. thesis, 1973).

17 The most familiar corpus of such material surviving from early modern England is the extensive rogue literature which flourished in the Elizabethan and Jacobean periods: two collections of this literature are *The Elizabethan underworld*, ed. A. V. Judges (1930); and *Cony-catchers and bawdy baskets*, ed. Gamini Salgado (Harmondsworth, 1972).

18 The pioneering study using such an approach is J. A. Sharpe, 'Crime and delinquency in an Essex parish 1600–1640', *Crime in England 1550–1800*, ed. J. S. Cockburn (1977). A more developed study, again based on Essex materials, is provided by Keith Wrightson and David Levine, *Poverty and piety in an English village: Terling 1525–1700* (New York, San Francisco and London, 1979).

19 A. H. A. Hamilton, *Quarter sessions from Queen Elizabeth to Queen Anne* (1878); *Middlesex county records*, ed. J. C. Jeaffreson (4 vols., Middlesex County Record Soc., 1886–92).

20 J. M. Beattie, 'The pattern of crime in England, 1660–1800', *Past and present*, 72 (1974), 47–95; J. S. Cockburn, 'The nature and incidence of crime in England 1559–1625: a preliminary survey', *Crime in England 1550–1800*, ed. J. S. Cockburn (1977). Such an approach was also used in the first doctoral thesis to study crime in the Stuart period: T. C. Curtis, 'Some aspects of the history of crime in seventeenth-century England, with special reference to Cheshire and Middlesex' (Manchester University Ph.D. thesis, 1973).

21 James Buchanan Given, *Society and homicide in thirteenth-century England* (Stanford, California, 1977); Barbara A. Hanawalt, *Crime and conflict in English communities, 1300–1348* (Cambridge, Mass., and London, 1979).

22 *Law and order in historical perspective: the case of Elizabethan Essex* (New York and London, 1974).

23 These are sketched economically and forcefully in a review by T. C. Curtis in *Social history*, 2 (1976), 261.

24 Cockburn, 'Nature and incidence of crime'; Beattie, 'Pattern of crime'.

25 It is worth noting that a number of historians of nineteenth-century crime have used such an approach, and their researches must be added to the medieval and early modern works mentioned above. See, for example, David Philips, *Crime and authority in Victorian England: the Black Country 1835–1860* (1977); and V. A. C. Gatrell, 'The decline of theft and violence in Victorian and Edwardian England', *Crime and the law*, ed. Gatrell, Lenman and Parker (1980).

26 The best introduction to current research being carried out abroad is the *Newsletter* of the International Association for the History of Crime and Criminal Justice.

27 *Crime and punishment in early Massachusetts* (Boston, 1966).

28 *Wayward puritans: a study in the sociology of deviance* (New York, 1966).

29 *Crime and law enforcement in the Colony of New York, 1691–1776* (Ithaca and London, 1976).

30 The more important of these have been collected in *Crimes et criminalité en France sous l'Ancien Régime, 17ᵉ et 18ᵉ siècles*, ed. F. Billaçois (Cahiers des Annales, 33, Paris, 1971), which also contains a bibliography of French writing on the subject, including articles in regional publications. Another

collection of relevant articles on French materials is *Deviants and the abandoned in French society*, ed. Robert Forster and Orest Ranum (selections from *Annales E.S.C.*, vol. 4, Baltimore and London, 1978).

31 *Justice et répression en Languedoc à l'époque des lumières* (Paris, 1980).
32 'Introduction: crime and the historian', *Crime in England 1550–1800*, ed. J. S. Cockburn (1977), p. 2.
33 Holdsworth, *History of English law*, vol. 5, pp. 302–3, suggests a growing differentiation in the sixteenth and seventeenth centuries.
34 Indeed, historians of a radical persuasion might reject such a definition altogether. Douglas Hay, for example, comments that 'to say that crime is what is forbidden by law is clearly not a helpful definition, unless as a reminder that criminology is ideology': see 'Crime, authority and the criminal law: Staffordshire 1750–1800' (University of Warwick Ph.D. thesis, 1975), fol. 9.
35 Essex records are described in F. G. Emmison, *Guide to the Essex Record Office* (Chelmsford, 1969). Essex borough documents not in the custody of the E.R.O. are listed in *Calendar of muniments in possession of the borough of Harwich with the report of the borough muniment committee* (Harwich, 1932), and in *Repertory of the records and evidence of the borough of Colchester*, ed. H. Harrod (Colchester, 1865). F. G. Emmison, *Elizabethan life: disorder* (Chelmsford, 1970) is based on the Elizabethan assize and quarter sessions records of the county, and gives a broad if unsystematic impression of their contents.
36 Blackstone, *Commentaries*, vol. 4, p. 299.
37 1 Hen. V cap. 5.
38 See Blackstone, *Commentaries*, vol. 4, pp. 301–2.
39 J. S. Cockburn, 'Early modern assize records as historical evidence', *Journal of the Society of Archivists*, 5 (1975), 215–31.
40 This assertion may be corrected by Cockburn's promised future examination of the subject: see 'Early modern assize records', p. 228.
41 This point is elaborated above, pp. 91–2, 146.
42 Cockburn has checked the dates given on indictments for Hertfordshire assizes against those given on recognizances, a class of document that does not survive on the Essex assize files. Examination of a sample of Essex quarter sessions rolls (those for 1624) indicated that similar problems existed for the dating of felony indictments tried at that court when checked against recognizances: E.R.O., Q/SR 243–6, *passim*.
43 The indictments were found in P.R.O., ASSI 44/13–18, *passim*.; the depositions in *ibid.*, 45/7/1–45/9/2, *passim*.
44 Alan Macfarlane, *The justice and the mare's ale: law and disorder in seventeenth-century England* (Oxford, 1981), chapter 4, 'Raising the hue and cry'. For a perceptive critique of Cockburn's views, see Macfarlane's review essay dealing with one of the volumes of *A calendar of assize records*, ed. J. S. Cockburn (in progress, 1975–   ), in *The American journal of legal history*, 24 (1980), 171–7.
45 See above, table 12, p. 124; table 4, p. 95, respectively.
46 Blackstone, *Commentaries*, vol. 4, pp. 313–16, describes the process upon indictments for misdemeanour.
47 See above, table 9, p. 117.
48 Sharpe, 'Crime and delinquency', pp. 98, 100–2; Wrightson and Levine, *Poverty and piety*, pp. 120–5.
49 'Early modern assize records', p. 230.

50 See J. S. Cockburn, 'Seventeenth-century clerks of assizes – some anonymous members of the legal profession', *The American journal of legal history*, 13 (1969), 315–32.

51 For this reason tables giving details of punishment of offenders do not include a detailed breakdown of punishment by social status. Details of the alleged social status of those accused are, however, given at the foot of such tables.

52 For good examples, see the investigations of alehouses and popish recusants in 1644, E.R.O., Q/SBa 2/6; and those attached to the Trinity 1671 assize file, P.R.O., ASSI 35/112/8.

53 Indictments following presentment have been classed as ordinary indictments. There were also a large number of draft indictments drawn up on paper in the first few years of the period covered by this study, E.R.O., Q/SBa 1/39–47, the last of these being from 1623. Their purpose is unclear, and there is only rare evidence of their having formed the basis for trial. They have not, therefore, been totalled with the standard indictments.

54 Dalton, *Countrey justice*, p. 457.

55 1 & 2 Philip and Mary cap. 13, which instituted the practice for persons being bailed, and 2 & 3 Philip and Mary cap. 10, which extended it to persons being committed to prison. The background to this legislation is described, and some wider issues relevant to it raised, in Langbein, *Prosecuting crime in the Renaissance*.

56 'Crime and the historian', p. 2.

2 Essex: a county and its government

1 The starting point for any discussion of the Essex economy during this period must be that provided by two doctoral theses, F. Hull, 'Agriculture and rural society in Essex, 1560–1640' (London University Ph.D. thesis, 1950), and K. H. Burley, 'The economic development of Essex in the later seventeenth and early eighteenth centuries' (London University Ph.D. thesis, 1957), neither of which has been much modified by more recent work. *V.C.H. Essex*, vol. 2, has dated (it was published in 1907), but still contains some useful information, and has some very apposite quotations from Tudor and Stuart sources. Of these John Norden, *Speculi Britanniae pars: an historical and chorographical description of the county of Essex* (Camden Soc., old ser., 9, 1840) has been used extensively by historians of the county, as have the relevant sections of a work by the Elizabethan incumbent of Radwinter parish, William Harrison, *The description of England*, ed. G. Edelen (Ithaca, New York, 1968). Daniel Defoe, *A tour through the whole island of Great Britain* (Harmondsworth, 1971), especially pp. 47–66, gives that author's impressions of the county in the early eighteenth century. A. F. J. Brown, *Essex at work 1700–1815* (Chelmsford, 1969) is a useful description of eighteenth-century conditions and contains much of relevance to the earlier period. A brief outline of Essex agriculture is given in Joan Thirsk, 'The farming regions of England', *The agrarian history of England and Wales, vol. 4, 1500–1640*, ed. Joan Thirsk (Cambridge, 1967), pp. 53–5, while further background to the county's economic life in the sixteenth century, much of it of an anecdotal nature, can be found in F. G. Emmison, *Elizabethan life: home, work & land* (Chelmsford, 1976). Further information on the life of the county in the period is given in B. W. Quintrell, 'The government of the county of Essex, 1603–1642' (London University Ph.D. thesis, 1965). See also map 1.

2 See those quoted in *V.C.H. Essex*, vol. 2, p. 358.

3 For the background to this process see F. J. Fisher, 'The development of the London food market, 1540–1640', *Econ. hist. rev.*, 5 (1935), 46–64.

4 The problem is discussed at length in E. F. Farrell, 'Essex rural settlement: some aspects of its evolution, with particular reference to the sixteenth century' (University of Wales M.A. dissertation, 1969).

5 Hull, 'Agriculture and rural society', fols. 474–80. The parish in question was Heydon.

6 Burley, 'Economic development of Essex', fols. 337–8.

7 Deeper insights into the farming life of this area are provided by *Farm and cottage inventories of mid-Essex, 1635–1749*, ed. F. W. Steer (Essex Record Office publications, 8, Chelmsford, 1950).

8 Neither of these developments was new, but the comments of Defoe, *Tour*, pp. 48–9, suggest that they accelerated considerably from the closing years of the seventeenth century.

9 Burley, 'Economic development of Essex', fol. 213.

10 The Essex textile industry is touched upon in most of the works cited in n. 1 above. More specialised are J. E. Pilgrim, 'The cloth industry in Essex and Suffolk, 1558–1640' (London University M.A. thesis, 1938), and L. Roker, 'The Flemish and Dutch communities in Colchester in the sixteenth and seventeenth centuries' (London University M.A. thesis, 1963). B. E. Supple, *Commercial crisis and change in England, 1600–1642: a study in the instability of a mercantile economy* (Cambridge, 1959), is essential to any understanding of the textile trade during this period, while Joan Thirsk, 'Industries in the countryside', *Essays in the economic and social history of Tudor and Stuart England*, ed. F. J. Fisher (Cambridge, 1961), not only raises some important general issues but also offers some pertinent observations on the Suffolk textile industries that may be equally applicable to Essex.

11 See D. C. Coleman, 'An innovation and its diffusion: the "new draperies" ', *Econ. hist. rev.*, 2nd ser. 12 (1969), 417–29; and J. E. Pilgrim, 'The rise of the "new draperies" in Essex', *University of Birmingham historical journal*, 7 (1959–60), 36–59.

12 The impact of some of the more serious of these is considered in chapter 11 above.

13 Quoted in Brown, *Essex at work*, p. 17.

14 This conclusion is based on a comparison of the estimates of population given by Hull, 'Agriculture and rural society', fol. 122, and Burley, 'Economic development of Essex', fol. 11. Farrell, 'Essex rural settlement', fol. 155, suggests that any excess population in the county would have been absorbed by London.

15 Farrell, 'Essex rural settlement', fol. 22.

16 Burley, 'Economic development of Essex', fol. 372, points out that the wage assessments of 1651, 1661 and 1705 were 'virtually identical'.

17 For a recent discussion of the operation of courts in this period, see J. H. Baker, 'Criminal courts and procedure at common law 1550–1800', *Crime in England 1550–1800*, ed. J. S. Cockburn (1977).

18 Essex quarter sessions records for this period are described in F. G. Emmison, *Guide to the Essex Record Office* (Chelmsford, 1969), pp. 1–47, *passim*. The only part of these records so far published is the *Essex quarter sessions order book 1652–1661*, ed. D. H. Allen (Essex edited texts, 1, 1974).

19 J. S. Cockburn, *A history of English assizes, 1558–1714* (Cambridge, 1972),

p. 91, suggests that it was customary in the late sixteenth century for JPs to refer 'difficult cases' to the assize judges, this procedure being regularised by C. J. Wray's reform of the Commission of the Peace in 1590. On the evidence of the Essex quarter sessions, after 1620 almost every case likely to involve capital punishment was classed as 'difficult'.

20 For the early development of petty sessions and similar justices' meetings in Essex see F. G. Emmison, *Elizabethan life: disorder* (Chelmsford, 1970), pp. 28–35; and Quintrell, 'Government of Essex', fols. 48–63.

21 33 Hen. VIII cap. 10.

22 This is printed in J. C. Cox, *Three centuries of Derbyshire annals as illustrated by the records of the quarter sessions of the county of Derby from Queen Elizabeth to Queen Victoria* (2 vols., 1890), vol. 2, pp. 4–6.

23 This order is reprinted in J. P. Kenyon, *The Stuart constitution, 1603–1688* (Cambridge, 1966), p. 499.

24 The location of the divisions and other elements in the county's administrative system is given on map 2.

25 P.R.O., S.P. 16/270/5; 16/271/30; 16/329/48; 16/364/83; 16/347/73.

26 See E.R.O., Q/SR 313/58; 423/20; 440/82.

27 E.R.O., Q/SBa 2/27; 2/30; Q/SR 314/63, respectively.

28 This may be inferred from the preamble to 37 Hen. VIII cap. 7, which repealed 33 Hen. VIII cap. 10.

29 Descriptions of the early history of the assizes can be found in F. Pollock and F. W. Maitland, *The history of English law before the time of Edward I*, 2nd edn (2 vols., Cambridge, 1968), vol. 1, pp. 136–49; S. F. C. Milsom, *Historical foundations of the common law* (1969), pp. 114–19; and the introduction to *Somerset assize orders, 1629–1640*, ed. T. G. Barnes (Somerset Record Soc., 65, 1959). Several county record societies have published medieval assize rolls, and the introduction to *The earliest Lincolnshire assize rolls, A.D. 1202–1209*, ed. D. M. Stenton (Lincoln Record Soc. publications, 22, 1926) was found very useful. A full picture of the workings of the assizes in the seventeenth century is provided by Cockburn, *History of English assizes*, which also contains a brief account of the origins of the court. Cockburn is engaged in editing *A calendar of assize records* in which details of Home circuit indictments (P.R.O., ASSI 35) for the Elizabethan and Jacobean periods are calendared.

30 The origins of gaol delivery are described in R. B. Pugh, *Imprisonment in medieval England* (Cambridge, 1968), chapter 12, 'The earlier history of gaol delivery', and chapter 13, 'The later history of gaol delivery'.

31 For an excellent description of the grand jury in another county see J. S. Morrill, *The Cheshire grand jury 1625–1659: a social and administrative study* (Leicester University, Department of English Local History, Occasional Papers, 3rd ser., 1, 1976). Morrill's findings, in terms of both the social composition of the grand jury and the scope of its interests, seem generally applicable to the Essex grand juries, whether of the assizes or of the quarter sessions.

32 The assizes already displayed the spectacle and ceremony which were so important in emphasising the majesty of the law in the eighteenth century, a phenomenon placed in its context in Douglas Hay, 'Property, authority and the criminal law', in *Albion's fatal tree*, ed. Hay *et al.* (1975), pp. 26–31; see the comments of Joel Samaha, *Law and order in historical perspective: the case of Elizabethan Essex* (New York and London, 1974), p. 95, on ceremony at the

Hilary 1594 assizes. The minister delivering the sermon at the Trinity 1678 assizes felt that 'The awful Solemnities which attend Courts of Judicature' could overawe defendants of 'low and common Education'; see Anthony Walker, *Say on: or, a seasonable plea for a full hearing betwixt man and man, and, a serious plea for the like hearing betwixt God and man, delivered in a sermon at Chelmsford in Essex, at the general assize holden for the said county, July 8 1678* (1679), p. 13.

33 The uncontroversial and conventional nature of the ideas found in assize sermons is stressed by Barbara White, 'Assize sermons 1660–1720' (C.N.A.A., Polytechnic of Newcastle-upon-Tyne, 1980, Ph.D. thesis), which also contains details of assize sermons preached in Essex in the period it covers. Pre-1660 sermons, often imbued with Calvinist ideas on human sinfulness, probably tended to be less bland than their post-Restoration successors: for a typical example, kindly brought to my attention by Keith Thomas, see N[ath] B[ownd], *Saint Paul's trumpet, sounding an alarme to iudgement. Warning all men to prepare themselves against their appearing before Christ's tribunall. Delivered in two sermons, commanded by publique authoritie to be preached: the one at Paul's Crosse: the other at the assizes at Chelmsford in Essex, July 24 1615* (1615).

34 A very full description is provided by the anonymous *The office of the clerk of assize, containing the form and method of the proceedings at the assizes as also on the crown and* nisi prius *side. Together with the office of the clerk of the peace* (1676); this may be supplemented by the list of 'Rules' to be observed at sessions noted down by Richard Bragge, a Chichester lawyer and deputy clerk of the peace for West Sussex, printed in *Quarter sessions order book 1642–1649*, ed. B. C. Redwood (Sussex Record Soc. publications, 54, n.d.), pp. 210–14. Dalton, *Countrey justice*, pp. 531–8, also describes the running of a sessions. These sources indicate that trial procedure at the assizes and quarter sessions was roughly similar. Cockburn, *History of English assizes*, chapter 6, 'Criminal proceedings', demonstrates that the actual conduct of trials was often less smooth than these accounts would suggest.

35 In theory the trial jury retired to consider its verdict, although it is probable that this practice was dispensed with if business was especially heavy. However, Cockburn, *History of English assizes*, p. 123, states that it was still customary for juries to retire in the seventeenth century, although they ceased to do so in the eighteenth. It is interesting to note in this connection a complaint made at the Hereford assizes in 1658 against 'the great obstruct[i]on of the proceedings att the Assizes for want of a convenient roome for the Grand Inquest & Jurye of life & death to consider of their verdicts, they being now sent to Innes & alehouses'; P.R.O., ASSI 2/1, fol. 6. See the comments of Samaha, *Law and order in perspective*, p. 93, on the speed of trials at the Essex assizes. The business of the assizes was normally completed in two days, that of the quarter sessions in three.

36 Cockburn, *History of English assizes*, p. 122.

37 The evolution of the concept of the misdemeanour is described by Holdsworth, *History of English law*, vol. 2, p. 360; vol. 3, p. 318. The use of the traverse is described by Dalton, *Countrey justice*, p. 552. The decision to traverse an indictment led to process which could continue over several sessions. Unfortunately, process records for the Essex assizes and quarter sessions are defective in this period, and the outcome of only a few cases can be determined.

38 Punishment is described at greater length in chapter 9 above.

39 Coke, *Third institute*, pp. 210–11.
40 See Stephen, *History of the criminal law*, vol. 1, pp. 298–301, for the history of this practice. Refusal to plead prevented the confiscation of goods that still, theoretically, could follow conviction for felony. In practice, juries normally resorted to the legal fiction that convicted felons were propertyless, and standing mute was a rare phenomenon. Only two examples have been found in the records consulted for the present study: P.R.O., ASSI 35/63/1/36–9; Colchester borough records, S/R 37/11, 16, 17.
41 The history of benefit of clergy is described in Blackstone, *Commentaries*, vol. 4, pp. 358–67, and Holdsworth, *History of English law*, vol. 3, pp. 293–302. A. L. Cross, 'The English criminal law and benefit of clergy during the eighteenth and early nineteenth centuries', *Am. hist. rev.*, 22 (1917), 544–65, has some useful observations on earlier practice, as does L. C. Gabel, *Benefit of clergy in England in the later middle ages* (Smith College studies in history, 14, Northampton, Mass., 1928–9). Convicted pregnant women enjoyed a suspension of execution until after the birth of the child: Radzinowicz, *History of English criminal law*, vol. 1, p. 12, n. 35.
42 4 Hen. VII cap. 13.
43 P.R.O., ASSI 35/96/1/1. The formula is a standard one.
44 A lively antiquarian account of these punishments, well illustrated, is W. Andrews, *Punishments in the olden time* (1881).
45 The standard account of the origins and significance of the King's Bench is G. O. Sayles, *The court of King's Bench in law and history* (Selden Society lecture, 1959). The court's history in the later middle ages has been subjected to a searching reappraisal by Marjorie Blatcher, *The court of King's Bench 1450–1550: a study in self-help* (University of London legal series, 12, 1978).
46 See Blackstone, *Commentaries*, vol. 4, pp. 315–16 on the use of the *certiorari*.
47 The King's Bench Ancient Indictments for this period (P.R.O., K.B. 9/757–931) were searched for Essex references.
48 *The third report of the Deputy Keeper of the Public Records* (1842), appendix 2, pp. 215–30.
49 The early development of manorial courts is described in S. and B. Webb, *English local government from the Revolution to the Municipal Corporations Act. Part two: the manor and the borough* (1908). A number of contemporary handbooks dealt with the running of the manorial courts, two of the most popular being William Sheppard, *The court keeper's guide for the keeping of courts leet and courts baron*, 7th edn (1685); and William Greenwood, Βουλευτηριον *or a practical demonstration of country judicatures, wherein is amply explained the judicial and ministerial authority of sheriffs and coroners*, 6th edn (1675). The continued vitality and importance of the leet in Stuart England has recently been stressed by Walter J. King, 'Leet jurors and the search for law and order in seventeenth-century England: "galling persecution" or reasonable justice?', *Histoire sociale – social history*, 13 (1980), 305–23, while the work of Essex manorial courts in the Elizabethan period is described at length in Emmison, *Home, work & land*, pp. 197–333.
50 S. and B. Webb, *Manor and borough*, p. 116.
51 Perhaps the most remarkable example of this phenomenon is Manchester; see *The court leet records of the manor of Manchester*, ed. J. P. Earwaker (12 vols., 1884–90), covering the period 1552–1846. For general comments on the importance of Essex leets see Emmison, *Guide to the Essex Record Office*, p. 90.

52 Emmison, *Guide to the Essex Record Office*, p. 90; S. and B. Webb, *Manor and borough*, p. 74.
53 This is one of the major themes of King, 'Leet jurors and the search for law'; the Essex leet materials listed in the bibliography support King's views, which are based mainly on Lancashire leet records, at least until the mid seventeenth century. After this date the quantity and variety of leet business declined in Essex: cf. the situation described at Earls Colne in Alan Macfarlane, Sarah Harrison and Charles Jardin, *Reconstructing historical communities* (Cambridge, 1977), pp. 56–7.
54 Sheppard, *The court keeper's guide*, p. 13.
55 E.R.O., D/DU 65/57, fol. 36.
56 The system of church courts is outlined by Holdsworth, *History of English Law*, vol. 1, pp. 598–632.
57 Studies of archdeaconry courts consulted include: J. P. Anglin, 'The court of the archdeacon of Essex, 1571–1609' (University of California Ph.D. thesis, 1965); Robert Peters, *Oculus episcopi: administration in the archdeaconry of St Albans 1580–1625* (Manchester, 1963); R. A. Marchant, *The church under the law: justice, administration and discipline in the diocese of York, 1560–1640* (Cambridge, 1969); and E. R. Brinkworth, 'The study and use of archdeacons' court records: illustrated from the Oxford records (1556–1759)', *Trans. Royal Hist. Soc.*, 4th ser., 25 (1943), 93–120. One aspect of the ecclesiastical courts' activities is illustrated, if a little unsystematically, in *Before the bawdy court: selections from church court and other records relating to the correction of moral offences in England, Scotland and New England, 1300–1800*, ed. Paul Hair (1972). F. G. Emmison, *Elizabethan life: morals & the church courts* (Chelmsford, 1973), is a wide-ranging if anecdotal study based mainly on archdeacons' court records from Essex. M. J. Ingram, 'Ecclesiastical justice in Wiltshire 1600–1640, with special reference to cases concerning sex and marriage' (Oxford University D.Phil. thesis, 1976), has a much sounder and more imaginative approach to the problem of the impact of the church courts on society.
58 Quintrell, 'Government of Essex', fols. 145–6.
59 The correction side of the archdeacon's court, of course, was only one aspect of its work. Like other church courts, it also dealt with suits between parties, as well as with testamentary and probate cases.
60 Emmison, *Elizabethan life: disorder, passim.*
61 E.R.O., Q/SR 286/39, 40.
62 See P.R.O., ASSI 35/84/9/43 for an aggrieved Colchester taxpayer who claimed that the assize judges had no right to apportion taxation in the borough.
63 E.R.O., Q/SR 227/22.
64 This impression is shared by Quintrell, 'Government of Essex', fol. 65.
65 Works consulted in connection with the history and powers of the JP include: J. H. Gleason, *The justices of the peace in England, 1558 to 1640* (Oxford, 1969); E. Moir, *The justice of the peace* (Harmondsworth, 1969); B. H. Putnam, 'The transformation of the keepers of the peace into the justices of the peace 1327–1380', *Trans. Royal Hist. Soc.*, 4th ser., 12 (1929), 19–48; and the two best-known justices' handbooks of the period, Lambarde, *Eirenarcha*, and Dalton, *Countrey justice*. For a recent description of justices at work see G. C. F. Forster, *The East Riding justices of the peace in the seventeenth century* (East Yorkshire local history series, 30, 1973).
66 The administrative duties imposed on the justices by statute are listed in Lambarde, *Eirenarcha*, pp. 189–205, 299–349.

67 Dalton, *Countrey justice*, p. 19.

68 Sir Edward Coke, *The fourth part of the institutes of the laws of England: concerning the jurisdiction of courts*, 4th edn (1669), p. 170.

69 See the comments of Gleason, *Justices of the peace*, especially pp. 66–7.

70 The development of the Essex bench in the Elizabethan period is traced by Joel Samaha in Emmison, *Elizabethan life: disorder*, appendix F, pp. 321–6. The justices of the early Stuart period are described in Quintrell, 'Government of Essex', fols. 38–45.

71 This is the impression given by Quintrell, 'Government of Essex', *passim*.; see also Clive Holmes, *The Eastern Association in the English Civil War* (Cambridge, 1974), pp. 21–3, 26, 28.

72 This conclusion is based on a study of the lists of JPs given in quarter sessions rolls between Epiphany 1648 and Michaelmas 1650, E.R.O., Q/SR 334–46.

73 *The autobiography of Sir John Bramston, K.B.*, ed. P. Braybrooke (Camden Soc., old ser., 32, 1844), *passim*.

74 The activities and origins of these and other justices in the years before the Civil Wars are discussed at length in Quintrell, 'Government of Essex', *passim*.

75 This impression is based on a search of the Essex quarter sessions rolls, 1650–4, and the sessions bundles for the same period; E.R.O., Q/SR 343–62, and Q/SBa 2/72–90.

76 For Alleyn's early involvement in local government in the county, see E.R.O., Q/SR 241/37; 318/14; for his immediate family background, see Morant, *Essex*, vol. 1, pp. 343–4.

77 This impression is based on a search of the Essex quarter sessions rolls 1665–9 E.R.O., Q/SR 403/21.

78 See S. T. Bindoff, *Tudor England* (Harmondsworth, 1950), p. 57, who comments that in the late sixteenth century 'the chief threat to the efficiency of the JP was the weight and complexity of his duties' and describes the JP of this period as 'a willing horse struggling with a gigantic burden'. Such men may have existed, in the shape of the Lambardes, the Herons and the Heighams, but they were the exception.

79 E.R.O., D/DU 262; D/DCv 1, respectively. It should be remembered that both these justices were active in other aspects of local government.

80 The standard work on the clerk of the peace is T. G. Barnes, *The clerk of the peace in Caroline Somerset* (Leicester University, Department of English Local History, Occasional Papers, 14, 1961). The duties of the office are set out in *The office of the clerk of assize*. As Barnes, *Clerk of the peace*, p. 7, points out, most of the routine work of the office was, by the early seventeenth century, carried out by the deputy clerk.

81 Quintrell, 'Government of Essex', fols. 40, 67. A list of Essex *custodes rotulorum* is given in R. B. Colvin, *The lieutenants and keepers of the rolls of the county of Essex* (1934).

82 See Quintrell, 'Government of Essex', fols. 68–9 for a favourable description of Eldred's work. For his will see E.R.O., D/ABV 45/13.

83 For Pulley's involvement in county administration see *Cal. S.P. Dom. 1633–4*, pp. 321–2, 323–4, 473, 488; *Cal. S.P. Dom., 1636–7*, p. 362; *Cal. Com. Comp.* vol. 1, p. 314; for his activities as informer see E.R.O., Q/SR 293/16, 17; 299/107; 311/25.

84 For Goldsborough's will see E.R.O., D/AER 21/125; for details of the family, *V.C.H. Essex*, vol. 4, p. 161.

85 The standard work on the sheriff for this period is C. H. Karraker, *The seventeenth-century sheriff* (Chapel Hill, 1930). A useful description of the

work of the sheriff in one English county is T. G. Barnes, *Somerset 1625–1640* (1961), chapter 5, 'Shrievalty'. A contemporary guide was John Wilkinson, *A treatise collected out of the statutes of this kingdom, and according to the common experience of the lawes, concerning the office and authorities of coroners and sherifes: together with an easie and plain method for the keeping of a court leet, court baron and hundred court &c.* (1618).

86 The problems of collecting ship money in Essex are recounted in V. A. Rowe, 'Robert, second Earl of Warwick, and the payment of ship money in Essex', *Transactions of the Essex Archaeological Society*, 3rd ser., 1 (1962), 160–3. After early troubles collection ceased to be a problem when the Earl was threatened with dismissal from the Lord Lieutenancy. For the sheriff's problems in a county where opposition was more tenacious, see Barnes, *Somerset 1625–1640*, chapter 8, 'Ship money'.

87 *Aubrey's brief lives*, ed. O. L. Dick (Harmondsworth,) 1972), p. 339; Josselin, *Diary*, p. 78, respectively.

88 Wilkinson, *A treatise*, p. 8. An Essex undersheriff in the 1680s entered into such a bond for £1,000: E.R.O., D/DFa 05.

89 Karraker, *Seventeenth-century sheriff*, p. 19. For a general background to the problem, see T. E. Hartley, 'Under-sheriffs and bailiffs in some English shrievalties, *c.* 1580 to *c.* 1625', *Bulletin of the Institute of Historical Research*, 47 (1974), 164–85.

90 E.R.O., Q/SR 342/26.

91 The early history of the English county gaol is covered by Pugh, *Imprisonment in medieval England*. He states that the sheriff was responsible for the gaol from the twelfth century.

92 P.R.O., ASSI 35/73/1/156–7; E.R.O., Q/CP, fol. 108, respectively.

93 P.R.O., K.B. 9/772/213–24; ASSI 35/68/1/114; K.B. 9/813/133–40; 9/817/340–1; 9/858/357–83.

94 P.R.O., ASSI 35/69/2/6–10, 13, 15–17, 30, 41, 46; 35/71/2/108; 35/71/3/62; 35/72/2/22.

95 *Ibid.*, 35/85/5/2.

96 E.R.O., Q/SO 1, fol. 182v.

97 The gaoler, like the bailiffs and the undersheriff, entered into a bond with the sheriff, in this case for 'the safe keeping of the prisoners': Wilkinson, *A treatise*, pp. 11–12.

98 E.R.O., Q/SR 262/26.

99 *Ibid.*, 259/9; 260/9, respectively.

100 E.R.O., Q/SBa 2/109.

101 P.R.O., K.B. 9/845/176, 177; 9/847/307, 312. All of these inquests resulted in verdicts of death by divine visitation.

102 A full list of Essex sheriffs is given in *P.R.O. lists and indexes, 9* (New York, 1963), pp. 43–8.

103 Quintrell, 'Government of Essex', fols. 91–3.

104 No adequate study of the seventeenth-century coroner exists. The early history of the office is given in R. F. Hunnisett, *The medieval coroner* (Cambridge, 1961). R. H. Wellington, *The king's coroner* (2 vols., 1905–6), includes a short history of the office and a list of relevant statutes, none of which was passed between 1585 and 1692. For the work of coroners in the early sixteenth century, see *Calendar of Nottinghamshire coroners' inquests, 1485–1558*, ed. R. F. Hunnisett (Thoroton Soc. record series, 25, 1969). A standard contemporary work was Wilkinson, *A treatise*.

105 For the history of the deodand, see Stephen, *History of the criminal law*, vol. 3, pp. 77–8.
106 Hunnisett, *Medieval coroner*, pp. 11–12.
107 They are preserved among the King's Bench Ancient Indictments, P.R.O., K.B. 9, *passim*.
108 Wilkinson, *A treatise*, pp. 6–8, gives the form of this charge.
109 Only one case of a disputed verdict following a coroner's inquest has been traced in the assize and quarter sessions records consulted in this study, P.R.O. ASSI 35/104/4. Other classes of document contain further examples, although it seems unlikely that they are very numerous. For two relevant cases in the Star Chamber see P.R.O., STAC 8/3/4; 8/125/16.
110 Morant, *Essex*, vol. 1, p. 161; *V.C.H. Essex*, vol. 4, p. 260; P.R.O., ASSI 35/80/3/3; e.g. P.R.O., K.B. 9/831/143–67, 9/834/210–26.
111 Appointments of high constables are listed in quarter sessions order books, notably E.R.O., Q/SO 2, *passim*. Draft lists of prospective candidates are found in some of the later sessions bundles; e.g. E.R.O., Q/SBa 2/108 contains such lists for Tendring, Hinckford, Lexden, Rochford, and Ongar Hundreds.
112 The early history of the constable is given in H. B. Simpson, 'The office of constable', *Eng. hist. rev.*, 10 (1895), 625–41. The constable's duties are set out in two contemporary handbooks, William Lambarde, *The duties of constables, borsholders, tithingmen, and such other low ministers of the peace. Whereunto be also adioyned the several offices of church wardens: of surveyors for amending the high waies: of distributors of the provision for noysome fowls & vermin: of the collectors: overseers: and governors of the poore: and of the wardens and collectors for the houses of correction* (1583); and William Sheppard, *The offices and duties of constables, borsholders, tything-men, treasurers of the county stock, overseers of the poore, and other lay ministers* (1641).
113 Lambarde, *Duties of constables*, p. 11.
114 Appointments by the bench were becoming more common by the 1670s: E.R.O., Q/SO 2, *passim*.
115 Sheppard, *The offices and duties of constables*, pp. 15–17.
116 Norden, *Speculi Britanniae pars*, p. 12.
117 J. A. Sharpe, 'Crime and delinquency in the Essex parish 1600–1640', *Crime in England 1550–1800*, ed. J. S. Cockburn (1977), pp. 94–5; Keith Wrightson and David Levine, *Poverty and piety in an English village: Terling 1525–1700* (New York, San Francisco and London, 1979), pp. 103–6.
118 E.R.O., Q/SR 243/34.
119 E.R.O., Q/SBa 2/76.
120 E.R.O., Q/SR 243/7.
121 E.R.O., Q/SBa 2/76.
122 See E.R.O., Q/SR 423/30, 31, 33, 34, 55, for reports of searches in five parishes.
123 Occasional *ex gratia* payments were made for exceptional devotion to duty, e.g. the £4 awarded to William Batsford, chief constable of Chelmsford Hundred, in 1650 for 'Good service done' by him: E.R.O., D/DMs 015.
124 For a typical example of this attitude see J. W. Draper, *Stratford to Dogberry* (Pittsburgh, 1961), chapter 30, 'Dogberry's due process of law'.
125 D. Ogg, *England in the reign of Charles II*, 2nd edn (2 vols., Oxford, 1956), vol. 2, p. 494. The most sophisticated appraisal of the role of the parish constable in the seventeenth century yet to appear is Keith Wrightson, 'Two

concepts of order: justices, constables and jurymen in seventeenth-century England', *An ungovernable people*, ed. John Brewer and John Styles (1980).
126 The standard work on this office is still G. Scott Thomson, *Lords lieutenants in the sixteenth century: a study in Tudor local administration* (1923) Quintrell, 'Government of Essex', provides a very clear picture of the functioning of the Essex lieutenancy during the first half of the seventeenth century.

3 The regulation of economic life

1 See table 19, p. 183 above.
2 5 Eliz. I cap. 4.
3 E. H. Sutherland, *White collar crime* (New York, 1949), p. 9. This work is the classic exposition of the concept.
4 For an elaboration of this viewpoint see J. B. Mays, *Crime and the social structure* (1963), chapter 14, 'Crime and prosperity'.
5 Daniel Defoe, *The complete English tradesman* (Dublin, 1726), pp. 178, 189.
6 *V.C.H. Essex*, vol. 2, p. 349. The offence was obviously thought to have been a serious one, for the accused was fined £1,000 and pilloried.
7 E.R.O., Q/SR 420/128; 273/89; 244/29; P.R.O., ASSI 35/104/11/21, respectively.
8 R. B. Westerfield, *Middlemen in English business, particularly between 1660 and 1760* (New Haven, 1915), p. 399.
9 Holdsworth, *History of English law*, vol. 4, p. 376.
10 E. P. Thompson, 'The moral economy of the English crowd in the eighteenth century', *Past and present*, 50 (1971), 79.
11 Fourteenth-century prosecutions before borough courts are given in Holdsworth, *History of English law*, vol. 2, p. 390.
12 N. S. B. Gras, *The evolution of the English corn market* (Cambridge, Mass., 1926), pp. 62–3.
13 Above, p. 183.
14 An excellent introduction to contemporary attitudes to dearth and to contemporary practice in dealing with it is provided by John Walter and Keith Wrightson, 'Dearth and the social order in early modern England', *Past and present*, 71 (1976), 22–42.
15 P.R.O., K.B. 9/793/51. Despite this lack of prosecutions of middlemen in times of dearth, popular opinion still regarded them as an aggravating influence in times of economic crisis; see, for example, petitions from the poor of Chelmsford in 1608 and 1647: E.R.O., Q/SR 183/62; 332/106, respectively.
16 *Cal. S.P. Dom., 1629–1631*, p. 500; *Acts P.C. June 1630 to June 1631*, pp. 226, 235, 243.
17 The activities of informers are described above, pp. 46–8.
18 P.R.O., ASSI 35/83/7/34–6; 35/83/8/15–18, 20–3.
19 E.R.O., Q/SR 386/9.
20 For Rochford Hundred's contribution to economic offences see table 20, p. 184 above.
21 E.R.O., Q/SR 314/37–43; P.R.O., ASSI 35/91/4/124–8, respectively.
22 E.R.O., Q/SR 314/37; 397/24, respectively.
23 P.R.O., ASSI 35/69/1/11–14; *Cal. S.P. Dom. 1619–1623*, p. 273, respectively.
24 Harwich borough records, Bundle 98/14, fol. 66; E.R.O., Q/CP 3, fol. 108, respectively.

25 E.R.O., Q/SBa 2/65.
26 For another example of small fines at the sessions see E.R.O., Q/SR 286/44.
27 This topic is discussed in general terms by M. G. Davies, *The enforcement of English apprenticeship, 1563–1642* (Cambridge, Mass., 1956).
28 K. H. Burley, 'The economic development of Essex in the later seventeenth and early eighteenth centuries' (London University Ph.D. thesis, 1965), fol. 379.
29 Even the rise in prosecutions in the 1660s seems to have been prompted by local initiatives, although the frequency with which those prosecuted were resident in or near Chelmsford suggests some encouragement from the county authorities: see E.R.O., Q/SR 389/11–13 (three bakers in Writtle); *ibid.*, 399/22–4 (three bakers from Moulsham); and *ibid.*, 393/30–1, 33 (three plumbers and a glazier from Chelmsford).
30 *Ibid.*, 249–57, 396/14, 301/32, respectively.
31 Richard Steele, *The tradesman's calling* (1684), p. 104.
32 Holdsworth, *History of English law*, vol. 10, p. 404.
33 A development discussed above, pp. 47–8.
34 E.R.O., D/B3/3/198.
35 E.R.O., D/DU 146/7, fols. 39ff.
36 See E.R.O., Q/SR 367/28; 388/27; 437/30.
37 John Powell's much reprinted *The assize of bread* describes these laws. The 1630 edition was consulted in connection with this work.
38 For a rare example, resulting in a 12d fine, see E.R.O., Q/SR 239/31.
39 See J. P. Kenyon, *The Stuart constitution, 1603–1688* (Cambridge, 1966), pp. 500–1, for this order, directed, incidentally, mainly to keepers of court leets.
40 These are included for analysis with drink offences, for which see table 19, p. 183 above.
41 E.R.O., D/DU 65/57, *passim*.
42 Although this offence has strong religious overtones, it was felt that it could be best fitted into a discussion of legal restraints on economic activity.
43 E.R.O., Q/SBa 2/76.
44 Discussions of this topic by R. H. Tawney and R. Keith Kelsall are collected with a useful introduction in *Wage regulation in pre-industrial England*, ed. W. E. Minchinton (Newton Abbot, 1972).
45 Burley, 'Economic development of Essex', fol. 374.
46 E.R.O., Q/SR 435/31; 436/12.
47 E.R.O., D/DCv 2/4.
48 E.R.O., Q/SR 450/60.
49 The best account of this subject is still R. H. Tawney's introduction to his edition of Thomas Wilson, *A discourse upon usury by way of dialogue and oration, for the better variety and more delight of all those that shall read this treatise* (1925).
50 13 Eliz. I cap. 8.
51 E.R.O., Q/SR 256/107; P.R.O., ASSI 35/83/7/23; 35/118/11/18–23, respectively.
52 The same conclusions for another area are reached by R. A. Marchant, *The church under the law: justice, administration and discipline in the diocese of York, 1560–1640* (Cambridge, 1969), p. 218.
53 Background to informers is provided by M. W. Beresford, 'The common informer, the penal statutes and economic regulation', *Econ. hist. rev.*, 2nd ser., 10 (1957–8), 221–38. For one area of their activities see Davies,

Enforcement of apprenticeship, chapters 1–6. For informers in another county see *Tradesmen in early Stuart Wiltshire*, ed. N. J. Williams (Wiltshire Archaeological and Natural History Soc., 15, 1960), pp. xv–xix.

54 Beresford, 'Common informer', p. 222.

55 E.R.O., Q/SR 252/129, 136, 135 respectively.

56 21 Jac. I cap. 28. Examination of the King's Remembrancer Rolls for late 1619 – early 1621, P.R.O., E. 157/9, suggests that prosecutions of Essex inhabitants before this court were comparatively infrequent in the early 1620s.

57 Coke, *Third institute*, pp. 191–4.

58 E.R.O., Q/SR 330/67.

59 E.R.O., Q/SBa 2/27.

60 E.R.O., Q/SR 241/17, 21; 242/38; Q/SBa 2/6. Two of the indictments were taken to the King's Bench, P.R.O., K.B. 9/771/116–17.

61 See above, p. 41.

62 P.R.O., ASSI 35/104/12/13–34.

63 E.R.O., Q/SPa 1/2.

64 E.R.O., Q/SR 236/84.

65 See table 19, p. 183 above.

66 For Nicholls's appointment see E.R.O., Q/SR 437/30. For indictments etc. in which he participated, *ibid.*, 417/34; 418/48, 49, 51, 53; 420/60–2, 64, 65, 70; 437/31–4; 438/51; 440/73; 441/20; 442/36; 443/40. For payments, E.R.O., Q/SO 2, fols. 9, 15, 35, 245 (where Nicholls is described as an informer), 269, 280, it being specified in these last two that Nicholls was concerned with weights and measures.

67 This point is elaborated on pp. 191–8 above.

68 The situation is further obscured, at least in the first third of the period under review, by the activities of the royal clerk of the market, whose supervision of weights and measures and other aspects of retailing caused growing resentment in the early Stuart period. An introduction to the clerk's activities is provided by *Tradesmen in early Stuart Wiltshire*, ed. Williams, pp. vii–x; for the hostility that the clerk of the market encountered in Essex, see F. Hull, 'Agriculture and rural society in Essex, 1560–1640' (London University Ph.D. thesis, 1950), fols. 146–51.

4 Drink offences

1 B. H. Harrison, *Drink and the Victorians: the temperance question in England, 1815–1872* (1971), pp. 69–70.

2 Contemporary literature on drunkenness was voluminous, some of the more accessible examples being cited below, *passim*. A typical example, by a writer of Essex origins, is Richard Younge, *The drunkard's character* (1638). A dated but still useful general survey is R. V. French, *Nineteen centuries of drink in England*, 2nd edn (1891). Contemporary unease about the problems of drunkenness and the alehouse is one of the major themes of Keith Wrightson, 'The puritan reformation of manners with special reference to the counties of Lancashire and Essex, 1640–1660 (Cambridge University Ph.D. thesis, 1973), especially chapter 4, 'Drink and drunkenness'. For evidence that this unease was not altogether unfounded see Peter Clark, 'The alehouse and the alternative society', *Puritans and revolutionaries: essays in seventeenth-century history presented to Christopher Hill*, ed. Donald Pennington and Keith Thomas (Oxford, 1978).

3 Joseph Rigbie, *An ingenious poem called the drunkards perspective of burning glass* (1656), p. 1.

4 4 Jac. I cap. 5.

5 William Prynne, *Healthes: sicknesse* (1628), sig. B3.

6 *The autobiography of Sir John Bramston K.B.,* ed. P. Braybrooke (Camden Soc., old ser., 32, 1844), pp. 18–19. The unfortunate wooer was Sir Anthony Browne.

7 A process described by French, *Nineteen centuries of drink,* pp. 214–17. The coffee house was an accepted feature of life in Chelmsford by 1677: E.R.O., Q/SR 435/41, 123.

8 1 Jac. I cap. 9; 21 Jac, I cap. 7.

9 1 Jac. I cap. 9.

10 Fynes Moryson, *An itinerary* (4 vols., Glasgow, 1908), vol. 4, pp. 174–5.

11 Joseph Bufton's Diary, quoted in Bryan Dale, *The annals of Coggeshall, otherwise Sunnedon, in the county of Essex* (Coggeshall, 1863), p. 272.

12 P.R.O., W/O 30/48, drawn up for military use in 1686, lists 173 locations in the county possessing inns or alehouses. Between them these contained 3,101 'guestbeds'.

13 B. W. Quintrell, 'The government of the county of Essex 1603–1642' (London University Ph.D. thesis, 1965), fol. 226.

14 E.R.O., Q/SBa 2/91.

15 Refusal to lodge travellers was illegal, although it was unclear how such cases should be dealt with: Dalton, *Countrey Justice,* p. 30. There are a few cases of alehouse-keepers being presented or indicted for this offence, e.g. P.R.O., ASSI 35/177/3/21.

16 See tables 19 and 22, pp. 183, 197 above. The implications of fluctuations in these figures is discussed above, pp. 191, 196.

17 There is scattered evidence of summary fining, e.g. E.R.O., Q/SR 360/77, 78; 365/65. Fines were paid into poor relief funds.

18 The first example of this practice comes from the Epiphany 1650 session, *ibid.*, 344/97.

19 E.R.O., Q/SBa 6.

20 John Walter and Keith Wrightson, 'Dearth and the social order in early modern England', *Past and present,* 71 (1976), 33–42, provide graphic evidence of this.

21 *Ibid.*, p. 40.

22 Walter and Wrightson, *ibid.*, p. 29, quote the Essex JP whose immediate reaction to the bad harvest of 1629 was to set about 'punishing 4 drunkards, 4 drinkers and 2 Alehousekeepers in one towne'.

23 P.R.O., S.P. 16/186/62.

24 Wrightson, 'Puritan reformation of manners', fol. 93.

25 E.R.O., Q/SBa 2/48. Disorder in alehouses is one of the major themes of Clark, 'The alehouse and the alternative society'.

26 Richard Allestree, *The whole duty of man* (1678), pp. 169–77.

27 *Ibid.*, p. 174.

28 E.R.O., D/AEA 36, fol. 177v.

29 *Ibid.*, 32, fol. 103.

30 See table 19, p. 183 above.

31 E.R.O., D/ACA 44, fol. 49.

32 E.R.O., D/AEA 38, fol. 226v.

33 E.R.O., Q/SBa 6/5.

34 David G. Hey, *An English rural community: Myddle under the Tudors and Stuarts* (Leicester, 1974), pp. 227–8, traces the decline in the fortunes of a number of families resulting from drunkenness, and makes some attempt to place the phenomenon in its context.
35 4 Jac. I cap. 5.
36 Younge, *The drunkard's character*, p. 63.
37 See table 20, p. 184 above.
38 E.R.O., Q/SR 271/8.
39 *Ibid.*, 259/11.
40 E.R.O., Q/SBa 2/9.
41 E.R.O., Q/SR 292/30. 41; Q/SBa 2/24.
42 E.R.O., Q/SR 378/11.
43 P.R.O., ASSI 35/76/3/59.
44 E.R.O., Q/SR 285/8.
45 *Ibid.*, 269/21.
46 *Ibid.*, 236/23.
47 *Ibid.*, 235/47.
48 E.R.O., Q/SBa 2/37.
49 4 Jac. I cap. 5.
50 E.R.O., D/B3/3/1/19, fol. 193v.
51 See table 19, p. 183 above.
52 See E.R.O., D/AEA 39, fol. 64, when five such drunkards from Hatfield Peverel were presented simultaneously.
53 Dalton, *Countrey justice*, p. 29.
54 E.R.O., D/B3/3/392/7.
55 See Younge, *The drunkard's character*, p. 20.
56 Modern sociologists have advanced the theory that drunken behaviour is to some extent socially determined by the expectations of the current 'conventional wisdom' of the society in which the drunkard grows up. For an elaboration of this theory, see C. MacAndrew and R. B. Edgerton, *Drunken comportment* (1970). It is interesting to speculate on the irony that the writings of Prynne, Younge and other moral commentators, with their catalogues of drunken sin, may have reinforced the very behaviour they attacked.
57 E.R.O., D/AEA 36, fol. 32.
58 E.R.O., Q/SR 268/54; D/AEA 32, fols. 153v, 343, respectively.
59 E.R.O., Q/SBa 2/78; Q/SR 351/24.
60 See E.R.O. Q/SBa 2/20; 2/57.
61 See p. 131 above.
62 'The wofull lamentation of William Purcas, who for murtherin his mother at Thaxted in Essex was executed at Chelmsford', *The Roxburghe ballads*, ed. W. Chappell and J. W. Ebsworth (9 vols., Hertford, 1871–9), vol. 3, pp. 28–35. The relevant indictment survives: P.R.O., ASSI 35/50/2/9.
63 N. J. Walker, *Crime and insanity in England* (2 vols., Edinburgh, 1968–73), vol. 1, pp. 177–81.
64 E.R.O., Q/SBa 2/10, Q/SR 269/17.
65 E.R.O., Q/SBa 2/20.
66 E.R.O., D/DCv 1, fol. 19v.
67 E.R.O., Q/SBa 2/41.
68 E.R.O., Q/SR 257/76.
69 E.R.O., Q/SBa 2/110.
70 E.R.O., Q/SR 259/28. Wrightson, 'Puritan reformation of manners', fol. 86,

comments that 'An ale licence . . . could be a pension which cost the parish nothing and allowed the poor the dignity of maintaining themselves in a manner useful to the community', an opinion confirmed by these examples.

71 E.R.O., Q/SR 412/62; 432/55; Q/SBa 2/100; 2/108 provide examples of this practice.
72 Dale, *Annals of Coggeshall*, p. 272.
73 E.R.O., D/DCv 1, fol. 4.

5 Sexual morality and sexual offences

1 The fullest general survey of the subject for the early modern period is Lawrence Stone, *The family, sex and marriage in England, 1500–1800* (1977), although it should be noted that this work is at its weakest when dealing with the lower orders. An earlier study, still stimulating, is G. May, *Social control of the sex expression* (1930). G. R. Taylor, *Sex in history* (1953), was also consulted, but found to be too anecdotal and prone to generalisation. Alan Macfarlane, 'The regulation of marital and sexual relationships in seventeenth-century England, with special reference to the county of Essex' (London University M.Phil. thesis, 1968), although useful is concerned mainly with the application of anthropological techniques to the problem, and makes no claim to be an exhaustive study. M. J. Ingram, 'Ecclesiastical justice in Wiltshire 1600–1640, with special reference to cases concerning sex and marriage' (Oxford University D.Phil. thesis, 1976), especially fols. 109–302, is more substantial. Another regional study, based on Somerset court materials, is G. R. Quaife, *Wanton wenches and wayward wives: peasants and illicit sex in early seventeenth-century England* (1979). One important aspect of the history of sexual behaviour in the past receives full treatment in *Bastardy and its comparative history: studies in the history of illegitimacy and marital nonconformity in Britain, France, Germany, Sweden, North America, Jamaica and Japan*, ed. Peter Laslett, Karla Oosterveen and Richard M. Smith (1980). Keith Wrightson, 'The puritan reformation of manners with special reference to the counties of Lancashire and Essex, 1640–1660' (Cambridge University Ph.D. thesis, 1973), discusses puritan attitudes to sexual morality in the general context of puritan thought.
2 The problem of bridal pregnancy is discussed by Paul Hair, 'Bridal pregnancy in rural England in earlier centuries', *Population studies*, 20 (1966), 233–43.
3 Essex materials, however, are used extensively in Alan Macfarlane, 'Illegitimacy and illegitimates in English history'; David Levine and Keith Wrightson, 'The social context of illegitimacy in early modern England'; and Keith Wrightson, 'The nadir of illegitimacy in the seventeenth century', all in *Bastardy and its comparative history*, ed. Laslett *et al.*
4 For examples of sexual offences presented before the archdeacon in the late Tudor period see F. G. Emmison, *Elizabethan life: morals & the church courts* (Chelmsford, 1973), pp. 1–47.
5 This calculation is based on figures given in J. A. Sharpe, 'Crime and delinquency in an Essex parish 1600–1640', *Crime in England 1550–1800*, ed. J. S. Cockburn (1977), p. 109.
6 *Middlesex sessions records*, ed. W. le Hardy (new ser., 4 vols., 1935–41), *passim.*
7 P.R.O., ASSI 35/76/3/61; E.R.O., Q/SR 230/3.
8 See *ibid.*, 229/47.

9 E.R.O., D/AEA 39, fol. 36.
10 *Ibid.*, 38, fol. 38v.
11 This is one of the themes of Peter Laslett, 'The bastardy-prone sub-society', *Bastardy and its comparative history*, ed. Laslett *et al.* Quaife's discussion of prostitution, *Wanton wenches and wayward wives*, pp. 146–52, confirms the impression given by a consultation of Essex court materials: there was little organised prostitution on the London scale, but there existed a stratum of semi-professional, casual, or vagrant, prostitutes. For Elizabethan examples of prostitutes and brothels presented before the archdeaconry courts see Emmison, *Morals & the church courts*, pp. 20–4.
12 E.R.O., Q/SR 441/24.
13 Colchester borough records, examination and recognizance book, 1619–45, unfoliated, 29 August 1622.
14 E.R.O., D/AEA 33, fol. 109; 34, fols. 1, 11; D/B3/3/392/59; D/B3/3/388.
15 18 Eliz. I cap. 3; 7 Jac. I cap. 4; 3 Car. I cap. 4; 13 & 14 Car. II cap. 12 s. 19.
16 See Colchester borough records, examination and recognizance book, 1647–84, unfoliated, 12 December 1668; E.R.O., Q/SBa 2/97.
17 See E.R.O., Q/SR 363/49.
18 See *ibid.*, 419/64.
19 See E.R.O., Q/SBa 2/75; Q/SR 242/118; 246/72, 73.
20 Colchester borough records, examination and recognizance book, 1619–45, unfoliated, 23 June 1645.
21 *Ibid.*, 11 March 1623; E.R.O., Q/SBa 2/27, 29.
22 See *ibid.*, 2/9, 27.
23 E.R.O., Q/SR 398/66.
24 *Ibid.*, 417/24.
25 These cases were found in *ibid.*, 344–80; and Q/SBa 2/73–101, *passim.* These materials form the basis of Wrightson, 'Nadir of illegitimacy', whose conclusions are broadly similar to those of the present writer.
26 E.R.O., Q/SR 329/69.
27 Somerset materials give much the same impression: Quaife, *Wanton wenches and wayward wives*, pp. 59–64.
28 For adverse puritan comment on this attitude see William Gouge, 'Of domesticall duties, eight treatises', *Workes* (1626), p. 118; and William Perkins, 'Oeconomy, or household government', *Workes* (1631), pp. 672–3.
29 E.R.O., D/AEA 38, fol. 50v.
30 It is instructive to note that in Plymouth Colony, New England, the normal penalty for fornication, a £10 fine or whipping, was reduced to a fine of £2/10/- if the couple involved were contracted to marry: John Demos, *A little commonwealth: family life in Plymouth Colony* (New York, 1970), p. 158.
31 This is reprinted in C. H. Firth and R. S. Rait, *Acts and ordinances of the Interregnum, 1642–1660* (3 vols., 1911), vol. 2, pp. 387–9. For a wide-ranging discussion of the background to this legislation, see Keith Thomas, 'The puritans and adultery: the Act of 1650 reconsidered', *Puritans and revolutionaries: essays in seventeenth-century history presented to Christopher Hill*, ed. Donald Pennington and Keith Thomas (Oxford, 1978).
32 A married couple accused of incest in 1653 were apparently convicted initially, although both were subsequently reprieved: P.R.O., ASSI 35/94/2/2–3.
33 Richard Burn, *Ecclesiastical law* (2 vols., 1763), vol. 2, p. 406.
34 Harwich borough records, Bundle 130/12.
35 E.R.O., Q/SBa 2/20.

36 E.R.O., D/AEA 32, fol. 153v.

37 Colchester borough records, examination and recognizance book, 1647–84, unfoliated, loose paper dated 28 February 1657.

38 E.R.O., Q/SR 335/44.

39 For a wider discussion of some of the implications of this problem, based on court materials dealing with another region, see J. A. Sharpe, *Defamation and sexual slander in early modern England: the church courts at York* (Borthwick papers, 58, 1980).

40 Wrightson, 'Puritan reformation of manners', fols. 67–8, reaches a similar conclusion after a lengthy discussion of both literary and archival sources.

41 *Ibid.*, fol. 43.

42 Peter Laslett and Karla Oosterveen, 'Long-term trends in bastardy in England: a study of the illegitimacy figures in the parish registers and the reports of the Registrar General, 1561–1960', *Population studies*, 27 (1973), 261, trace a 'very striking rise in the illegitimacy ratio' in the late sixteenth century.

43 The existence of such a group is postulated in Laslett, 'The bastardy-prone sub-society'. It seems likely that a 'sub-society' of this type did exist, and further research will doubtless confirm the impression that these bearers of several bastards were atypical.

44 See the general oblivion and pardon of February 1652, for which see Firth and Rait, *Acts and ordinances*, vol. 2, pp. 568–9.

45 Leon Radzinowicz, *Sexual offences* (English studies in criminal science, 9, 1957), p. xv. This is, of course, partly a reflection of the more diversified range of behaviour which can constitute a modern sexual offence.

46 Colchester borough records, examination and recognizance book, 1647–84, unfoliated, 8 November 1669.

47 See the comments of Radzinowicz, *Sexual offences*, pp. xv–xvi.

48 Coke, *Third institute*, p. 60.

49 P.R.O., ASSI 35/76/3/60.

50 Hale, *Pleas of the crown*, vol. 1, p. 634.

51 Blackstone, *Commentaries*, vol. 4, p. 211. See also the comments of Dalton, *Countrey justice*, p. 392.

52 E.R.O., Q/SBa 2/11; 2/55; 2/82; 2/97.

53 Dalton, *Countrey justice*, p. 392.

54 E.R.O., Q/SR 324/103; Q/SBa 2/56.

55 E.R.O., D/DCv 2/16.

56 P.R.O., STAC 8/64/23; 8/140/7.

57 See p. 118 above.

58 E.R.O., Q/SBa 2/57.

59 *Ibid.*, 2/92.

60 *Ibid.*, 2/4.

61 Colchester borough records, examination and recognizance book, 1619–45, unfoliated, 19 August 1624.

62 *Ibid.*, 4 December 1624.

63 *Ibid.*, 12 July 1640.

64 E.R.O., Q/SR 301/122.

65 P.R.O., ASSI 35/62/1/24–7. There is, however, no overall connection between conviction for rape and the age of the alleged victims in the sample of Essex cases studied.

66 E. Powers, *Crime and punishment in early Massachusetts* (Boston, 1966), pp. 264–5. Remarkably, however, rape in Massachusetts was usually

punished by whipping after this scandal. Whipping was even the penalty inflicted on an Indian who had raped a white woman, since 'hee was but an Indian, and is therefore in an incapacity to know the horribleness and wickedness of this abominable act': *ibid.*, p. 303.

67 Coke, *Third institute*, p. 58.
68 Blackstone, *Commentaries*, vol. 4, p. 215.
69 1 Mary cap. 1.
70 P.R.O., ASSI 35/110/2/12; 110/8/28.
71 E.R.O., Q/SR 286/49; P.R.O., ASSI 35/105/2/1–2, respectively.
72 *Ibid.*, ASSI 35/68/1/14.
73 Colchester borough records, examination and recognizance book, 1619–45, unfoliated, 20 August 1643.
74 E.R.O., Q/SBa 2/79; Q/SR 352/128.
75 E.R.O., Q/SBa 2/57.
76 For a discussion of this topic, pivoting on the *cause célèbre* of the Earl of Castlehaven's case, see Coral Bingham, 'Seventeenth-century attitudes towards deviant sex', *Journal of interdisciplinary history*, 1 (1971), 447–72.
77 1 Jac. I cap. 11.
78 P.R.O., ASSI 35/64/1/49.
79 Blackstone, *Commentaries*, vol. 4, p. 164.
80 Macfarlane, 'Marital and sexual regulation', fol. 119.
81 Colchester borough records, examination and recognizance book, 1619–45, unfoliated, 19 August 1623.
82 E.R.O., Q/SR 346/61.
83 Colchester borough records, examination and recognizance book, 1647–84, unfoliated, 4 June 1667.
84 Holdsworth, *History of English law*, vol. 1, pp. 622–4.
85 P.R.O., ASSI 35/108/9/12.
86 Keith Thomas, 'Women and the Civil War sects', *Past and present*, 13 (1958), 42–62, especially 49–50.
87 Colchester borough records, examination and recognizance book, 1647–84, unfoliated, 30 October 1649.
88 P.R.O., ASSI 35/85/5/15.
89 The subject is discussed at length in Macfarlane, 'Marital and sexual regulation', chapter 2.
90 Taylor, *Sex in history*, pp. 149–50.
91 For Elizabethan cases brought before the Essex church courts see Emmison, *Morals & the church courts*, pp. 36–44.
92 Macfarlane, 'Marital and sexual regulation', fol. 28. For a list of the prohibited degrees see Burn, *Ecclesiastical law*, vol. 2, pp. 441–5.
93 Macfarlane, 'Marital and sexual regulation', fol. 64.
94 E.R.O., D/ACA 32, fols. 226, 339.
95 *Ibid.*, 34, fol. 52v.
96 E.R.O., D/AEA 29, fol. 177.
97 Firth and Rait, *Acts and ordinances*, vol. 2, pp. 387–9.
98 P.R.O., ASSI 35/92/1/97.
99 *Ibid.*, 35/94/2/2–3.
100 E.R.O., Q/SR 377/46.
101 Sharpe, 'Crime and delinquency', p. 109, gives a statistical analysis of these presentments.

6 Riot and popular disturbances

1 The only general survey covering this period so far produced is C. S. L. Davies, 'Les révoltes populaires en Angleterre (1500–1700)', *Annales E.S.C.*, 29 (1969), 24–60. Buchanan Sharp, *In contempt of all authority: rural artisans and riot in the west of England, 1586–1660* (Berkeley, Los Angeles, and London, 1980), although concentrating on events outside Essex, raises a number of interesting general points about the popular disturbances of the period. John Walter and Keith Wrightson, 'Dearth and the social order in early modern England', *Past and present*, 71 (1976), 22–42, is a stimulating study of one aspect of the problem, and is based to a large extent on Essex materials relating to 1629–31. A number of limited local studies of rioting and disorder have appeared, of which perhaps the most detailed is Peter Clark, 'Popular protest and disturbance in Kent, 1558–1640', *Econ. hist. rev.*, 2nd ser., 29 (1976), 365–82.

2 Interesting comparisons are provided by research on French materials, the two best-known works on the problem being R. Mousnier, *Peasant uprisings in seventeenth-century France, Russia and China* (1971), and B. Porchnev, *Les soulèvements populaires en France de 1623 à 1648* (Paris, 1963).

3 Lambarde, *Eirenarcha*, p. 181.

4 17 Rich. II cap. 8. The *posse comitatus* was used as late as 1839 to suppress Chartist risings: see Radzinowicz, *History of English criminal law*, vol. 4, p. 107.

5 13 Hen. IV cap. 7; 2 Hen. V Stat. 1 cap. 8 respectively.

6 3 & 4 Edw. VI cap. 5; 1 Mary Sess. 2 cap. 12.

7 1 Geo. 1 Stat. 2 cap. 5.

8 Radzinowicz, *History of English criminal law*, vol. 4, p. 131, who states that 13 and 14. Car. II cap. 11 s. 32 was the first statutory authority for the use of regular forces to aid the civil power, in this case for the suppression of seditious conventicles. Troops were used for this purpose in Essex in the 1660s, e.g. E.R.O., Q/SR, 399/98.

9 It will become apparent, however, that the trial of those involved in popular disturbances subsequent to the suppression of the outbreaks in question was frequently entrusted to special commissions of Oyer and Terminer. J. Bellamy, *Crime and public order in England in the later middle ages* (1973), p. 95, points out that this method was used to suppress both the Peasants' Revolt of 1381 and Cade's Rebellion, and suggests that it reflected an unwillingness on the part of the central government to depend on local justices. On the evidence of the records consulted for the present study, JPs by the seventeenth century welcomed the assistance of the central government in trying rioters. B. W. Quintrell, 'The government of the county of Essex, 1603–1642' (London University Ph.D. thesis, 1965), fols. 134–5, comments that the county's deputy lieutenants had a similar attitude when faced with disturbances among the soldiery. It is hoped that John Walter's research (in progress) on rioting will throw greater light on the workings of commissions of Oyer and Terminer in the seventeenth century.

10 This total ignores cases of closebreaking or forcible disseisin committed by three or more people, and therefore technically riotous. Large-scale poaching expeditions are discussed pp. 168–9 above.

11 P.R.O., K.B. 9/758/125.

12 *Ibid.*, 9/842/246.

13 *Ibid.*, 9/914/203.

14 E.R.O., Q/SR 274/37; 407/28, respectively.
15 Blackstone, *Commentaries*, vol. 4, p. 147.
16 A. Harding, *A social history of English law* (Harmondsworth, 1966), p. 41.
17 See H. S. Bennett, *The Pastons and their England* (Cambridge, 1922), pp. 183–4, who comments that attempts to disseize the Pastons involved them in three full-scale sieges, one of them involving the Duke of Norfolk and 3,000 men.
18 F. G. Emmison, *Elizabethan life: disorder* (Chelmsford, 1970), p. 119.
19 Some idea of the complexity of the seventeenth-century land law can be gained from the descriptions of the action of ejectment given in Holdsworth, *History of English law*, vol. 7, pp. 4–23; and S. F. C. Milsom, *Historical foundations of the common law* (1969), pp. 136–8. A general background is provided by A. W. B. Simpson, *An introduction to the history of the land law* (Oxford, 1961).
20 5 Rich. II Stat. 1 cap. 8. This legislation was, of course, enacted in the aftermath of the Peasants' Revolt.
21 Lambarde, *Eirenarcha*, p. 144; Dalton, *Countrey justice*, p. 298, respectively.
22 E.R.O., Q/SR 403/28, 84–5. The accused in this case also stated under examination that his neighbours had advised him that carrying a stool across the threshold was enough to justify a claim for possession.
23 Bellamy, *Crime and public order in the later middle ages*, p. 29.
24 E. Kerridge, *Agrarian problems in the sixteenth century and after* (Historical problems, studies and documents, 6, 1969), p. 82.
25 E.R.O., Q/SBa 2/80.
26 E.R.O., Q/SR 355/12.
27 E.R.O., Q/SR 400/16, 128–30.
28 See *ibid.*, 414/51; 359/17–19; P.R.O., K.B. 9/87/224–5, 9/849/384, 388, respectively.
29 E.R.O., Q/SR 432/51.
30 Holdsworth, *History of English law*, vol. 7, p. 47, n. 1.
31 P.R.O., K.B. 9/910/292; E.R.O., Q/SR 234/33, respectively.
32 E.R.O., Q/SR 347/23; 260/163, respectively.
33 P.R.O., ASSI 35/95/12/121.
34 For the presentments against Alston see E.R.O., Q/SR 292/16, 364/23, 366/30, 31. That Alston had served as highway surveyor for the parish (E.R.O., Q/SR 317/40) adds a certain irony to them. For the background to the case see Morant, *Essex*, vol. 2, pp. 393–4; U. Simmon, *small beer: an Essex village from Elizabeth I to Elizabeth II* (Braintree, n.d.), p. 13; E.R.O., Q/SBa 2/78; and Josselin, *Diary*, p. 24. For the false accusation, E.R.O., Q/SBa 2/56–8; Q/SR 324/118, extracts from this last being printed in Alan Macfarlane, *Witchcraft in Tudor and Stuart England* (1970), pp. 306–7.
35 E.R.O., D/DMs 036; 037/1–3.
36 P.R.O., K.B. 9/780/2, 3.
37 *Cal. S.P. Dom., 1637–8*, p. 610.
38 P.R.O., ASSI 35/118/12/17. Details of the Walfleet dispute are given in K. H. Burley, 'The economic development of Essex in the later seventeenth and early eighteenth centuries' (London University Ph.D. thesis, 1957), fols. 88–9. For the licences see E.R.O., D/DGe M 165.
39 It was probably the irregularities in the investigation of this death, attributed by local opinion to venereal disease, that brought the case to the Star Chamber.
40 P.R.O., STAC 8/125/16. For the background to the Denny family, who had based their fortunes on the purchase of monastic lands after the Dissolution,

see *D.N.B.* Waltham manor was one of their earlier acquisitions, having come into their possession in 1541: *V.C.H. Essex*, vol. 5, p. 157. F. Hull, 'Agriculture and rural society in Essex, 1603–1642' (London University Ph.D. thesis, 1950), fols. 361–5, indicates that this was the only example of popular disturbance in Essex to be recorded in the Star Chamber in the period covered by this study.

41 Colchester borough records, examination and recognizance book, 1619–45, unfoliated, 8 February 1624.
42 *Ibid.*, 26 July 1624.
43 Bodleian MS Firth c. 4, fols. 488–91.
44 *Ibid.*, fol. 120.
45 *Ibid.*, fols. 146–7.
46 *Ibid.*, fol. 347.
47 *Ibid.*, fol. 237.
48 P.R.O., S.P. 16/96/39, fols. 6–7.
49 E.R.O., D/B 3/1/19, fol. 240v.
50 Bodleian MS Firth c. 4, fol. 455. P.R.O., S.P. 16/96/39. For a discussion of the wider implications of the incident see G. E. Aylmer, 'St Patrick's Day 1628 in Witham, Essex', *Past and present* 61 (1973), 139–48. Both the documentation and Professor Aylmer's findings correct the reports of heavy fatalities resulting from this incident given in T. Birch, *The court and times of Charles the First*, ed. R. F. Williams (2 vols., 1848), vol. 1, p. 331.
51 These incidents and their backgrounds are described at length in Walter and Wrightson, 'Dearth and the social order'; and John Walter, 'Grain riots and popular attitudes to the law: Maldon and the crisis of 1629', *An ungovernable people*, ed. John Brewer and John Styles (1980).
52 P.R.O., S.P. 16/133/19/1.
53 E.R.O., D/B3/3/208.
54 P.R.O., ASSI 35/71/3/97.
55 E.R.O., Q/SR 264/21.
56 Colchester borough records, examination and recognizance book, 1647–84, unfoliated, 3 March 1674.
57 *Ibid.*, 14 October 1675.
58 P.R.O., S.P. 16/497/6.
59 E.R.O., Q/SR 316/2.
60 Colchester borough records, sessions book, 1630–63, unfoliated, 19 March 1630.
61 Cf. Walter and Wrightson, 'Dearth and the social order', pp. 26–7, 42, where the rarity of riots caused by food shortages is commented upon.
62 See the conclusion of Mousnier, *Peasant uprisings*, pp. 307–9.
63 E.R.O., Q/SBa 2/60.
64 *Ibid.*, 2/91.
65 E.R.O., Q/SR 400/21.
66 P.R.O., ASSI 35/121/8/84.
67 The problems of collecting the tax nationally are discussed in L. M. Marshall, 'The levying of the hearth tax, 1662–1688', *Eng. hist. rev.,* 51 (1936), 628–46.
68 E.R.O., Q/SR 421/87. Poole was tried at the assizes and acquitted, P.R.O., ASSI 35/111/7/3.
69 E.R.O., Q/SR 405/72.
70 *Ibid.*, 399/108.

71 *Ibid.*, 421/122.
72 *Ibid.*, 418/43–5, 56. Another collector was indicted for unlawful distraint, *ibid.*, 434/34.
73 Colchester borough records, examination and recognizance book, 1647–84, unfoliated, 1 March 1668.
74 E. J. Hobsbawm, 'The machine breakers', *Past and present*, 1 (1952), 59. See also G. Rudé, *Paris and London in the eighteenth century* (New York, 1969), chapter 1, 'The "pre-industrial" crowd'. A good local example of the 'industrial' riot, which occurred a few years after the period covered in the present study, is described by K. H. Burley, 'A note on a labour dispute in early eighteenth-century Colchester', *Bulletin of the Institute of Historical Research*, 29 (1956), 220–30.
75 Bodleian MS Firth c. 4, fol. 495.
76 P.R.O., K.B. 9/765/17; 9/928/307 respectively.
77 E.R.O., Q/SR 328/102, 114.
78 P.R.O., ASSI 35/117/2/12. For the London rioting that formed the background to this case see R. M. Dunn, 'The London weavers' riot of 1675', *Guildhall studies in London history*, 1 (1973), 13–23.
79 This account is based mainly on the depositions in Colchester borough records, examination and recognizance book, 1647–84, unfoliated, 13–14 October, 1675. Details of punishments are found in P.R.O., P.C. 2/65, fol. 20; *Cal. S.P. Dom., 1675–6*, p. 513. Burley, 'Economic development of Essex', fol. 150, comments that the years 1675–6 were bad for the Colchester textile trade.
80 For the general background to the popular disturbances of this period see Brian Manning, *The English people and the English revolution, 1640–1649* (1976).
81 Emmison, *Elizabethan life: disorder*, pp. 38–65; cf Joel Samaha, 'Gleanings from local criminal court records: sedition among the "inarticulate" in Elizabethan England', *The journal of social history*, 8 (1975), 61–79. Clark, 'Popular protest in Kent', p. 380, is probably correct in taking a sceptical view of the revolutionary implications of such utterances.
82 E.R.O., Q/SR 388/26; 389/26–9. The rarity of such cases probably demonstrates the extent of the divergence between actual and reported attitudes rather than a universal satisfaction with the restoration of the Stuart monarchy.
83 H. Smith, *The ecclesiastical history of Essex under the Long Parliament and the Commonwealth* (Colchester, n.d.), pp. 6–74, gives an outline of the development of puritanism in the county before the Civil War.
84 E.R.O., Q/SR 432/36, 45, 59–62.
85 *Ibid.*, 400/133–9; 401/50. Hickeringill was also allegedly the victim of a forcible expulsion at the hands of some sixty persons in May 1666, *ibid.*, 409/18. For his career see *D.N.B.*
86 Alan Macfarlane, *The family life of Ralph Josselin* (Cambridge, 1970), p. 186.
87 P.R.O., ASSI 35/81/1/72.
88 *A true and exact relation of the severall informations, examinations, and confessions of the late witches, arraigned and executed in the county of Essex* (1645), p. 27.
89 P.R.O., P.C. 2/52, fol. 616. The following account is based on *ibid.*, fols. 616, 634, 674, 699, and *Cal. S.P. Dom., 1640*, pp. 500, 516–17. See also map 3.
90 J. K. Gruenfelder, 'The election of knights of the shire for Essex in the spring of 1640', *Transactions of the Essex Archaeological Society*, 3rd ser., 2 (1967), 143–6.

91 See p. 86 above.
92 Smith, *Ecclesiastical history*, p. 69. The long-suffering vicar of Radwinter, Nicholas Drake, was in Cambridge at the time, perhaps fortunately.
93 A. Kingston, *East Anglia and the Great Civil War* (1897), p. 28.
94 E.R.O., Q/SR 311/46–51.
95 E.R.O., Q/SBa 2/41.
96 P.R.O., ASSI 35/84/10/24.
97 *Ibid.*, 35/84/9/12–17. These indictments tally with Drake's account of the troubles, the relevant section of his diary being translated in Smith, *Ecclesiastical history*, pp. 179–91.
98 E.R.O., Q/SR 312/136.
99 *Ibid.*, 318/33–42; 319/23–40.
100 For the background to these events see W. L. F. Nuttall, 'Sir Thomas Barrington and the Puritan Revolution', *Transactions of the Essex Archaeological Society*, 3rd ser., 2 (1966), 60–82.
101 Josselin, *Diary*, p. 13. These disturbances are described at greater length in Manning, *English people and English revolutions*, pp. 171–8.
102 Colchester borough records, examination and recognizance book, 1619–45, unfoliated, 26 May 1640; *Cal. S.P. Dom., 1640*, pp. 342–3.
103 E.R.O., Q/SR 311/14. Ferman was committed to the house of correction.
104 Colchester borough records, examination and recognizance book, 1619–45, unfoliated, 19 June 1641.
105 P.R.O., ASSI 35/83/7/7.
106 Stephen, *History of the criminal law*, vol. 2, p. 242.
107 B. Dale, *The annals of Coggeshall, otherwise Sunnedon, in the county of Essex* (Coggeshall, 1863), p. 268.
108 See C. S. L. Davies, 'Peasant revolt in France and England: a comparison', *Ag. hist. rev.*, 21 (1973), 122–34, especially 130–1.
109 Sir John Oglander, *A royalist's notebook*, ed. F. Bamford (1936), p. 61. Cf. Sharp, *In contempt of all authority*, pp. 215–19, where the helplessness of the government in the face of determined rioting in the Forest of Dean is stressed.
110 Sharp, *In contempt of all authority*, pp. 104, 130–1, where Sharp is similarly sceptical about the involvement of 'outside agitators' or ringleaders from the upper strata of society in seventeenth-century riots.
111 For an introduction to this subject see Christopher Hill, 'The many-headed monster in late Tudor and early Stuart political thinking', *From the Renaissance to the Counter-Reformation: essays in honour of Garrett Mattingly*, ed. C. H. Carter (1966).
112 It is hoped that John Walter's Cambridge University Ph.D. thesis (in progress) will provide considerable illumination on the topic.

7 Property offences

1 Joel Samaha, *Law and order in historical perspective: the case of Elizabethan Essex* (New York and London, 1974), table 2, p. 20; J. S. Cockburn, 'The nature and incidence of crime in England 1559–1625', *Crime in England 1550–1800*, ed. J. S. Cockburn (1977), pp. 60–70; J. M. Beattie, 'The pattern of crime in England, 1660–1800', *Past and present*, 72 (1974), 73–8.
2 Barbara A. Hanawalt, *Crime and conflict in English communities 1300–1348* (Cambridge, Mass., and London, 1979), pp. 66–7.
3 Cockburn, 'Nature and incidence of crime', p. 60; Beattie, 'Pattern of crime', p. 73.

4 Coke, *Third institute*, p. 107.
5 For the evolution of the law relating to larceny, see Holdsworth, *History of English law*, vol. 3, pp. 360–8.
6 D. Veall, *The popular movement for law reform, 1640–1660* (Oxford, 1970), pp. 127–30.
7 Holdsworth, *History of English law*, vol. 3, p. 367.
8 Blackstone, *Commentaries*, vol. 4, p. 238.
9 Radzinowicz, *History of English criminal law*, vol. 1, pp. 95–6.
10 See above, pp. 144–6.
11 See above, tables 2–5. All figures about thefts quoted in this chapter are derived from these tables unless otherwise stated.
12 P.R.O., ASSI 35/72/1/14–17; 35/72/1/28; 35/76/1/65, respectively. The accused in each of these cases was hanged.
13 E.R.O., Q/SR 252/7, 25.
14 *Ibid.*, 351/16; Q/SBa 2/78.
15 P.R.O., ASSI 35/76/2/65, 71.
16 See E.R.O., Q/SBa 2/81, a reference to a sheep bearing 'Both tarre markes and flesh markes'.
17 *Ibid.*, 2/68. See also *ibid.*, 2/19, for an allegedly stolen sheep being mixed with strays.
18 *Ibid.*, 2/7.
19 E.R.O., D/B3/3/388.
20 See E.R.O., Q/SBa 2/78.
21 See *ibid.*, 2/73; Q/SR 396/93; 403/90; 405/162.
22 1 Edw. VI cap. 12; 2 & 3 Edw. VI cap. 33; 31 Eliz. I cap. 12.
23 William Harrison's 'Description of England', *Shakespere's youth*, ed. F. J. Furnival (New Shakespere Soc., 6th ser., 1, 1877) p. 308.
24 T. Dekker, 'Lantern and candlelight, or the bellman's second night's walk', *The Elizabethan underworld*, ed. A. V. Judges (1930), pp. 351–6. The statute 31 Eliz. I cap. 12, entitled 'An Act to avoid Horse-stealing', was concerned mainly with the regulation of horse markets.
25 Colchester borough records, examination and recognizance book, 1619–45, unfoliated, 8 August 1629; cf. E.R.O., Q/SR 399/110, for evidence of four men being examined to ascertain if a horse on sale at Smithfield market was stolen. Late seventeenth-century depositions from the northern assizes and the Palatinate of Lancaster give the impression that those suspected of stealing horses were often horse-traders: P.R.O., ASSI 45/7–9; P.R.O., Records of the Palatinate of Lancaster, Depositions, 27/1–2.
26 E.R.O., Q/SBa 2/80.
27 *Ibid.*, 2/14; Q/SR 265/37.
28 P.R.O., ASSI 35/62/1/27.
29 Three cases of stealing hops and four of stealing hay have been included in this total for convenience.
30 P.R.O., ASSI 35/91/1/50–1.
31 *Ibid.*, 35/63/1/64.
32 *Ibid.*, 35/91/1/17.
33 E.R.O., Q/SR 272/44.
34 See W. O. Ault, 'By-laws of gleaning and the problems of harvest', *Econ. hist. rev.*, 2nd ser., 14 (1961), 215–16.
35 See p. 110 above.
36 P.R.O., ASSI 35/76/2/51.

37 These figures are based on an analysis of the Colchester borough records, S/R 26–37, *passim.*

38 F. G. Emmison, *Elizabethan life: disorder* (Chelmsford, 1970), appendix B, pp. 311–14.

39 See Colchester borough records, examination and recognizance book, 1647–84, unfoliated, 18 December 1667; 19 October 1669.

40 See E.R.O., D/B3/3/392/14, 24; P.R.O., ASSI 35/68/1/35. Similarly, a London gentleman stealing cloth at Chelmsford, P.R.O., ASSI 35/92/2/44, was probably guilty of commercial malpractice rather than theft proper.

41 P.R.O., ASSI 35/105/2/4.

42 E.R.O., Q/SR 286/39; P.R.O., ASSI 35/105/1/2, respectively.

43 P.R.O., ASSI 35/81/1/77–8.

44 See E.R.O., Q/SBa 2/22; 2/73; 2/76; 2/80; Q/SR 411/100.

45 E.R.O., Q/SBa 2/4.

46 *Ibid.,* 2/17.

47 See *ibid.,* 2/9; 2/17.

48 See *ibid.,* 2/73; Q/SR 345/23.

49 E.R.O., Q/SBa 2/2.

50 E.R.O., Q/SR 266/27; 282/28; 295/14; 304/41; 402/20, respectively.

51 J. S. Cockburn, 'Early modern assize records as historical evidence', *Journal of the Society of Archivists,* 5 (1975), 222, suggests that this could be explained by accusations in larceny cases being brought against receivers of stolen goods rather than against the thief proper. The hypothesis is an interesting one, and may account for some of the cases in which craftsmen and tradesmen were accused of theft; on the evidence of Essex quarter sessions depositions, however, such cases were virtually unknown, at least at that court.

52 P.R.O., ASSI 35/71/2/54; 35/72/2/39, respectively.

53 8 Eliz. I cap. 4.

54 Blackstone, *Commentaries,* vol. 4, p. 241.

55 8 Eliz. I cap. 4.

56 Colchester borough records, examination and recognizance book, 1619–45, unfoliated, 22 June 1629.

57 William Kemp, *Kemp's nine days wonder* (1600), sig. B1.

58 Colchester borough records, examination and recognizance book, 1647–84, unfoliated, 10 October 1662; 11 October 1680, respectively.

59 E.R.O., Q/SBa 2/23.

60 See E.R.O., Q/SR 228/3 (8d); 264/13 (8d); 277/8 (4d).

61 P.R.O., ASSI 35/116/2/6.

62 *Ibid.,* 35/90/8/9; 35/88/10/49; 35/63/1/44, respectively.

63 *Ibid.,* 35/75/1/37; 35/76/2/73, respectively.

64 *Ibid.,* 35/75/1/78, 62; 35/78/1/52, respectively.

65 *Ibid.,* 35/68/1/83; 35/69/2/38, respectively.

66 *Ibid.,* 35/72/2/69.

67 *Ibid.,* 35/61/1/48; 35/72/1/18, respectively.

68 *Ibid.,* 35/75/1/70; 35/94/11/1, 35/94/1/30, respectively.

69 *Ibid.,* 35/85/5/47.

70 *Ibid.,* 35/71/3/24.

71 Holdsworth, *History of English law,* vol. 3, p. 301.

72 As it had been in the Elizabethan period; Emmison, *Elizabethan life: disorder,* p. 257.

73 E.R.O., Q/SR 237/7.

74 *Ibid.*, 366/103; 367/23, respectively.
75 P.R.O., ASSI 35/64/1/30–1; 35/69/2/40.
76 Emmison, *Elizabethan life: disorder*, appendix A, pp. 308–10.
77 It may not be irrelevant to point out that at least one historian of eighteenth-century Essex and its economy does not think that the highwayman constituted a great problem in the county during this period: E. F. J. Brown, *Essex at work 1700–1815* (Chelmsford, 1969), p. 85.
78 *Diary of John Rous*, ed. M. A. E. Green (Camden Soc. old ser., 66, 1856), p. 83.
79 He was named on an Essex assize indictment in 1669, although it would appear that he never came to trial: P.R.O., ASSI 35/110/1/7. For Duval's biography, and those of many other highwaymen, see Alexander Smith, *A complete history of the lives and robberies of the most notorious highwaymen, footpads, shoplifts and cheats of both sexes*, ed. A. L. Hayward (1926).
80 *Memoirs of the Verney family from the Restoration to the Revolution, 1660 to 1696*, ed. F. P. and M. M. Verney (4 vols. 1892–9), vol. 4, pp. 307–13. Isolated examples of highwaymen connected with gentle families are given in Joan Parkes, *Travel in England in the seventeenth century* (1925), pp. 163–4.
81 E.R.O., D/DCv 1, fol. 15.
82 E.R.O., Q/SBa 2/22. For another ineffective attempt at highway robbery see E.R.O., D/B3/3/388.
83 P.R.O., ASSI 35/97/8/153; 35/73/1/113, respectively.
84 Fynes Moryson, *An itinerary* (4 vols., Glasgow, 1908), vol. 3, p. 408.
85 Parkes, *Travel in England*, p. 173.
86 P.R.O., ASSI 35/109/2/10–11.
87 Smith, *Complete history*, p. 280, records an incident in which the Earl of Albemarle's coach was attacked between Manningtree and Colchester by a gang headed by Frank Osborn, son of a Colchester Quaker family. Two horses were killed and two footmen injured.
88 E.R.O., Q/SR 430/106.
89 E.R.O., Q/SBa 2/123.
90 See table 19, p. 183 above.
91 A view put forward by Parkes, *Travel in England*, p. 154.
92 Dalton, *Countrey justice*, p. 359.
93 As Dalton's definition reminds us, burglary could comprehend breaking and entering by night with intent to commit felonies other than theft. Only one such case, breaking and entering with intent to murder, has been found in sources consulted for this study: P.R.O., ASSI 35/95/12/26. Generally, burglary was aggravated theft.
94 Coke, *Third institute*, p. 63.
95 F. Pollock and F. W. Maitland, *The history of English law before the time of Edward I*, 2nd edn (2 vols., Cambridge, 1968), vol. 2, p. 493.
96 Holdsworth, *History of English law*, vol. 3, p. 369; vol. 8, pp. 304–5.
97 A. Harding, *A social history of English law*, (Harmondsworth, 1966), pp. 82–3.
98 39 Eliz. I cap. 15.
99 Hale, *Pleas of the crown*, vol. 1, p. 565.
100 See P.R.O., ASSI 35/72/2/79; 35/73/1/118; 35/90/7/41; 35/91/1/68.
101 *Ibid.*, 35/91/1/47. Both the accused were acquitted.
102 *Ibid.*, 35/117/3/2; 35/117/4/19, respectively.
103 *Ibid.*, 35/69/1/3–7.

104 *Ibid.*, 35/95/1/23, 32–3.
105 Colchester borough records, examination and recognizance book, 1619–45, unfoliated, 16 February 1634.
106 P.R.O., ASSI 35/103/1/6. He was subsequently hanged, *ibid.*, 35/103/1/16.
107 See E.R.O., Q/SR 235/18; Q/SBa 2/2; Q/SR 345/26; Q/SBa 2/74.
108 Colchester borough records, examination and recognizance book, 1647–84, unfoliated, 1 December 1651.
109 E.R.O., 343/36; Q/SBa 2/72.
110 Colchester borough records, examination and recognizance book, 1619–45, unfoliated, 12 May 1631; 6 July 1631.
111 E.R.O., Q/SR 235/10; Q/SBa 2/2.
112 E.R.O., Q/SR 395/26, 67.
113 P.R.O., ASSI 35/117/3/2.
114 *Ibid.*, 35/108/1/15.
115 This is evident from a close reading of *Middlesex sessions records*, ed. W. le Hardy (new ser., 4 vols., 1935–41), *passim.*
116 Richard Allestree, *The whole duty of man* (1678), p. 230.
117 See E.R.O., Q/SR 402/124A; P.R.O., ASSI 35/62/1/1, 3.
118 E.R.O., Q/SR 423/73.
119 E.R.O., Q/SBa 2/22.
120 E.R.O., Q/SR 435/117; Q/SBa 2/17, respectively.
121 E.R.O., Q/SBa 2/74.
122 *Ibid.*, 2/94.
123 *Ibid.*, 2/73.
124 *Ibid.*, 2/19.
125 *Ibid.*, 2/2.
126 E.R.O., Q/SR 430/104.
127 *Ibid.*, 393/75; E.R.O., D/B3/3/392/45, respectively.
128 This situation is much like that obtaining in medieval England: Hanawalt, *Crime and conflict*, pp. 92–6. It should be noted, however, that Middlesex records reveal numerous examples of thieves from the metropolitan area operating in Essex, and of Essex thieves being apprehended on the peripheries of the capital. This suggests that thieves living in those parts of Essex adjacent to London had access to outlets for stolen goods in the capital or in its growing suburbs: see *Middlesex sessions records* vol. 1, pp. 206, 294, 297, 298, 329, 412, 453, for isolated examples.
129 P.R.O., ASSI 35/62/1/26, 28, 53–6.
130 Colchester borough records, examination and recognizance book, 1619–45, unfoliated, 13 August 1631.
131 Evidence from a detailed study of one Essex township suggests that thieves were drawn from these two elements in roughly equal numbers: J. A. Sharpe, 'Crime and delinquency in an Essex parish 1600–1640', *Crime in England 1550–1800*, ed. J. S. Cockburn (1977), pp. 100–2. Similarly, Keith Wrightson and David Levine, *Poverty and piety in an English village: Terling 1525–1700* (New York, San Francisco and London, 1979), p. 122, concluded that 'theft accusations . . . were primarily initiated by more substantial, established villagers against their poorer, less established, and more marginal neighbors'.
132 The existence of such a group in the period under consideration is discussed above, pp. 179–81.
133 The connection between these phenomena is discussed above, pp. 198–200.

8 Crimes of violence

1 See Alan Macfarlane, *The justice and the mare's ale: law and disorder in seventeenth-century England* (1980).
2 See table 19, p. 183 above.
3 E.R.O., D/DU 65/57, fol. 10.
4 E.R.O., D/AEA 32, fols. 95v–6.
5 Assault, like other forms of trespass, could form the grounds for a suit at Common Pleas as an alternative to being indicted at a criminal court: see M. J. Ingram, 'Communities and courts: law and disorder in early seventeenth-century Wiltshire', *Crime in England 1550–1800*, ed. J. S. Cockburn, p. 114. Ingram's investigations suggest that the total of such suits arising at any one time from a given county would not be very high.
6 Lambarde, *Eirenarcha*, pp. 76–118; Dalton, *Countrey justice*, pp. 263–86.
7 Lambarde, *Eirenarcha*, p. 77.
8 *Ibid.*, p. 119.
9 *Ibid.*, p. 123.
10 Dalton, *Countrey justice*, p. 293.
11 E.R.O., D/B3/1/11, *passim.*, and especially fols. 164–6.
12 E.R.O., Q/SR 236/73.
13 E.R.O., Q/SBa 2/91. The complaint seems to have been justified; for further details of Warner's violence see E.R.O., Q/SR 329/24; 335/30; 358/87; 364/19; P.R.O., ASSI 35/91/10/29.
14 Lambarde, *Eirenarcha*, p. 128.
15 For which see N. D. Walker, *Crime and punishment in Britain* (Edinburgh, 1965), p. 18.
16 E.R.O., Q/SR 353/126, 149; Q/SBa 2/80.
17 E.R.O., Q/SR 308/46; P.R.O., ASSI 35/104/11/1, respectively.
18 Blackstone, *Commentaries*, vol. 4, p. 379. No direct evidence of this practice has been found in assault cases analysed in this study. It is however, interesting to note a letter of 1606 from a Kent JP to his county bench requesting that a man convicted of forcible entry should not be fined above 2/- 'for he ys a very poore body': *Kentish sources; 6. Crime and punishment*, ed. E. Melling (Maidstone, 1969), p. 199.
19 E.R.O., Q/SR 301/23, 25.
20 *Ibid.*, 415/8.
21 E.R.O., Q/SBa 2/45.
22 Keith Wrightson and David Levine, *Poverty and piety in an English village: Terling 1525–1700* (New York, San Francisco and London, 1979), p. 123. For isolated examples which support this assertion see J. A. Sharpe, 'Crime and delinquency in an Essex parish 1600–1640', *Crime in England 1550–1800*, ed. J. S. Cockburn (1977), pp. 97–8, 103.
23 For an elaboration of this view see M. E. Wolfgang and F. Farracuti, *The subculture of violence: towards an integrated theory in criminology* (1967).
24 See B. Wootton, *Social science and social pathology* (1959), p. 29. Aspects of family violence in this period are discussed in J. A. Sharpe, 'Domestic homicide in early modern England', *The historical journal*, 24 (1981), 29–48.
25 Bronislaw Malinowski, cited in Lewis A. Coser, *The functions of social conflict* (1956), p. 63.
26 William Gouge, 'Of domesticall duties, eight treatises', *Workes* (1626), p. 203.

27 See pp. 126–8 above.
28 P.R.O., ASSI 35/114/9/24; 35/90/3/32, respectively.
29 For isolated examples see E. P. Thompson, ' "Rough music": le charivari anglais', *Annales E.S.C.*, 27 (1972), 288, 293; Sharpe, 'Domestic homicide', p. 32.
30 E.R.O., Q/SBa 2/58.
31 E.R.O., Q/SR 432/63.
32 E.R.O., Q/SBa 2/60.
33 Colchester borough records, examination and recognizance book, 1647–84, unfoliated, 20 December 1672.
34 William Perkins, 'Oeconomy, or household government', *Workes* (1631), p. 697.
35 See E.R.O., Q/SO 1 fols. 60, 183v, 245v.
36 E.R.O., Q/SR 427/49, 61.
37 E.R.O., Q/SBa 2/32.
38 See *ibid.*, 2/45, Q/SR 391/65.
39 For comparison see T. G. Barnes, *Somerset 1625–1640* (1961), pp. 184–7.
40 See E.R.O., Q/SBa 2/27, 84.
41 *Ibid.*, 2/30.
42 Colchester borough records, examination and recognizance book, 1619–45, unfoliated, 12 April 1647.
43 E.R.O, Q/SBa 2/44.
44 Colchester borough records, examination and recognizance book, 1619–45, unfoliated, 26 June 1626.
45 E.R.O., Q/SBa 2/100.
46 *Ibid.*, 2/97.
47 At Thorpe, for example, between 1644 and 1652, where numerous bindings over to keep the peace and indictments for assault give the impression of a divided community: E.R.O., Q/SR 322/88, 89; 325/106; 326/32, 74, 100; 327/24, 34, 72; 328/54, 55; 328/11; 329/141; 332/109; 353/30, 31.
48 See *ibid.*, 382/2, 4; 386/4, 17; 394/16, 22; 415/13, 14.
49 E.R.O., Q/SBa 2/94. For more on the connection between drink and violence see pp. 54–5 above.
50 E.R.O., Q/SBa 2/80.
51 E.R.O., Q/SR 326/28; Q/SBa 2/55.
52 E.R.O., Q/SR 376/16, 17.
53 *Ibid.*, 425/44, 106.
54 For the rules governing the typology of homicide at this time see Coke, *Third institute*, pp. 55–7; and Hale, *Pleas of the crown*, pp. 23–48.
55 The early development of the law of homicide is traced in Holdsworth, *History of English law*, vol. 2, pp. 358–9; vol. 3, pp. 313–14; and J. M. Kaye, 'The early history of murder and manslaughter', *Law quarterly review*, 83 (1967), 365–95, 569–601. James Buchanan Given, *Society and homicide in thirteenth-century England* (Stanford, California, 1977), is a useful survey of the problem in that period, and is based on court materials similar to those employed in the present study.
56 A process described in T. A. Green, 'Societal concepts of criminal liability for homicide in medieval England', *Speculum*, 47 (1972), 669–94.
57 Coke, *Third institute*, p. 47.
58 P.R.O., ASSI 35/97/3/31.
59 Zachary Babington, *Advice to grand jurors in cases of blood* (1677),

especially sig. A4. It should be noted, however, that the conviction rate in seventeenth-century Essex was higher than that obtaining in medieval England: Given, *Society and homicide*, pp. 97–102. In the later period, of course, the law relating to manslaughter meant that it was possible for a jury to convict for homicide without necessarily putting the convicted person at risk of execution.

60 P.R.O., ASSI 35/73/1/4; for the other example, *ibid.*, 35/76/3/6.
61 Green, 'Societal concepts of criminal liability for homicide', pp. 675ff.
62 P.R.O., ASSI 35/92/11/51.
63 For details of this case see above, p. 131.
64 P.R.O., ASSI 35/124/1/9.
65 See *ibid.*, 45/7/2/47–52, 126–30; 45/9/1/26.
66 This defect is partly remedied by the presence of depositions in the Essex borough archives. Further qualitative insights were gleaned from Northern circuit assize depositions for the years 1664–9; P.R.O., ASSI 45/7/1–45/9/3. This source yielded information on a total of sixty-four cases.
67 Gouge, 'Domesticall duties', pp. 234–5, 276–7.
68 Such relationships will probably only become apparent when the victim and the offender are studied in the context of their own communities. For one case where such research has shown a 'family' relationship which was not evident from the relevant court materials, see Josselin, *Diary*, p. 539, n. 1.
69 P.R.O., ASSI 35/99/1/30. Even in this instance the killer was merely branded. Much the same situation existed in late Tudor Essex: see F. G. Emmison, *Elizabethan life: disorder* (Chelmsford, 1970), p. 155.
70 Blackstone, *Commentaries*, vol. 4, p. 182.
71 One student of this phenomenon in sixteenth-century Essex has concluded that 'the courts were bending the rules of the common law in order to maintain the employer–employee status quo': Jeremy C. M. Walker, 'Crime and capital punishment in Elizabethan Essex' (University of Birmingham B.A. dissertation, 1971), fol. 32. J. S. Cockburn, 'The nature and incidence of crime in England 1559–1625', *Crime in England 1550–1800*, ed. J. S. Cockburn (1977), p. 57, after comparing Essex homicide cases with those of Sussex and Hertfordshire, suggests that the 'relatively common' killing of servants in Essex was a distinctive feature of homicide patterns within the county in that period.
72 *The full and true relation of all the proceedings at the assizes late holden at Chelmsford in the countie of Essex* (1680), p. 3. The assize files for 1680 are missing, so no corresponding indictment can be traced.
73 P.R.O., ASSI 35/98/2/29; 35/99/1/32, respectively.
74 Colchester borough records, examination and recognizance book, 1619–45, unfoliated, 23 November 1638.
75 E.R.O., Q/SBa 2/56.
76 *Ibid.*, 2/97.
77 E.R.O., D/B3/3/210.
78 Colchester borough records, S/R 35/2; 39/2; 48/1, 2.
79 P.R.O., ASSI 35/100/2/25; 35/100/7/132.
80 25 Edw. III Stat. 5 cap. 2.
81 P.R.O., ASSI 35/70/1/51; 35/104/2/2, respectively.
82 *Ibid.*, 35/117/3/3; 35/77/1/22, respectively.
83 T. Morris and L. Blom-Cooper, *A calendar of murder: criminal homicide in England since 1957* (1964), pp. 279–80; Walker, *Crime and punishment in Britain*, p. 18. It should be noted that while the proportion of homicides

involving family members was lower in Stuart Essex than in modern England, it was still much higher than that obtaining in the medieval period: Given, *Society and homicide*, pp. 55–7, shows that only 6.5% of the 2,434 victims in his sample were killed by relatives.

84 Josselin, *Diary*, p. 1.
85 Doubts about the reliability of details of the method of killing as given on indictments were allayed by checking Northern circuit indictments for the period 1664–9 (in P.R.O., ASSI 44/12–16) against the sample of homicide depositions for that period, *ibid.*, 45/7/1–45/9/3. In twenty-eight cases an indictment or coroner's inquisition could be matched with a detailed deposition, and in every case the method of killing as described by the former was found to correspond with that given in the latter.
86 Perhaps as a result of the Jacobean statute against stabbing, 2 Jac. I cap. 8.
87 Essex gentry were probably at times involved in duels in the capital, a member of the Wiseman family being killed in one in 1684: Morant, *Essex*, vol. 2, p. 563.
88 P.R.O., ASSI 35/89/6/18; 35/116/2/3, respectively.
89 E.R.O., Q/SBa 2/91.
90 P.R.O., ASSI 35/103/1/20; 35/95/12/5; 35/108/1/13, respectively.
91 Coke, *Third institute*, p. 47.
92 Reginald Scot, *Discoverie of witchcraft*, ed. Brinsley Nicholson (1886), p. 83.
93 E.R.O., Q/SR 390/32.
94 E.R.O., Q/SBa 2/85.
95 Colchester borough records, S/R 37/14, 15, 22, 23; Colchester borough records, examination and recognizance book, 1619–45, unfoliated, 12 November 1638.
96 It is noteworthy that only three of the sixty-four northern depositions consulted for comparison refer to homicide as a means of furthering or concealing another crime. Cockburn, 'Nature and incidence of crime', p. 59, could find only thirteen such cases in his sample of 364 homicides. Macfarlane, *The justice and the mare's ale*, argues that English criminals in the seventeenth century rarely inflicted casual violence on their victims. This seems to contrast with thirteenth-century England, where over 9% of killings were homicides in pursuit of robbery: Given, *Society and homicide*, p. 133.
97 P.R.O., ASSI 35/73/1/138, 88.
98 For the background to this case see *The complete Newgate calendar*, ed. J. L. Rayner and G. T. Crook (5 vols., 1926), vol. 1, pp. 161–9. The corresponding indictment survives, P.R.O., ASSI 35/108/1/3.
99 *Ibid.*, 35/80/3/37.
100 See Josselin, *Diary*, p. 539, who attributes a murder in which an Earls Colne man was thrown into a tub of scalding beer wort to 'the sad effect of dronkeness'; for the relevant indictment see P.R.O., ASSI 35/108/1/13.
101 P.R.O., ASSI 45/7/1/83–90; 45/7/92–7; 45/8/1/44–50, respectively.
102 *Ibid.*, 35/71/3/1, 13; *Cal. S.P. Dom., 1629–1631*, pp. 4, 68, 70; E.R.O., D/B3/3/210; D/B3/1/19, fol. 103v.
103 P.R.O., ASSI 35/83/3/62.
104 *Ibid.*, 45/7/2/69–70.
105 *Ibid.*, 45/8/1/61.
106 *Ibid.*, 45/7/2/22, 25.
107 *Ibid.*, 35/80/3/66–7.
108 *Ibid.*, 45/8/2/55–7; 45/7/2/51; 45/9/2/179–85, respectively.

109 *Ibid.*, 45/8/1/158.
110 *Ibid.*, 45/8/2/113.
111 J. Dod and R. Cleaver, *A treatise or exposition upon the ten commandments grounded upon the scriptures canonical* (1603), pp. 38, 39.
112 An exhaustive study of the problem in modern England is provided by D. J. West, *Murder followed by suicide* (1965).
113 P.R.O., K.B. 9/794/253–4.
114 Colchester borough records, examination and recognizance book, 1619–45, unfoliated, 9 July 1636.
115 See M. E. Wolfgang, *Patterns in criminal homicide* (Philadelphia, 1958), part III, 'The victim–offender relationship', and D. Chapman, *Sociology and the stereotype of the criminal* (1968), chapter 5, 'The role of the victim in the crime'.
116 This is given in Wootton, *Social science and social pathology*, p. 29. Homicide rates seem to have been considerably higher in the middle ages than in Stuart Essex: see the figures provided by Given, *Society and homicide*, table 2, p. 36; and the comments of Barbara A. Hanawalt, *Crime and conflict in English communities 1300–1348* (Cambridge, Mass., and London, 1979), p. 98.
117 Walker, *Crime and punishment in Britain*, p. 21. Given makes much the same point, *Society and homicide*, p. 38.
118 This view is shared by Cockburn, 'Nature and incidence of crime', p. 57. Students of medieval homicide have come to much the same conclusion: see R. F. Hunnisett, *The medieval coroner* (Cambridge, 1961), p. 31; J. Bellamy, *Crime and public order in England in the later middle ages* (1973), p. 106; and Hanawalt, *Crime and conflict*, p. 101.
119 R. W. Malcolmson, 'Infanticide in the eighteenth century', *Crime in England 1550–1800*, ed. J. S. Cockburn (1977), is an important recent discussion of the subject. Malcolmson's work is based on a wide range of sources, which have allowed him to come to firmer conclusions than those reached here. Even so, his findings are consistent with those based on seventeenth-century Essex court materials. Keith Wrightson, 'Infanticide in earlier seventeenth-century England', *Local population studies*, 15 (1975), 10–22, is a slighter study based largely on Essex assize materials, with some evidence from Lancashire.
120 P.R.O., ASSI 35/110/8/26; she was acquitted, *ibid.*, 35/110/2/4.
121 43 Geo. III cap. 58.
122 Blackstone, *Commentaries*, vol. 4, p. 198.
123 E.R.O., D/B3/3/210.
124 Colchester borough records, examination and recognizance book, 1619–45, unfoliated, 6 January 1620.
125 See E.R.O., Q/SBa 2/59.
126 Malcolmson, 'Infanticide', p. 206, states that 'fewer than a dozen' of the 350 cases in his sample involved legitimate children being killed by their mothers.
127 The sources consulted for the present study give the impression that it was these considerations, rather than any desire to control population, which prompted infanticide in early modern England. This conclusion concurs with those of Malcolmson and Wrightson: see *ibid.*, p. 207, and Wrightson, 'Infanticide', p. 19.
128 For England, see Malcolmson, 'Infanticide', pp. 202–4; for France, Olwen H. Hufton, *The poor of eighteenth-century France, 1750–1789* (Oxford, 1974), p. 350. Occasionally, those indicted for infanticide in Essex in the period under

review can be proved to have been servants; for example Josselin, *Diary*, p. 349, states that Martha Wade, tried at the Trinity 1655 assizes, was one. She was acquitted, P.R.O., ASSI 35/96/2/19.

129 The Northern circuit assize depositions searched for homicide cases, P.R.O., ASSI 45/7/1–/9/3, contained insufficient depositions relating to infanticide for any conclusions to be reached.

130 See p. 60 above.

131 E.R.O., Q/SBa 2/57. The background to this case is discussed in Wrightson, 'Infanticide', pp. 13–14, where it is argued that prosecution was initiated some years after the offence was committed, largely at the instigation of a local minister.

132 For an example see C. Bridenbaugh, *Vexed and troubled Englishmen* (Oxford, 1968), p. 369. Wrightson, 'Infanticide', p. 21, n. 34, found many more examples of what he terms 'infanticidal nursing' in Lancashire than in Essex. The Essex assize files, however, contain one indictment of a widow allowing a bastard placed in her care to die of neglect, and a similar case of a couple who furthered the death of a bastard offspring of their daughter: P.R.O., ASSI 35/97/3/38; 35/111/9/4, respectively.

133 Colchester borough records, examination and recognizance book, 1619–45, unfoliated, 12 November 1638.

9 Punishment

1 That a major shift of this type occurred is one of the fundamental presuppositions of George Rusche and Otto Kirchheimer, *Punishment and social structure* (New York, 1939), and Michael R. Weisser, *Crime and punishment in early modern Europe* (Hassocks, Sussex, 1979).

2 S. F. C. Milsom, *Historical foundations of the common law* (1969), p. 361.

3 Radzinowicz, *History of English criminal law*, vol. 1, p. 5.

4 Blackstone put the total at about 160 in the third quarter of the eighteenth century, the period in which he was writing: *Commentaries*, vol. 4, p. 18.

5 It should be stressed, of course, that the infliction of the *peine forte et dure* was not, strictly speaking, a punishment.

6 See Radzinowicz, *History of English criminal law*, vol. 1, pp. 165–205, for a description of the ceremonies accompanying executions at Tyburn.

7 J. Bellamy, *Crime and public order in England in the later middle ages* (1973), p. 189, states that the custom was not established in his period of study.

8 See L. B. Smith, 'English treason trials and confessions in the sixteenth century', *Journal of the history of ideas*, 15 (1954), 471–98.

9 *The true narrative of the execution of John Marketman, chyrurgian, of Westham in the county of Essex, for committing a horrible & bloody murther* (n.d.), pp. 3–4. The pamphlet can be dated from another dealing with the case, *The full and true relation of all the proceedings at the assizes late holden at Chelmsford in the countie of Essex* (1680).

10 This will be discussed further in chapter 11 above.

11 For the survival of assize files see above, pp. 12–13.

12 One study, using a similar system of extrapolating an estimated figure from surviving evidence, has postulated that there were on average seventeen executions per year in Elizabethan Essex; see Jeremy C. M. Walker, 'Crime

and capital punishment in Elizabethan Essex' (University of Birmingham B.A. dissertation, 1971), fol. 41.

13 See Radzinowicz, *History of English criminal law*, vol. 1, pp. 139–64, for the background to this trend; Radzinowicz suggests (p. 149) that only thirteen felons were hanged per year at all of the Home circuit assizes by the mid eighteenth century, as compared to the average of seventeen per year for one county calculated by Walker.

14 For a discussion of the eighteenth-century situation, much of which is equally applicable to the seventeenth-century Essex assizes, see J. M. Beattie, 'Crime and the courts in Surrey 1736–1753', *Crime in England 1550–1800*, ed. J. S. Cockburn (1977), especially pp. 164–74.

15 Blackstone, *Commentaries*, vol. 4, p. 19.

16 For an outline of the history of benefit of clergy see p. 24 above.

17 Blackstone, *Commentaries*, vol. 4, p. 372.

18 For the figures upon which these calculations are based see table 3, p. 94 above; table 7, p. 109 above; and table 12, p. 124 above.

19 There are, however, a number of cases in which men granted benefit of clergy for theft were only able to sign depositions with a mark, which is at least an indication that they were illiterate: e.g. E.R.O., Q/SR 235/20; Q/SBa 2/2; Q/SR 287/25; Q/SBa 2/22.

20 5 Anne cap. 6.

21 'I.B.', *The psalme of mercy, or, a meditation upon the 51 Psalme, by a true penitent* (1625), sig. A5. The relevant verse ran: 'Have mercy upon me, O God, according to thy living kindness, according unto the multitude of thy tender mercies blot out my transgressions.'

22 Sir Thomas Smith, *De republica Anglorum* (1583), p. 83.

23 Quoted in D. Veall, *The popular movement for law reform, 1640–1660* (Oxford, 1970), p. 4, n. 4.

24 Quoted by A. L. Cross, 'The English criminal law and benefit of clergy during the eighteenth and early nineteenth centuries', *Am. hist. rev.*, 22 (1916–17), 554.

25 *The diary of John Manningham, of the Middle Temple, and of Bradbourne, Kent, barrister-at-law, 1602–1603*, ed. W. Tite (Camden Soc., old ser., 99, 1868), p. 40. For another example of the circumstances surrounding the granting of clergy see p. 24. I owe this reference to Peter Clark.

26 See P.R.O., ASSI 35/76/2/65; 35/91/1/17; 35/93/2/20, 29; E.R.O., Q/SR 272/44–7 (one husbandman on four indictments); Colchester borough records, S/R 34/9; 35/1. All these involved theft. Walker, 'Crime and capital punishment', fol. 21, states that only 9 of the 790 pleas of clergy known to have been made in Elizabethan Essex were refused on the grounds of the accused's inability to read.

27 See pp. 91–2 above.

28 Zachary Babington, *Advice to grand jurors in cases of blood* (1677), pp. 55–6.

29 The figures upon which these calculations are based are given in table 3, p. 94 above.

30 See P.R.O., ASSI 35/75/1/55; 35/76/2/60.

31 Radzinowicz, *History of English criminal law*, vol. 1, pp. 120–1. The use of the pardon and other aspects of judicial clemency are placed in a wider ideological context by Douglas Hay, 'Property, authority and the criminal law', *Albion's fatal tree*, ed. Hay *et al.* (1975), pp. 40–9.

32 The early history of pardoning is described in N. D. Hurnard, *The king's*

pardon for homicide before A.D. 1307 (Oxford, 1969), chapter 1, 'The origin of the medieval system of pardoning'.

33 See pp. 91–2 above.

34 Alexander Smith, *A complete history of the lives and robberies of the most notorious highwaymen, footpads, shoplifts and cheats of both sexes*, ed. A. L. Hayward (1926), pp. 375–6.

35 It has, indeed, been suggested that any county notable would regard the ability to obtain pardons for those petitioning him as one of the marks of his status: Douglas Hay, 'Crime, authority and the criminal law: Staffordshire, 1750–1800' (University of Warwick Ph.D. thesis, 1975), fol. 503.

36 12 Car. II cap. 11. Coke, *Third institute*, p. 233, remarks that these offences were not usually included in general pardons.

37 See P.R.O., ASSI 35/68/1/29; 35/73/1/141; 35/93/1/3–5; 35/101/3/36–41.

38 Blackstone, *Commentaries*, vol. 4, p. 394.

39 The file for the Essex Hilary assizes of 1620, the first to fall within the timespan covered by this work, includes a reprieve granted to a labourer convicted of theft: P.R.O., ASSI 35/62/1/12. Walker, 'Crime and capital punishment', fol. 30, finds the use of reprieves to be standard practice in the late sixteenth century.

40 P.R.O., ASSI 35/74/1/40; 35/86/1/27; 35/85/5/62; 35/86/1/53, 58, 66, 75, respectively.

41 Transportation in this period is discussed in A. E. Smith, *Colonists in bondage: white servitude and convict labour in America, 1607–1776* (Chapel Hill, 1947), especially part 2, 'Penal transportation'. A. G. L. Shaw, *Convicts and the colonies* (1966), chapter 1, 'Crime and transportation before the American Revolution', was also consulted.

42 Shaw, *Convicts and the colonies*, p. 24.

43 4 Geo. I cap. 11.

44 Shaw, *Convicts and the colonies*, p. 32.

45 Close analysis of Elizabethan court archives for the borough of Colchester, for example, indicates that the processes uncovered by historians of eighteenth-century crime were already operating in the late sixteenth century, at least in an embryonic form: see Joel Samaha, 'Hanging for felony: the rule of law in Elizabethan Colchester', *The historical journal*, 21 (1978), 763–82.

46 The epithet is suggested by a very informed study of one such punishment, J. W. Spargo, *Juridical folklore in England, illustrated by the cucking-stool* (Durham, North Carolina, 1944).

47 This is not to deny, of course, that the humiliation of the criminal was part of the objectives of both public hangings and public whippings.

48 P.R.O., ASSI 35/63/7, apparently the outcome of a decision made at a private session held before Sir Nicholas Coote and Sir Thomas Fanshawe in 1622, as a result of which a spinster accused of witchcraft was sentenced to stocking at Barking and Chelmsford, to be followed by committal to the house of correction.

49 *Ibid.*, 35/68/1/55, when a man allegedly resident in Middlesex was convicted of cheating an Essex man at a game called 'My carde before thy carde', and was sentenced to stand in the pillory with a placard announcing his fault.

50 E.R.O., T/A 419/1, fol. 58.

51 Colchester borough records, examination and recognizance book, 1619–45, unfoliated, 30 May 1639. However, the order that the couple should be

paraded 'w[i]th papers upon their heads accordinge to the Custome of this towne' suggests that the punishment was more frequently employed than references to it suggest: see W. J. Petchey, 'The borough of Maldon, Essex, 1500–1668: a study in sixteenth- and seventeenth-century urban history' (University of Leicester Ph.D. thesis, 1972), fol. 222, for an example of carting at Maldon in 1592.

52 See E.R.O., D/B3/1/19, fol. 193v, for an example of a petty thief being stocked on the orders of Maldon borough sessions.

53 Colchester borough records, examination and recognizance book, 1647–84, unfoliated, 18 December 1667.

54 See 18 Eliz. I cap. 3, 35 Eliz. I cap. 5.

55 7 Jac. I cap. 4.

56 J. P. Kenyon, *The Stuart constitution, 1603–1688* (Cambridge, 1966), p. 501.

57 B. W. Quintrell, 'The government of the county of Essex, 1603–1642' (London University Ph.D. thesis, 1965), fols. 206–7.

58 *V.C.H. Essex*, vol. 5, pp. 243–4.

59 See Colchester borough records, sessions book, 1630–63, for details of its work.

60 E.R.O., Q/SBa 2/76.

61 E.R.O., Q/SO 1, fol. 246v.

62 See E.R.O., Q/SR 236/102.

63 *Ibid.*, 258/95; 345/70.

64 Josselin, *Diary*, p. 587.

65 See E.R.O., Q/SR 337/65; P.R.O., ASSI 35/97/9/1, 79.

66 Particularly instructive in this respect are those occasions on which spinsters acquitted of infanticide were sent to the house of correction for a year, the obvious justification being that they should suffer the standard punishment for bearing bastards, even if they had not killed them: see P.R.O., ASSI 35/97/3/1, 16, 17, 22.

10 Crime and the local community

1 J. A. Sharpe, 'Crime and delinquency in an Essex parish 1600–1640', *Crime in England 1550–1800*, ed. J. S. Cockburn (1977); Keith Wrightson and David Levine, *Poverty and piety in an English village: Terling 1525–1700* (New York, San Francisco and London, 1979); John Walter, 'Grain riots and popular attitudes to the law: Maldon and the crisis of 1629', *An ungovernable people*, ed. John Brewer and John Styles (1980); and the research in progress on Earls Colne sources by Alan Macfarlane and his research team.

2 These requirements were laid down by 2 & 3 Philip and Mary cap. 8. For a general account of the difficulties of road repair in this period see S. and B. Webb, *English local government from the Revolution to the Municipal Corporations Act. Part five: the story of the king's highway* (1913), pp. 52–4.

3 See table 19, p. 183 above.

4 K. H. Burley, 'The economic development of Essex in the later seventeenth and early eighteenth centuries' (London University Ph.D. thesis, 1965) fols. 194–5.

5 E.R.O., Q/SR 379/36.

6 By the late seventeenth century the county bridge rate ran at £500 per year: E.R.O., Q/SO 2, fol. 28v.

7 E.R.O., Q/SR 287/14.

8 On one occasion fouling a ditch was an important incident in the build-up of tensions that preceded a witchcraft accusation: E.R.O., Q/SBa 2/60.

9 P.R.O., K.B. 9/759/23–30; E.R.O., Q/SR 333/39; 313/36, respectively.

10 F. G. Emmison, *Elizabethan life: disorder* (Chelmsford, 1970), p. 164.

11 E.R.O., Q/SR 240/17; 314/59; 245/32; Q/SO 1, fol. 206. It is worth mentioning in this connection a recognizance issued in 1675 against a London man for 'his keeping a lion to show, which lyon hath dangerously wounde[d] a child': E.R.O., Q/SR 429/112.

12 Josselin, *Diary*, pp. 352–3.

13 E.R.O., D/AEA 38, fol. 5.

14 *Ibid.*, 39, fol. 16. For Cutford's previous ambitions to witchcraft see Alan Macfarlane, *Witchcraft in Tudor and Stuart England* (1970), p. 286.

15 E.R.O., D/B3/3/388.

16 R.A. Marchant, *The church under the law: justice, administration and discipline in the diocese of York, 1560–1640* (Cambridge, 1969), p. 61.

17 For a description of the changes in the law relating to defamation see Theodore F. T. Plucknett, *A concise history of the common law*, 5th edn (1956), book 2, chapter 5, 'Defamation'.

18 Blackstone, *Commentaries*, vol. 4, p. 150.

19 Colchester borough records, examination and recognizance book, 1619–45, unfoliated, 24 January 1623.

20 E.R.O., Q/SR 367/12.

21 *Ibid.*, 435/41, 123; *The autobiography of Sir John Bramston, K.B.*, ed. P. Braybrooke (Camden Soc., old ser., 32, 1844), pp. 158–60.

22 For a recent discussion of the social implications of ecclesiastical defamation suits see J. A. Sharpe, *Defamation and sexual slander in early modern England: the church courts at York* (Borthwick papers, 58, 1980). Analysis of an Archdeaconry of Essex deposition book for 1626–42 reveals that, as in Yorkshire, sexual slander was central to church court defamation: E.R.O., D/AED 8, *passim.* Cf. F. G. Emmison, *Elizabethan life: morals & the church courts* (Chelmsford, 1973), pp. 48–68, for similar Elizabethan cases.

23 E.R.O., Q/SR 319/74; 307/80, respectively.

24 *Ibid.*, 322/40.

25 *Ibid.*, 372/5.

26 P.R.O., K.B. 9/871/403.

27 Dalton, *Countrey justice*, p. 38.

28 E.R.O., Q/SR 244/8.

29 Interestingly enough, these King's Bench cases include one sent up from Castle Hedingham court leet: P.R.O., K.B. 9/881/78.

30 Dalton, *Countrey Justice*, p. 39.

31 Blackstone, *Commentaries*, vol. 4, p. 133.

32 E.R.O., Q/SO 2, fol. 153v. Cudmore's last appearance as grand juror was at the Trinity assizes of 1675: P.R.O., ASSI 35/116/13/4.

33 P.R.O., ASSI 35/71/1/10; E.R.O., Q/SR 171/22; 172/43; 230/38; 234/114, 153.

34 E.R.O., Q/SR 350/28; 351/41–2; 358/56; 362/61.

35 *Ibid.*, 320/118; 324/65–6, 98, 108.

36 Witchcraft in Essex in the sixteenth and seventeenth centuries has been described in considerable depth by Macfarlane, *Witchcraft*, and the present writer is broadly in agreement with his conclusions. Wider background to the problem is provided by Keith Thomas, *Religion and the decline of magic*

(1971), especially chapters 14–18 which deal with witchcraft. Mention must also be made of an excellent pioneering study, C. L. Ewen, *Witch hunting and witch trials* (1929).

37 This is discussed in Macfarlane, *Witchcraft*, chapter 9, 'The witch-finding movement of 1645 in Essex'.

38 P.R.O., ASSI 35/86/1, *passim.*

39 See table 20, p. 184 above.

40 P.R.O., ASSI 35/68/2/51. Another witch was stocked and sent to the house of correction after apparently being tried by two JPs at a special sessions: *ibid.*, 35/63/7.

41 Macfarlane, *Witchcraft*, table 11, p. 150.

42 For a discussion of this point in a European context see Christina Larner 'Crimen exceptum? The crime of witchcraft in Europe', *Crime and the law: the social history of crime in western Europe since 1500*, ed. V. A. C. Gatrell, Bruce Lenman and Geoffrey Parker (1980).

43 Coke, *Third institute*, pp. 66–7.

44 Some of the more serious town fires of the period are mentioned in *Crisis and order in English towns, 1500–1700*, ed. P. Clark and P. Slack (1972), p. 7.

45 E.R.O., D/DM M9, mem. 4v.

46 E. J. Hobsbawm and E. Rudé, *Captain Swing* (1969), pp. 79–80; W. S. Amos, 'Social discontent and agrarian disturbances in Essex, 1795–1850' (Durham University M.A. thesis, 1971), fols. 15–18, 86–92.

47 Thomas, *Religion and the decline of magic*, pp. 531–4.

48 P.R.O., ASSI 35/86/1/27–8. He was subsequently reprieved.

49 E.R.O., Q/SR 358/27. The indictment was found *ignoramus*.

50 Colchester borough records, examination and recognizance book, 1619–45, unfoliated, 11 July 1631.

51 For example, a petition for relief from a victim of a fire in 1641 blamed 'a Tobacco pipe att the haystacke where the fire first kindled', which was thought to have been left by a vagrant: E.R.O., Q/SBa 2/43.

52 E.R.O., Q/SR 406/23. For similar examples see E.R.O., D/B3/3/125; Q/SBa 2/9; Colchester borough records, S/R 40/2.

53 Macfarlane, *Witchcraft*, p. 154, states that 431 various animals were recorded as having been bewitched in Essex assize indictments for witchcraft between 1560 and 1680.

54 E.R.O., Q/SR 406/69; 228/84, respectively.

55 Hobsbawm and Rudé, *Captain Swing*, p. 80.

56 This process is one of the major themes of Michael R. Weisser, *Crime and punishment in early modern Europe* (Hassocks, Sussex, 1979).

57 Sharpe, 'Crime and delinquency', pp. 95–9.

58 E.R.O., Q/SR 319/85, 98; 347/52; 349/116; 353/89; 366/43, 45; 373/28; 389/70, 73; 396/20, 59; D/AER 22/80; 23/42; P.R.O., ASSI 35/111/2/26; 35/115/4/8.

59 Cases involving the Osbournes include: E.R.O., Q/SR 305/24, 43; 317/28; 321/8; 327/29; 345/23; 397/11; 389/30; 398/46, 74; 418/97; 421/122; 420/66, 92–6; 448/41; 450/7; Q/SBa 2/73; P.R.O., ASSI 35/86/1/54; 35/88/2/84, 88. These offences were committed between 1639 and the early 1680s.

60 See the comments of Lawrence Stone, *The crisis of the aristocracy 1558–1641* (Oxford, 1965), pp. 240–2.

61 M. J. Ingram, 'Communities and courts: law and disorder in early seventeenth-

century Wiltshire', *Crime in England 1550–1800*, ed. J. S. Cockburn (1977), p. 116, comments on how in the early seventeenth century the taste for litigation 'penetrated deep into society as a whole'.

62 E.R.O., Q/SBa 2/27.

63 *Ibid.*, 2/76.

64 *Ibid.*, 2/126.

65 This is the conclusion of Ingram, 'Communities and courts', p. 119.

66 Alan Macfarlane, Sarah Harrison and Charles Jardin, *Reconstructing historical communities* (Cambridge, 1977), pp. 181–2.

67 Wrightson and Levine, *Poverty and piety*, p. 181.

68 Sharpe, 'Crime and delinquency', p. 108.

69 This is described in *The Elizabethan underworld*, ed. A. V. Judges (1930) pp. xxxi–xxxvii.

70 See the comments of J. F. Pound, *Poverty and vagrancy in Tudor England* (1971), pp. 35–6. For two important breaks from the uncritical use of pamphlet literature see P. A. Slack, 'Vagrants and vagrancy in England, 1598–1664', *Econ. hist. rev.*, 2nd ser., 27 (1974), 360–79; and A. L. Beier, 'Vagrants and the social order in Elizabethan England', *Past and present*, 64 (1974), 3–29.

71 P.R.O., K.B. 9/871/245.

72 Colchester borough records, sessions book, 1630–63, *passim.*

73 P.R.O., S.P. 16/329/48; 16/364/83.

74 E.R.O., Q/SR 251/79.

75 *Ibid.*, 426/53.

76 J. S. Cockburn, 'The nature and incidence of crime in England 1559–1625', *Crime in England 1550–1800*, ed. J. S. Cockburn (1977), p. 63, thinks that vagrant crime, 'though premeditated in a general sense, was essentially opportunistic'. Seventeenth-century Essex material supports this view.

77 E.R.O., D/B3/3/392/5.

78 A family group of 'Tellers of Destenyes' equipped with counterfeit passes was taken at Brentwood in 1639, and justice Holcroft encountered a similar group in the 1680s: E.R.O., Q/SR 304/152; D/DCv 1, fol. 24, respectively.

79 E.R.O., Q/SR 240/76.

80 *Ibid.*, 394/88.

81 E.R.O., Q/SBa 2/2.

82 E.R.O., Q/SR 235/16; Q/SBa 2/2.

83 See p. 60 above.

84 Dalton, *Countrey justice*, p. 413.

85 Many of the themes, and some of the material, used in the remainder of this chapter form the basis of J. A. Sharpe, 'Enforcing the law in the seventeenth-century English village', *Crime and the law*, ed. Gatrell, Lenman and Parker (1980). I am grateful to Europa Publications Limited for permission to draw so heavily on that essay.

86 E.R.O., Q/SR 233/128.

87 *Ibid.*, 399/120.

88 E.R.O., Q/SBa 2/44.

89 13 Rich. II Stat. 1 cap. 13. For the history of the game laws and the legal position on poaching see C. Kirby, 'The English game law system', *Am. hist. rev.*, 38 (1933), 240–62; and C. and E. Kirby, 'The Stuart game prerogative', *Eng. hist. rev.*, 46 (1931), 239–54. For two important local studies of eighteenth-century poaching see Douglas Hay, 'Poaching and the game laws on Cannock Chase', *Albion's fatal tree*, ed. Hay *et al.* (1975), and P. B.

Munsche, 'The game laws in Wiltshire 1750–1800', *Crime in England 1550–1800*, ed. J. S. Cockburn (1977).
90 Blackstone, *Commentaries*, vol. 4, pp. 174–5.
91 1 & 2 Jac. I cap. 27.
92 J. P. Kenyon, *The Stuart constitution 1603–1688* (Cambridge, 1966), p. 494.
93 Essex petty sessions do not survive for the seventeenth century; see the comments of Munsche, 'Game laws in Wiltshire', pp. 224–7, on the use of this source in a later period.
94 See table 19, p. 183 above.
95 E.R.O., Q/SR 318/33–42; 319/23–40.
96 By the early seventeenth century the sale to the capital of game poached in Essex was attracting the attention of the central government: P.R.O., S.P. 14/48/23.
97 E.R.O., D/DCv 1, *passim*.
98 W. R. Fisher, *The forest of Essex: its history, laws, administration and ancient customs, and the wild deer which lived in it* (1887), p. 87.
99 E.R.O., Q/SBa 2/49; Q/SR 399/100, respectively.
100 P.R.O., ASSI 35/87/2/78.
101 *Ibid.*, 35/99/11/14; 35/101/1/1, respectively.
102 *Ibid.*, 35/11/3/92; 35/110/7/37–8, respectively.
103 E.R.O., Q/SR 411/99.
104 For some comments on the importance of gleaning to the rural poor in a later century see Jennie Kitteringham, 'Country work girls in nineteenth-century England', *Village life and labour*, ed. Raphael Samuel (1975), pp. 54–6.
105 Thomas Tusser, *Five hundreth points of good husbandry* (1577), p. 54.
106 E.R.O., Q/SBa 2/81.
107 E.R.O., Q/SR 395/37, 71; 396/29, 30; P.R.O., ASSI 35/103/9/22; 35/105/2/15.
108 A few such thefts were prosecuted, however; e.g. Q/SR 265/25; 310/15, both of which concerned pieces of wood valued at one penny.
109 *Ibid.*, 258/95; 344/97; Colchester borough records, sessions book, 1630–63, unfoliated, 13 April 1631; E.R.O., T/A 419/1, fol. 35; F. G. Emmison, *Early Essex town meetings* (Chichester, 1970), p. 108.
110 R. Gough, *Antiquities and memoires of the parish of Myddle, county of Salop* (Shrewsbury, 1875), p. 61.
111 See E.R.O., Q/SR 241/12.
112 See E.R.O., Q/SBa 2/74.
113 43 Eliz. I cap. 7.
114 A. E. Everitt, 'Farm labourers', *The agrarian history of England and Wales. Vol. 4, 1500–1640*, ed. Joan Thirsk (Cambridge, 1967), especially, pp. 462–4.
115 See, for example, the uncritical acceptance of this view in Christopher Hill, *The world turned upside down: radical ideas during the English Revolution* (1972), pp. 35–40.
116 *Ibid.*, p. 35.
117 E. F. Farrell, 'Essex rural settlement: some aspects of its evolution, with particular reference to the sixteenth century' (University of Wales M.A. dissertation, 1969), fol. 139.
118 *Ibid.*, fol. 143.
119 See table 20, p. 184 above.
120 *Cal. S.P. Dom, 1623–1625*, p. 41.

121 Farrell, 'Essex rural settlement', fol. 23, describes Aveley in these terms.
122 E.R.O., D/D Th M12, fols. 6, 7.
123 David G. Hey, *An English rural community: Myddle under the Tudors and Stuarts* (Leicester, 1974), p. 224. T. C. Curtis, 'Some aspects of the history of crime in seventeenth-century England' (Manchester University Ph.D. thesis, 1973), fols. 171–84, experiences similar divergences between the pattern of recorded criminal prosecutions and Professor Everitt's hypothesis.
124 See table 20, p. 184 above.
125 Joan Thirsk, 'The farming regions of England', *The agrarian history of England and Wales. Vol. 4, 1500–1640*, ed. Joan Thirsk (Cambridge, 1967), p. 54.
126 Bodleian MS Firth c. 4, fol. 494.
127 *Cal. S.P. Dom., 1640–1641*, p. 362.
128 This view coincides with that of Buchanan Sharp, *In contempt of all authority: rural artisans and riot in the west of England, 1586–1660* (Berkeley, Los Angeles and London, 1980), pp. 1, 6–7.
129 Josselin, *Diary*, pp. 160–1.
130 *Minutes of proceedings in quarter sessions held for the parts of Kesteven in the county of Lincoln, 1674–1695*, ed. S. A. Peyton (2 vols., Lincoln Record Soc. publications, 25–6, 1931), vol. 1, pp. xxv–xxvi.
131 Quoted in C. Bridenbaugh, *Vexed and troubled Englishmen* (Oxford, 1968), p. 242.
132 For a full discussion of this tendency and its implications see Wrightson and Levine, *Poverty and piety*, pp. 103–6.
133 Particularly by Wrightson and Levine, *ibid., passim.* Cf. the comments of Sharpe, 'Enforcing the law', pp. 100–2.
134 See Keith Wrightson, 'Two concepts of order: justices, constables and jurymen in seventeenth-century England', *An ungovernable people*, ed. John Brewer and John Styles (1980).
135 See the comments of M. Cain, 'On the beat: interactions and relations in rural and urban police forces', *Images of deviance*, ed. S. Cohen (Harmondsworth, 1971).
136 Joseph Rigbie, *An ingenious poem called the drunkards perspective or burning glass* (1656), p. 22.
137 E.R.O., Q/SR 399/122; 435/53, respectively.
138 *Ibid.*, 242/43.
139 E.R.O., Q/SBa 2/48.
140 *Ibid.*, 2/2.
141 E.R.O., Q/SR 391/67.
142 *Ibid.*, 403/20, 88.
143 E.R.O., Q/SBa 2/95.
144 Both these cases are found in *ibid.*, 2/30.
145 *Tudor economic documents*, ed. R. H. Tawney and E. Power (3 vols., 1924), vol. 2, p. 341. More than a century after Hext wrote, an anonymous pamphleteer commented disapprovingly that 'some have refused to own their Goods (when taken on a thief) before a Maiestrate, for fear of forfeiting their Recognizance, and of long Journies that may sometimes more than double the loss': *Hanging not punishment enough for murtherers, high-way men, and house-breakers* (1701), p. 11.
146 E.R.O., Q/SBa 2/80.
147 E.R.O., D/B3/3/392/1.

148 E.R.O., MSS Morant, vol. 46, p. 153.
149 The tolerance evidently afforded to some known local offenders was probably complemented by a more immediate reaction against unknown offenders or the more marginal members of society, especially vagrants. This point is discussed at length in Ingram, 'Communities and courts', pp. 127–34. Essex materials do not permit the detailed analysis which Ingram has made, but isolated evidence can be found of a sharp reaction to outsiders, e.g. E.R.O., Q/SBa 2/4 for a vagrant thief apprehended after a hue and cry. Sharpe, 'Crime and delinquency', p. 101, suggests that about half the admittedly small sample of thieves tried for offences committed in Kelvedon between 1600 and 1640 were strangers to the parish.
150 Fees at assizes are discussed in J. S. Cockburn, *A history of English assizes 1558–1714* (Cambridge, 1972), pp. 72–4. A list of fees charged on the Western circuit can be found in *Somerset assize orders, 1629–1640*, ed. T. G. Barnes (Somerset Record Soc., 65, 1959), appendix 3, pp. 72–3. Fees at the Essex quarter sessions are discussed in B. W. Quintrell, 'The government of the county of Essex, 1603–1642' (London University Ph.D. thesis, 1965), fols. 75–6.
151 E.R.O., Q/SR 279/4.
152 Quintrell, 'Government of Essex', fol. 75.
153 *Ibid.*
154 Quintrell, for example, *ibid.*, fol. 76, points out that the costs of litigation at the quarter sessions were roughly comparable with those charged for causes of office at the archdeacon's court.
155 Cockburn, *History of English assizes*, p. 73.
156 Quintrell, 'Government of Essex', fol. 87, n. 3.
157 *Ibid.*, fol. 75.
158 *Hanging not punishment enough*, p. 12.
159 See E.R.O., Q/SR 434/35.
160 Colchester borough records, examination and recognizance book, 1647–84, unfoliated, 14 March 1670.
161 Treatment of petty crime at the workplace is one of the themes currently interesting criminologists. See, for example, Jason Ditton, *Part-time crime: an ethnography of fiddling and pilferage* (1977).
162 E.R.O., D/Ba 4497 bundle G.
163 E.R.O., Q/SBa 2/37.
164 *Ibid.*, 2/31; 2/37; 2/39.
165 Wrightson, 'Two concepts of order', p. 42.
166 Keith Wrightson, 'The puritan reformation of manners with special reference to the counties of Lancashire and Essex, 1640–1660' (Cambridge University Ph.D. thesis, 1973), fols. 104–5.
167 Keith Wrightson, 'Terling study: working paper 1. An Essex village and the courts, 1590 to 1650' (unpublished paper presented to the National Criminology Conference at Cambridge, 1975), fol. 13.
168 E.R.O., Q/SBa 2/91. An earlier example is provided by a charity established by a local yeoman at Terling in 1626, which not only led to the badging of the poor, but also forbade the granting of relief to those poor who were pilferers, habitual drunkards, swearers, idlers, vagrants, or entertainers of inmates: David Levine, *Family formation in an age of nascent capitalism* (New York, San Francisco and London, 1977), p. 119.
169 For a preliminary discussion of this question see J. A. Sharpe, 'Was er een

"criminal class' in het vroeg–moderne Europa? Enig Engels materiaal' (trans. Pieter Spierenburg), *Tijdschrift voor Criminologie*, 20e jaargang (mei–augustus 1978), 211–22.

170 A point emphasised by J. J. Tobias, *Crime and industrial society in the nineteenth century* (1967), p. 52.

171 This tendency has, of course, attracted considerable adverse comment from radical criminologists: for an early critique see D. Chapman, *Sociology and the stereotype of the criminal* (1968), pp. 52–3.

172 *Middlesex sessions records*, ed. W. le Hardy (new ser., 4 vols., 1935–41), contain numerous references to both these phenomena.

173 M. McIntosh, 'Changes in the organization of thieving', *Images of deviance*, ed. S. Cohen (Harmondsworth, 1971), p. 109.

174 A detailed impression of such offenders can be gained from Alan Macfarlane, *The justice and the mare's ale: law and disorder in seventeenth-century England* (1980), which quotes extensively from contemporary court archives.

175 Peter Clark, 'The migrant in Kentish towns 1580–1640', *Crisis and order in English towns 1500–1700*, ed. P. Clark and P. Slack (1972), p. 144; cf. Cockburn, 'Nature and incidence of crime', p. 64, where the existence of 'a sizeable local population for whom petty pilfering was almost instinctive' is postulated.

176 F. Hull, 'Agriculture and rural society in Essex, 1603–1642' (London University Ph.D. thesis, 1950), fol. 501, comments that 'it is impossible to decide on what these labourers depended for their livelihood'.

177 The term was, of course, popularised by a monograph dealing with the impact of urbanisation on France: Louis Chevalier, *Labouring classes and dangerous classes in Paris during the first half of the nineteenth century* (1973).

178 Wrightson and Levine, *Poverty and piety*, p. 185.

11 Overall patterns of crime in Essex, 1620–80

1 J. S. Cockburn, *A history of English assizes, 1588–1714* (Cambridge, 1972), p. 113.

2 See above, p. 144, and table 16, p. 143.

3 For an introduction to this proliferation of capital statutes see Radzinowicz, *History of English criminal law*, vol. 1, chapter 1, 'Extension of capital punishment'.

4 See table 14, p. 134 above.

5 It is probable, indeed, that such a transition never took place in England: as Alan Macfarlane, *The justice and the mare's ale: law and disorder in seventeenth-century England* (1980) pp. 196–9, argues, English crime was already 'modern' or 'capitalist' in the seventeenth century.

6 Perhaps the most dramatic example of this is provided by the presentment of numerous unlicensed alehouses during an intensification of the efficiency of local government in 1644: E.R.O., Q/SBa 6.

7 A trend discussed in Keith Wrightson, 'The puritan reformation of manners, with special reference to the counties of Lancashire and Essex, 1640–1660' (Cambridge University Ph.D. thesis, 1973).

8 See J. P. Kenyon, *The Stuart constitution, 1603–1688* (Cambridge, 1966), pp. 493–5, for a statement of this view.

9 B. W. Quintrell, 'The government of the county of Essex, 1603–1642'

(London University Ph.D. thesis, 1965), fols. 228–9, thinks that the Book of Orders still had a moderate influence in promoting diligence in local government in the county as late as 1638.

10 As they belong essentially to religious history, recusancy and failing to attend church have been excluded from this study. However, some general comments on fluctuations in the prosecution of these offences are offered above, p. 198.

11 This conclusion must, of course, make an exception of the unusual crusade against the unlicensed alehouse of 1644, of which Q/SBa 6 provides ample evidence.

12 See table 19, p. 183 above.

13 For a discussion of regulative prosecution in periods of bad harvest see John Walter and Keith Wrightson, 'Dearth and the social order in early modern England', *Past and present*, 71 (1976), 22–42, especially 29, 35–42.

14 M. James, *Social problems and policy during the Puritan Revolution 1640–1660* (1930), chapter 2, 'Economic conditions 1640–1660', still constitutes a useful introduction to these years. For a more recent approach to the general problem see J. P. Cooper, 'Social and economic policies under the commonwealth', *The Interregnum: the quest for settlement 1646–1660*, ed. G. E. Aylmer (1972).

15 This is the conclusion of Cooper, 'Social and economic policies', pp. 140–1. See Wrightson, 'Puritan reformation of manners', for the view that the impact of puritanism in this period produced a new ethos among the officers of county and parish government; however, Walter and Wrightson, 'Dearth and the social order', p. 40, seem to suggest that the dearth of 1648–52, in Lancashire at least, was met by traditional methods, and Wrightson himself, 'Puritan reformation of manners', p. 207, comments that no sustained local government activity on the scale of 1629–31 was found in Essex during the Interregnum.

16 For an easily accessible example of such articles see W. E. Tate, *The parish chest*, 3rd edn (Cambridge, 1969), pp. 178–9.

17 In some instances large numbers of people might be indicted together, e.g. forty-nine at the Trinity assizes of 1670: P.R.O., ASSI 35/111/12/13.

18 The main outlines of this topic are given in Charles Wilson, 'The other face of mercantilism', *Trans. Royal Hist. Soc.*, 5th ser., 9 (1959), 81–101.

19 J. S. Cockburn, 'The nature and incidence of crime in England 1559–1625', *Crime in England 1550–1800*, ed. J. S. Cockburn (1977), there were 168 indictments for vagrancy at the Essex assizes, 1559–1603.

20 A search of the Essex assize files for 1620–1629 revealed no examples of indictments of vagrants: P.R.O., ASSI 35/62/1–35/71/3, *passim*. An examination of the quarter sessions rolls for the same period produced two such indictments: E.R.O., Q/SR 229/39; 324/20.

21 It is, however, possible that the development of the house of correction presented the county with a method of dealing with vagrants that was felt to be more appropriate than indictment.

22 This appears to be at variance with the conclusions reached in Cockburn, *History of English assizes*, p. 187. It should be noted, however, that Cockburn's findings are based on the evidence of Western circuit order books, a class of document which has been lost for the Home circuit, thus preventing direct comparison.

23 For example, thirty-seven at the Hilary 1621 assizes: P.R.O., ASSI 35/63/1/2–12; and twenty-five at the Trinity 1627 assizes: *ibid.*, 35/69/2/5.

24 E.R.O., Q/SR 247–51, *passim*.
25 *Ibid.*, 252–5, *passim*.
26 *Ibid.*, 264–8, *passim*.
27 *Ibid.*, 343–66, *passim.*; P.R.O., ASSI 35/91/1–35/97/8, *passim*.
28 E.R.O., Q/SR 387–403, *passim*.
29 For a description of the activities of the criminal poor in the county see pp. 160–73 above.
30 W. G. Hoskins, 'Harvest fluctuations and English economic history 1620–1759', *Ag. hist. rev.* 16 (1968), 15–31. Connecting property offences and wheat prices is, of course, open to the objection that the poor would have eaten inferior grain during this period. Unfortunately the terminal date of C. J. Harrison, 'Grain price analysis and harvest qualities, 1465–1634', *Ag. hist. rev.*, 19 (1971), 135–55, which provides details of the harvests of other cereals, is too early to make it useful to the present study. Even so, Harrison's figures suggest that a disastrous wheat harvest was rarely offset by bumper harvests of inferior grains, an impression confirmed by the figures given by Peter Bowden, 'Statistical Appendix', *The agrarian history of England and Wales. Vol. 4, 1500–1640*, ed. Joan Thirsk (Cambridge, 1967), pp. 820–1, which go up to 1649. Other evidence supports this view; Josselin, for example, normally linked the prices of various foods when commenting on food prices and twice linked the prices of wheat and rye: *Diary*, pp. 152, 167, 184. Similarly, a letter from Sir Thomas Barrington in March 1631 described how barley, upon which the poor subsisted, was at 6/4d a bushel: *Cal. S.P. Dom., 1629–1631*, p. 532. As figure 6 shows, the price of wheat was also high at that time.
31 Josselin, *Diary*, pp. 72, 73, 95, 104, 110, 125, 130, 131, 152, 156, 163, 167, 181, 184, 237.
32 *Ibid.*, p. 484.
33 *Ibid.*, p. 492.
34 For an impression of the impact of bad harvests on criminal statistics in the 1590s see Joel Samaha, *Law and order in historical perspective: the case of Elizabethan Essex* (New York and London, 1974), pp. 22, 168–9, and Cockburn, 'Nature and incidence of crime', pp. 67–70.
35 This impression is supported by an examination of the Essex assize files for the 1690s, which demonstrates that property offences never reached the levels of the bad years of the 1590s or of 1631; nevertheless, over forty property offences were tried at the Hilary 1698 assizes, and over fifty at the Hilary 1699 assizes: P.R.O., ASSI 35/139/1; 35/140/1 respectively, with a further forty-nine tried at the Trinity 1699 assizes: *ibid.*, 35/140/2. These were the only years in which a high number of property offences was tried at the assizes during this decade, despite the recurrent bad harvests that it experienced.
36 See pp. 18–19 above.
37 J. E. Pilgrim, 'The rise of the "new draperies" in Essex', *University of Birmingham historical journal*, 7 (1959–60), 55.
38 *Cal. S.P. Dom., 1619–1623*, p. 480.
39 *Cal. S.P. Dom., 1640–1641*, p. 362.
40 For a recent description of these disturbances see Brian Manning, *The English people and the English revolution 1640–1649* (1976), pp. 171–8.
41 *Cal. S.P. Dom., 1651*, p. 10.
42 *Cal. S.P. Dom., 1651–1652*, pp. 479–80.
43 No complete history has yet been written of fluctuations in the textile industry during this period, but a useful introduction is provided by D. W. Jones, 'The

"Hallage" receipts of the London cloth markets, 1562–1720', *Econ. hist. rev.*, 2nd ser., 25 (1972), 567–87.

44 See pp. 80–2 above.

45 This contrasts with the situation in the years 1559–1625 as portrayed by Cockburn, 'Nature and incidence of crime', p. 52, where it is asserted that London provided 'by far the most significant influence on crime in Essex'. The apparent reversal of this situation in the period 1620–80 is difficult to explain, although the constant troubles of the new draperies must have served to shift the centre of gravity of crime in the county away from the London peripheries towards the clothing areas. As table 21 demonstrates, this tendency was already marked by the end of the period dealt with by Cockburn.

46 F. Hull, 'Agriculture and rural society in Essex, 1560–1640' (London University Ph.D. thesis, 1950), fol. 123; and K. H. Burley, 'The economic development of Essex in the later seventeenth and early eighteenth centuries' (London University Ph.D. thesis, 1957), fols. 21, 137.

47 For a stark portrayal of the connection in another pre-industrial society see Olwen H. Hufton, *The poor of eighteenth-century France, 1750–1789* (Oxford, 1974), especially part 3, 'The crimes of the poor'.

48 See E.R.O., Q/SBa 2/22; 2/32; 2/73; 2/84; Q/SR 394/97; 418/69; 428/144; Colchester borough records, examination and recognizance book, 1619–45, unfoliated, 11 January 1639.

49 B. E. Supple, *Commercial crisis and change in England, 1600–1642: a study in the instability of a mercantile economy* (Cambridge, 1959), p. 107; Bodleian MS Firth c. 4, fol. 138.

50 E.R.O., Q/SBa 2/43; 2/45; 2/46; one hundred-and-forty families were put out of work by this visitation, apart from those infected.

51 W. G. Bell, *The Great Plague in London in 1665*, 2nd edn (1951), pp. 186, 201.

52 J. F. D. Shrewsbury, *A history of the bubonic plague in the British Isles* (Cambridge, 1970), p. 502.

53 T. C. Glines, 'Politics and government in the borough of Colchester, 1660–1693' (University of Wisconsin Ph.D. thesis, 1974), fol. 124; cf. I. G. Doolittle, 'Population growth in Colchester and the Tendring Hundred', *Essex journal*, 7 (1972), 31–6.

54 I. G. Doolittle, 'The plague in Colchester 1579–1666', *Transactions of the Essex Archaeological Society*, 3rd ser., 4 (1972), 143, states that the Colchester textile trade was effectively stopped until 1668.

55 Glines, 'Politics and government', fol. 130, comments on the rapid repopulation of Colchester, this being almost complete by 1675. He attributes this to 'the powerful attraction of urban employment in the seventeenth century for those living in the surrounding rural hinterland'.

56 The classic account of the impact of the war upon Essex and the area adjacent to it is A. Kingston, *East Anglia and the Great Civil War* (1897). This has been supplemented recently by Clive Holmes, *The Eastern Association in the English Civil War* (Cambridge, 1974).

57 One contemporary, quoted in Kingston, *Great Civil War*, p. 260, commented that the townspeople of Colchester in 1648 were 'distracted with the noveltie of their business, having never seene an army before'.

58 Holmes, *Eastern Association*, pp. 21–3, 26, 28, attributes this early unity largely to the influence of the Earl of Warwick.

59 Cockburn, *History of English assizes*, p. 241.

60 E.R.O., Q/SBa 2/53.
61 It is worth remembering, however, that the royalists believed that they had 10,000 supporters in the county willing to rise on their behalf should they attack it; see Kingston, *Great Civil War*, pp. 140–1.
62 Alan Macfarlane, *Witchcraft in Tudor and Stuart England* (1970), p. 142.
63 E.R.O., Q/SBa 2/48.
64 Josselin, *Diary*, p. 185. It should be noted that Josselin related this development to economic hardship rather than to the aftermath of war.
65 *Cal. S.P. Dom., 1649–50*, p. 392.
66 See Josselin, *Diary*, p. 91; for an example of his fears, *ibid.*, p. 94.
67 E.R.O., Q/SBa 2/80.
68 Kingston, *Great Civil War*, pp. 270–1.
69 This term is used by Hull, 'Agriculture and rural society', fol. 471.
70 Walter and Wrightson, 'Dearth and the social order', p. 29. See also the comments of Hull, 'Agriculture and rural society', fol. 493.
71 Colchester borough records, examination and recognizance book, 1619–45, unfoliated, 8 February 1624.
72 Bodleian MS Firth c. 4, fol. 494.
73 Manning, *English people and English revolution*, p. 176, quotes the Earl of Warwick's steward who reported that 'no man appeared like a gentleman, but was made a prey to that ravenous crew'.
74 See above, pp. 80–2, for an account of this incident.
75 Quoted in Buchanan Sharp, *In contempt of all authority: rural artisans and riot in the west of England, 1586–1660* (Berkeley, Los Angeles and London, 1980), p. 34. Sharp's work emphasised the contribution of textile workers to the popular disturbances of the period, and it is now evident that this was just one aspect of widespread lawlessness in the clothing areas. It is interesting to note in this connection that Barbara A. Hanawalt, *Crime and conflict in English communities 1300–1348* (Cambridge, Mass., and London, 1979), p. 259, attributes the high incidence of theft in fourteenth-century Norfolk, in part at least, to the existence of a developed rural cloth industry in the county.
76 *V.C.H. Essex*, vol. 2, p. 394.
77 It should be remembered, however, that Bodleian MS Firth c. 4 might distort the evidence by constituting an unusually vivid source for the earlier period.
78 This opinion is shared by Quintrell, 'Government of Essex'.
79 For a recent discussion of this point see Jason Ditton, *Controlology: beyond the new criminology* (1979), especially chapter 2, 'Crime waves or control waves? A recipe for atheistic statisticians'.

12 Concluding observations

1 There are, of course, a number of other historians of crime who have produced works based on the county as a unit of study: two of the most relevant, for our immediate purposes, are Joel Samaha, *Law and order in historical perspective: the case of Elizabethan Essex* (New York and London, 1974), and T. C. Curtis, 'Some aspects of the history of crime in seventeenth-century England' (Manchester University Ph.D. thesis, 1973).
2 For two recent attempts at a synthesis of current writing on the history of crime, neither of them entirely successful, see Michael R. Weisser, *Crime and punishment in early modern Europe* (Hassocks, Sussex, 1979), and Bruce Lenman and Geoffrey Parker, 'The state, the community and the criminal law

in early modern Europe', *Crime and the law*, ed. Gatrell, Lenman and Parker (1980).

3 In particular, a very useful study could be based on the records of the Northern circuit of the assizes, which include both indictments (P.R.O., ASSI 44) and depositions (P.R.O., ASSI 45) in a good series from the 1650s onwards. Alan Macfarlane, *The justice and the mare's ale: law and disorder in seventeenth-century England* (1980), is based on these materials and demonstrates their usefulness.

4 These are discussed at length in T. C. Curtis, 'Quarter sessions appearances and their background: a seventeenth-century regional study', *Crime in England 1550–1800*, ed. J. S. Cockburn (1977), and J. A. Sharpe, 'Enforcing the law in the seventeenth-century English village', *Crime and the law*, ed. Gatrell, Lenman and Parker (1980). Curtis's ideas are developed further in his 'Explaining crime in early modern England', *Criminal justice history* (1980), vol. 1, pp. 117–37.

5 In *Poverty and piety in an English village: Terling 1525–1700* (New York, San Francisco and London, 1979), especially chapter 5, 'Conflict and control: the villagers and the courts'.

6 This impression is based on Barbara A. Hanawalt, *Crime and conflict in English communities 1300–1348* (Cambridge, Mass., and London, 1979); J. S. Cockburn, 'The nature and incidence of crime in England 1559–1625', *Crime in England 1550–1800*, ed. J. S. Cockburn (1977); Samaha, *Law and order in historical perspective*; and J. M. Beattie, 'The pattern of crime in England, 1660–1800', *Past and present*, 72 (1974), 47–95.

7 This notion was first popularised by a group of scholars working on French provincial archives, normally using only very small samples of cases: the relevant references and some criticisms are given in Lenman and Parker, 'The state, the community and the criminal law', p. 47, n. 80.

8 Beattie, 'Pattern of crime', p. 61.

9 This seems to be the conclusion to draw from comparing the data given in table 14, p. 134 above, with those provided by Cockburn, 'Nature and incidence of crime', p. 55. For an early, and extremely shaky, attempt to look at long-term fluctuations of this type see Paul Hair, 'Deaths from violence in Britain. A tentative secular survey', *Population studies*, 25 (1971), 5–24.

10 Cockburn, 'Nature and incidence of crime', p. 68.

11 Beattie, 'Pattern of crime', p. 77.

12 The use of the death penalty in the eighteenth century is discussed by Douglas Hay, 'Property, authority and the criminal law', *Albion's fatal tree*, ed. Hay *et al*, (1975), and J. M. Beattie, 'Crime and the courts in Surrey 1736–1753', *Crime in England 1550–1800*, ed. J. S. Cockburn (1977).

13 I owe this notion to A. E. Soman, who was good enough to discuss with me some of the early findings of his research on cases tried by the Parlement of Paris in the late sixteenth and early seventeenth centuries. The idea of a 'judicial revolution' also intrudes at certain points into Lenman and Parker, 'The state, the community and the criminal law'.

14 The fullest discussion of this theme is to be found in Radzinowicz, *History of English criminal law*, vol. 1.

15 For example, 25 Henry VIII cap. 6 (buggery); 1 Edw. VI cap. 12, 2 & 3 Edw. VI cap. 33, and 31 Eliz. I cap. 12 (horse-theft); and 8 Eliz. I cap. 4 (pickpocketing).

16 It would be otiose to reiterate a full bibliography of works dealing with

vagrancy at this point; however, for an extremely stimulating article discussing perhaps the harshest of the Tudor statutes dealing with the offence see C. S. L. Davies, 'Slavery and Protector Somerset: the Vagrancy Act of 1547', *Econ. hist. rev.*, 2nd ser., 16 (1966), 533–49.

17 This is one of the major themes of J. H. Langbein, *Prosecuting crime in the Renaissance: England, Germany, France* (Cambridge, Mass., 1974).

18 For example, 1 Jac. I cap. 9; 21 Jac. I cap. 7.

19 Puritan attitudes towards crime and delinquency await full investigation, and it seems likely that study of what might be termed the 'social control' aspects of puritanism would lead to a useful reassessment of that phenomenon. Keith Wrightson, 'The puritan reformation of manners, with special reference to the counties of Lancashire and Essex, 1640–1660' (Cambridge University Ph.D. thesis, 1973), is a stimulating initial survey.

20 Even the radical critics of the law during the Interregnum were unable to achieve much by way of reform; the limited nature of such reforms as were brought about is described by D. Veall, *The popular movement for law reform, 1640–1660* (Oxford, 1970).

21 S. F. C. Milsom, *Historical foundations of the common law* (1969), pp. 353, 361.

22 Douglas Hay, 'Crime, authority and the criminal law: Staffordshire 1750–1800' (University of Warwick Ph.D. thesis, 1975), fol. 22, comments that 97% of executions on the Western circuit between 1770 and 1779 were punishments of infringements of the common law or pre-1742 legislation.

23 Radzinowicz, *History of English criminal law*, vol. 1, p. 35. For the background to one of the most notorious of these statutes, where the situation was rather more complex, see E. P. Thompson, *Whigs and hunters: the origin of the Black Act* (1975).

24 Attitudes to the law form one of the major themes of *Albion's fatal tree: crime and society in eighteenth-century England*, ed. Hay *et al.* (1975); Thompson, *Whigs and hunters*; and *An ungovernable people*, ed. John Brewer and John Styles (1980), all of which focus mainly on the eighteenth century. For some comments on attitudes to the law and litigation in the Stuart period see M. J. Ingram, 'Communities and courts: law and disorder in early seventeenth-century Wiltshire', *Crime in England 1550–1800*, ed. J. S. Cockburn (1977), and J. A. Sharpe, 'Litigation and human relations in early modern England: ecclesiastical defamation suits at York', *Law and human relations* (papers presented to the Past and Present Society conference, 1980).

25 Hay, 'Property, authority and the criminal law', *passim.*

26 Laurie Lee, *Cider with Rosie* (Harmondsworth, 1973), pp. 205–6.

Bibliography

MANUSCRIPT SOURCES

Essex Record Office

Quarter sessions records
Quarter sessions rolls, Epiphany 1620 – Michaelmas 1680: Q/SR 227–441
Draft indictments from presentments, Epiphany 1620 – Easter 1623: Q/SBa
   1/39–47
Quarter sessions bundles, main series, Michaelmas 1621 – Michaelmas 1680:
   Q/SBa 2/1–127
Returns of recusants and alehouses, 1644: Q/SBa 6
Sessions book, 1632–43: Q/SMg/1
Order books, 1652–61: Q/SO 1 (printed as *Essex quarter sessions order book
   1652–1661*, ed. D. H. Allen (Essex edited texts, 1, 1974))
            1671–86: Q/SO 2
Process and related documents: Q/SPa 1/1–2
                               Q/SPa 2/1–4
                               Q/SPa 3
                               Q/SPa 4/1–13
'Bridge book': Q/CP 3 (a manuscript book, drawn up in the early eighteenth
   century, comprising material abstracted from most of the above sources)

Maldon borough records
Sessions books, 1606–31: D/B3/1/19
            1631–64: D/B3/1/20
            1664–90: D/B3/1/21
Sessions papers and related documents: D/B3/3/125; 144; 147; 148; 167; 177;
   198; 208; 210; 211; 214; 388; 392; 422

Saffron Walden borough records
Microfilm of sessions book, 1657–73: T/A 419/1

Archdeaconry of Essex
Act books, 1618–32: D/AEA 31–8 (searched primarily for references to Maldon
   inhabitants)
Deposition book, 1626–42: D/AED 8 (searched for defamation cases)

Archdeaconry of Colchester
Act books, 1596–41: D/ACA 24–54 (searched primarily for references to
   Kelvedon Easterford inhabitants)

Manorial records
Manor of Kelvedon Hall, court roll, 1511–1647: D/DU 19/31–3 Manor of
    Braintree, abstract of court roll, 1616–1769: D/DU 65/57
Manor of Rochford Hall, court roll, 1632–70: D/DU 183/2
Manor of Burnham, licences to fish Walfleet, 1677: D/DGe M. 165
Manor of Earls Colne Priory, court roll, 1605–29: D/DPr 21/4–21
Manor of Aveley, notes on previous entries in manorial rolls, *c.* 1625: D/D Th
    M12

Family records
Barrington Papers (temporary reference): D/Ba Acc. 4497 Bundle G
Diary of William Holcroft, JP, 1661–89: D/DCv 1
Papers relating to Holcroft Diary: D/DCv 2/1–20
Deed and bonds between Thomas Dawtrey, sheriff, and his undersheriff, 1681:
    D/DFa 05
Record book of Sir Humphrey Mildmay while sheriff of Essex, 1635–6: D/DU
    146/7
Copy of *Gallen's Almanack* for 1669 annotated with details of official business by
    Carew Mildmay: D/DU 262
Papers relating to official work of Carew Harvey Mildmay, JP: D/DMs 07-011;
    036–7
Diary of unknown member of Clopton family of the Essex–Suffolk border: D/DQs
    18
Original charter confirming incorporation of Thaxted: D/Dsh 03

Wills
Edward Eldred: D/ABV 45/13
Cawood family: D/AER 22/80; 23/42

Chelmsford churchwardens' accounts, 1557–1668: D/P 94/5/1

Public Record Office

Assize Records
Home circuit indictments, ASSI 35, were searched for Essex references. The series
was not unbroken; the following files survive and were used in this study:

	Hilary file	Trinity file	Hilary (general) file	Trinity (general) file
1620	62/1	62/2	—	—
1621	63/1	63/7	—	—
1622	64/1	—	—	—
1623	—	—	—	—
1624	66/7	66/8	—	—
1625	67/9	67/1	—	—
1626	68/1	68/2	—	—
1627	69/1	69/2	—	—
1628	70/1	—	—	—
1629	71/2	71/3	—	—
1630	72/1	72/2	—	—

	Hilary file	Trinity file	Hilary (general) file	Trinity (general) file
1631	73/1	—	—	—
1632	74/1	74/2	—	—
1633	75/1	—	—	—
1634	76/2	76/3	76/1	76/11
1635	—	77/1	77/8	77/9
1636	78/1	78/2	78/10	—
1637	—	—	79/1	79/2
1638	—	80/3	80/11	80/10
1639	—	81/1	81/6	81/7
1640	—	82/2	82/6	82/7
1641	83/9	83/3	83/7	83/8
1642	—	84/2	84/10	84/9
1643	—	—	—	—
1644	—	85/5	85/3	—
1645	—	86/1	—	86/5
1646	—	—	—	87/2
1647	88/9	88/4	88/2	88/6
1648	89/10	89/6	89/1	89/7
1649	90/3	90/7	—	90/8
1650	91/1	91/8	91/4	91/10
1651	92/1	92/2	92/11	92/12
1652	93/1	93/2	93/10	93/11
1653	94/1	94/2	94/11	94/12
1654	95/1	95/2	95/11	95/12
1655	96/1	96/2	96/11	96/12
1656	97/3	97/1	97/8	—
1657	98/1	98/2	98/11	98/12
1658	99/1	99/2	99/11	99/12
1659	—	100/2	—	100/7
1660	—	101/3	—	—
1661	—	102/2	—	102/8
1662	103/1	103/2	103/9	103/10
1663	104/1	104/2	104/11	104/12
1664	105/1	105/2	105/10	105/11
1665	—	106/1	106/4	106/12
1666	107/1	—	107/9	107/10
1667	108/1	108/2	108/9	108/10
1668	109/1	109/2	109/7	109/8
1669	110/1	110/2	110/7	110/8
1670	111/7	111/9	111/11	111/12
1671	112/10	112/8	112/2	112/9
1672	—	113/10	113/10	113/11
1673	—	114/1	114/9	114/10
1674	115/2	115/3	—	115/10
1675	116/1	116/2	116/12	116/13
1676	117/2	117/3	117/11	117/12
1677	118/1	118/2	118/11	118/12

	Hilary file	Trinity file	Hilary (general) file	Trinity (general) file
1678	119/2	119/3	119/1	—
1679	120/1	120/2	120/9	—
1680	—	—	121/8	—

Home circuit cause book, 1673–81: ASSI 34/1
Western circuit crown book, 1656–78: ASSI 2/1
Northern circuit indictment rolls, *c.* 1664–9: ASSI 44/12–16
Northern circuit depositions, *c.* 1664–9: ASSI 45/7/1–45/9/3

King's Bench records
Ancient Indictments, 1620 – Hilary 1675: K.B. 9/757–931, and Indictments,
    Hilary 1675 – Hilary 1681: K.B. 11/1–5, were searched for Essex references

Exchequer records
King's Remembrance rolls, 1619–21: E. 157–9, were searched for Essex
    references

State Papers
S.P. 16/96/39; 133/19; 186/62; 270/5; 271/30; 329/48; 347/73; 364/83

Privy Council records
P.C. 2/52
P.C. 2/65

Star Chamber records
STAC 8/3/4; 8/64/23; 8/125/16; 8/140/7

War Office
W.O. 30/48, 'Abstract of a particular account of all the inns, alehouses, &c., in
    England with their stable-room and bedding in the year 1686' (covers Essex
    with other counties)

Colchester borough records (Town Hall, Colchester)

Sessions rolls, 1620–59: S/R 17–48 (imperfect series)
Examination and recognizance books, 1619–45 and 1647–84
Sessions book, 1630–63

Harwich borough records (Town Hall, Harwich)

Sessions books, 1601–39: Bundle 98/14
              1640/95: Bundle 98/15
Miscellaneous sessions documents: Bundle 130

Bodleian Library, Oxford

The Essex Lieutenancy letter book, 1608–39: MS Firth c. 4

PRINTED SOURCES

The place of publication of books and pamphlets is London unless otherwise stated. It was decided, because of the constraints of space, not to give a simple listing of all the works consulted in the preparation of this book, and, in consequence, a number of general works are omitted in the select bibliography which follows. The most relevant of the works consulted fall under seven main headings.

1 Contemporary works relating to Essex, including assize sermons

The autobiography of Sir John Bramston, K.B., ed. P. Braybrooke (Camden Soc., old ser., 32, 1844)

B[ownd], N[ath]. *Saint Paul's trumpet, sounding an alarme to iudgement, Warning all men to prepare themselves against their appearing before Christ's tribunall. Delivered in two sermons, commanded by publique authoritie to be preached: the one at Paul's Crosse: the other at the assizes at Chelmsford in Essex, Iuly 24 1615* (1615)

The diary of Ralph Josselin, 1616–1683, ed. Alan Macfarlane (Records of social and economic history, new ser., 3, 1976)

The full and true relation of all the proceedings at the assizes late holden at Chelmsford in the countie of Essex (1680)

Hardy, Nathaniel. *An apostolical liturgy revived. A sermon preached at the assizes held in the county of Essex, March 18 1660* (1661)

Norden, John. *Speculi Britanniae pars: an historical and chorographical description of the county of Essex* (Camden Soc., old ser., 9, 1840)

Scott, John. *A sermon preached at the assizes at Chelmsford in the county of Essex, August 31 1685* (1685)

A true and exact relation of the severall informations, examinations, and confessions of the late witches, arraigned and executed in the county of Essex (1645)

The true narrative of the execution of John Marketman, chyrurgian, of Westham in the county of Essex, for committing a horrible & bloody murther (n.d.)

Walker, Anthony. *Say on: or, a seasonable plea for a full hearing betwixt man and man, and, a serious plea for the like hearing betwixt God and man, delivered in a sermon at Chelmsford in Essex, at the general assize holden for the said county, July 8 1678* (1679)

2 Collections of pamphlets, etc., relating to crime in the period

The complete Newgate calendar, ed. J. L. Rayner and G. T. Crook (5 vols., 1926)

The Elizabethan underworld ed. A. V. Judges (1930)

Smith, Alexander. *A complete history of the lives and robberies of the most notorious highwaymen, footpads, shoplifts and cheats of both sexes*, ed. A. L. Hayward (1926)

3 Printed court records from counties other than Essex

Quarter sessions and other court records have been printed for a substantial number of English counties. Those listed below are a selection of the most useful, in terms either of their introductions or of the breadth of the material they contain.

Before the bawdy court: selections from church court and other records relating to the correction of moral offences in England, Scotland and New England, 1300–1800, ed. Paul Hair (1972)

A calendar of assize records, ed. J. S. Cockburn (in progress, 1975–)
Calendar of Nottinghamshire coroners' inquests, 1485–1558, ed. R. F. Hunnisett (Thoroton Soc. record series, 25, 1969)
Calendar of the quarter sessions papers, ed. J. Willis Bund (Worcestershire County Records, 2 vols., 1900)
The court leet records of the manor of Manchester, ed. J. P. Earwaker (12 vols., 1884–90)
Cox, J. C. *Three centuries of Derbyshire annals as illustrated by the records of the quarter sessions of the county of Derby from Queen Elizabeth to Queen Victoria* (2 vols., 1890)
The earliest Lincolnshire assize rolls, A.D. 1202–1209, ed. D. M. Stenton (Lincoln Record Soc. publications, 22, 1926)
Hamilton, A. H. A. *Quarter sessions from Queen Elizabeth to Queen Anne* (1878)
Kentish sources: 6. Crime and punishment, ed. E. Melling (Maidstone, 1969)
Middlesex county records, ed. J. C. Jeaffreson (4 vols., Middlesex County Record Soc., 1886–92)
Middlesex sessions records, ed. W. le Hardy (new ser., 4 vols., 1935–41)
Minutes of proceedings in quarter sessions held for the parts of Kesteven in the county of Lincoln, 1674–1695, ed. S. A. Peyton (2 vols., Lincoln Record Soc. publications, 25–6, 1931)
Quarter sessions order book, 1642–1649, ed. B. C. Redwood (Sussex Record Soc. publications, 54, n.d.)
Somerset assize orders, 1629–1640, ed. T. G. Barnes (Somerset Record Soc. publications, 65, 1959)
The third report of the Deputy Keeper of the Public Records (appendix 2, pp. 215–30, 1842)
Western circuit assize orders 1629–1648, ed. J. S. Cockburn (Camden Soc., 4th ser., 17, 1976)

4 Contemporary works on law and legal institutions, etc.

Babington, Zachary. *Advice to grand jurors in cases of blood* (1677)
Blackstone, William. *Commentaries on the laws of England*, 4th edn (4 vols., 1771). Book 4, 'Of public wrongs', was the most useful part for the purposes of the present work
Burn, Richard. *Ecclesiastical law* (2 vols., 1763)
Coke, Sir Edward. *The third part of the institutes of the laws of England: concerning high treason, and other pleas of the crown, and criminal causes* (1644)
Coke, Sir Edward. *The fourth part of the institutes of the laws of England: concerning the jurisdiction of courts*, 4th edn (1669)
Dalton, Michael. *The countrey justice: containing the practice of the justices of the peace out of their sessions: gathered for the better help of such justices of peace, as have not been much conversant in the study of the laws of this realm*, 10th edn (1677)
Firth, C. H. and Rait, R. S. *Acts and ordinances of the Interregnum, 1642–1660* (3 vols., 1911), especially vol. 2, pp. 387–9, giving the ordinance of 10 May 1650 'for suppressing the detestable sins of Incest, Adultery, and Fornication'
Greenwood, William Βουλευτηριον *or a practical demonstration of county judicatures, wherein is amply explained the judicial and ministerial authority of sheriffs and coroners*, 6th edn (1675)
Hale, Sir Matthew. *Pleas of the crown, or a brief, but full account of whatsoever*

can be found relating to that subject (1678). T. Dogherty's edition of 1800 was also consulted

Hanging not punishment enough for murtherers, high-way men, and house-breakers (1701)

Lambarde, William. *The duties of constables, borsholders, tithingmen, and such other low ministers of the peace. Whereunto be also adioyned the several offices of church wardens: of surveyors for amending the high waies: of distributors of the provision for noysome fowls & vermin: of the collectors: overseers: and governors of the poore: and of the wardens and collectors for the houses of correction* (1583)

Lambarde, William. *Eirenarcha: or of the office of the justices of peace in foure bookes, gathered 1579: first published 1581: and now secondly revised, corrected, and enlarged agreeably to the reformed commission of the peace,* 7th edn (1592)

March, John. *Actions of slaunder, or, a methodicall collection under certain grounds and heads, of what words are actionable at law, and what not?* (1647)

The office of the clerk of assize, containing the form and method of the proceedings at the assizes as also on the crown and nisi prius *side. Together with the office of the clerk of the peace* (1676)

Powell, John. *The assize of bread, newly corrected and enlarged* (1630)

Sheppard, William. *The court keeper's guide for the keeping of courts leet and courts baron,* 7th edn (1685)

Sheppard, William. *The offices and duties of constables, borsholders, tything-men, treasurers of the county stock, overseers of the poore, and other lay ministers* (1641)

Wilkinson, John. *A treatise collected out of the statutes of this kingdom, and according to the common experience of the lawes, concerning the office and authorities of coroners and sherifes: together with an easie and plain method for the keeping of a court leet, court baron and hundred court, &c.* (1618)

5 Secondary works on the history of Essex

Amos, W. S. 'Social discontent and agrarian disturbances in Essex, 1795–1850' (Durham University M.A. thesis, 1971)

Anglin, J. P. 'The court of the archdeacon of Essex, 1571–1609' (University of California Ph.D. thesis, 1965)

Aylmer, G. E. 'St Patrick's Day 1628 in Witham, Essex', *Past and present*, 61 (1973), 139–48

Brown, A. F. J. *Essex at work 1700–1815* (Chelmsford, 1969)

Burley, K. H. 'The economic development of Essex in the later seventeenth and early eighteenth centuries' (London University Ph.D. thesis, 1957)

Burley, K. H. 'A note on a labour dispute in early eighteenth-century Colchester', *Bulletin of the Institute of Historical Research*, 29 (1956), 220–30

Colvin, R. B. *The lieutenants and keepers of the rolls of the county of Essex* (1934)

Dale, B. *The annals of Coggeshall, otherwise Sunnedon, in the county of Essex* (Coggeshall, 1863). Contains extracts from the late seventeenth-century diary of Joseph Bufton

Doolittle, I. G. 'Population growth in Colchester and the Tendring Hundred', *Essex journal*, 7 (1972), 31–6

Doolittle, I. G. 'The plague in Colchester 1579–1666', *Transactions of the Essex Archaeological Society*, 3rd ser., 4 (1972), 134–47

Emmison, F. G. *Early Essex town meetings* (Chichester, 1970)
Emmison, F. G. *Elizabethan life: disorder* (Chemlsford, 1970)
Emmison, F. G. *Elizabethan life: home, work & land* (Chelmsford, 1976)
Emmison, F. G. *Elizabethan life: morals & the church courts* (Chelmsford, 1973)
Emmison, F. G. *Guide to the Essex Record Office* (Chelmsford, 1969)
Farm and cottage inventories of mid-Essex, 1635–1749, ed. F. W. Steer (Essex
    Record Office publications, 8, Chelmsford, 1950)
Fisher, W. R. *The forest of Essex: its history, laws, administration and ancient
    customs, and the wild deer which lived in it* (1887)
Glines, T. C. 'Politics and government in the borough of Colchester, 1660–1693'
    (University of Wisconsin Ph.D. thesis, 1974)
Gruenfelder, J. K. 'The election of the knights of the shire for Essex in the spring of
    1640', *Transactions of the Essex Archaeological Society*, 3rd ser., 2 (1967),
    143–6
Holmes, Clive. *The Eastern Association in the English Civil War* (Cambridge,
    1974)
Hull, F. 'Agriculture and rural society in Essex, 1560–1640' (London University
    Ph.D. thesis, 1950)
Hunt, W. A. 'The godly and the vulgar: puritanism and social cleavage in
    seventeenth-century Essex, England' (Harvard University Ph.D. thesis, 1974)
Kingston, A. *East Anglia and the Great Civil War* (1897)
Levine, David. *Family formation in an age of nascent capitalism* (New York, San
    Francisco and London, 1977), especially chapter 8, 'Proletarianization and
    pauperism: .the case of Terling'
Macfarlane, Alan. *The family life of Ralph Josselin* (Cambridge, 1970)
Morant, Philip. *The history and antiquities of the county of Essex*, (2 vols., 1816)
Nuttall, W. L. F. 'Sir Thomas Barrington and the Puritan Revolution', *Transactions
    of the Essex Archaeological Society*, 3rd ser., 2 (1966), 60–82
Petchey, W. J. 'The borough of Maldon, Essex, 1500–1668: a study in sixteenth-
    and seventeenth-century urban history' (University of Leicester Ph.D. thesis,
    1972)
Pilgrim, J. E. 'The cloth industry in Essex and Suffolk, 1558–1640' (London
    University M.A. thesis, 1938)
Pilgrim, J. E. 'The rise of the "new draperies" in Essex', *University of Birmingham
    historical journal*, 7 (1959–60), 36–59
P.R.O. lists and indexes, 9 (New York, 1963), pp. 43–8 (list of Essex sheriffs)
Quintrell, B. W. 'The divisional committee for southern Essex in the Civil War and
    its part in local administration' (Manchester University M.A. thesis, 1962)
Quintrell, B. W. 'The government of the county of Essex, 1603–1642' (London
    University Ph.D. thesis, 1965)
Roker, L. 'The Flemish and Dutch communities in Colchester in the sixteenth and
    seventeenth centuries' (London University M.A. thesis, 1963)
Rowe, V. A. 'Robert, second Earl of Warwick, and the payment of ship money in
    Essex', *Transactions of the Essex Archaeological Society*, 3rd ser., 1 (1962),
    160–3
Simmon, U. *small beer: an Essex village from Elizabeth I to Elizabeth II*
    (Braintree, n.d.)
Smith, H. *The ecclesiastical history of Essex under the Long Parliament and the
    Commonwealth* (Colchester, n.d.)
The Victoria history of the counties of England: a history of Essex (6 vols., in
    progress, 1903–   )
Wrightson, Keith and Levine, David. *Poverty and piety in an English village:
    Terling 1525–1700* (New York, San Francisco and London, 1979)

6. Secondary works on the history of crime and the law

Albion's fatal tree: crime and society in eighteenth-century England, ed. Douglas Hay, Peter Linebaugh, John G. Rule, E. P. Thompson and Cal Winslow (1975)

Andrews, W. *Punishments in the olden time* (1881)

Ault, W. O. 'By-laws of gleaning and the problems of harvest', *Econ. hist. rev.*, 2nd ser., 14 (1961), 210–17

Barnes, T. G. *The clerk of the peace in Caroline Somerset* (Leicester University, Department of English Local History, Occasional Papers, 14, 1961)

Bastardy and its comparative history: studies in the history of illegitimacy and marital nonconformity in Britain, France, Germany, Sweden, North America, Jamaica and Japan, ed. Peter Laslett, Karla Oosterveen and Richard M. Smith (1980)

Beattie, J. M. 'Crime and the courts in Surrey 1736–1753', *Crime in England 1550–1800*, ed. J. S. Cockburn (1977)

Beattie, J. M. 'The pattern of crime in England, 1660–1800', *Past and present*, 72 (1974), 47–95

Beier, A. L. 'Vagrants and the social order in Elizabethan England', *Past and present*, 64 (1974), 3–29

Bellamy, J. *Crime and public order in England in the later middle ages* (1973)

Beloff, Max. *Public order and popular disturbances 1660–1714* (Oxford, 1938)

Bercé, Y-M. 'Aspects de la criminalité au XVIIᵉ siècle', *Revue historique*, 239 (1968), 33–42

Beresford, M. W. 'The common informer, the penal statutes and economic regulation', *Econ. hist. rev.*, 2nd ser., 10 (1957–8)

Bingham, Coral. 'Seventeenth-century attitudes toward deviant sex', *Journal of interdisciplinary history*, 1 (1971), 447–72

Blatcher, Marjorie. *The court of King's Bench 1450–1550: a study in self-help* (University of London legal series, 12, 1978)

Bridenbaugh, C. *Vexed and troubled Englishmen* (Oxford, 1968)

Brinkworth, E. R. 'The study and use of archdeacons' court records: illustrated from the Oxford records (1566–1759)', *Trans. Royal Hist. Soc.*, 4th ser., 25 (1943), 93–120

Clark, Peter. 'Popular protest and disturbance in Kent, 1558–1640', *Econ. hist. rev.*, 2nd ser., 29 (1976), 365–82

Cockburn, J. S. 'Early modern assize records as historical evidence', *Journal of the Society of Archivists*, 5 (1975), 215–31

Cockburn, J. S. *A history of English assizes, 1558–1714* (Cambridge, 1972)

Cockburn, J. S. 'The nature and incidence of crime in England 1559–1625: a preliminary survey', *Crime in England 1550–1800*, ed. J. S. Cockburn (1977)

Cockburn, J. S. 'Seventeenth-century clerks of assizes – some anonymous members of the legal profession', *The American journal of legal history*, 13 (1969), 315–32

Crimes et criminalité en France sous l'Ancien Régime, 17ᵉ et 18ᵉ siècles, ed. F. Billaçois (Cahiers des Annales, 33, Paris, 1971)

Cross, A. L. 'The English criminal law and benefit of clergy during the eighteenth and early nineteenth centuries', *Am. hist. rev.*, 22 (1916–17)

Curtis, T. C. 'Quarter sessions appearances and their background: a seventeenth-century regional study', *Crime in England 1550–1800*, ed. J. S. Cockburn (1977)

Curtis, T. C. 'Some aspects of the history of crime in seventeenth-century England, with special reference to Cheshire and Middlesex' (Manchester University Ph.D. thesis, 1973)

Davies, C. S. L. 'Les révoltes populaires en Angleterre (1500–1700)', *Annales E.S.C.*, 29 (1969), 24–60

Davies, C. S. L. 'Peasant revolt in France and England: a comparison', *Ag. hist. rev.*, 21 (1973), 122–34

Dunn, R. M. 'The London weavers' riot of 1675', *Guildhall studies in London history*, 1 (1973), 13–23

Erikson, K. T. *Wayward puritans: a study in the sociology of deviance* (New York, 1966)

Ewen, C. L. *Witch hunting and witch trials* (1929)

Forster, G. C. F. *The East Riding justices of the peace in the seventeenth century* (East Yorkshire local history series, 30, 1973)

Gabel, L. C. *Benefit of clergy in England in the later middle ages* (Smith College studies in history, 14, Northampton, Mass., 1928–9)

Gatrell, V. A. C. 'The decline of theft and violence in Victorian and Edwardian England', *Crime and the law: the social history of crime in western Europe since 1500*, ed. V. A. C. Gatrell, Bruce Lenman and Geoffrey Parker (1980)

Given, James Buchanan. *Society and homicide in thirteenth-century England* (Stanford, California, 1977)

Gleason, J. H. *The justices of the peace in England, 1558 to 1640* (Oxford, 1969)

Green, T. A. 'Societal concepts of criminal liability for homicide in medieval England', *Speculum*, 47 (1972), 669–94

Hanawalt, Barbara A. *Crime and conflict in English communities 1300–1348* (Cambridge, Mass., and London, 1979)

Harding, A. *A social history of English law* (Harmondsworth, 1966)

Hartley, T. E. 'Under-sheriffs and bailiffs in some English shrievalties, *c.* 1580 to *c.* 1625', *Bulletin of the Institute of Historical Research*, 47 (1974), 164–85

Hay, Douglas. 'Crime, authority and the criminal law: Staffordshire 1750–1800' (University of Warwick Ph.D. thesis, 1975)

Hay, Douglas. 'Poaching and the game laws on Cannock Chase', *Albion's fatal tree: crime and society in eighteenth-century England*, ed. Douglas Hay, Peter Linebaugh, John G. Rule, E. P. Thompson and Cal Winslow (1975)

Hay, Douglas. 'Property, authority and the criminal law', *Albion's fatal tree: crime and society in eighteenth-century England*, ed. Douglas Hay, Peter Linebaugh, John G. Rule, E. P. Thompson and Cal Winslow (1975)

Hobsbawm, E. J. 'The machine breakers', *Past and present*, 1 (1952), 57–70

Hobsbawm, E. J. and Rudé, G. *Captain Swing* (1969)

Holdsworth, W. S. *A history of English law*, ed. A. L. Goodhart and H. G. Hanbury (17 vols., 1903–72)

Holt, F. J. *The law of libel* (1813)

Hone, N. J. *The manor and manorial records* (1912)

Hunnisett, R. F. *The medieval coroner* (Cambridge, 1961)

Hurnard, N. D. *The king's pardon for homicide before A.D. 1307* (Oxford, 1969)

Ingram, M. J. 'Communities and courts: law and disorder in early seventeenth-century Wiltshire', *Crime in England 1550–1800*, ed. J. S. Cockburn (1977)

Ingram, M. J. 'Ecclesiastical justice in Wiltshire 1600–1640, with special reference to cases concerning sex and marriage' (Oxford University D.Phil. thesis, 1976)

Karraker, C. H. *The seventeenth-century sheriff* (Chapel Hill, 1930)

Kaye, J. M. 'The early history of murder and manslaughter', *Law quarterly review*, 83 (1967), 365–95, 569–601

Kenyon, J. P. *The Stuart constitution, 1603–1688* (Cambridge, 1966)

King, Walter J. 'Leet jurors and the search for law and order in seventeenth-century England: "galling persecution" or reasonable justice?', *Histoire sociale – social history*, 13 (1980), 305–23

Kirby, C. 'The English game law system', *Am. hist. rev.*, 38 (1933), 240–62

Kirby, C. and Kirby, E. 'The Stuart game prerogative', *Eng. hist. rev.*, 46 (1931), 239–54

Langbein, John H. *Prosecuting crime in the Renaissance: England, Germany, France* (Cambridge, Mass., 1974)

Langbein, John H. *Torture and the law of proof: Europe and England in the ancien régime* (Chicago and London, 1977)

Lenman, Bruce and Parker, Geoffrey. 'The state, the community and the criminal law in early modern Europe', *Crime and the law: the social history of crime in western Europe since 1500*, ed. V. A. C. Gatrell, Bruce Lenman and Geoffrey Parker (1980)

Macfarlane, Alan. *The justice and the mare's ale: law and disorder in seventeenth-century England* (Oxford, 1981)

Macfarlane, Alan. *Witchcraft in Tudor and Stuart England* (1970)

Malcolmson, R. W. 'Infanticide in the eighteenth century', *Crime in England 1550–1800*, ed. J. S. Cockburn (1977)

Marchant, R. A. *The church under the law: justice, administration and discipline in the diocese of York, 1560–1640*, (Cambridge, 1969)

Milsom, S. F. C. *Historical foundations of the common law* (1969)

Moir, E. *The justice of the peace* (Harmondsworth, 1969)

Morrill, J. S. *The Cheshire grand jury 1625–1659: a social and administrative study* (Leicester University, Department of English Local History, Occasional Papers, 3rd ser., 1, 1976)

Mousnier, R. *Peasant uprisings in seventeenth-century France, Russia and China* (1971)

Munsche, P. B. 'The game laws in Wiltshire 1750–1800', *Crime in England 1550–1800*, ed. J. S. Cockburn (1977)

Peters, Robert. *Oculus episcopi: administration in the archdeaconry of St Albans 1580–1625* (Manchester, 1963)

Philips, David. *Crime and authority in Victorian England: the Black Country 1835–1860* (1977)

Pike, L. O. *A history of crime in England* (2 vols., 1873–6)

Pollock, F. and Maitland, F. W. *The history of English law before the time of Edward I*, 2nd edn (2 vols., Cambridge, 1968)

Porchnev, B. *Les soulèvements populaires en France de 1623 à 1648* (Paris, 1963)

Powers, E. *Crime and punishment in early Massachusetts* (Boston, 1966)

Pugh, R. B. *Imprisonment in medieval England* (Cambridge, 1968)

Putnam, B. H. 'The transformation of the keepers of the peace into the justices of the peace 1327–1380', *Trans. Royal Hist. Soc.*, 4th ser., 12 (1929), 19–48

Quaife, G. R. *Wanton wenches and wayward wives* (1979)

Radzinowicz, Leon. *A history of English criminal law and its administration from 1750* (4 vols., 1948–68). The most relevant part for the purposes of the present study was *The movement for reform*

Rule, John G. 'Social crime in the rural south in the eighteenth and early nineteenth centuries', *Southern history*, 1 (1979), 135–53

Samaha, Joel. 'Gleanings from local criminal court records: sedition among the "inarticulate" in Elizabethan England', *The journal of social history*, 8 (1975), 61–79

Samaha, Joel. 'Hanging for felony: the rule of law in Elizabethan Colchester', *The historical journal*, 21 (1978), 763–82

Samaha, Joel. *Law and order in historical perspective: the case of Elizabethan Essex* (New York and London, 1974)

Sayles, G. O. *The court of King's Bench in law and history* (Selden Society lecture, 1959)

Sharp, Buchanan. *In contempt of all authority: rural artisans and riot in the west of England, 1586–1660* (Berkeley, Los Angeles, and London, 1980)

Sharpe, J. A. 'Crime and delinquency in an Essex parish 1600–1640', *Crime in England 1550–1800*, ed. J. S. Cockburn (1977)

Sharpe, J. A. *Defamation and sexual slander in early modern England: the church courts at York* (Borthwick papers, 58, 1980)

Sharpe, J. A. 'Domestic homicide in early modern England', *The historical journal*, 24 (1981), 29–48

Sharpe, J. A. 'Enforcing the law in the seventeenth-century English village', *Crime and the law: the social history of crime in western Europe since 1500*, ed. V. A. C. Gatrell, Bruce Lenman and Geoffrey Parker (1980)

Shaw, A. G. L. *Convicts and the colonies* (1966), especially chapter 1, 'Crime and transportation before the American Revolution'

Simpson, A. W. B. *An introduction to the history of the land law* (Oxford, 1961)

Simpson, H. B. 'The office of constable', *Eng. hist. rev.*, 10 (1895), 625–41

Slack, P. A. 'Vagrants and vagrancy in England, 1598–1664', *Econ. hist. rev.*, 2nd ser., 27 (1974), 360–79

Smith, A. E. *Colonists in bondage: white servitude and convict labour in America, 1607–1776* (Chapel Hill, 1947)

Smith, L. B. 'English treason trials and confessions in the sixteenth century', *Journal of the history of ideas*, 15 (1954), 471–98

Spargo, J. W. *Juridical folklore in England, illustrated by the cucking-stool* (Durham, North Carolina, 1944)

Stephen, J. F. *A history of the criminal law of England* (3 vols., 1883)

Thompson, E. P. 'The moral economy of the English crowd in the eighteenth century', *Past and present*, 50 (1971), 76–136

Thompson, E. P. *Whigs and hunters: the origin of the Black Act* (1975)

Tobias, J. J. *Crime and industrial society in the nineteenth century* (1967)

Veall, D. *The popular movement for law reform, 1640–1660* (Oxford, 1970)

Walker, Jeremy C. M. 'Crime and capital punishment in Elizabethan Essex' (University of Birmingham B.A. dissertation, 1971)

Walter, John. 'Grain riots and popular attitudes to the law: Maldon and the crisis of 1629', *An ungovernable people: the English and their law in the seventeenth and eighteenth centuries*, ed. John Brewer and John Styles (1980)

Walter, John and Wrightson, Keith. 'Dearth and the social order in early modern England', *Past and present*, 71 (1976), 22–42

Webb, S. and Webb, B. *English local government from the Revolution to the Municipal Corporations Act. Part two: the manor and the borough* (1908)

Webb, S. and Webb, B. *Ibid. Part five: the story of the king's highway* (1913)

Weisser, Michael R. *Crime and punishment in early modern Europe* (Hassocks, Sussex, 1979)

Wellington, R. H. *The king's coroner* (2 vols., 1905–6)

Westman, Barbara Hanawalt. 'The peasant family and crime in fourteenth-century England', *Journal of British studies*, 13, no. 2 (1974), 1–18

Wilson, J. S. 'Sheriffs' rolls of the sixteenth and seventeenth centuries', *Eng. hist. rev.*, 47 (1932), 31–45

Wrightson, Keith. 'Infanticide in earlier seventeenth-century England', *Local population studies*, 15 (1975), 10–22

Wrightson, Keith. 'The puritan reformation of manners, with special reference to the counties of Lancashire and Essex, 1640–1660' (Cambridge University Ph.D. thesis, 1973)

Wrightson, Keith. 'Terling study: working paper 1. An Essex village and the courts, 1590 to 1650' (unpublished paper presented to the National Criminology Conference at Cambridge, 1975)

Wrightson, Keith. 'Two concepts of order: justices, constables and jurymen in seventeenth-century England', *An ungovernable people: the English and their law in the seventeenth and eighteenth centuries*, ed. John Brewer and John Styles (1980)

7 Modern works on criminology

The lack of sufficiently detailed source material, and the limited state of our present knowledge of crime as a historical phenomenon make the application of modern criminological theory to early modern materials difficult. The following works, however, were found to provide insights beneficial to the historian.

Chapman, D. *Sociology and the stereotype of the criminal* (1968)

Cohen, S. *Folk devils and moral panics* (1972)

Coser, Lewis A. *The functions of social conflict* (1956)

Images of deviance, ed. S. Cohen (Harmondsworth, 1971)

MacAndrew, C. and Edgerton, R. B. *Drunken comportment* (1970)

McClintock, F. H. and Avison, N. H. *Crime in England and Wales* (1968)

Mays, J. B. *Crime and the social structure* (1963)

Morris, T. and Blom-Cooper, L. *A calendar of murder: criminal homicide in England since 1957* (1964)

Radzinowicz, Leon. *Sexual offences* (English studies in criminal science, 9, 1957)

Walker, N. D. *Crime and punishment in Britain* (Edinburgh, 1965)

Walker, N. D. *Crime and insanity in England* (2 vols., Edinburgh, 1968–73)

West, D. J. *Murder followed by suicide* (1965)

Wolfgang, M. E. *Patterns in criminal homicide* (Philadelphia, 1958)

Wolfgang, M. E. and Farracuti, F. *The subculture of violence: towards an integrated theory in criminology* (1967)

Wootton, B. *Social science and social pathology* (1959)

Index

adultery, 27, 57, 60–2
alehouses: disorderly, 52, 167; licensing of, 50; receiving of stolen goods in, 112–13, 167; unlicensed, 50–3, 196, 197
Alleyn, Isaac, 29
Amsterdam, 150
apprentices: and alehouses, 53–4; violence against, 121, 130; *see also* servants
apprenticeship regulations, 39, 42–3, 46
archdeaconry courts, 26–7, 45, 46, 116
Ardleigh, 83
arson, 116, 147, 154, 160–1, 162
assault, 11, 114–23, 189–90; indecent, 64–5
assizes, functioning of, 21–4
assizes of bread and ale, 44
Aveley, 35, 158, 172

bailiffs, 32
Baker, J. H., 3
Barbados, 164
Barking, 17, 150, 171, 207
Barling, 36
barratry, 158–9
Barrington, Sir John, 178
Barrington, Sir Thomas, 29, 51, 86
Barstable Hundred, 31
bastardy, 57, 59–60, 62–3
Beattie, J. M., 7, 214
Beccaria, Cesare, 141
Becontree Hundred, 201–6
Bellamy, J., 4
benefit of clergy, 24, 154–6
Berden, 72
bigamy, 57, 63, 67–8, 147
binding over, 11–12, 51, 116–17, 218; *see also* recognizances
Birchanger, 97
Blackmore, 167
Blackstone, Sir William, 64, 67, 92, 102, 126, 136, 145, 147, 157
blasphemy, 27
Bocking, 18, 40, 53, 78, 80, 81, 84, 101, 110, 122, 161, 201, 208; The White Hart, inn at, 56

Boreham, 45, 131, 157
Bowes, Sir Thomas, 30
Boxted, 83, 101, 117
Bradwell, 85
Braintree, 18, 26, 44, 78, 101, 122
Bramston, Sir John, 157
Brentwood, 17, 103, 166
bridal pregnancy, 57
Bridewell, 150
bridges, upkeep of, 155
Brightlingsea, 79
brothels, 58
buggery, 27, 57, 63, 65–6, 147
Bulmer, 103
burglary, 106–12; defined, 106; goods taken by, 110
Burrow Hills, 77–9
Buttsbury, 47

Cambridgeshire, 130
Canewdon, 76
carting, 61
Castan, Nicole, 7
cattle-maiming, 161–2
Chelmsford, 17, 41, 53, 65, 101, 112, 127, 157, 172; assizes held at, 22; county gaol moved to, 32–3; court leet of, 26, 160; house of correction in, 150, 151, 164, 170; quarter sessions held at, 20; riots in, 84, 85, 86
Chevely, William, 34
Chignall Smealley, 72
Chrishall, 112
Civil Wars, 8, 29, 31, 68, 106, 159, 201, 206–9; riots preceding, 82–6
Clark, Peter, 180
class consciousness, 87, 208–9
Clavering, 45
clergy, 83–4, 178
clerk of the peace, 30–1, 119
Cockburn, J. S., 7, 9, 10
Colchester, 17, 41, 45, 58, 62, 64, 65, 66, 67, 103, 120, 122, 127, 133, 136, 157, 161, 176, 177, 186, 202, 208; castle, location of county gaol in, 32, 33, 98;

285

Colchester (*cont.*)
  cloth trade in, 18, 40, 100, 101; house of
    correction in, 150, 164, 170; plague in,
    206; riots in, 77, 79, 81, 83, 84, 85, 86,
    87, 208; sessions at, 20, 92, 115, 130,
    144, 149, 182
constables, 34–6, 173–6, 192; high
    constables, 34; violence against, 122
Coote, Nicholas, 30
coroner, 33–4
Corringham, 112
Cressing, 166
crime: definition of, 7–8; professional,
    113–14, 180; white collar, 39
criminal class, concept of, 114, 179–81
cucking-stool, 149
cuckolds, popular attitudes towards, 62
custos rotulorum, 22

Dagenham, 55
Dalton, Michael, 54, 64, 73, 106, 116, 158,
    166–7
Danbury, 116
Dedham, 101
defamation, 27, 62, 156–8
Defoe, Daniel, 17, 39
Dengie Hundred, 186
Denny, Sir Edward, 76
depositions, 12
divorce, 68, 120
Doddinghurst, 69
dogs, dangerous, 156
Dorset, 80
drink offences, 27, 51–6, 191, 196
drunkenness, 53–6, 57; and theft, 55; and
    violence, 54–5, 122, 131
duelling, 129
Dunkirk, 17
Dunmow Hundred, 204
Duval, Claude, 105

Earls Colne, 163, 173
East Hanningfield, 127
ecclesiastical courts, 26–7, 196
Eldred, Edward, 31
Elmdon, 74, 85
Elmstead, 126
Elsenham, 166
Elton, G. R., 7, 14
embezzlement, by outworkers, 100, 149
engrossing, 39, 40–1, 46
Epping, 157, 207
Essex: agriculture in, 15–19; distribution
    of poverty and crime in, 204–5; economy
    of, 15–19; population of, 15, 203–4; socio-
    economic change in, 6, 160, 162, 174,

178; textile industry in, 17, 80–1, 172–3,
    200–1, 204, 208–9; turnpikes in, 155

fees, payable in court, 177
Felstead, 121
Finchingfield, 170, 176
Fobbing, 58
forcible disseisin, 72–4
forcible entry, 72–4
forestalling, 39, 40, 41, 43, 46
fornication, 27, 57, 60–3
fortune-tellers, 165
France, 7, 79
fraud, 40
Freshwell Hundred, 204
Freud, Sigmund, 120
Frinton, 103
Furly, John, 81

gambling, 53, 131
gaol, 32–3, 152; and gaoler, 33
Gent, Henry, 29
gleaning, 98, 99, 169–70
Goldhanger, 35
Goldsborough, Thomas, 31
Gouge, William, 120
Great Baddow, 72
Great Bardfield, 113, 122
Great Braxted, 85, 101
Great Bromley, 122, 127
Great Burstead, 35, 54, 176, 178
Great Coggeshall, 18, 55, 61, 74, 81, 87,
    101, 116, 200
Great Dunmow, 84
Great Holland, 85, 155
Great Horkesley, 72, 177
Great Maplestead, 66
Great Oakley, 163
Great Totham, 78, 111
Great Yeldham, 74
Greenburg, Douglas, 7
Greenstead, 101
Grimston, Sir Harbottle, 86

Hale, Sir Matthew, 64
Hamilton, A. H. A., 6
Hampshire, 87
Harlackenden, Richard, 31
Harlow, 99
Harlow Hundred, 204
harvests, 41, 51, 196, 198–200, 208, 267
    n30
Harwich, 17, 20, 43, 61, 77, 79, 115, 182,
    183
Hatfield Broad Oak, 66
Hatfield Forest, 76
Hatfield Peverel, 60, 130

Havering Liberty, 20, 186
Hay, Douglas, 217
hearth-tax, 79–80
hedgebreaking, 98
Heigham, Thomas, 30
Heron, James, 29
Hertfordshire, 9, 80, 106
Hext, Edward, 176
Heybridge, 74
Heydon, 133
Hickeringill, Edmund, 83
highway robbery, 104–6, 213
highways, upkeep of, 155
Hinckford Hundred, 17, 19, 29, 53, 201–6, 208
Hockley, 99, 169
Holcroft, William, 30, 55, 64, 169
Holdsworth, Sir William, 40
homicide, 10, 123–35, 214; and the family, 126–8, 130; *see also* manslaughter, murder, violence
Hopkins, Matthew, 159
Hornchurch, 75
Horndon, 65
Hoskins, W. G., 198
house of correction, 51, 59, 149–52, 218
House of Lords, 145
Hoy, Stephen, 33
Hull, 78
Hutton, 112

idleness, 57
incest, 27, 57, 60–2, 68–70
indictments, 9–10, 216
infanticide, 135–7, 147
informers, 41, 46–7
Ingatestone, 17
Ingrave, 157
Inworth, 69, 111
Isle of Rhé, 77

Jeaffreson, J. C., 6
Jonson, Ben, 31
Josselin, Ralph, 31, 75, 83, 86, 128, 156, 173, 200, 207
justices of the peace, 28–30

Kelvedon, 17, 52, 57, 69, 85, 101, 158, 163; The Angel, inn at, 50
Kemp, William, 103
Kent, 9
Kenyon, J. P., 168
King's Bench, court of, 25, 34, 41, 115, 123, 131, 155, 158
Kirby, 67

Lambarde, William, 28, 35, 71, 73, 116

Lancaster, County Palatine of, 49, 175
Langbein, J. H., 4
Langdon, 111
Langham, 101
larceny, 91–104; defined, 91; grand, 142; undervaluing of goods in, 92, 146; *see also* pilfering, theft
Latton, 85, 99
Leeds (Yorkshire), 132
Leicestershire, 16
Leigh, 64, 161, 162
Levine, David, 213
Lexden Hundred, 17, 186, 201–2, 208
Leytonstone: The Robin Hood, inn at, 56
Lincolnshire, 16
litigation, vexatious, 163
Little Baddow, 158
Little Coggeshall, 101, 113
Little Stambridge, 103
London, 74, 81, 93, 130, 202, 205, 210; crime in, 105, 112, 113, 130, 179–80; executions in, 142; influence on Essex economy of, 15, 16, 17, 29, 41, 92, 212
Low Countries, 17, 18, 50
Lucas, Sir John, 85, 86

Macfarlane, Alan, 10, 69, 114, 160
Maitland, F. W., 106
Maldon, 17, 127, 136, 182, 186; offences in, 44, 54, 60, 62, 97, 113, 156, 164; riot in, 78, 79; sessions at, 20, 92, 115, 116, 176
manslaughter, 123; *see also* homicide, murder
marriage, popular attitudes to, 60, 68
Marrion, Robert, 46–7
Massachusetts (United States), 7, 65
Maxie, Sir William, 75
mayhem, 142
Melford, 86
Middlesex, 58, 180
Mildmay: family of, 157; Carew, 30; Carew Hervey, 105; Sir Henry, 33; Sir Robert, 55
Milsom, S. F. C., 141
Moryson, Fynes, 105
murder, 123–37, 142, 147; attempted, 118; defined, 123; followed by suicide, 133; *see also* homicide, manslaughter, violence
Muschamp, Christopher, 30
Myddle, 170, 172

Nazeing, 76
Newcastle upon Tyne, 17
New York (United States), 7
Nicholls, Nicholas, 44, 47–8
Norden, John, 35, 172

North Fambridge, 165
Norwich, 103

Oyer and Terminer, commissions of, 78, 84, 85, 87, 241 n9

Panfield, 84, 99
Panfield Hall, 29
pardon, 147
peine forte et dure, 24, 142
Perkins, William, 121
Petre: family of, 169; Augustine, 125
petty sessions, 21, 55–6
pickpocketing, 102–3
Pike, Luke Owen, 3
pilfering, 57, 152
pillory, 24, 149, 152
plague, bubonic, 210, 214–6, 209
poaching, 48, 98, 168–9
Pollock, F., 106
poor relief, 179
popular disturbances, 8, 72–88
posse comitatus, 71
Powers, Edwin, 7
presentment, 11, 193–6
Privy Council, 21, 41, 77, 81, 84, 86, 192, 200, 209
property offences, 91–114, 188, 198–214; *see also* burglary, highway robbery, larceny, pickpocketing, robbery, theft
prostitution, 58–9, 62, 180
Prynne, William, 49
Pulley, Richard, 31
punishment, 23–4, 141–53; at ecclesiastical courts, 27, 152; at manorial courts, 26
puritanism, 8, 52, 61, 144, 178, 196, 210, 213
Purleigh, 111

Quakers, 198
quarter sessions, functioning of, 19–20

Radwinter, 84, 85
Radzinowicz, Sir Leon, 3, 4, 217
rape, 57, 63–5, 142, 147; attempted, 118
recognizances, 11–12, 193–4; *see also* binding over
recusants, 198
regratting, 39, 40
religious offences, 198
Restoration, the, 8, 29, 30, 100, 193
Rettendon, 79, 84, 113, 120
riding the stang, 132
Rigby, Joseph, 49
riot, 71–88; defined, 71–2; and enclosure, 76; and grain, 40, 76–9; and industrial workforces, 80–2; and taxation, 79–80;

see also popular disturbances
Rivenhall, 101
Rivers, Countess, 86
robbery, 104, 142; *see also* highway robbery
Rochford Hundred, 41
Romford, 45, 54, 98, 207
Roxwell, 176
Roydon, 65, 129

sabbath offences, 27, 39, 44–5
Saffron Walden, 19, 20, 84, 149, 182, 183
St Lawrence, 164
St Osyth, 17, 84, 86
Samaha, Joel, 6
scolding, 156
sedition, 82–3
servants, 166, 177–8; and bastardy, 60; and homicide, 126–7, 132; and infanticide, 137; and sexual relations with master, 66–7; thefts by, 102, 121; violence against, 121
sexual morality, 57–63, 66–7, 70
sexual offences, 63–60; *see also* adultery, bigamy, buggery, fornication, prostitution, rape, sodomy
sheriff, 31–3
Short Parliament, the, 86
Sible Hedingham, 158
Smith, Sir Thomas, 145
Smithfield, 98
sodomy, 65–6
soldiers, 84, 207, 209
Somerset, 80, 146, 176
sorcery, 27
South Ockenden, 167
South Shoebury, 17
South Weald, 162
Southchurch, 110
Southminster, 170
Spain, 18
Springfield, 54, 163
Stambourne, 118
Stansted Mountfitchet, 79
Stapleford Abbots, 173
Star Chamber, 40, 64
Stebbing, 52, 58, 84
Steeple Bumpstead, 29
Stifford, 120
Stisted, 74, 85
Stock, 19
stocks, 24, 54, 149
stolen goods, receiving of, 112–13, 180, 247 n51
Stowmarket, 67
Stratford, Langthorne, 76, 118, 158
suicide, 132
Surrey, 7, 9, 214

Sussex, 7, 9, 64, 214
swearing, 57

Takely, 178
Tendring Hundred, 122, 149, 186, 201–2
Terling, 163, 179
Thaxted, 20
theft, 10, 91–104; of cloth, 100–1; of
    clothes and household linen, 101–2; of
    foodstuffs, 99–100; of grain, 99; of horses,
    97–8, 213; of money, 102–3; of pigs, 98;
    of poultry, 98–9; of sheep, 92–7; of tools
    and materials, 102; *see also* larceny,
    pilfering, property offences
Tiptree Heath, 97, 172
Tobias, J. J., 3
Tollesbury, 97
Tolleshunt Major, 127
Toppesfield, 55
transportation, 147–8
treason, 142
trial procedure, 23

Ulting, 111
usury, 27, 45–6
Uttlesford Hundred, 186, 201–2

vagrants, 164–6, 196–8; and burglary, 110–
    11; and theft, 101
Vange Island, 111
venereal disease, 58, 242 n39
Verney family, 105
violence, 115–38; and family, 119–20, 123,
    126–8; and parish officers, 122; and
    servants, 121; social distribution of, 118–
    19, 123, 125–6, 135

violent offences, 115–37; *see also* assault
    homicide, infanticide, manslaughter,
    murder, riot

wages, regulation of, 45, 48
Walfleet oyster beds, 76
Waltham Abbey (Holy Cross), 66
Waltham Forest, 85, 169, 171
Waltham Hundred, 172
Walthamstow, 63, 207
Warwick, Robert Rich, 2nd Earl of, 29, 31,
    82
Webb, Sidney and Beatrice, 25, 26
weights, false, 39, 43–4, 48
Weisser, Michael R., 4
West Bergholt, 67, 101, 111
West Ham, 52, 81, 105, 142, 155
West Hanningfield, 52, 161
Westminster, 22, 25, 31, 80, 173, 201
Westmorland, 10
White Colne, 179
Wickford, 69
Wickham Bishops, 74
Wiltshire, 163
Wiseman, Sir William, 31
witchcraft, 147, 154, 156, 159–60, 161,
    162, 207
Witham, 18, 77, 84, 85, 170, 205
Wivenhoe, 17, 101, 168; The Cross Keyes,
    inn at, 113
Wray, Sir Christopher, CJ, 27
Wren, Matthew, Bishop of Ely, 86; soldier
    nicknamed after, 84
Wrightson, Keith, 51, 178, 179, 213
Writtle, 103, 113

York, 131
Yorkshire, 16; vagrant from, 97